Minnesota, *Real & Imagined*

MINNESOTA
Real & Imagined

Essays on the State and Its Culture

Edited by Stephen R. Graubard
with an Introduction by Nina M. Archabal

Minnesota Historical Society Press

Minnesota Historical Society Press
345 Kellogg Blvd. West
St. Paul, MN 55102-1906

www.mnhs.org/mhspress

The paper used in this publication meets the minimum requirements of the
American National Standard for Information Sciences—Permanence for Printed
Library Materials, ANSI Z39.48-1984.

A Cataloging-in-Publication record for this book is available from the Library of
Congress.

International Standard Book Number 0-87351-397-5
Manufactured in Canada
10 9 8 7 6 5 4 3 2 1

CONTENTS

NINA M. ARCHABAL

Introduction

MINNESOTA, REAL & IMAGINED was originally published as the Summer 2000 issue of *Dædalus*, the journal of the American Academy of Arts and Sciences. An anomaly in the volumes of this distinguished periodical, it focused on a single state. As editor Stephen Graubard explained, the idea for the issue had originated in discussions with European colleagues who wanted to understand the United States but found that Europe's mass media concentrated on events in a few major American cities and overlooked the Midwest and Southwest.

Initially, Graubard intended to produce two *Dædalus* issues: one about Minnesota, the other about Texas. These states were of particular interest— Minnesota, for having produced two vice presidents, and Texas, for having produced two (now three) recent presidents. Graubard also noted that the states are strategically located at opposite ends of the north-south Interstate 35. He found that support for the project "quickly developed in Minnesota" but "there was no comparable support for a study of Texas."

Having lived here for some thirty-seven years now—a transplant from New England—I am not surprised that Minnesotans rallied to Graubard's challenge to examine their state. Of all the impressions that I recall from my first days here as a graduate student in 1965, Minnesotans' sense of place and particularity remains the most vivid. Everyone I met seemed to have grown up on a farm. As time went on, I became aware of the great number of historical organizations in the state, surprising in light of a certain arrogance I had about New Englanders owning the nation's history. Bostonians are certainly not shy about asserting that their place in the world is "the hub of the universe," but I learned that Minnesotans have their own way of claiming to be above average. When outsider Graubard asked, "Minnesota: A Different America?" we set out to answer the question.

The effort began with a meeting called by then-University of Minnesota President Nils Hasselmo. The assembled faculty members and other individuals

NINA M. ARCHABAL *is director of the Minnesota Historical Society.*

showed interest in Graubard's proposal and agreed with his declaration that the issue should not be a puff for Minnesota. In the preface, Graubard laid out the purpose:

> to analyze what has happened to this state since its founding less than a century and a half ago, what has happened more recently since the time of the Depression and World War II . . . whether the Minnesota of Sinclair Lewis and Charles Lindbergh, Sr. and Jr., is long dead, whether a state capable of electing a Hubert Humphrey to the U.S. Senate is essentially transformed, at least politically, in a time when an ex-professional wrestler has come to occupy the governor's chair.

I don't know if all of the answers were of interest to Graubard's European friends, but they are likely to intrigue Minnesotans who focus so intently on their state. Perhaps this is why Garrison Keillor created a mythical place we could share. Lake Wobegon appeals to us just because it is so close to the reality of some of Minnesota's most endearing places. Who wouldn't want to stop for coffee and danish at the Chatterbox Cafe? But in some parts of Minnesota we would find the cafe boarded up—a symptom of a dying town, where, it turns out, only the woe remains. So what is the real Minnesota today? By asking this question, we hope to raise awareness of some of the factors that have brought Minnesota to its present reality; perhaps the answers will help us ensure a future that incorporates the best of Minnesota's past.

Inevitably, a collection is something of a patchwork, but many of the essays complement each other in surprising and interesting ways. Although produced by individuals from a wide variety of disciplines, professions, and perspectives, the picture of Minnesota that develops has considerable coherence. This is not to say that the state is a place whose history and culture are easily characterized or understood in the same way by all the essayists. There are some strikingly different points of view.

Consider Joseph and Anthony Amato's warning that a fundamental change is occurring in Minnesota, brought on by the decreasing importance of agriculture and the fragmentation of rural life. The Amatos see growing separation between urban and rural areas, where "One anticipates a future of limitless possibilities, and the other endures decline." Perhaps most ominous is the "disconnection" occurring in rural Minnesota as towns dissolve and communities unravel.

Contrast the Amatos' view with the more optimistic vision offered by John Brandl. Although sharing a concern for the loss of the local and a "corresponding sense of inability to affect public affairs," Brandl imagines that Minnesota will be able to draw upon a long tradition of discourse to revive the state's civic life.

He looks hopefully at legislators, who are well positioned "to ask what is best for the whole state."

In characterizing Minnesota, several of the writers look to the ethnic and religious origins of its people. The earliest culture, as Rhoda Gilman discusses, was Native American, while later contact with Europeans produced a "mutual accommodation" of lifestyles that lasted until settlers arrived in numbers. John Adams describes the state, founded in 1858, as "a distinctive cultural island" created by first Yankees and later Germans and Scandinavians who immigrated between 1830 and 1930. Richard Chapman observes that the role of the state's dominant Christian churches "helped shape the state's communal ethos in fundamental ways." He notes, too, that the state's relatively small Jewish community has "gained national recognition for the dynamism of its community-service organizations." While acknowledging the role of European immigrants in establishing the state's culture, Michael O'Keefe finds a force for renewal of traditional values in recent immigrants with their "strong religious sense, a commitment to family, a thirst for education, and a willingness to work hard for themselves and their children."

The greatest accord among the writers arises in their conception of Minnesota's distinctiveness being the result of an unusually vibrant civic culture, one in which the citizens engage in widespread discourse and action on matters of common interest. Minnesotans are willing to make sacrifices to support the state's quality of life and demonstrate what Virginia Gray and Wyman Spano describe as a "proclivity for participation." They are engaged in their communities to an unusually high degree, active in a long list of groups ranging from church circles to the Citizens League, an organization known for its role as a convener, helping Minnesotans identify and resolve the challenges of their society. As Brandl notes, "Over the last forty years many of the state's important policy innovations have originated in the league," which stands against the prevailing national norm of "interest group liberalism."

Perhaps the most powerful evidence of the state's civic culture is Minnesota's abiding commitment to education and social welfare. Gray and Spano note the widely held belief that students and citizens have "the right to expect the highest quality, active educational and general governmental services, regardless of the wealth of the local community." Over the years, government has acted generously to provide for the people's welfare. What seems to set the state apart is Minnesota's willingness to innovate. In many instances, the private sector has joined state government to create new ways to provide a beneficial social climate for the state's people.

Concern for the common good is expressed in other ways through Minnesota's philanthropic community, which includes individuals and corporations as well as foundations. Writing about the dynamics of corporate philanthropy, Jon Pratt and Edson Spencer highlight George Draper Dayton's commitment in 1909 to set aside 5 percent of his company's pretax profits for charitable gifts. In 1976 the Minneapolis Chamber of Commerce institutionalized Dayton's giving standard by creating the Five Percent Club, an action that elicited reactions from the business community across the nation. Pratt and Spencer tell us that John D. Rockefeller III came to Minneapolis in 1977 to learn more and said, "I feel a bit like Dorothy in the Land of Oz. I had to come to the Emerald City myself to see if it really exists."

A healthy civil culture is also nourished by the arts and humanities. Speaking for the cultural community, Joe Dowling comments on Minnesota's "proud record in the matter of arts funding." A study of the arts in the state, published by the McKnight Foundation in 1996, found that Minnesota supports about 1,700 arts groups; sixty percent of these are outside the metropolitan area.[1]

But there are crosscurrents. In her historical survey, Gilman finds that some Minnesotans seem to have lost faith in political parties and others register a growing cynicism about politics in general. Thomas Peacock and Donald Day observe that many Indian people continue to feel marginalized and are "still struggling to exist in two worlds." Annette Atkins strips away the façade of generalized success and progress to show us specific examples of human experience that reveal Minnesota as "a place of complicated and conflicting truths." David Lanegran describes the state as "nature's playground," but discovers considerable disagreement about nature's uses. And Robert White finds a disquieting contradiction between Minnesotans' concerns about helping each other while remaining only somewhat committed to helping those beyond U.S. borders.

Several writers ask whether or not the election of Governor Jesse Ventura signals a change in Minnesota's civic culture. It is too soon to know. What we do know is that culture is resilient and durable, evolving and changing over time. Although these essays cannot provide conclusions about the future, the writers present a fairly optimistic view. The image appears of a resilient and distinctive Minnesota. Perhaps some underlying sense of the state's special nature and its durability explains Minnesotans' abiding interest in preserving both their quality of life and their history.

Former Governor Elmer L. Andersen, a past president of the Minnesota Historical Society and a major force in the state's civic culture for more than six decades, speaks often of the responsibility to preserve and know our history, and to pass on our cherished values to the next generations. He has frequently described the establishment of the historical society as a reflection of its founders' commitment to ensuring the state's future. At the groundbreaking in 1988 for the society's Minnesota History Center in St. Paul, Andersen moved the audience with these words:

> our future depends on our ability to preserve and transmit the rich heritage of values that is the foundation of our state. Early Minnesotans had visions of building a great state for their children. That vision is the foundation of our state today. There is no question that the values that built our past are essential to our future. But we cannot assume they will be automatically adopted by future generations.[2]

The essays in this book have the potential to help us make decisions that will affect Minnesota's future. They remind us of our strong civic traditions and open our imaginations to think about what we ought to cherish and preserve of Minnesota's unique culture as we move into a new century.

Minnesota, Real & Imagined benefited from the assistance of many people. We are grateful to the Europeans who want to know us better and to Stephen Graubard for asking us to help answer their questions. Financial support from the McKnight Foundation and the Blandin Foundation was essential in the creation of this work. Numerous individuals spent long hours discussing subjects to include and writers to address them. Especially valuable contributions came from Cheryl Dickson, director of the Minnesota Humanities Commission, Lou Bellamy, founder and artistic director of the Penumbra Theatre Company, James P. Shannon, senior consultant for the national Council on Foundations, Clarke Chambers, professor emeritus at the University of Minnesota, Charles I. Mundale, former college professor and journalist, and Deborah Miller, Patrick Coleman, and Ann Regan of the Minnesota Historical Society. Rhoda Gilman provided invaluable guidance based on her many years at the society spent in researching and writing the state's history. Greg Britton, director of the Minnesota Historical Society Press, saw the value of bringing these essays in their new form to a broader audience. Deborah Swanson and Jeri Niedenfuer ably shepherded them into print.

But the greatest credit goes to the essay writers, each with a distinct vision, who accepted the challenge to depict what has happened to Minnesota since its beginnings and to search out what is distinctive in the picture that emerges. They and their ideas truly bring Minnesota to life as a different America.

Notes

1. McKnight Foundation, *Here and Now: A Report on the Arts in Minnesota* (Minneapolis, 1996), 15.
2. Minnesota Historical Society, *Minnesota's History: A Story Worth Preserving and Sharing* (St. Paul, 1991), 1.

Minnesota, *Real & Imagined*

RHODA R. GILMAN

The History and Peopling of Minnesota: Its Culture

THE STATE OF MINNESOTA has been described as being "at the top of the North American hill."[1] Its waters flow south to the Gulf of Mexico, east to the Atlantic Ocean, and north to Hudson Bay. Its environment mirrors this three-way division. If it were a milking stool, Minnesota would have one leg in the northern pine forests, one leg in the corn belt, and one on the Great Plains. It is a transition zone, and its human history reflects the diversity of its geography.[2]

Just as the story of the southwestern states cannot be told without reference to Mexico, so Minnesota's history is interwoven with that of Canada. First described by French traders and missionaries in the 1600s, the region was for practical purposes a part of British territory until well into the nineteenth century. Today it shares with the Province of Ontario a coastline on Lake Superior and a vast wilderness canoe country. With Manitoba it shares the agricultural wealth and the flood problems of the Red River Valley, and it depends on the prairie provinces for vital energy resources—oil from Alberta and Saskatchewan, and hydroelectricity from northern Manitoba. In human terms it shares the Ojibwe people, whose language and culture were a seamless whole for generations before they were divided into Canadians and Americans.

Ahead of the first Frenchmen to reach the area came an inrush of Indians from the St. Lawrence Valley and what is now southern Ontario. In the mid-1600s bands of Huron, Ottawa, and Ojibwe, fleeing the onslaught of the Iroquois, sought refuge west of Lakes Michigan and Superior. The Huron and Ottawa eventually returned eastward, but the Ojibwe stayed. This migration forced the Cheyenne, the Dakota, and the Assiniboine westward from the forests onto the open prairies.

For the next century and a half the land now comprising Minnesota was included in the Canadian fur-trade system—a continent-spanning network that linked American Indian cultures and resources with the commercial world

RHODA R. GILMAN *is senior research fellow emerita at the Minnesota Historical Society.*

of Europe. Indian people handled production on their own terms, while transportation and marketing were dominated first by licensees of the French crown and later by large British-managed monopolies.

The culture that developed in Minnesota and other Great Lakes states during that era has been called "the middle ground"—a mutual accommodation of Indian and European lifestyles, technologies, and attitudes.[3] Its common language was French, and it included an influential population of mixed-blood families that served as go-betweens and local traders. Among other things, it left a legacy of French place-names scattered across the land and French surnames among Indian tribes.

Minnesota Becomes an American State

After the War of 1812 the United States asserted control over its territory by establishing forts along the northwestern frontier. One of them stood high on a bluff at the confluence of the Mississippi and Minnesota Rivers. Named for its builder, Colonel Josiah Snelling, the fort was located at the head of steamboat navigation on the Mississippi and close to the Falls of St. Anthony, where the army immediately built a sawmill. Fort Snelling radiated U.S. power and Anglo-American influence throughout the region, and was the cradle of what became the Twin Cities Metropolitan Area.

As the tide of European migration surged westward, the middle ground was erased and Indians were expropriated through a series of treaties. North of the international boundary people of mixed blood—the Métis—resisted; in Canada they still maintain a distinct identity, but in Minnesota as elsewhere in the United States they faced a stark choice between the white and Indian worlds. Minnesota became an organized territory in 1849, and only nine years later it was admitted to statehood. Those nine years saw its European-American population soar from less than 5,000 to more than 150,000. Prairies were surveyed into acres and forests were estimated in board feet of lumber; a natural habitat of animals and humans was transformed into commodities, subject to ownership and exchange.[4]

Statehood came on the eve of the American Civil War, and within four years Minnesota received two baptisms of blood—one on southern battlefields, and one on its own frontier. In what nineteenth-century writers called "the great Minnesota massacre," the Dakota tribe, starving and cheated, made a desperate effort to reclaim their homeland. Vengeance was swift and ruthless. The Dakota were driven from the state and hunted across the plains, initiating a generation of sporadic warfare that ended only with the slaughter at Wounded

Knee in 1890. The Ojibwe, confined to reservations across the northern part of the state, remained Minnesota's largest racial and cultural minority until the second half of the twentieth century.

Canadian and New England lumbermen, following the stands of white and red pine, were the vanguard of the state's new inhabitants. Lumber replaced hides and furs as the leading export. Anglo-Americans built mill towns along the rivers and took charge of business and government. They were soon outnumbered by farmers and laborers, many fresh from across the Atlantic. Within thirty years, three out of every four white Minnesotans came from northern Europe or had parents who were immigrants.

Most immigrant farmers were drawn by the dream of owning land— land in which they could root their own lives and those of their descendants. But roots often proved shallow in the new soil. Subsistence farming and local market gardening never became important in Minnesota. High wartime prices and a booming wheat market in the 1860s immediately tied Minnesota's agriculture to world markets and a cash-crop system. With luck, a new settler could pay for his acres in one or two seasons, but on the heels of the oxen that broke the prairie sod came expensive horse-drawn mowers, reapers, and cultivators. Single-crop farming also exhausted the soil, and diversification demanded capital for buildings, fences, and stock. Those who had it or could borrow it stayed; those without it sold out and moved on.

Until late in the nineteenth century, rivers provided not only power for mills but transportation for marketing lumber. The spread of agriculture throughout Minnesota had to await the expansion of railroads; by 1879 they reached north and west to the wheat fields of Manitoba, and by 1883 they linked Lake Superior with Puget Sound. Minnesota was shaped by the railroad era. The steel rails dictated the value of land and the location—and survival or failure—of towns. The power of railroad corporations created fortunes and government subsidies along with waves of agrarian revolt, which produced the state's volatile politics.

As the turn of the century approached, Minnesotans could look back on forty years of statehood. A generation of grinding toil had turned the oak savannas and tall-grass prairies into a land of farm fields and small towns. Distant horizons were constricted by barns and wood lots, silos and grain elevators. To the never-ending work had been added grasshopper plagues, prairie and forest fires, and killing blizzards, but a community had been forged that could (and did) boast of its free public schools, its influential churches, its numerous small colleges, and a land-grant university. An overflowing supply of local newspapers in English and other languages testified to its literacy, and the great clusters of Scandinavian and German people were beginning to assert civic leadership.

The Minnesota economy was still rooted in raw materials and processing. Agricultural products and the shrinking stands of timber were already being supplemented by iron ore from a line of hills in the northeast known to Ojibwe as the Mesabi, or "sleeping giant." The state capital and commercial hub of St. Paul and the flour and sawmill center of Minneapolis had both seen dramatic growth in the 1880s. Jobs in the expanding cities were drawing unmarried women from the region's farms and a wave of new immigrants, including many from southern and eastern Europe. Unions were reaching out from their narrow base of skilled craftsmen to take in workers in transportation and industry. Joining with hard-pressed farmers in the grim 1890s, the new labor movement brought a surge of populism that threatened to end thirty years of unbroken Republican rule.

The Early Twentieth Century and World War I

The first quarter of the twentieth century saw the cresting of small-town culture and the reforms of the Progressive Era, which reshaped government and politics in response to rapid urbanization. To this scene were added the turbulent bonanza years of iron and steel on the Mesabi Range, and the profoundly alienating impact of World War I in Minnesota.

The years before the war established a long-remembered norm for farmers, when the prices they received reached parity with those they paid for manufactured goods. Stimulated by agricultural prosperity, rural centers continued to grow in number and size, and nearly all were served by a network of rail lines that reached into every corner of the state. By the 1920s, however, farm depression along with automobiles and improved roads brought changing patterns of rural life. Smaller towns were withering under the competition of larger shopping centers, and the attractions of urban culture were beckoning to the young. A bitter blow to small-town self-esteem was dealt in 1920 by the novel *Main Street*, in which Minnesota author Sinclair Lewis satirized the smug shallowness of Gopher Prairie, a thinly disguised version of his native Sauk Centre.

Meanwhile, in northeastern Minnesota three mining districts collectively known as the Iron Range produced a unique industrial frontier. On the Mesabi, by far the largest of the three, strip mining turned the remote forest and swampland into a sixty-mile swath of yawning pits and hills of red mine waste. Mining camps, or "locations," and a chain of small towns housed thousands of unskilled laborers. By 1900 the population of Mesabi communities was more than fifteen thousand; in 1910 it had reached sixty-eight thousand. Early arrivals included Canadians and Cornishmen from older mines in Michigan, but most of the newcomers were immigrants from eastern Europe. The largest single group was the Finns.

Local mine owners had been forced out in the depression of the 1890s, and in 1901 the formation of the United States Steel Company established monolithic control over most of the Mesabi. The steel trust did little to improve the conditions of labor or to reduce the danger of the work, which claimed the lives of five in every one thousand men between 1905 and 1910.[5] A bitter strike in 1907, organized by the Western Federation of Miners and led largely by Finnish workers, was defeated through mass importation of strike breakers from the Balkan countries and Italy. By 1916 the new labor force itself had been radicalized, and a second strike, led by the Industrial Workers of the World (IWW), was crushed. After that an uneasy industrial peace was enforced with labor spies and blacklisting, supplemented by gradual improvement in working and living conditions. This situation prevailed until passage of the National Labor Relations Act in 1935.

Taxation on the wealth of iron ore being extracted was a long-disputed issue in Minnesota, but while the legislature temporized local governments moved ahead, assessing and taxing mining land at its real value. This resulted in schools and public services for the Range towns that were unmatched elsewhere in the state. Along with churches and a variety of fraternal organizations, these educational and social benefits slowly drew the polyglot ethnic population into the mainstream of American life. Nevertheless, the Range, with its onion-shaped steeples, ravaged landscape, and submerged streak of radicalism, remained for most of the century a world apart within Minnesota.

The outlet for iron was through the Great Lakes, and the ever-hopeful town of Duluth, which had been through an earlier cycle of boom and bust in the 1870s, emerged as Minnesota's third major city. Shipbuilding brought prosperity in the 1890s, and railroad yards and ore docks continued to multiply after the turn of the century. In 1916 a massive steel mill was built in West Duluth, and by 1920 the port city and its environs had a population of more than 150,000.

Urban growth in the Twin Cities kept pace. By the turn of the century Minneapolis had pulled well ahead of St. Paul in wealth, industry, and population. Its financial sway over the region was symbolized after 1912 when it became the seat of the Ninth Federal Reserve District, extending from Upper Michigan to Montana. Its daily papers served readers across roughly the same area, and beginning in the 1920s its radio stations dominated the airwaves. St. Paul's earlier start and its role as the center of state government helped it to retain a separate identity. The first quarter of the twentieth century, however, saw the spread of suburbs that would eventually merge the cities into a single metropolis.

Yet the two communities continued to have distinct characters, both visually and socially. St. Paul, built on terraces and bluffs that look onto the majestic valley of the Upper Mississippi, was clearly a river town. In Minneapolis the Mississippi's narrow, rocky gorge was scarcely visible from the flat prairies that spread away from it, and the chains of small lakes that dotted those prairies gave the town its image as a "City of Lakes."

Catholicism, established in St. Paul by its French Canadian founders, remained firmly rooted in a large German population and a vocal Irish minority. Except among the Swedes and Norwegians clustered on the city's East Side, St. Paul was a place where neighborhoods were defined by parish and parochial school. Minorities—Jewish, black, and later Mexican—remained small and found easy (although far from complete) acceptance. In Minneapolis, where the population was heavily Scandinavian and Protestant, the expanding mills and factories attracted a large influx of eastern European immigrants, including many Polish and Russian Jews. Cultural contrasts raised social barriers, and by the 1920s Minneapolis was becoming widely known for its anti-Semitism.[6]

Through the first third of the century Minneapolis also maintained a reputation as one of the country's most strongly antiunion towns. A semisecret association of businessmen, called the Citizens Alliance, enforced nonunion contracts among employers and enlisted the support of city authorities when trouble erupted. Wages remained below the national average, and as labor became more militant, conflict became bitter.[7]

In St. Paul, craft unions had gained an early start. Catholic influence played a moderating role among both workers and employers, and the long-established business community was open to compromise. With a few exceptions, the labor movement remained essentially conservative, and the city boasted of a peaceable partnership in the workplace.

In state politics the Progressive movement succeeded the strident wave of populism. Earnest attempts by Progressive reformers to rein in the power of corporations and the corruption of political parties were supported by the Minnesota business community, which was still locally controlled and suspicious of eastern domination. The Progressive Era reshaped municipal governments and extended nonpartisan elections to the judiciary, to local offices, and even to the state legislature—a dubious experiment that was finally reversed in 1973. Suffrage for women, associated with the temperance movement, was blocked by the state's strong German vote and its brewing lobby. Ironically, however, Minnesota became a symbol of prohibition through the name of Congressman Andrew Volstead, author of the bill that implemented the Eighteenth Amendment.

Meanwhile, Norwegian and Swedish voters, reinforced by a fresh wave of urban immigration in the 1890s, sent candidates to the statehouse, Congress, and the Senate. Men such as Knute Nelson, John Lind, John A. Johnson, Charles A. Lindbergh Sr., Henrik Shipstead, and Magnus Johnson drew national attention. Along with novelist Ole Rølvaag and social theorist Thorstein Veblen, they established the state's image as a Scandinavian stronghold.

Although Germans outnumbered any other single nationality, they produced few political or cultural leaders. The rift between Protestant and Catholic, northern and southern, divided them, and the wave of nativism and red-baiting that swept the nation during World War I reached a feverish crescendo in Minnesota. Deep-running antiwar sentiment in German communities was met with verbal abuse and mob violence that was openly sanctioned by the state government. A Minnesota Commission of Public Safety with dictatorial powers banned expressions of German culture and required aliens of any kind to register with the state. At the same time, a militia was organized to break strikes, and when farmers united politically in the Nonpartisan League, their candidates were silenced as traitors and occasionally jailed. For a while, civil liberties ceased to exist.[8]

The Interwar Decades

The reaction to the excesses of World War I created new alliances and did much to shape Minnesota politics until the end of World War II. Marginalized farmers and normally conservative ethnic voters united with Labor to support the left-leaning Farmer-Labor Party. Although challenged at first by a vigorous Communist movement among miners, lumberjacks, and immigrant Finns in northern Minnesota, the Farmer-Labor coalition gathered strength. It replaced the Democrats as Minnesota's second major party when it captured the governorship in 1930.

Minnesota's industry, meanwhile, was adapting to changed conditions. The last of the pine forests had been cut early in the century, and lumber operations belonging to the Weyerhaeuser family, Minnesota's largest timber interest, had moved to the West Coast. What remained was papermaking and the manufacture of various other wood products. By the 1920s Minnesota had also lost its commanding lead in flour making, and the two largest milling firms, Washburn-Crosby and Pillsbury-Washburn, were turning increasingly to brand-name consumer products. By the end of the 1930s Washburn-Crosby had become General Mills. Its breakfast cereals, baking mixes, and advertising symbol—Betty Crocker—were known nationwide. Meatpackers and other food processors followed the same pattern of diversification and increased marketing, along with consolidation of corporate control.

As the 1920s closed, the state's farmers could look back on nearly a decade of agricultural depression. Defeated in their political drive to regain price parity, many of them united in cooperatives of various kinds. Not new to Minnesota, farm co-ops had been introduced as early as the 1870s and had spread during the Populist era. By the end of the 1920s they had become a significant social and economic force in the state. Nevertheless, farm families had seen few of the new amenities that were transforming towns and cities. Telephones, paved roads, and electricity still bypassed rural areas. Only with the creation of the Rural Electrification Administration in 1935 and the organization of REA co-ops did life on the farm change significantly.

The early 1930s brought not only deepening depression but also a devastating drought, and many farmers who had barely hung on through the 1920s lost their land. United in the Farm Holiday Movement, they blocked highways to protest low prices and gathered at auctions to prevent foreclosure sales. Although elsewhere these actions were sometimes marked by violence, in Minnesota the Farmer-Labor governor, Floyd B. Olson, avoided confrontation and supported militant farmers in their demand for a state moratorium on mortgage foreclosures.

Olson used the same restraint as labor unrest erupted, declining to send the National Guard in 1933 when packinghouse workers on strike in Austin occupied the plant of the Hormel company. He was forced to call out troops in 1934, however, when employers in Minneapolis refused to recognize or negotiate with the Teamsters union. Dragging on for several months, the Teamsters strike led to rioting and open warfare on the streets of the city. The standoff ended only when the Roosevelt administration put sub-rosa pressure on Minneapolis banks associated with the Citizens Alliance. The historic confrontation brought to a close the city's longtime status as an open-shop town and played a role in the passage of the National Labor Relations Act the following year.[9]

The charismatic Olson became a legend in Minnesota. More radical in words than in actions, he drew support from far beyond the ranks of his own party, and the entire state mourned his early death from cancer in 1936. Without his unifying influence, the Farmer-Labor Party split between radical and more conservative wings. A bitterly fought election in 1938 was muddied by charges of corruption and overtones of red-baiting and anti-Semitism. It saw Farmer-Labor governor Elmer A. Benson defeated by Harold E. Stassen, a young political newcomer who embodied the moderate Republicanism that had held sway in Minnesota through much of its history.

For at least one group in the state, the grim 1930s had brought a glimmer of new hope. Ojibwe people on reservations across northern Minnesota had suffered more than fifty years of oppression, broken promises, timber theft, and fraud in land sales. Disease, destitution, and despair were widespread, and U.S. citizenship, granted in 1924, had done little to change things. However, federal Depression-era programs such as the Civilian Conservation Corps offered the Ojibwe people employment near their own homes, while the Indian Reorganization Act, passed in 1934, allowed the creation of tribal governments and a measure of self-determination.

With the approach of World War II, Minnesotans showed a long memory for their bitter experience in World War I. Antiwar sentiment, defined as "isolationism" by the press, reached across party lines. The America First campaign of Charles A. Lindbergh Jr. drew widespread support, for although the famous aviator had long since left Minnesota, the state still claimed him and recalled his father's courage when widely vilified as the Nonpartisan League candidate for governor in 1918. Until 1940 both of Minnesota's U.S. senators stubbornly fought the Roosevelt administration in its moves toward intervention. One of them, Henrik Shipstead, a Farmer-Laborite turned Republican, held office long enough to cast his vote against ratification of the UN charter in 1945. His defeat in the Republican primary the following year, however, signaled a sea change in the state's attitude toward foreign involvement.

The Postwar Era: 1948–1968

As Minnesota emerged from World War II and approached its territorial centennial in 1949, the future looked promising. There had been none of the divisive bitterness that had accompanied World War I and, in spite of the conflict's pain and sacrifice, it had brought the state unmatched prosperity. Agricultural prices had soared, and farmers who had weathered the depression were rapidly mechanizing their operations. Wages had risen, and unions, protected by the National Labor Relations Act, had become established both in cities and along the Iron Range, where the United Steelworkers had achieved general acceptance. The conversion of industry to war production had left large local enterprises such as Northern Pump Company, Minnesota Mining and Manufacturing (3M), and Minneapolis-Honeywell in stronger positions than ever before. An economic watershed had been crossed, and the foundations for a manufacturing economy had been laid.

It was also a time of new political consensus. Under liberal Republican governors like Stassen and his successors, Edward J. Thye and Luther W. Youngdahl, state government had been modernized and cleaned up. A system of merit-based civil service for state employees had been adopted, and state services were being improved and expanded. In Minneapolis a similar housecleaning had been pushed by the young Democratic mayor, Hubert H. Humphrey. In 1944 the Farmer-Labor Party merged with the weaker Democrats, and the new Democratic-Farmer-Labor (DFL) party matched the liberal Republicans in commitment to internationalism.

Conflict remained to be settled, however, within the DFL. Its radical wing, still led by Benson, opposed the anti-Soviet Cold War policies of the Truman administration, and in 1948 Benson and his followers supported Henry A. Wallace in his bid for the presidency. In a bitter battle, Humphrey and a group of liberal Democrats won control of the DFL. That year saw Humphrey elected to the U.S. Senate and the beginning of three decades during which Minnesotans of both parties achieved unprecedented prominence in national politics and government.

Party rivalry was keen between 1948 and 1968, and power was closely balanced, but Minnesota Republicans and DFL leaders united in their support of the Cold War. During the Eisenhower administrations Stassen was a top advisor to the president, and on most foreign-policy issues he and Humphrey were in substantial agreement. A more conservative voice, especially on Asia, was Republican Congressman Walter H. Judd, a former missionary. During the wave of political persecution in the 1950s, Humphrey himself authored a bill outlawing the Communist Party, and many of the state's Communists and Communist sympathizers were hounded by federal agencies. Minnesota authorities, however, were comparatively restrained. Loyalty oaths were never required of state employees, and academic freedom was preserved.[10]

The tone of state politics was exemplified in 1962, when DFL candidate Karl F. Rolvaag defeated Republican governor Elmer L. Andersen in an election so close that the actual outcome was not known for months. During the time of indecision, Andersen held office but provided quarters in the capitol for Rolvaag and kept him informed on essential matters of state business. The meticulous combing of all ballots cast in the state revealed virtually no cases of deliberate fraud. Thus Minnesota's growing reputation for clean, citizen-based politics was triumphantly vindicated.[11]

These same decades saw deep-running changes within the state. Some were demographic. Minnesota's African American community had always been relatively small, well educated, and solidly rooted in service jobs, many of them on the railroads. This changed when a flood of black Americans, driven off the land by mechanization of agriculture in the postwar years, headed toward northern cities. Soon the black population centered in the Twin Cities rivaled Indians as Minnesota's dominant minority.

Meanwhile, Indians themselves were moving. In the 1950s the U.S. government actively encouraged relocation to urban areas far from reservation communities. This policy, along with the never-ending search for jobs, brought Indians to Minneapolis, St. Paul, and Duluth, not only from northern Minnesota but from the Dakotas and Wisconsin as well. Many of them lived a divided existence, alternating between city employment and seasonal residence on their home reservations.

Indians and African Americans were soon joined by Hispanics. The employment of migratory farm workers—mostly single men—dated back to the bonanza wheat harvests of the 1880s, but in the 1920s the patterns of migratory employment had begun to change. Whole families of Mexicans appeared in the sugar-beet fields of western Minnesota. Already a small community of Mexicans had found permanent employment in the giant packinghouses of South St. Paul, and each year they were joined by a few migrants who chose to wait out the winter in Minnesota. With the surge of large-scale agriculture in the postwar years, the number of migrant workers increased, and so did the number who stayed. Like other immigrant groups throughout Minnesota's history, they turned to their church for a sense of identity and cohesion. In St. Paul the parish of Our Lady of Guadalupe became the center of their community.

Women in Minnesota, like those elsewhere, were expected to give up wartime jobs and return to homemaking. Many did not. A few barriers, especially those inhibiting the employment of married women, had fallen during the war, but others remained in place. Nevertheless, by 1950 nearly a third of Minnesota women worked at jobs outside the home. Barriers also remained in politics, where, as in the earlier struggle for suffrage, the state demonstrated a deep reluctance to give women equal standing. Their representation in the legislature had fallen from a high point of four after passage of the Nineteenth Amendment to none between 1945 and 1950. From then until 1962 there were no more than two women in the legislature at any time. The first of only two Minnesota women ever elected to Congress, Coya Knutson, was sent to Washington in 1954 and served two terms with distinction, until she proved too independent for leaders of her own DFL Party.[12]

The postwar years also saw fundamental economic changes. In agriculture, mechanization was supplemented by the so-called Green Revolution in plant genetics and by new chemical pesticides and fertilizers. Crop yields expanded along with the capital required for successful farming, and the family farm, a Minnesota social and political icon, was subjected to ever-mounting pressure.

In industry the wartime development of precision manufacturing opened the door to a whole new world of high technology, much of it supported by the country's continuing military buildup. One such venture was the upper atmosphere research conducted by General Mills and others with towering polyethylene balloons in advance of the era of rocketry and satellites. Another was the development of massive mainframe computers for industry and the military. The manufacture of medical devices also became important, bolstered by the state's longstanding reputation as home of the Mayo Clinic and as a center for medical research conducted at the University of Minnesota.

At the same time, the state's second great extractive industry faced a crisis. Two world wars had exhausted the reserves of high-grade ore on the Mesabi, and open-pit mining was drawing to a close. Efforts to exploit the iron locked into the hard rock known as taconite took a step forward in 1955 when the first taconite plant went into operation. Two years later a second one opened. The process, however, required acres of heavy machinery for crushing rock and separating out the ore, then shaping it into pellets usable in blast furnaces. Steel companies refused to make further investment unless guaranteed against an increase in state taxes. Anxiety and unemployment on the Range deepened and debate throughout the state mounted until 1964, when Minnesota voters approved a constitutional amendment establishing a twenty-five-year moratorium on additional taconite taxes.

By the late 1960s nearly half of the state's population lived in the Twin Cities Metropolitan Area—a shift that led to a long struggle between rural and urban Minnesota over legislative reapportionment. It ended in 1966 when a redrawing of legislative district lines gave the metropolitan area additional representation. One immediate result was a new state focus on metropolitan planning and the creation in 1967 of the Twin Cities Metropolitan Council to oversee and coordinate area-wide public services that had been divided among a jumble of local governments. One of the first such regional authorities in the nation, the council was greeted as further evidence of Minnesota's political creativity.

"A State That Works"

In the summer of 1968, just twenty years after Hubert Humphrey had become the leading figure in Minnesota politics, he found himself challenged for the Democratic presidential nomination by a fellow Minnesotan. Senator Eugene J. McCarthy had become the spokesperson for a nationwide tide of protest against the U.S. war in Vietnam. Humphrey, then vice president under Lyndon B. Johnson, defended the war, but in doing so he barely held onto his own state's delegation to the Democratic convention. Thus, the bitter confrontation on the streets of Chicago that summer had a special meaning for Minnesota and was a measure of its pivotal position in national politics.

Despite Humphrey's defeat for the presidency, his DFL Party reached the summit of its power in Minnesota with the election of Wendell R. Anderson as governor in 1970 and of the first DFL-controlled legislature in 1972. These years saw the enactment of a sweeping program of liberal legislation. It included everything from partial public financing of political campaigns and a stringent open meetings law to the lowering of the voting age to eighteen and unionization rights for public employees. The most substantial of the changes was a multifaceted program of tax reform that altered the fiscal relationship of the state to local governments and involved shifting a share of the overall tax burden from real property to state-levied income and sales taxes. At the same time, the state's biennial budget leaped from $1 billion in 1967 to $4 billion in 1973.

A principal beneficiary of this program was public education, which was groaning under the weight of the postwar baby boom. The plan bolstered and equalized school financing throughout Minnesota. This "Minnesota Miracle" capped an all-out commitment to modernized education that had received bipartisan support since World War II. Part of this effort was directed to closing rural schools through enforced consolidation. Bitterly opposed by some local communities, consolidation had reduced the number of districts from 1,700 in 1945 to fewer than 450 in 1972. Still unchanged, however, was a tradition of strict local autonomy among school districts, which limited the state's department of education to a role of advice and support.

The same years had seen steady expansion in higher education. A network of area vocational-technical schools, started in 1947, numbered twenty-eight by the late 1960s. The five state teachers' colleges existing at the end of World War II had been transformed into seven state universities by 1975, and the University of Minnesota had grown proportionately.

The cover of *Time* magazine for August 13, 1973, said it all. Above the words "The Good Life in Minnesota" was a picture of the youthful Governor Anderson, a former Olympic hockey champion, triumphantly displaying a large fish. Minnesota was, *Time* announced, "a state that works."

Most Minnesotans agreed, for it was a period of prosperity. Industrial methods were transforming traditional agriculture, and farmers were being told to "get big or get out." Many, faced with skyrocketing land prices, were getting out, but they found new opportunities plentiful in the sprawling metropolitan suburbs that were fast outgrowing the cities they surrounded. The state's postwar start in computers had blossomed into a booming electronics industry; taconite plants had mushroomed across northern Minnesota; the opening of the St. Lawrence Seaway in 1959 had made Duluth an ocean port; and new oil and gas pipelines and nuclear plants were countering Minnesota's perennial lack of energy sources.

In other respects, too, the state's "good life" was manifold. For sports fans it was the arrival of major league baseball, football, and hockey in the early 1960s. For concert-, theater-, and gallerygoers it was the spectacular multiplying of arts organizations, led most conspicuously by the Tyrone Guthrie Theater and the Minnesota Orchestra. For writers and literary critics it was the growing number of small presses and publications with a regional imprint. For out-of-doors enthusiasts it was the burgeoning snowmobile industry, and for lovers of nature it was the steady expansion of the Boundary Waters Canoe Area and the creation of Voyageurs National Park on the state's northern border.

Meanwhile, in U.S. popular culture the often scathing image of the state sketched in the 1920s by such expatriate Minnesota authors as Sinclair Lewis and F. Scott Fitzgerald was being replaced. In the 1950s, St. Paul-reared cartoonist Charles Schulz launched a comic strip that caught the heart of the nation, and in the 1960s *Peanuts* soared to unprecedented popularity. At the same time, the wailing folk tunes and protest songs of Bob Dylan were carrying to a new generation and distant places the isolation and aspirations of his native Iron Range. Then, in 1974, a modest program of music and sly humor called *A Prairie Home Companion* premiered on Minnesota Public Radio. By the 1980s, Garrison Keillor's mythical Lake Wobegon—"The little town that time forgot"—with its gently eccentric folk had eclipsed Gopher Prairie as a symbol of the state and its culture.

Deepening Rifts

In Minnesota as elsewhere, the social revolution of the 1960s had raised new issues and with them new definitions of what was "liberal" and what "conservative." A generation of young people who identified with the counterculture of the 1960s experienced deep alienation from the mainstream values and materialist goals of American society. In Minnesota they looked for inspiration to a nostalgic vision of the state's rural and sometimes radical past. Many headed back to the land, hoping not so much to create as to reconnect with community, simplicity, and economic and environmental sustainability. They became organic farmers, small shopkeepers, artists, craftspersons, and rural activists.[13]

In the cities they achieved community and some economic support in a new wave of cooperatives. The anarchic lifestyle and antipathy to business culture out of which this movement emerged in 1970 is seen in the fact that no accurate count was ever made of the number of organizations (or nonorganizations) to which it gave birth. By 1975, however, there was an ever-shifting network of nearly seventy small food co-ops that radiated out from the Twin Cities and were supplied from a central warehouse in Minneapolis. Torn apart in that year by conflicting ideologies, the movement survived as a collection of health-food stores, still committed to general principles of environmentalism and communal control.[14]

No less alienated than those of the alternative culture were conservatives of the religious Right. Like their counterparts on the Left, they could connect with a long Minnesota tradition, for religion had always been a powerful force in the state's rural and immigrant communities. Although most mainstream churches had become liberalized in the twentieth century, charismatic fundamentalists kept Minnesota anchored within the Bible Belt. One was William B. Riley, for forty-five years the popular pastor of the First Baptist Church in Minneapolis and founder of the Northwestern Bible Schools. His protégé, Billy Graham, became president of the schools in 1947, and although Graham left in 1952 to carry his evangelical crusades to a wider world, the headquarters of his association remained in Minneapolis along with his influence and image.

For religious conservatives the new sexual and social mores that swept the country in the 1960s were a sign of moral disintegration, and the New Age mysticism of the 1970s was a return to heathenism. The fiercest controversy, in Minnesota as elsewhere, was over legalized abortion. It began in 1969 with efforts to reform the state's antiabortion law and entered a new phase after January of 1973, when the U.S. Supreme Court struck down such laws in a decision written by Minnesotan Harry A. Blackmun. The issue, cutting across party lines, has played a divisive role in nearly every legislative session since that time.

While the conflict over abortion became central and symbolic, the new feminism that emerged from the civil-rights struggle of the 1960s also addressed a broader range of questions. For the first time, women laid claim to leadership roles in politics, business, civil administration, and the nonprofit world. The election of 1976 sent eleven women to the Minnesota legislature, a number that reached a peak of sixty-one (30.4 percent) in 1996.[15] Since 1976 the office of secretary of state has been held by women, and since 1982 women have generally been assigned the slot of lieutenant governor on party tickets. Two women, both nominated by the DFL, have been defeated in statewide elections for U.S. Senate seats. In the metropolitan area, however, a victory was won for women as well as for African Americans when Sharon Sayles Belton was elected mayor of Minneapolis in 1993.

In some other aspects of women's rights Minnesota has shown national leadership. Domestic abuse became a public issue in 1974 when the nation's first shelter for battered women opened in St. Paul. Women's representation in the state's judicial system took a leap forward in 1977 with the appointment of Judge Rosalie Wahl to the Minnesota Supreme Court. More appointments followed, and in December of 1990, Minnesota became the first American state with a majority of women on its highest court. This majority held until August of 1994.

The civil rights struggle also led to new militancy among Native Americans, especially in urban communities. The American Indian Movement, formed in Minneapolis in 1968, became a radical voice for the young and disaffected. Six years later the eyes of the nation focused on St. Paul, where AIM leaders Dennis Banks and Russell Means were tried in federal court (and acquitted) for their part in the violent confrontation at Wounded Knee in South Dakota.

Less noticed by the press and public was the growing influence of tribal governments. A statewide commission, created in 1963, evolved by 1983 into the Minnesota Indian Affairs Council, which focused Indian power within the state. Of particular concern have been education and tribal control over reservation schools and community colleges, as well as some areas of law enforcement. The 1980s and 1990s saw a fierce struggle over long-ignored treaty rights in both Wisconsin and Minnesota, reflecting a fundamental shift toward cultural separatism and demands for greater tribal sovereignty.

The environmental movement, which had achieved organization and some forward-looking laws in the late 1960s, took on a more urgent tone in the 1970s. One of the longest environmental court cases on record concerned the dumping of taconite tailings into Lake Superior. The economic stakes were high, but they were outweighed when it was shown in 1974 that the asbestos-like fibers were entering Duluth's drinking water. Even so, the battle dragged on until 1980.

Meanwhile, controversy was building around issues of energy. In 1973, public utilities proposed a long-distance high-tension line to deliver power from generating plants in central North Dakota to the metropolitan area of Minneapolis–St. Paul. Without opposition the massive line of steel towers marched through North Dakota and western Minnesota, once hotbeds of radical farm protest, but in the conservative heartland of central Minnesota it met a wall of resistance. Local governments refused permits, and when state authorities overruled them, public hearings were packed with protesters. As it became clear that the decision had been made in early discussions between utilities and state agencies, and no alternatives would be seriously considered, farmers blocked construction sites, and state troopers were forced to arrest them as they stood in their own fields.[16]

Alarm was also mounting over the state's two nuclear plants, both operated by Northern States Power Company (NSP) and located on the Mississippi River. Environmental groups demanded conservation efforts and a shift to more benign local sources of power, such as wind, solar energy, and biomass. A legislative compromise measure in 1994 allowed limited above-ground storage of high-level nuclear wastes but required the company to develop other energy supplies. As a result, wind farms have become part of the landscape on Buffalo Ridge in southwestern Minnesota, where the corn belt meets the open sweep of the Great Plains. Another alternative already tapped in the mid-1970s was hydroelectricity generated through the Churchill River diversion project in northern Manitoba. By 1999, NSP was receiving 14 percent of its daily fuel load from Manitoba Hydro and seeking permission to buy more.[17]

By the end of the 1970s, farmers again felt the effects of economic depression. Agricultural prices were down, and inflated land values had collapsed. Those who had borrowed heavily to expand were in trouble. A new wave of foreclosure sales recalled the protests of the 1930s, but despite "tractorcades" and other demonstrations, both Washington and St. Paul were unresponsive. Agribusiness—loosely defined as the chemical, seed, feed, and machinery manufacturers that supply farms, along with the grain buyers, packinghouses, canneries, and other processors that buy from them—wielded far more political power than the shrinking fraction of independent farmers in the state's population.

Displaced farmers could still become "human resources" on the labor market, but options were narrowing. Although industry remained varied and strong, with high technology employing nearly a sixth of the state's industrial workers in 1980, Minnesota's dreams of becoming a "Silicon Valley North" were fading. The need for huge research budgets favored national and international companies over locally based innovators like Control Data, and the spread of the personal computer had to some extent bypassed the mainframes that were the specialty of state firms.

Depression was also returning to the Iron Range, where global competition in steel was fast closing down the new taconite plants. Tourism offered a way to diversify the economy, and in this nature cooperated. Twenty years of neglect had allowed most of the open pit mines to become lakes; new vegetation covered the barren red hills; birds and fish were coming back. The state added its own efforts at reforestation and built new recreational facilities. Yet many workers on the Iron Range resisted having their region become a playground for affluent visitors. Their woes were heard, for in 1976 one of their own had become governor.

Rudolph Perpich inherited the state's top office when Wendell Anderson resigned to take the Senate seat vacated by Walter Mondale, who became the second Minnesotan to serve as U.S. vice president. Perpich, the son of a Croatian miner, was the first Iron Ranger (and the first Catholic) to serve as governor. He filled out Anderson's term but was defeated when Republicans swept the state in 1978. In 1982 he was returned to office, and reelection in 1986 made him the state's longest-serving governor. During that time he moved steadily from populist beginnings toward promotion of global trade and support of Minnesota-based corporations, staying in line not only with national trends, but with much of the DFL.

This and other changes in the world were brought home in 1985 to meatpackers of Local P-9 of the United Food and Commercial Workers (UFCW) at the Hormel plant in Austin. A bitter strike, protesting speedups and wage cuts by one of the state's most profitable companies, drew intense sympathy in Minnesota and among rank-and-file members of the labor movement. There was no support, however, from the UFCW or the National Labor Relations Board, and when Hormel hired permanent replacements for the strikers, Perpich sent National Guard troops to keep the plant open. It was a stark contrast to the action of Farmer-Laborite Floyd Olson at the same place in 1933.[18]

The DFL was not alone in migrating to the right. Minnesota Republicans had reacted to the Nixon scandals by adding "Independent" to their name, but more fundamental changes were brewing. To the conservative sweep of the national party under Ronald Reagan was added a powerful bloc of religious activists within Minnesota. Through the 1980s and into the 1990s, state Republicans struck an uneasy balance between fiscal conservatism and a relatively liberal stand on social issues such as abortion and gay rights. Arne Carlson, who succeeded to the Republican nomination for governor when scandal swamped a party-endorsed religious conservative, walked the tightrope successfully. Elected in 1990, Carlson went on to serve as governor until 1998, but in that year the Republican candidate, Norman Coleman, moved further to the right—and lost.

New Diversity and New Dissent

The demographic changes that followed World War II have continued and accelerated, although by 1998 the Census Bureau estimated that Minnesota still had a nonwhite and Hispanic population of only 8 percent, as against a national figure of 28 percent. Its racial and cultural minorities are increasingly diverse. While African Americans still make up the largest single group (146,000), Asians and Pacific Islanders are second (124,000), followed by Hispanics (87,000) and American Indians (57,000). But projections indicate that Hispanic people will outstrip all other minorities within the next quarter century.[19]

Until World War II, Asians in Minnesota were only a scattered handful, mostly men, divided among Chinese, Japanese, and Filipinos. This changed with the easing of anti-Asian immigration laws in the 1940s and the wartime relocation of Japanese American citizens from the West Coast. Nevertheless, significant Asian immigration to Minnesota did not begin until the late 1970s, when the end of war in Southeast Asia sent a stream of refugees and displaced people to the United States. Despite its harsh climate, the state attracted a disproportionate number of Southeast Asians, drawn by social services, jobs, and housing, as well as by the absence of severe racial and ethnic conflict.

By 1990 Minnesota's Asian population numbered nearly seventy-eight thousand, most of whom lived in the metropolitan area. The largest single group were Hmong from the northern highlands of Laos. A tightly organized and cohesive community, the Hmong have concentrated in St. Paul, where Hmong is now the second most spoken language in the city's schools. As the decade advanced, the state's booming economy and a labor shortage continued to draw newcomers. In addition to more Hispanic people and Southeast Asians, these have included small but significant groups of refugees from the Balkan countries, Somalia, and Tibet. In the past five years an estimated fifteen thousand immigrants have made Minneapolis the Somali capital of the United States. Not only the face but the spirit of Minnesota has become more varied as Buddhist temples and meditation centers and Islamic mosques have been added to the churches and synagogues that previously defined religion in the state.[20]

How growing diversity will affect Minnesota and its culture is an open question. The accommodation of this "New England of the West," as it was sometimes called, to the great tide of foreign-born immigrants that arrived in the settlement years may not be a pattern for the future. Nineteenth-century Minnesota communities were often ethnic enclaves. Some carried their identities in their names—Holland, Caledonia, New Prague, Vasa, New Ulm, Karlstad, Clontarf, Toimi, Little Canada—but varied as they were, they shared the common traditions and blond complexions of northern Europe. Even at the end of the century, the mills and factories of the Twin Cities received fewer laborers from southern and eastern Europe than did other midwestern industrial centers.

Ojibwe and Dakota, African Americans, Jews, Mexicans, and even Germans—all can testify that prejudice exists in the state. Hate crimes have been isolated, but they have occurred. The aftermath of the Dakota War in 1862 brought the largest mass hanging in U.S. history, and it would have been far larger without the restraining hand of President Lincoln. Yet today, by comparison with other places, tensions are moderate, and perhaps the greatest source of hope lies in the very extent of the state's diversity. There is no single deep cleavage along racial or cultural lines, and if barriers of poverty and social class can be overcome, some sort of new middle ground may be achieved. The importance of education is one thing on which native Minnesotans and newcomers are solidly united.

No single factor accounts for Minnesota's exceptional prosperity in the 1990s, but much of it rested on expanding global markets. Manufacturing of paper and other wood products remained strong. Taconite was once more in demand, and plants were being reopened and modernized, with a corresponding effect on Great Lakes shipping. High-technology industries held their own, partly through growth in the manufacture of medical devices. Tourism played a role, for its increase was substantial, both in the scenic north and in the Twin Cities, where the Mall of America, a monument to American consumerism, became a major national and international attraction.

In agricultural areas, crisis continued and deepened. Crops were bountiful, but prices lagged. Huge poultry and hog production facilities multiplied in the southern parts of the state, raising worries about environmental effects and questions as to whether the term "farming" could still apply. At the same time, the population continued to shrink in the once-rich agricultural counties along Minnesota's southern and western borders.

The greatest growth was in the metropolitan suburbs and the north-central parts of the state. In the area around the Twin Cities, the population increased by 11.5 percent between 1990 and 1998, outstripping other midwestern urban centers. Demographic projections portray a semi-urban triangle that will include a broad belt extending from St. Cloud to Rochester and a metropolitan area spilling over into western Wisconsin. Outlying points will be Duluth-Superior in the northeast, La Crosse-Winona in the southeast, and Fargo-Moorhead to the west. Within this triangle, a growing commuter population will gradually blur the lines between country and city.[21]

Although the historic division between urban and rural lifestyles has faded in recent decades, the interwoven social fabric that has made the state "work" seems increasingly threatened. As global trade has widened in the 1990s, capital has migrated even faster than people, and while industry thrives in Minnesota, control and management are becoming less rooted in the state and no longer identified with its future. Many of the largest corporations have subdivided and moved part of their operations elsewhere, while mergers have produced complex layers of distant ownership. The ties of business to place and community and the sense of interdependence that were strong in the state have begun to dissolve.

Whether Minnesota is part of the American West has often been debated. At the end of the twentieth century it shares at least some cultural traits with that region. Among those who have lost the American dream of independence and self-sufficiency along with the family farm and the mom-and-pop business, there is denial, nostalgia—and anger. The phenomenon of "organized" militias has been largely absent from Minnesota, but its seedbed can be seen in rampant individualism, in hostility to wilderness preserves, in attacks upon resource conservation, and in the mystique of the hunter. No question in Minnesota politics stirs more fury than gun control, and in 1998 the citizen's eternal right to hunting and fishing was written into the state constitution. In other parts of the West an imagined frontier, where there is still an uncrowded, limitless world for human exploitation, lies over mountains or across deserts; in Minnesota it is somewhere "up north."

Despite a moralistic reputation, Minnesota has long been near the top among states in the incidence of alcoholism (and also in its treatment). An antigambling bastion as recently as the 1940s, Minnesota has now become a center for the pursuit of Lady Luck. It was the first state to sign agreements with Indian tribes for the opening of casinos under the federal Indian Gaming Act of 1988, and in the same year voters authorized a state lottery. The reasons for this turnaround have been widely debated. Some see it as a protest against taxes; others see a decline in habits of hard work, thrift, and planning for the future. The question seldom asked is whether gambling is not itself a symptom that confidence in a future of stability and just rewards has waned.

Yet there is also a stubborn clinging to traditions associated with Minnesota's quality of life. Although its forms and structures are hotly debated, education still draws overwhelming political support; in 1992 the state adopted its own health-care plan to provide for at least some of the thousands without coverage; home ownership in the Twin Cities outstrips that of most urban areas; welfare programs are strong; and in charitable giving Minnesota leads the nation. Preservation, both of history and the environment, also receives generous support. A host of nonprofit groups work at protecting and cleaning up the state's scenic waters, and in 1999 citizen protests delayed for months the construction of a new highway through historic Minnehaha Park in south Minneapolis.

Finally, the tradition of maverick politics has been resoundingly upheld. Although, as elsewhere in the nation, voter participation has declined steadily, Minnesota is still a leader among the states in the number of registered voters casting ballots. In 1990 a decrepit green school bus in which Paul Wellstone toured the state symbolized his upstart campaign against an incumbent senator widely thought to be unbeatable. In Washington, Wellstone reasserted Minnesota's reputation for liberal leadership and populist politics in a decade of booming prosperity and growing conservatism. At the opposite extreme stood the state's second senator, Rod Grams, a voice for the Christian Right and corporate advancement. And in 1998 Minnesotans astounded the nation by once again electing a third-party governor. In a time when campaign funds in the tens of millions seem a requirement for public office, Reform Party candidate Jesse Ventura spent less than a million dollars and even made a public appeal to pay for his inaugural celebration. His victory was widely interpreted as a rejection of both major parties in the state—and, perhaps more deeply, of American politics as a whole.

Notes

1. To the best of the author's recollection, this description originated with John Parker, former curator of the James Ford Bell Library of the University of Minnesota Libraries and an authority on the literature of exploration. The name Minnesota is a Dakota Indian word meaning "cloud-colored water," but more popularly interpreted as "sky-blue water."

2. Unless otherwise noted, information for this essay is drawn from four general works on Minnesota's history. They are: Theodore C. Blegen, *Minnesota, A History of the State*, 2d ed. (Minneapolis: University of Minnesota Press, 1975); William E. Lass, *Minnesota: A History*, 2d ed. (New York: W. W. Norton & Co., 1998); Clifford E. Clark Jr., ed., *Minnesota in a Century of Change: The State and Its People Since 1900* (St. Paul:

Minnesota Historical Society Press, 1989); and June Drenning Holmquist, ed., *They Chose Minnesota: A Survey of the State's Ethnic Groups* (St. Paul: Minnesota Historical Society Press, 1981).

3. The term "middle ground" has been put forward in a volume by Richard White, *The Middle Ground: Indians, Empires, and Republics in the Great Lakes Region, 1650–1815* (Cambridge: Cambridge University Press, 1991). The same cultural interlude, with particular reference to Minnesota, was examined in 1982 by the Minnesota Historical Society in St. Paul in an exhibition and accompanying book. See *Where Two Worlds Meet: The Great Lakes Fur Trade*, by Carolyn Gilman, with essays by Alan R. Woolworth, Douglas A. Birk, and Bruce M. White.

4. On the abrupt transformation of Minnesota from an Indian and mixed-blood community into a European-American commonwealth, along with the role of national expansion and regional tensions, see Anne R. Kaplan and Marilyn Ziebarth, eds., *Making Minnesota Territory, 1849–1858* (St. Paul: Minnesota Historical Society Press, 1999).

5. Population and fatality figures are from Arnold R. Alanen, "Years of Change on the Iron Range," in Clark, ed., *Minnesota in a Century of Change*, 159, 180.

6. By 1946 Minneapolis was referred to as "the capital of anti-Semitism in the United States." See Hyman Berman, "The Jews," in Holmquist, ed., *They Chose Minnesota*, 500.

7. For the role of the Minneapolis Citizens Alliance from 1903 to 1935, see Lois Quam and Peter J. Rachleff, "Keeping Minneapolis an Open-Shop Town: The Citizens Alliance in the 1930s," *Minnesota History* 50 (Fall 1986): 105–117.

8. Carl H. Chrislock, *Watchdog of Loyalty: The Minnesota Commission of Public Safety During World War I* (St. Paul: Minnesota Historical Society Press, 1991).

9. For the role played by the Reconstruction Finance Corporation in settling the strike, see Thomas E. Blantz, "Father Haas and the Minneapolis Truckers' Strike of 1934," *Minnesota History* 42 (Spring 1970): 5–15.

10. The most significant challenge to academic freedom at the University of Minnesota came in 1963–1965, when Professor Mulford Q. Sibley, an outspoken socialist and pacifist, was attacked by a longtime St. Paul city commissioner and others as being unfit to teach. In several public debates, Sibley (himself a Quaker) kept the focus of the argument on academic freedom, defending the rights of both Communists and atheists to a place in the educational system. His antiwar activism continued, and he was never fired.

11. Ronald F. Stinnett and Charles H. Backstrom, *Recount* (Washington, D.C.: National Document Publishers, 1964).

12. Barbara Stuhler and Gretchen Kreuter, eds., *Women of Minnesota*, rev. ed. (St. Paul: Minnesota Historical Society Press, 1998), 280–291; Gretchen Urnes Beito, *Coya Come Home: A Congresswoman's Journey* (Los Angeles: Pomegranate Press, Ltd., 1990).

13. A small magazine, published between 1972 and 1989 in Millville, Minnesota, served as one voice for this movement. See Rhoda R. Gilman, ed., *Ringing in the*

Wilderness: Selections from the "North Country Anvil" (Duluth: Holy Cow! Press, 1996).

14. Craig Cox, *Storefront Revolution: Food Co-ops and the Counterculture* (New Brunswick, N.J.: Rutgers University Press, 1994).

15. Figures compiled by the Legislative Commission on the Economic Status of Women, at <http://www.leg.state.mn.us>.

16. Barry M. Casper and Paul David Wellstone, *Powerline: The First Battle of America's Energy War* (Amherst, Mass.: University of Massachusetts Press, 1981).

17. Information from Minnesota Public Utilities Commission and NSP web site at <http://www.nspco.com>.

18. Peter Rachleff, *Hard-Pressed in the Heartland: The Hormel Strike and the Future of the Labor Movement* (Boston: South End Press, 1993).

19. Minnesota Planning State Demographic Center, *Turn of the Century: Minnesota's Population in 1900 and Today* (St. Paul: November 1999), 8, at <http://www.mnplan.state.mn.us/pdf/1999/demog/century0.pdf>; *Faces of the Future: Minnesota Population Projections 1995–2025* (St. Paul: May 1998), 5, at <http://www.mnplan.state.mn.us/press/cntypop.html>.

20. Minneapolis Foundation, *Immigration in Minnesota* (n.d.), at <http://www.mplsfoundation.org/overview/publicationstop.html>.

21. Minnesota Planning State Demographic Center, *Faces of the Future: Minnesota County Population Projections 1995–2025* (September 1998); *Star Tribune*, 17 December 1999, sec. B, 1.

Facing Minnesota

I QUIT MY JOB AT THE Sunshine food stores in Sioux Falls, South Dakota, on August 12, 1968—my eighteenth birthday—and spent the next month sewing name tags on my clothes and packing and repacking my boxes of stuff to take to school. I could hardly wait. "I'm going to college, I'm going to college," I kept repeating to myself. And I was going to Minnesota. Like 80 percent of college-age kids of my generation in South Dakota, I was leaving the state. If we wanted to get somewhere in life, we had learned, we had to get away.

I picked a college where I knew no one, where I could escape the local memory of my widely known (and well-liked) parents and the accumulated school and neighborhood memories of my four older sisters and my older brother. I did not want to be "an Atkins girl" anymore. I wanted to be me, though I had little idea who that was. I was going to Minnesota to find out.

Like most immigrants to the state for the past two hundred years I knew better what I was leaving than what I was entering. I knew about Hubert Humphrey and Eugene McCarthy, about Minnesota lakes (my family had stayed at one once), and about Minneapolis (I had never been there, though I have a vague childhood memory of the Edina water tower). I had listened to WCCO radio and, from time to time, had even seen the *Minneapolis Tribune*. In short, I had some images of the state, but not much more.

Minnesota has an ability to draw people—not all, of course, and it sends some people running away without looking back. Just ask Bob Dylan, who even scorned Duluth's offer to name a street after him. For me, though, it has been an immigrant's dream.

In another essay in this collection, Rhoda Gilman offers an overview of the state's history, filled with information essential to seeing the sweep of the

ANNETTE ATKINS *is author of* We Grew Up Together: Brothers and Sisters in Nineteenth-Century America *and* Harvest of Grief: Grasshopper Plagues and Public Assistance in Minnesota, 1873–78. *She is professor of history at St. John's University/College of St. Benedict in Minnesota.*

state's past. She has taken the burden of telling the big story; I am afforded the pleasure of a more eclectic task: to pick out a few people whose stories reveal some truths that do not normally factor in our collective state memory. These stories suggest the complexity of racial issues in the state, the variation among immigrants, the nature of pioneering, the vitality of American Indian culture, the power of politics and politicians to do good and not to, the seductions and the perils of hero-worship.

Of the issues highlighted in this essay, none is more complicated, subtle, or tangled than relations between American Indians and Euro-Americans. Never so simple—then or now—as indigenous people honoring Mother Earth while whites mindlessly exploited it; never so simple as altruistic whites saving uncivilized Indians; never so simple as whites cruelly tricking trusting native people. These stereotypes hide more than they reveal, and they all overlook the period in Minnesota's past when racial categories were more blurred and when Dakota and Euro-American people lived on more common grounds.

Little Crow and Philander Prescott lived in those times and on those grounds. Little Crow (about 1810–1863) was born in the Mdewakanton village of Kaposia on the Minnesota River, near what is today South St. Paul. Philander Prescott (1801–1862) was born in upstate New York and made his way to Little Crow's country in 1820 when he was nineteen years old. Like most white men in the fur trade, Prescott married an Indian woman—Nag-he-no-Wenah, or Spirit in the Moon. In his autobiography, Prescott referred to his nine children by their western names. They, no doubt, also had American Indian names. They lived among their mother's people much of the time and their mother continued to participate in her band's traditional life, especially while Prescott was gone for months at a time buying trading goods in St. Louis or elsewhere.[1]

Prescott learned to speak Dakota. His wife could understand both French and English; she reputedly did not speak either. As a "sutler" (storekeeper), an interpreter at Fort Snelling, and a government-appointed supervisor of Dakota farming, he had a life and a livelihood dependent on Little Crow's people.

Prescott was not living an "Indian" life, but his was not a white life either. He was one of many whites—and then mixed-blood people—before 1862 who stood between the two cultures. His loyalty to his own was strong and, as more whites made their way to Little Crow's territory and he was re-Christianized by the missionaries to the Dakota, his world became more and more white. But living with an Indian wife and doing business primarily with Dakota people, Prescott operated largely in an Indian world.[2]

When Prescott arrived, the Eastern Dakota had been in contact with Europeans and Euro-Americans—a few explorers, but mostly fur traders—for about 150 years. Nonetheless, Little Crow's life was still a Dakota life and his people were living much as they had for generations. Like Dakota men before him, Little Crow experienced a purification ritual with a shaman; he had his own sacred bundle; he was given the crow as his sacred animal guide; he joined his band's medicine society. He, like the Dakota people around him, had incorporated into their traditional ways the new goods that the traders offered — iron pots and knives, blankets, beads, guns, alcohol. With the exception of liquor, these goods largely supported the native culture and did not radically alter its basic order. The Dakota engaged in the trade because it suited their interests; they judged the trade goods to be useful and helpful. Cooking with iron kettles, for example, was better than cooking without them.

Little Crow grew up knowing many white people. Through marriages like the one between Prescott and Nag-he-no-Wenah, he was related to a great many of them. They were his kin. Moreover, Little Crow found it helpful to be schooled by white missionaries for a short time and to know the rudiments of reading and writing in his own language, as well as arithmetic, at which he was quite adept. He developed, too, into quite a good poker player.[3]

Little Crow tried to understand and work with whites, an effort born out of the realization after mid-century of the ultimately greater power of whites. He was among the Dakota who went to Washington, D.C., in 1858 to seek redress, or so they thought, for unmet and broken promises after the Treaty of 1851, when the Dakota had ceded much of their land in Minnesota. The commissioner of Indian Affairs, however, had a different purpose in mind: to get yet more Dakota land. The commissioner's agenda prevailed. He acquired the land he wanted at an irresponsibly low price (most of which never made its way into Dakota hands), and he disregarded the Dakota's complaints. These meetings exacerbated the Dakota grievances that, when combined with starvation and withheld rations, finally erupted in furious violence in August of 1862. It was a Dakota/white conflict that was once called the Sioux Massacre and now, more accurately, is called the Dakota War, for war it was.

When the Dakota War exploded in Minnesota in 1862 both Prescott and Little Crow were caught up in the rage. Whatever territory they had shared was ripped into two separate and explicitly racial camps. There was no middle ground to meet or stand on. When a band of Mdewakanton attacked the Lower Sioux Agency on the second day of the war, Prescott walked into the line of their fire. He faced up to a group of his wife's people, presuming that his long association with them would protect him. It did not. He was shot and killed.

Although certain of defeat, Little Crow assumed leadership, reluctantly and yet loyally. He assented to the dictum that Prescott's killers are reputed to have invoked: "Our orders are to kill all white men. We cannot spare you." When defeat of the Indians—always a given, but only conceded by the Dakota after a month of fighting and eluding white soldiers and civilian guards—was assured, Little Crow, like many other Dakota, fled Minnesota. A year later, he returned and was shot while picking berries near Hutchinson. His killers were motivated by their acid-etched memories of the previous year and by the unspoken, but no less powerful, white imperative to kill all Indians. Prescott had not been spared. Little Crow could not be spared, either.

The deaths of these two men—relatives, certainly friendly if not friends, and mutually dependent—signaled the end of one phase of Indian-white relations and ushered in another much more hostile to the Dakota. Following the hanging of thirty-eight Dakota at Mankato at the conclusion of the war, the remainder of the Dakota were removed, mostly to the Santee Reservation in Nebraska. Only a few returned.

Until 1837 the lives of Indians and whites overlapped, often awkwardly and without subtle understandings of each other. From 1837 to 1858, animosities that had been at the periphery of relations became the centerpiece, but kinship ties still mattered on both sides. What changed most dramatically in 1862 was the disappearance of any shared territory—literally and figuratively. It was a tragedy.

The story of the Dakota War inclined nineteenth-century readers to focus on the brutality of the Dakota; it inclines modern-day readers to pay closer attention to the crimes committed against the Dakota. There is a kind of emotional whiplash that occurs when we turn to the Civil War, in which Minnesota men (white as well as mixed-blood sons of couples like the Prescotts) distinguished themselves in the Union Army.

The men of the First Minnesota Regiment fought in many of the most important battles in the Civil War in 1861 and 1862: Bull Run, Antietam, Fredericksburg. When General Winfield Scott Hancock found himself without reinforcements at Gettysburg on July 2, 1863, and with a hole in his line, he turned to the First Minnesota Regiment and ordered them to block that hole. They were experienced enough to know that they faced "death or wounds to us all," as one survivor reported. What mutinous thoughts might have filtered through their heads we do not know. We do know, however, that the men of the First did as they were ordered; they poured themselves into the breach, knowing that their main job was simply to buy a few minutes with their lives. They did. The reinforcements arrived, the skirmish was won, the battle was won, the war was won. The casualties? By one account 272 men charged, by another 315; by all accounts, however, 215 lay dead or wounded. The same survivor recalled, "every man saw and accepted the necessity for the sacrifice."[4] These heroes were in the same army as the men who defeated the Dakota in Minnesota.

The Civil War ended in 1865, but only on the battlefields. The war shaped much of what happened in Minnesota and in the United States for the rest of the century. Men who ran for public office had to be veterans or have a good reason why they were not. Virtually every family in Minnesota in the 1860s had been touched by the war—soldiers, of course, by their own service; but also every wife, child, brother, sister, or parent who stayed behind and tended farms, stores, businesses, and the affairs of daily life while the soldiers were away. Some men certainly came home with what we would now call post-traumatic stress syndrome, but most in the nineteenth century had neither the language nor the inclination to call it anything. What did those men do with their memories of the savagery of that war?

Some blotted them out and clutched their memories of glory. Alexander Christie, an Irish-born Scotsman whose family settled in Minnesota, was bereft when his three older brothers went off to war together and left him at home with the women. He was only fifteen. He longed to grow up fast so that he could join up, and, finally, in 1865 just before the war ended, he enlisted and served briefly. Nothing he did in the rest of his life rivaled for him the intensity of those few months. It was the high point of his life—as for many another veteran.[5]

Virtually every small town in Minnesota built a GAR (Grand Army of the Republic) hall and most erected as well some kind of memorial to its local veterans, like the Union soldier carved by a local stonemason in 1901 that still guards the Pipestone County Courthouse grounds. The most common reminders of the war, however, were the hundreds of veterans who were without an arm or a leg.

In 1897—on the thirty-fourth anniversary of the charge—a state-funded memorial to the First Minnesota Regiment was dedicated on the Gettysburg battlefield. Dozens of politicians turned up, as well as survivors and a few widows, all transported on railroad cars supplied by St. Paulite James J. Hill. The ceremony had all the hallmarks of a nineteenth-century Fourth of July celebration—extraordinary rhetoric, pomp and circumstance, the aged but venerable veterans. People relieved not to have been called on to sacrifice their lives and grateful to those who did offered thanks and praise, in huge quantities. The memorial plaque reads, in part: "In self-sacrificing desperate valor their charge has no parallel in any war." Minnesotans felt triumphant and agreed that a good thing had been done; men had fought bravely; slavery had been eliminated.

The wounds and the triumphs of the Dakota and Civil Wars are all integral to the state's story. Pioneers are also central to Minnesota's identity. Minnesotans have honored pioneers for their individualism, for their hard work, for their ability to do what we imagine is impossible and somehow triumph over the odds. One version of the story happened often enough, but is only rarely recounted: the tale of those who tried as hard as they could and still did not make it. Mary Carpenter's life gives that account as well as anyone's in Minnesota.

In 1873, Mary (1840–1889) had been married for thirteen years. She and her husband, George, living on a small farm in southeastern Minnesota, dreamed that Lyon County, in southwestern Minnesota, offered them better prospects and a brighter future. They packed up their things and made the two-week, two-hundred-mile journey by wagon. George walked most of the way, tending the stock. Their three surviving children—of the seven she had borne already—took turns riding and walking. Mary, thirty-three years old and pregnant with her eighth child, drove the wagon. Mary later reported that she "was not romantic enough to enjoy it much, but endured it better than I feared."

In a letter to her Aunt Martha shortly after arriving, Mary described their already battered dream. They had planned to sell their horse, milk the cows and use the stock, eat from the garden. They found, though, no buyer for the horse; the best cow got sick en route; grasshoppers had eaten their way through everyone's gardens. Mary needed help of whatever kind her aunt could offer: clothes, money, newspapers, books. "Mother said when we started, 'you are going there to freeze and starve next winter.' I thought not, but George said today it might prove so."

Mary and her family settled on land from which the Dakota had been removed. To the Dakota, the land was certainly stolen. To Mary, she and her husband had acquired their land legally and legitimately from the ostensible owners—the U.S. government. Perhaps she should have been smarter, more sensitive, and more aware of Dakota culture and government injustice, but in the context of the time it would have been virtually impossible. Such ideas were simply not available, even to the whites who were the smartest, the most sensitive, and the most interested in American Indian ways. There is no evidence that Mary was any of these.

Mary knew, though, that she was a "pioneer" and was supposed to act and talk like a pioneer. She could not quite transform herself into what had already become in the American imagination a mythic legend. "You hope a double portion of the pioneering spirit descends to me. I am endowed with very little of it. My taste runs the other way, to conveniences, elegancies, comforts and all the paraphernalia of civilized life."[6]

She and George returned to Rochester for the winter of 1873–1874, then back to Marshall in 1874 to try again, a strategy that they used at least two more times before they finally were able to stay on their new land for the whole year. They settled down, then, in Lyon County and worked their farm. Mary bore three more children and lost another.

Despite their determination and effort, Mary and George did not prosper. Their most serious problem was that they could not get out of debt, not matter how hard they worked. Mary despaired. "George is hopeful, as usual," Mary wrote, but, she confessed, "I have spells of being 'very blue.'"[7]

In 1889 her "terrible hypochondria"—what she called her depression—deepened and Mary died, perhaps by her own hand. Suicides were not identified as such in the nineteenth century; they were called by some other name. The cause of death offered in her obituary (more explicit than most obituaries then or now) was "melancholy, tending to derangement." Historian Sara Brooks Sundberg observed that it would be wrong to call Mary "a reluctant, stoic pioneer." She was more complex than that, more mixed, more human, more three-dimensional than the icon of "pioneer" or "pioneer woman" normally allows.[8] Unless you read Ole Rølvaag's accounts; he knew the costs of migration.

Ole Edvart Rølvaag (1876–1931) was one drop in the tidal wave of Scandinavian immigrants that washed into Minnesota. Another was Carl Skoglund (1884–1960). Two men could hardly have lived lives more different from each other than did these two. The category "Scandinavian immigrant" has to be big to hold them both.

Rølvaag was born in a Norwegian fishing village in 1876; at nineteen he landed in South Dakota with an uncle from whom he had borrowed the money for the passage. Within a few years, Rølvaag enrolled at St. Olaf, a Norwegian-Lutheran college in Northfield, Minnesota. He graduated, returned to Norway for a year of further study at Christiania, then returned again to Northfield to take up teaching and writing. He chaired the department of Norwegian language and literature and stayed in Northfield until his death in 1931. He became a citizen, married, and had four children. Two died before reaching adulthood; a third, Karl, was elected governor of Minnesota and served from 1963 to 1967.[9]

Rølvaag published six novels about the immigrant experience. He is best known for *Giants in the Earth,* his novel of rural pioneering life. I prefer—and recommend—his quieter, less well-known *The Boat of Longing.* This tale opens in Norway, in a fishing village, and tells of how Nils Vaag—Nils of the Sea—decides to leave his mother and father to find his future in Minneapolis. The words in the first hundred pages, when Nils is in Norway, lap against each other like the water against Nils's scow on a dreamy day: languid and easy. It is poetry. When Nils gets to Minneapolis, the book's language speeds up and mimics the blare of voices and sounds on the streets and in his boarding house they called Babel. He shares the house with the Norwegian Mrs. Andersen (married to and later abandoned by a Dane); the Pinskys, she a Russian-Pole, he a Russian Jew; the German Mrs. Hoffman and her two daughters; Mike Sullivan and his wife Maria; Gustaf Soderblom, his wife, and their five children; Dagny and Marie, clerks in a Minneapolis department store; and his friend the poet. Nils works in the city, then up north in the woods; then he simply vanishes.

In the book's last section, "Hearts That Ache," Nils's parents grieve their son's disappearance. No word. No news. They wait. Driven finally to despair at hearing nothing, Nils's father sets out from Norway to find his son in Minnesota. Immigration officials stop him at the port of New York. He had neither the right documents nor enough money to be allowed into the country. So, without ever setting foot in the United States, he is sent back. On the boat he happens upon a woman who has just come from Minneapolis. Had she, the old man asks, seen his son? He was a tall, light-haired man with blue eyes and broad shoulders. She thinks for a minute then remembers, yes, she did; he was "well dressed" and "unusually busy," and, she is sure, "he lived in a marble palace." Hearing this report, Rølvaag wrote, Jo is "the happiest passenger on board."[10] He never sees his son again.

Rølvaag's Scandinavian past haunted him; Carl Skoglund's past radicalized him. Born in 1884, he was eight years younger than Rølvaag. He grew up not in rural Norway, as Rølvaag had, but in a Swedish town. When he was twelve he took his first job as an unskilled laborer in a paper mill. And he became an activist early. He organized a union and then a strike in his paper mill when he was in his early twenties. This earned him his first blacklisting—hardly so poetic a story as Rølvaag's. In 1911, when he was twenty-seven, he migrated to the United States and ended up in Minneapolis. He did not go to college; he did not marry; he did not become a citizen, though in 1918 when asked to what country he claimed allegiance, he replied, "America."

He worked for the Pullman railroad company as a mechanic, but when he helped organize a rail strike he found himself blacklisted again. He joined the Communist Party in Minnesota and the Minnesota branch of the Scandinavian Socialist Federation. When his politics had resulted in blacklisting him from almost any job he sought, he bought a truck and went into the coal-hauling business. Then, of course, he organized the coal-haulers. He was one of the chief strategists in the Minneapolis truckers' strike in 1934. He was almost deported twice. Once he was held at Ellis Island and slated to be loaded on the next ship bound for Sweden before friends managed to get him released. He served sixteen months in jail for advocating the overthrow of the American government. He was always a Marxist, believing fundamentally in the centrality of the class struggle, and a Trotskyist, committed to the world spread of communism.[11]

For all their differences both men offered critiques of American life. Rølvaag emphasized the high cost of leaving one's own land and despaired of American materialism. Minnesota does not fare too well in his depictions. It is the place where people lose themselves. Skoglund despaired of America's class divisions that left the rich richer and working people desperate. Of course, he advocated the overthrow of American capitalism. While Rølvaag rowed his boat of longing, Skoglund was marching, marching onward.

Another pair of Minnesotans—native-born, African American—offered one more critique of America and of Minnesota. Nellie Griswold Francis (1874–1969) and William T. Francis (1870?–1929) played starring roles in St. Paul life for the first three decades of the twentieth century. A lawyer, William Francis worked first for the Northern Pacific Railway, and then when Fredrick McGhee, the most prominent black criminal lawyer in Minnesota—and reportedly the first one west of the Mississippi—died suddenly, Francis took over McGhee's office, practice, and prominent place in the community.[12]

Francis belonged to the Twin Cities Protective League—a black self-help organization—but when it decided to affiliate itself with the National Association for the Advancement of Colored People in 1912, he initially opposed the move. Blacks all over the United States had before them in this period two very strong, very different spokesmen who held conflicting solutions to the race problem. W. E. B. Du Bois, northern-raised and Harvard-educated and -employed, argued that blacks must work for their political rights, and his philosophy infused the NAACP. Booker T. Washington, born into slavery and the founder of the Tuskegee Institute, urged blacks to look to their economic interests (and clout) and to pursue their political rights only gradually. Francis was neither docile nor "accommodating," but he found himself more in accord with Washington. When Washington came to St. Paul in 1913, it was Francis who entertained him socially.

The Francises lived in a world circumscribed by their race, in the midst of which they helped create—and benefited from—a strong black community: black churches, clubs, fraternal organizations, stores, restaurants, and several black newspapers. They did not have to go far, however, to encounter discrimination and racial hatred. Both of the Francises took on those outside forces. William often worked on discrimination cases. He regularly gave speeches on race issues to black and mixed audiences. He spoke in a Washington-like voice of cooperation and reconciliation—"we are glad to fight our country's battles and we bear no malice for the wrongs we have suffered"—but he, like Washington, also fought back. He spoke out against a ban on interracial marriage; he worked to end discrimination in schools of hairdressing (black barbers being the largest single category of black professionals in St. Paul in the 1920s); and he spoke against the ban on interracial boxing. He resented and spoke out against the YMCA's decision to discontinue black memberships when it moved into a new building in downtown Minneapolis. During World War I he was especially bitter about the treatment of black soldiers who, even though in service to their country, "had to wait in dark and dingy separate Negro waiting rooms to board Jim Crow cars."[13]

Nellie Francis worked for some years as a stenographer at West Publishing Company in downtown St. Paul, quite a good position for a black woman in St. Paul at the beginning of the twentieth century. Afterwards, she taught stenography to young women in her home. Like many middle-class women of her generation she made a career out of public service. From the 1890s to the 1920s she belonged to virtually every major black women's organization in Minnesota as well as to the National Association of Colored Women's Clubs and to a few racially mixed organizations as well, such as the Tri-State Women's Baptist Convention and the Schubert Club. When Mrs. B. T. Washington visited St. Paul, Nellie Francis served as her escort. Nellie and her husband protested the showing of D. W. Griffith's racist 1915 movie *The Birth of a Nation*. She was the state president of the Federation of Negro Women's Clubs. She became deeply engaged in the drive for women's suffrage and was a founder and first president of the Everywoman Suffrage Club, a black women's group. After women won the vote she led the Republican Colored Women for Minnesota Campaign in 1920. She also worked especially hard for the passage of an anti-lynching law, an effort intensified by the lynching in 1920 of three black men in Duluth. In part because of the persistent efforts of the Francises, the 1921 Minnesota state legislature passed the anti-lynching law that Nellie Francis had written.[14]

In 1927 W. T. Francis was appointed consul to Liberia, but within a year of taking the post he contracted and died of yellow fever. Nellie returned to Tennessee, where she had been born and spent her first ten years and where most of her family still lived. She died there in 1969, having visited Minnesota only a few times in forty years. She must have felt more at home in Tennessee, despite all she had invested in Minnesota.

It is quite probable that through their political work the Francises knew at least one of the two Charles Lindberghs. Charles Lindbergh Sr. (1859–1924) was a two-time congressman from Minnesota and twice ran for governor. He played an active role in state politics and championed particularly the rights of farmers against what he called the commercial interests. He defended communists, labor unionists, and radicals of all kinds (and was often accused of being one himself). Believing that bankers and business interests were pushing the United States into World War I, he adamantly counseled neutrality, then actively opposed America's entry into the war.

Given that much of Minnesota was erupting in a frenzy of anti-German sentiment and xenophobia at the beginning of World War I, Lindbergh's stand required courage. The state-appointed Minnesota Commission of Public Safety was authorized, among other things, "to check or suppress all efforts interfering with the mobilization of the man power of the state." This somehow included pulling down statues of German figures, allowing to go unpunished the tarring and feathering of conscientious objectors, and outlawing public questioning of the American war effort. The state legislature barred teaching in and of German in the public schools, shaming an entire generation of German Americans simply for their ancestry. Lindbergh lost his bid for the governorship. His stance provoked questions about his loyalty and his patriotism and ended his political career. It also ensured his enshrinement in Minnesota's cathedral of radicals.[15]

His son, Charles Lindbergh Jr. (1902–1974)—partly in response to the treatment of his father and partly in sympathy with his Detroit mother's longtime disdain for the state—left Minnesota as early as he could. He was long gone when in 1927 he gathered up his courage and five sandwiches (if he made it, he explained, five would be enough; if he did not, he would not need any more than that) and flew from New York to Paris, the first person to do so solo. People all over the world cheered the man many called "Lucky Lindy," though, as one biographer reports, Lindbergh hated the nickname, grumbling that there was nothing lucky about it.[16]

This Lindbergh may have rejected Minnesota, but Minnesota claimed him. We needed him. Minnesota had not offered up many romantic figures. We specialized, instead, in grimmer images. Rølvaag's, yes, but also Sinclair Lewis's. In 1920, Lewis published *Main Street,* his novel about stultifying small-town life in Gopher Prairie, Minnesota, not too unlike the Sauk Centre of his childhood. His heroine Carol Kennicott chafed at the boundaries and barriers of Main Street. Lamenting that "everything crushes me so," she tried to push them back, but was eventually broken by the town's conventionalities and small-mindedness. The narrator grimly concluded: "a hundred generations of Carols will aspire and go down in tragedy . . . the humdrum inevitable tragedy of struggle against inertia."[17]

Lewis described his own life as "quite unromantic and unstirring" and proved that he could lack a little imagination himself. According to Garrison Keillor, when the Nobel Prize committee representative called from Sweden to tell Lewis that he was the first American to win the prize in literature, Lewis, certain that one of his Minnesota friends was putting on a Scandinavian accent and playing a joke on him, made a joke of his own and hung up on him.

But Lindbergh was different: Scandinavian, but neither morose nor a communist; from a small town, but worldly; romantic and quite stirring and with movie-star good looks; triumphant but also bashful and charmingly self-effacing. He was ours. In his grand American tour after his trans-Atlantic flight, Lindbergh stopped twice in Minnesota: once in the Twin Cities and once in Little Falls where the water tower had been repainted to announce that this was his hometown.[18]

A decade later, in the late 1930s, he was invited by the führer to inspect the German air strength. When Lindbergh returned home, he endorsed neutrality and opposed America's entry into World War II. In expressing views similar to his father's of World War I, Lindbergh Jr. believed he was speaking with the same dignity and honor that had earned his father respect in many quarters. The world had turned, however. Words that sounded courageous when they came from the father sounded fascist and anti-Semitic when spoken by the son. Many of the same people who had showered him with confetti and praise a decade earlier now vilified him. Little Falls repainted its water tower. Minnesota did not need him anymore. Lindbergh lived out his life mostly in Hawaii, engaged in environmental causes. He only rarely returned to Minnesota.

One of the most prominent and popular people in Minnesota in the 1940s was Elizabeth Kenny (1886–1952). Sister Kenny, as she was called, was a sister in the British sense of "nurse," though not quite that either. She invented her nursing credentials along with her nurse's costume. Born and raised in Australia, she taught herself to see what medical training taught others in her time *not* to see—how to treat polio victims. While virtually all doctors were immobilizing their afflicted patients, Sister Kenny developed a method of applying heat and then stretching the muscles to release polio's lock on the patient's limb. She brought her methods to the United States and met nearly universal opposition until 1940, when she met up with Dr. Wallace H. Cole, the head of orthopedics at the University of Minnesota. After watching her work with several of his patients, he is reported to have said, in a characteristically Minnesota understatement, "I think you had better stick around for a while."

She did. First she managed a ward at the Minneapolis General Hospital. Then, after it was built for her, the Elizabeth Kenny Institute. Since the creation of the Salk and then the Sabine vaccines, the incidence of polio has virtually disappeared and today the Sister Kenny Institute, a part of Abbott Northwestern Hospital systems, operates as a rehabilitation center for people with all sorts of physical difficulties and stands as a monument to her stubbornness.[19]

Sister Kenny, by all reports, could be a difficult woman except with her patients, with whom she exercised extraordinary patience and kindness. She affected an intimidating public presence, dramatic hats and all. Americans voted her their second-most-admired woman consistently through the 1940s (behind Eleanor Roosevelt), and grateful recipients of the Kenny treatment deluged her with letters of thanks. RKO Pictures made a movie of her life that starred Rosalind Russell, screenplay by Mary McCarthy. The movie poster "She won fame . . . but lost love!" told one story, but the fuller story is that she revolutionized the treatment of polio in Minnesota and in the rest of the United States. She returned to Australia in 1951 and died there a year later.

She was not a Minnesotan—how long does a person have to live in the state before being one, I wonder?—but we claim her as partly ours. She demonstrates a kind of stubbornness that Minnesotans admire, at least sometimes.

Hubert Humphrey (1911–1978) had a long political career as a mayor of Minneapolis, senator, and vice president. He is part of what makes Minnesota Minnesota. In 1948 Humphrey was mayor of Minneapolis—like the St. Paul of the Francises, a city with a reputation for being quite insensitive on matters of race. He was also an aspiring Senate candidate and member of the platform committee at the Democratic National Convention.

The national Democratic Party had been, since the days of the Civil War, a predominantly white and southern party. Whenever black men had been allowed a political voice it had been in the Republican Party, the party of Abraham Lincoln. But in 1936 that changed. In that election, one leading black newspaper called on black voters to turn Lincoln's picture to the wall and to vote for Franklin Roosevelt. They did. Thus northern blacks and southern whites found themselves—oddly—in the same political party. This was a fragile coalition, and FDR and other Democratic leaders, who were most afraid of alienating the southerners, walked softly on civil rights issues. That blacks nonetheless still found the Democratic Party more appealing than the Republican hints at how hostile the entire process must have felt to black voters.

In 1948, the platform committee, too, was in the grip of the southern Democrats. Humphrey's efforts to get the committee to adopt a strong civil rights plank failed. Against the advice of many colleagues and against the majority of the committee, but with the help of several close friends (especially Orville Freeman and Humphrey's father, a delegate to the convention from South Dakota), Humphrey forced a vote on the convention floor between the committee's wording and his wording. His dramatic speech called on the Democrats "to get out of the shadows of state's rights to walk forthrightly into the bright sunshine of human rights." He won. The Southern Dixiecrats bolted the party. For the remainder of his political career, Humphrey lived in the shadow of that floor fight with his southern colleagues in the Senate, and he lived in the proud memories of many Minnesotans. Not, though, Coya Knutson.

Coya Gjesdal Knutson (1912–1996) was the first of only two woman elected to serve in the U.S. Congress from Minnesota. The oldest daughter in a Norwegian-speaking farm family, she sang her way into political office—literally. A talented singer who trained briefly at the Julliard School of Music, she could give a rousing stump speech, but sang an even more rousing stump song. She was elected to the state house in 1950 and 1952. In 1954 she was elected to the U.S. Congress, and was reelected in 1956. She was the first woman to serve on the House Agriculture Committee. She was a prime mover of federal defense student loans and of federal funding of cystic fibrosis research. She took her adopted son with her to Washington and raised him alone. She hired a male assistant/secretary who was often rumored to have been her lover (what other relationship could a woman and man have, it was wondered in the 1950s), and her husband eventually sued the aide for the alienation of his wife's affection.[20]

She was politically smart enough to get elected—she was popular with the voters—but not astute enough to keep her bridges secure. She burned an important one in 1956. Believing that he would address the agricultural needs of her rural constituents, she backed Senator Estes Kefauver's bid for the vice-presidential nomination against her fellow Minnesotan, Senator Humphrey. Two years later, in 1958, Coya's husband, a too-often drinker who had eschewed Washington life, wrote—and gave a copy to the newspapers—a letter that pleaded "Coya, Come Home." Her political ship began to sink under the weight of his pathos and of gender-role expectations in the 1950s. Her state political colleagues—including Senator Humphrey—did not throw her a lifeline. In the "you help me, I will help you" world of politics, she had not and they did not. She was defeated in 1958; her political career was finished.

At her funeral in Minneapolis in 1996, her grandchildren wept openly; Martin Olaf Sabo and Bill Luther, two sitting Minnesota congressmen, memorialized her; her biographer Gretchen Beito put her life into context; a gospel singer lamented her passing; and dozens of Minnesotans who had never known her showed up to honor her. Coya had tried to sing her own song. Theodore Blegen's encyclopedic *Minnesota: A History of the State* (1963 and 1975) does not mention her.

Women have risen to elected leadership roles against the dictates of tradition in other Minnesota settings as well. There are eleven American Indian reservations and communities in Minnesota: seven Ojibwe reservations (Fond du Lac, Grand Portage, Leech Lake, Mille Lacs, Bois Forte, Red Lake, White Earth) and four Dakota communities (Prairie Island, Lower Sioux, Shakopee-Mdewakanton, Upper Sioux). Marge Anderson (1938–) was appointed chief executive of the Mille Lacs band of Ojibwe in 1991 (filling out the term of the chief executive who died in office), elected to the post in 1992, reelected in 1996, and defeated in 2000. She held office at a time when her band and other American Indians in Minnesota and the United States are in the midst of reimagining themselves and their choices for understanding and living out their identity. As Anderson herself put it, "Our elders teach us that without our culture, we are not Ojibwe people—we are only the descendants of Ojibwe people."[21]

An especially contentious issue between the Ojibwe and many white Minnesotans—including many in the state legislature—has been Ojibwe hunting and fishing rights. In brief, in an 1837 treaty the federal government granted to the Ojibwe people special rights to hunt, fish, and gather in lands that they were ceding to the federal government. On various grounds, the federal government, first, and then the state of Minnesota contested these rights, but a 1999 U.S. Supreme Court ruling upheld the Ojibwe rights. It has been a bitter argument with both sides claiming cultural prerogative. Anderson spoke neither to, nor from, that bitterness, but instead, in the tense months before the Supreme Court issued its decision, she called on her people in a letter to "carry yourselves with the dignity that is your heritage." The tone of the letter taught by example.[22]

Another contentious issue within the Ojibwe community has been casinos and how to distribute their proceeds. The result of contact between American Indian and Euro-American peoples has been that Indians have faced crushing, grueling poverty in the nineteenth and twentieth centuries. But the legalization of gaming on Indian lands has blown in change, even improvement. The Mille Lacs band runs two casinos: Grand Casino Mille Lacs and Grand Casino Hinckley (about 50 miles apart). The annual attendance at the two casinos exceeds seven million people, which translates into big profits. Anderson had a clear vision about the place of Indian gaming and the proper use of those profits. At Mille Lacs, she and the other elected officials put most of the proceeds back into the community: paving the streets on the reservation, renovating and building homes, putting in a sewer system, and building schools, community centers, water treatment plants, and clinics. In addition, band members received small cash payments.

In the 1996 election Anderson faced opposition from band members who argued that the lot of individual Indians had little improved despite the inrush of funds into the tribal coffers. About 40 percent of the Mille Lacs band members live off the reservation land and, the critics argued, did not benefit from improvements to the reservation; they needed a larger and more direct allotment of tribal profits—as is the case in some other Native American communities. Anderson, however, remained vehemently committed to improving the lot of the community. Perhaps she remembered that the effects of the Nelson Act in 1889, which, in effect, divided Ojibwe tribal lands among individual members, resulted in the loss of much of that land. She knew that what is held in common survives; she also knew that good fortune can turn bad.[23]

Although she could be mild-mannered, she could also be fierce and sharp—as in her criticism of the state's consideration of extending gaming rights to non-Indians, in her zero-tolerance of drinking among tribal employees, in her defense of Indian rights ("We've waited 161 years. How much longer should we wait?") and of Indian sovereignty, and in her criticism of the racist remarks of a KSTP broadcaster. She made some enemies along the way. Whatever the criticism and whatever the rewards, of which there have been many, Anderson steered by her own vision: to create at Mille Lacs "a place where people can dare hope for a better life."[24] She reminded even those who might care to forget that American Indians live today, that their culture did not ultimately collapse under white pressure, that theirs remains a strong community that, like every community, faces internal conflict.

My original assignment for this essay had been to identify some Minnesota heroes. Certainly the essay embraces a number of people I consider admirable; but heroic? I could not do it. In 1968, when I got to Southwest Minnesota State College, I found that those name tags I had sewn into my clothes were the only things around me not unraveling. In Marshall, students, faculty, and town activists—such as the remarkable Polly Mann—marched to city hall in protest against the Vietnam War. People went on hunger strikes; some were arrested for staging a sit-in in front of the police station (we actually did think that we would end the war this way and maybe it made a difference). Some students demonstrated to change dorm hours for women; some white students met black people for the first time. Me, I found the women's movement. Right there in Marshall. And I found books, real books, hard-to-read books, books that questioned everything I had ever known, including the definition of hero. I majored in history and learned that the job of the historian is not to pat down the wrinkles of the past, but to explore them, to understand their texture, shape, and meaning.

I do not know if Minnesota is a better place to live than most other places; it is certainly different from South Dakota. At my husband's fortieth class reunion at Cretin High School in St. Paul, I met a remarkably large number of his classmates who still lived in the houses they had grown up in; some of the more adventuresome ones had moved to Minneapolis; not more than a handful had left the state. Like many Minnesotans, these men did not think they had to go away to get somewhere. They found that somewhere right here.

But it can be a hard somewhere to be, too. I knew a Hmong student a few years ago who had spent the summer before he came to Minnesota in a refugee camp in Laos and the summer before college earning money for his family. His mother spoke only a few words of English; his father's oldest brother, in the Hmong tradition, made most of the family rules, including whom his nephew could date and would marry. The nephew spoke English quite well, especially slang, had a secret American girlfriend, and worked hard to fit into his new life. Everyone at school was very nice to him, he reported, but he wondered why none of the students ever asked him about his past or his life, which had been and was so obviously different from their own. It might have been, as he suspected, that they were not interested. I suspect, however, that they pretended not to notice that he was different from them and, moreover, that they intended their ignorance as an act of kindness. I could not help but wonder if this was the kind of disappearance Rølvaag meant in his *Boat of Longing*.

So, Minnesota, a place historically of comings and goings, of entrances and exits. A place, like every place, of complicated and conflicting truths.

Notes

1. Philander Prescott, "Autobiography and Reminiscences of Philander Prescott," *Collections of the Minnesota Historical Society* 6 (1894): 475–491; and Donald Dean Parker, ed., *Recollections of Philander Prescott: Frontiersman of the Old Northwest, 1819– 1862* (Lincoln: University of Nebraska Press, 1966).

2. Gary Anderson has written an excellent biography of Little Crow, on which this portrait is largely based. Gary Clayton Anderson, *Little Crow: Spokesman for the Sioux* (St. Paul: Minnesota Historical Society Press, 1986). See also his *Kinsman of Another Kind: Dakota-White Relations in the Upper Mississippi Valley, 1650–1862* (Lincoln: University of Nebraska Press, 1984; reprinted St. Paul: Minnesota Historical Society Press, 1997).

3. Interview with Alan Woolworth, research fellow, Minnesota Historical Society, 16 February 2000.

4. The *Minneapolis Times*, the *St. Paul Pioneer Press*, and other newspapers throughout the state gave over their front pages to the story of the First Minnesota and the dedication ceremony of their memorial on July 2 and 3, 1897. The best, single account of the regiment is Richard Moe, *The Last Full Measure: The Life and Death of the First Minnesota Volunteers* (New York: Henry Holt, 1993; St. Paul: Minnesota Historical Society Press, 2001), 258–297; quotes on 268.

5. See James C. Christie Family Papers, Minnesota Historical Society, St. Paul.

6. Mary Carpenter to Aunt Martha, 10 July 1873, Mary Lovell Carpenter Papers, Minnesota Historical Society, St. Paul.

7. Ibid., 31 March 1887.

8. Sara Brooks Sundberg, "A Farm Woman on the Minnesota Prairie: The Letters of Mary E. Carpenter," *Minnesota History* 51 (Spring 1989): 186–193.

9. Paul Reigstad, *Rølvaag: His Life and Art* (Lincoln: University of Nebraska Press, 1972).

10. O. E. Rølvaag, *The Boat of Longing*, reprint ed. (St. Paul: Minnesota Historical Society Press, 1985), 294–295.

11. See David Riehle, "A Life We Can Learn From," in *Carl Skoglund, 1884–1960: Remembered in Struggle*, pamphlet, October 1984, Minnesota Historical Society; and Philip A. Korth, *The Minneapolis Teamsters Strike of 1934* (East Lansing: Michigan State University Press, 1995), 24–27, 53–60, 190–193. The record of his 1918 claim of American loyalty is included in the Public Safety Commission, Alien Registration and Declaration of Holdings Forms, 1918, Hennepin County, Ward 4, Precinct 5, Minnesota Historical Society, St. Paul.

12. See Earl Spangler, *The Negro in Minnesota* (Minneapolis: T. S. Dennison & Co., 1961); and David V. Taylor, "The Black Community in the Twin Cities," *Roots* 17 (Fall 1988): 3–22. I found especially helpful a "Minnesota Black Newspaper Index," compiled by Brendan Henehan, producer at KTCA, Minnesota Public Television, typescript, 24 October 1999.

13. "Francis Condemns Wrongs Against Negro Americans," *Twin City Star*, 6 April 1918, 2. "Atty. Francis Addresses Social Service Club," *Twin City Star*, 11 May 1918, 1.

14. Mary Dillon Foster, comp., *Who's Who Among Minnesota Women* (St. Paul, Mary Dillon Foster, 1924), 111. See also Barbara Stuhler, *Gentle Warriors: Clara Ueland and the Minnesota Struggle for Woman Suffrage* (St. Paul: Minnesota Historical Society Press, 1995), 81.

15. Carl Chrislock, *Watchdog of Loyalty: The Minnesota Commission of Public Safety During World War I* (St. Paul: Minnesota Historical Society Press, 1991). See also Minnesota Commission of Public Safety, *Report* (St. Paul: Dow and Co., 1919).

16. A. Scott Berg, *Lindbergh* (New York: Putnam's, 1998).

17. Sinclair Lewis, *Main Street and Babbitt* (New York: Library of America, 1992), 399, 485, 486.

18. Bruce L. Larson, "Lindbergh's Return to Minnesota, 1927," *Minnesota History* 42 (Winter 1970): 141–152.

19. Victor Cohn, *Sister Kenny: The Woman Who Challenged the Doctors* (Minneapolis: University of Minnesota Press, 1975). See also Cohn, "Sister Kenny's Fierce Fight for Better Polio Care," *Smithsonian* 12 (November 1981): 180–200.

20. See Gretchen Beito, *Coya Come Home: A Congresswoman's Journey* (Los Angeles: Pomegranate Press, 1990). See also "Coya Knutson, A Minnesota Legend," *St. Paul Pioneer Press*, 15 October 1996, 4A; Chuck Haga, "'Come Home' Coya Dies," *Star Tribune*, 11 October 1996, 1A; and Mary C. Pruitt, "Knutson Obit Gave Her Career Short Shrift," *Star Tribune*, 26 October 1996, 23A. Betty McCollum was elected to the U.S. House in November 2000. See Kevin Diaz, "Women Infuse McCollum with the Ghost of Coya," *Star Tribune*, 13 November 2000 (online version).

21. Larry Oakes, "A Rare Talk with Chippewa Leader," *Star Tribune*, 29 November 1998, 14A.

22. Doug Grow, "Chippewa Leader Radiates Diplomacy," *Star Tribune*, 24 February 1999, 2B.

23. Deborah Locke, "Mille Lacs Chief Executive Keeps Pace with the Wind," *St. Paul Pioneer Press*, 11 December 1997, 11A. See also a week-long series of articles, "A Change of Luck," *St. Paul Pioneer Press*, 2–9 August 1998.

24. Marge Anderson, "Indian Casinos Are a Boon, On Reservations and Off," *Star Tribune*, 4 July 1998, 15.

JOSEPH A. AMATO & ANTHONY AMATO

Minnesota, Real and Imagined: A View from the Countryside

MINNESOTA IS A DECENT PLACE TO LIVE. It is both big enough to be big and small enough to be small. Blessed with rivers and lakes, and three distinct ecological zones (prairie, coniferous forest, and deciduous forest), it abounds with parks and wilderness.[1] The state has a tradition of progressive politics, and its Twin Cities, Minneapolis and St. Paul, boast of a prosperous and balanced economy. While other midwestern states struggle with brain drain and population loss, Minnesota is vibrant and growing. For many the state offers all the qualities that make for an attractive home.

Despite the state's beauty and vitality, there is nothing particularly compelling about Minnesota. Its significance is not quite national or global, not regional or local; Minnesota warrants little attention. This appraisal is further reinforced in an age when distinct places and unique localities matter less and less in shaping human experience, sensibility, and memory. Over the course of the past two centuries, the industrial revolution, the central state, global markets, and nationalism have taken control of and transformed local landscapes and minds, leaving little room for variation and peculiarities.

The notion of a Minnesota culture immediately strikes observers as counterfeit. Minnesota, never a natural or cultural unit, was born and nurtured by continuous artifice. At the time of its founding, Minnesota was a fanciful invention used to draw immigrants to the state with the enticement of all the land they wanted in a "bracing and invigorating climate." Since then, various public and private agencies (some educational, some philanthropic, some commercial) have increased their power, prestige, and profit by fostering select

JOSEPH A. AMATO, *dean of rural and regional studies at Southwest State University in Marshall, Minnesota, is the author of* Dust: A History of the Small and the Invisible *and* Rethinking Home: Fresh Ideas and Themes for Writing Local History *(forthcoming)*. ANTHONY AMATO *is assistant professor of rural and regional studies at Southwest State University.*

representations of the state. From Hollywood to National Public Radio, promoters have turned Minnesota into a consumable and profitable commodity.

Like other states' cultures, Minnesota's is a jumble of odd and discordant images accreted over time. It entails putting Charles Lindbergh, Walter Mondale, and Eric Sevareid in the same bag, along with such different companies as 3M, Pillsbury, Honeywell (which just recently passed into alien hands), and Schwan's Sales Enterprises (located in Marshall). Even the contemporary media in Minnesota wear Janus faces, with its two best-known masks, Governor Jesse Ventura and Garrison Keillor, taking turns mugging for the camera. In sum, Minnesota culture constantly composes and recomposes itself, and knowledge of it proves only as certain as the insights garnered from anecdotes, statistics, and select opinion polls.

Nevertheless, certain images of Minnesota have displayed some remarkable continuity over time, and one metaphor threads its way through Minnesota culture: the North Star State. Minnesota, the true North Star State, is about being pure, with a surface covered by water, snow, and ice; it is about being northern, being close to Canada. It is the land of purity and the pure—a moral beacon for the nation.

The quest for purity dates back to the state's beginnings. As historians of the state are fond of noting, early promoters of the territory mistranslated the name "Minnesota" from the Dakota language. "Minnesota," which referred to the "sky-colored" (i.e., "cloudy") waters of the territory's rivers, was rendered as "sky-blue," suggesting "clear," "clean," and "pure."[2] Purity also came to characterize the state's climate, usually described solely in terms of dry, cold winters, which made for a "healthy," "vigorous" environment.[3] The purity of a white land of ice and snow stood in sharp contrast to the sultry, decadent South.

Minnesotans did not limit their obsessions with purity and whiteness to landscape or climate. Late-nineteenth-century Minnesotans embraced the popular racial theories of the time, and they heralded their home state as the most Aryan of societies. The state's Scandinavian, German, and other northern European leaders envisioned their state as a bastion against the waves of Jews, Mediterranean peoples, and Latinos then entering the United States. Some members of Minnesota's Nordic population, convinced that their race conferred not only physical and intellectual superiority but a moral superiority as well, routinely cast themselves as being more honest, hardworking, and virtuous than all others. Long after racial theories had fallen out of fashion, the inclination to think in these terms persisted. As late as the 1970s, commentators cited the state's large Anglo-Saxon and Nordic populations as the basis for the state's supposed honesty, efficiency, and work ethic.[4]

Many still describe the state as clean and pure. Minnesota fights pollution. It escapes inclusion in the Rust Belt. It avoids the decadence and corruption of Chicago and Detroit, without succumbing to the lethargy and dullness of Des Moines or suffering the vacuity of the Dakotas.[5] Minnesota, the healthiest state in the union, stays young.[6] It keeps pace with medicine and computers. It has sent young, reforming politicians to Washington, like Hubert Humphrey and Eugene McCarthy. Singled out by commentators as unusually "liberal" or "progressive," Minnesota has provided the best the nation has to offer.[7] Unblemished by sins against nature, it truly shines as the moral guardian to the north.[8]

For many residents and nonresidents, Minnesota embodies the best of all possible worlds. The state has a rich natural heritage. The Twin Cities crown a mixed and balanced state economy.[9] They constitute an amenity-rich metropolitan area, worthy of envy throughout the nation, and the state and its smaller showcase cities routinely top livability surveys.[10] At the dawn of the television era, one sixth-grade textbook, stressing the state's exceptionalism and multiple blessings, taught: "We who live in Minnesota feel proud and happy to be here. It is not a perfect land in which to live . . . but we know that ours is a good land in many ways."[11]

Residents and outsiders herald Minnesota as a state of efficient and clean industry.[12] Contrasting their state with the Rust Belt to the east, they are quick to boast about the integrity, cleanliness, and environmental sensitivity of their state's leading employers. In doing so, they forget that one of the state's largest enterprises was a leader in the development of the mass-killing technologies of the twentieth century, that the famous megamall is an undeniable expression of crass consumerism, and that the state's agribusiness giants have been repeatedly accused of a number of questionable practices and ruinous trends. Minnesotans conveniently choose to ignore these facts.

Despite such numerous contradictions, Minnesotans still presume that their state is "The Star of the North." Although short on humor, wit, and irony (Howard Mohr, Bill Holm, and other writers notwithstanding), Minnesota's leaders lay claim to all virtuous wares—political, aesthetic, and commercial alike. They take for granted that their state outclasses the states of the Midwest and the nation. In fact, alarms sounded in 1996 when for the first time since 1982 the percentage of Twin Cities residents who believed that their quality of life was much better than in other urban areas dropped below 50 percent.[13]

This "I-am-as-good-as-they-come-yet-I-can-and-should-be-better"-ism accounts for Minnesotans' earnest moralism.[14] Minnesotans are moral about the smallest and seemingly least significant things—taxpayers' use of their tax rebates and complimentary cups of coffee for legislators. At the same time, no number of discoveries of corruption in business, government, sports, and education convinces Minnesotans that human nature is alive and thriving at home. Even in light of numerous recent scandals, one Democratic-Farmer-Labor political analyst insisted, "We don't have scandals to speak of."[15] The state and its admirers continue to confine corruption to the distant past, arguing that its last traces were rooted out decades ago.[16]

At the same time, Minnesota endlessly preoccupies itself with eliminating every possible vestige of injustice, real and remembered. Victims are included among Minnesota's liberals (with Paul Wellstone being the elected proof of it) and produce in them the most hollow moral rhetoric. At the same time, every national reactionary or conservative platform decked in "morality" and "purity" (including vicious attacks on liberals) has been utilized as a rhetorical gangplank to bridge the wanting and the having of political power in the state.

Moments of self-inflation followed by episodes of self-laceration are a well-established Gopher State ritual. By the time F. Scott Fitzgerald and Sinclair Lewis were writing, Minnesotans, told once too often that their state was a pretty darn good place to live, had already begun to wonder aloud about the onset of self-satisfaction in their state; ever since then, residents have had to endure periodic bouts of self-doubt followed by public outbursts of self-criticism. Any occasion to praise Minnesota is also occasion to attack its residents' smugness and complacency.[17] Year after year, Minnesotans and outsiders fall in love with the state's success and then come to hate it, each thinking that he or she has discovered the truly dirty underside of the proverbially clean state.[18]

Despite its many contradictions, the idea of Minnesota is solid enough to provoke, motivate, and incite. Minnesota can be counted as one of the many virtual or "imagined" communities around which inhabitants order their lives.[19] Minnesota, like any other imagined community, is an absurd combination of places, characteristics, and qualities. Its imagined geography includes Fargo and places like lakeless Rock County (in its southwestern corner) in the "Land of 10,000 Lakes." The state is the epitome of both evolved urbanity and simple rusticity. It embraces the fields and farms of its southwest and the bogs and boreal forests of its northeast as well as the lofts, cafés, malls, and bike paths of the Twin Cities. The state has many faces and embraces many images.[20]

"Imagined" Minnesota has its roots in electronic media. As the birth of the imagined community of the nation was part and parcel of the print medium and print as a commodity, the rise of imagined Minnesota is a product of the talk medium and talk as a commodity.[21] In an era when there is even a magazine entitled *Talk*, the talk medium dominates, producing a continuous stream of chat and prattle that is marketed, sold, and resold. While television, film, radio, and the Internet have helped erode public confidence in the nation by advertising the scandals, shortcomings, and failures of the federal government, they have elevated the idea of Minnesota to unprecedented importance. References to the state abound throughout the nation, including Jeff Foxworthy–style "You-might-be-a-Minnesotan-if" lists circulated over the Internet. The state, a cozy hut in the global village, has taken on many of the functions once carried out by the now-discredited nation, and imagined Minnesota, grounded by its political system, demands recognition.

The culture of this imagined community is a mixture of nineteenth-century ideals and twenty-first-century fantasies. While the image of a pure and rich North Star State thrived for more than a century after the state's admission to the union, it was not until the television era that the idea of Minnesota, drummed into its residents' minds, took off. Writers, producers, and executives celebrated the very life that their media were accused of wiping out. Television and radio offered up images of homey and wholesome places like Lake Wobegon, the Little House on the Prairie, and Mary Tyler Moore's Minneapolis, juxtaposing them with the impersonal, fast-paced, and rootless side of America.[22] At the same time, "local" television news and variety shows broadcast from the Twin Cities nurtured another view of the state with constant references to mosquitoes, wind chills, and walleyes. Shaped by earlier ideas of purity and moderation, the television images of Minnesota and Minnesotans were earthy, authentic, and well-balanced.[23]

The task of constructing Minnesota falls on both insiders and outsiders. Like all other communities, Minnesota requires common traditions, and residents do not hesitate to invent them where none have existed. Dying small towns affirm their existence and their place within the larger imagined community by holding centennials and annual town celebrations. Based on cursory references to ethnic, economic, and historical peculiarities, the annual celebrations range from Boxelder Bug Days in Minneota to Aebleskiver Days in Tyler. Almost all consist of a coronation, a parade, and three days of carnival rides. The creation of various "days" throughout the state is not the only result of the search for traditions. Although Minnesota cuisine does not yet exist, it may not be far off. The need for this particular tradition in the imagined community of Minnesota is so great that it has already prompted some to speculate on whether the state has shaped its inhabitants' foodways.[24] The idea of Minnesota precedes the reality of Minnesota.

Minnesotans and outside aficionados have readily embraced the symbols and images of the state created by authors, screenwriters, and media moguls. To appreciate how much contemporary Minnesota is a child of television and radio, one need only look to professional sports, an outgrowth of the electronic media. Minnesota was the first state to have teams. (Prior to the Vikings, Twins, and North Stars, only cities had teams.) Impressed by this, one author went so far as to suggest that the state teams, dependent on new media, had the potential to reduce the metro/outstate versus Minneapolis/St. Paul struggles that had denied the state unity.[25] The media also heavily influence Minnesota politics. Citizen involvement and active citizen participation, distinguishing features of the state's politics, depend heavily on electronic media. While party caucus attendance has plummeted, the Twin Cities public-television program *Almanac* is the most watched local public-affairs program in the nation.[26]

The connection of imagined Minnesota to media is also evident in discussions about threats to the state. One of the Twin Cities' best-known journalists recently sounded the alarm in his column that the state was in danger. He ignored the ever-present menaces of floods, voter apathy, and farm crises, and focused instead on unfavorable images and references in the nation's news and entertainment industry as the most pressing threat to the state. Locating the idea of Minnesota in the realm of talk, the author reminisced about the good old days of *The Mary Tyler Moore Show*, when the state was described as sensible and civilized. In his opinion, Minnesota and Minnesotans had taken some "heavy hits" from recent unfavorable portrayals of the state.[27]

Imagined Minnesota's dependence on the talk medium and on Minnesotans' presumption of the superiority of their state raises questions about the durability and utility of the state as an idea. How will this Minnesota stand up over time against a range of forces suggesting that the state does not control its own destiny? What will become of it when the vast majority of its citizens believe they have no effect either at home or nationwide? Will belief in Minnesota, chic and fashionable today, go the way of the flag-waving patriotism of yesteryear? One answer to these questions may come from two processes in rural Minnesota: the decline of the small farm and small town and the transformation of the countryside.

SOMETHING MOMENTOUS IS HAPPENING—or has perhaps already happened— in the Gopher State. Much of agricultural and rural Minnesota has fallen into decline. As farms and villages die not just demographically but as ways of life, does the concept of Minnesota as homey, independent, and communal perish along with them? Can the Minnesota ideal survive dominating markets, engulfing mass media, and intrusive federal government? Do these forces introduce a fatalism deadly to the state's progressive culture? Do they leave even a shred of the illusion that citizens' wishes and deeds matter?

As outlined in *The Decline of Rural Minnesota*, there are two Minnesotas: one is growing; the other is diminishing.[28] Eastern Minnesota and western Minnesota, divided by a line running just west of Rochester, Minneapolis, and St. Cloud, are two different states. The Minnesota on the east side of the line imitates the Metropolis; the Minnesota on the other side imitates the Dakotas. One anticipates a future of limitless possibilities, and the other endures decline. As these two Minnesotas separate, they deny the state the balance it once had, not just between farm and industry, countryside and metropolis, but between community and disconnection, place and flux.

Demographic decline in the Minnesota countryside is traceable from the 1950s on. In the 1980s, population losses reached percentages in the middle and high teens in many rural counties. These losses, due in large part to the flight of youth, have resulted in lopsided communities, such as southwestern Minnesota's Hendricks, which had a median age of 64.7 in 1990.[29] In 1995, natural decline appeared in a dozen of the state's southern and western counties.[30] The number of those dying—testifying to the age of its residents— exceeds the number of births. Decline looms large.

The current decline, a long time in the making, has overpowered numerous efforts to curtail its progression. By the 1980s, the momentum of economic and demographic decline was so great in the Upper Midwest that trade centers of all sizes in a six-county area of northern Iowa experienced population loss and drops in business volume.[31] Although Minnesota's trade centers fared better, the story in southwestern Minnesota was quite similar.[32] Even the go-go economy of the late 1990s has not stopped the flow of people out of southern and western Minnesota.[33] From 1990 to 1999, southwestern Minnesota's Lac qui Parle County led the state in population decline, losing 12.4 percent of its population.[34] Dashing any hope that smaller losses in the 1990s signal a turnaround, some have pointed out that the rate of population decline has slowed only because those prone to migrate moved away in the 1980s.[35] The countryside embodied in family farm and small town is vanishing.

At the same time, southern and western Minnesota appear to be in a state of metamorphosis. During the last two decades, closings, relocations, and consolidations of rural institutions have occurred at accelerating rates, with mergers of businesses, newspapers, hospitals, schools, and churches increasing geometrically.[36] The turnover and turbulence in the countryside's lead cities is accelerating. [37] The most visible face of this churning transformation is the stream of newcomers who come from across the world to fill out the workforce of the region's expanding meat-processing industry. Mexicans and Mexican Americans, Hmong and Lao, Somalis and Ethiopians provide essential labor to the pork and poultry plants that dot the countryside. Mirroring the dramatic turnover rate in the meatpacking industry itself, these populations are the most visible face of the countryside in transformation.[38]

With talent imported from across the country and with promotions tied to relocation outside the region, other industries also account for high employee turnover rates and the turbulence of regional populations. New employees staff multiplying franchises and burgeoning courthouses, along with the expanding services and administrations created to fulfill increased wants and rights. Collectively these processes produce unprecedented population movements in and out of the countryside. Turbulence jeopardizes community coherence and coalescence.

Regional leadership lacks the numbers, the energy, and the hope needed to form communities. The once all-important merchant retail class has all but disappeared from village, town, and lead city. The Main Street merchant ignominiously went broke, or died, or retired just in the nick of time. He no longer commands either Main Street or city hall. Merchants' wives no longer enrich the town's library, arts associations, and clubs, nor stir reform. City government has passed to better paid and more secure public employees, and it benefits only from the occasional newcomer whose curiosity or job encourages him or her to tread where newcomers once dared not tiptoe. With councils composed of itinerants, funding mandated, and anything worth doing taking too long to accomplish, small-town politics no longer engenders identity, pride, and the hope of getting something done.

The small group of leaders that remains is increasingly disconnected from a vital culture. By the early 1970s, the absence of young, energetic political leaders in small towns was evident to many.[39] Tradition and memory, enthusiasm and hope fizzle. There is no one to glean the past or seed the future. The keepers of the past, county historical societies, aged and gerontological, invariably indulge the most irrelevant nostalgia, guarding sentimental memories about the short-lived pioneer days and "the good old bad days" of dust storms and the Depression.

As diminished numbers undermine communal autonomy in townships, villages, and small towns, so turbulence in larger towns and regional centers challenges communal identity, continuity, and leadership. In the most severe instances, motions of people and leaders exceed the synthetic process of group affiliation and cohesion. Bankers, ministers, school superintendents, and hospital heads enroll themselves on the list of new arrivals. Formal and informal associations fail to rally new arrivals (one can only put so much new wine into old bottles), and the traditional clubs of Masons, Moose, Legionnaires, Lions, and Optimists disband.

This dissolution of small-town politics unfolds against the backdrop of the second agricultural crisis in two decades, a crisis that may mark the end of the countryside as known since European-American settlement. The crisis demonstrates that markets over the long term will not support the agriculture we are accustomed to, and proves that agriculture undermines the countryside that has been built around it. Laws of scale are not always insisting but ever abiding. As prices diminish, volume must correspondingly be increased, and as volume increases, prices diminish. As farms (receptive to and dependent on new technologies and expanded capital) correspondingly get bigger, farm communities (townships, villages, and small towns) get smaller and smaller. So, as the principal and formative industry of the countryside retreats, agriculture leaves the countryside—its people and institutions—a shell of its former self.

Here another remorseless law dominates the course of contemporary rural life. Abstractly, the law reads: "As the mass increases at the center of a society, so do its functions. As the functions increase at the center, so they are, by both law and desire, demanded in the periphery. The periphery, with correspondingly fewer people to carry out more obligations and desires, finds itself having to do more with less."[40] This process ultimately spawns a sense of inferiority. Individuals and institutions, from medicine and law to social services and education, find they have neither the means nor the resources to respond to increased demands. They feel themselves to be the hapless servants of a remote and abstract order, and certainly not bearers of a vital, organic culture.

Decline and subordination become pervasive conditions of mind. The countryside acknowledges its inability to keep pace with the mounting array of goods, services, and opportunities that flash across the television screen. The countryside (especially where its villages and towns are smallest and distances the greatest to lead cities) suffers decline in the face of civilization's multiplying needs and desires. With resources shrinking and wants increasing, even towns designated "complete shopping centers" are faced with the prospect of sliding down the trade-center hierarchy and becoming "minimum convenience centers" or mere "hamlets."[41] Amidst empty storefronts and abandoned buildings, minor victories take on great significance. In two villages near Marshall, a handful of town boosters take considerable pride in the reopening of a coffee shop. Villages and towns, once proud of self-sufficiency and completeness, are all diminished. They fail to keep up with their city cousins.

Decline strips the smallest villages and towns of economic and social functions. Towns support fewer affiliations and associations, and older family and ethnic bonds weaken. The towns lose their schools, churches, and co-ops. They no longer have bars, pool halls, restaurants, gas or service stations, and other gathering places that traditionally nurtured local culture. They find themselves to be without a doctor, lawyer, or even a mechanic; without a bank, hardware store, movie theater, ball field, or library. Residents depend on the highway convenience store for their daily bread and videos, and they trust their cars for their employment, shopping, medical care, and the "big events" of their lives. Towns that once sustained vital societies have become bedroom communities where residents have little knowledge of or contact with one another.[42] Dissolving towns no longer form vital units. They no longer absorb the lives and concerns of their residents. If small towns once constituted a culture, they now are fragments of a broken order.

The matrix of the decline in the countryside is best reflected in the modulations of the word "access." Access, the all-important intersection between rights and convenience, is at the center of the decline and transformation of rural Minnesota. Access opens a portal to worlds far removed from the main street and the farmhouse. As the railroad eliminated space in the nineteenth century, access to forms of telecommunication is eliminating landscape and place in the twenty-first century. Whether instantaneously through electronic media, in a couple of hours' travel by car, or in several hours by plane, rural Minnesotans are transported to metropolitan oases and pleasure palaces. The calls for access, heard more and more, carry with them a concession: the countryside simply cannot keep up.

THE CURRENT TRANSFORMATION of the countryside was incipient in its very origins. The American countryside sprang from the metropolis.[43] The agents of its conception and birth—the state, law, national culture, the market, and outside capital—mentored its growth. From the beginning they disciplined the natural and human environments to respond to demands. As this civilization, with its myriad agents and conflicting ideals, shaped the region's lands and waters, so it simultaneously formed rural peoples and communities.

Two opposing local groups with entirely different attitudes came together in the midwestern countryside. At one extreme, town leaders actively imitated and propagated what they took to be the best that civilization had to offer. They presumed themselves to be its legitimate representative. The wives of the town's prominent leaders (aptly described in Sinclair Lewis's *Main Street*) did what they could to hang civilization's curtains in dusty and dirty small towns. They established theaters and libraries, formed reading clubs, and organized moral and civic groups to win the war, banish strangers, stop drinking, and even win the right to vote for themselves. Along with their husbands, they took the issues of the nation, fashion, and their "spiritual selves" seriously, yet they had little understanding of or interest in their opposites, the people who inhabited the farms and villages of the surrounding countryside.

At this opposite extreme stood certain rural ethnic communities. Their hold on the countryside grew in scope and strength from the last decades of the nineteenth century onward. Perpetuating their farms and sustaining the adjacent towns for a century, they overcame the ordeals of bad times and avoided the temptations of good times. A narrow focus shielded these farmers from the dangers of the external world. At all times, they clung steadfastly to family, farm, and faith—the holy trinity at the heart of their folkways. The desire to stay on the land defined their lives and was the active principle by which they both resisted and accepted the outside world. Up until World War II and even beyond, these groups lived not only largely sealed off from one another but from the towns, which claimed to be the lords of the land. These groups retained their own languages and followed their own ways. They worked, saved, prayed, and ate as their grandparents taught them. They baptized, married, and buried their own. They built homes, schools, and churches to imitate the European communities they had left behind but still idealized.[44] Free of modern sensibilities, they harnessed their wives and children to the mutually recognized duty of supporting the all-important, all-consuming farm. They limited their contact with the town and its people. In fact, they harshly judged their own kind who spent time idling in town. They did not seek office, and instead of co-ops, they had their own families that formed de facto buying, selling, and service groups.[45] The market was near, but the farm and community of their making were closer yet. While never free of the demands of market or the laws of state and nation, they formed largely autonomous farms and communities, which were deemed worthy of a lifetime's endeavors.

The lords of regional centers and the masters of farms and villages were strangers to one another, although both defined the countryside and its culture. Indifference and exclusiveness were assumed. Rivalry and competition, which showed in battles on and off baseball diamonds and dance floors, were presumed. Being apart and separate was natural. There were always tasks at home. Distances between places were greater then, as cars were fewer and spending money was scarcer than today. With their own churches, schools, banks, and stores, small towns formed little worlds, around which emotions and interests clustered, and knowledge and business were jealously sought. Boundaries and borders, drawn between families, townships, and villages, stood strong (in much of this countryside) for the first half of the century. They started to come down in the second half of the century, and they have collapsed completely in the last two decades.

Even the strongest ethnic farmers and their communities, which constituted the nucleus of the countryside until the 1970s, are disappearing. Those who remain—apart from being lucky, as every farmer must in measure be, by either inheritance, or marriage, or, most of all, timing—have been bred for survival and prosperity on the land. They are the most wily and seasoned in battles with market, family, and self. But now, even when they number among the most aggressive and prosperous individuals in the contemporary countryside, these survivors have begun increasingly to concede that farming is just another way to make a living—and a nonrewarding one at that.

The children and grandchildren of these ethnic farmers no longer partake in the old ways. Two generations of goods, education, and leisure have bred them for a different life. Time and circumstances have made them good Americans. Their parents' successful battles against need and the market have elevated them to being full-fledged consumers. Freedom from the discipline of work coupled with the pervasive cult of the child have turned them into individuals who value personal choice and cherish private sentiment over the old trinity of farm, family, and faith. They are a different breed, another culture. In just the past twenty years, they have progressed a long way in becoming typical members of an advanced secular commercial society.

The cultural metamorphosis at hand can be measured by the distance that separates grandparents and great-grandparents from their grandchildren. This distance can be best described not by the years that separate generations but by entirely different orders of experience and mind—by the altered behavior, beliefs, and values of the sons and daughters of the region's most traditional peoples. They are the heirs of the German, Dutch, Czech, Belgian, and Polish farmers (to mention a few prominent groups in southwestern Minnesota) who a century ago took the land, worked it, and held on to it. These ethnic cultivators constituted a type of market-savvy peasant who did not surrender or quit no matter what the times brought. A stubborn duty to crops and animals defined their culture, with routines and responsibilities defining what it meant to be a real man or woman. Husband, wife, and child—even God and cousins—all were expected to serve the farm.

The promise of education and careers now opens a thousand roads for those who have desires and ambitions, or for those who simply wish to leave.

At the same time, the farm is subject to ever more scrutiny. Accounting and ledgers test the viability of farm and rural life, and the farm no longer equals or is worthy of a destiny. The price of sacrificing to stay on the farm has become too high, and the struggle often seems futile. Families that just a generation before did everything in their power to keep their children on the land are now for the first time encouraging them to leave it.

Even those who stay behind on the farm must tread a different and less illuminated path than their parents and grandparents. They live on altered land; they work with increasingly diverse tools; they inhabit a transformed farmstead. The elements of experience itself have been changed. The space of the farm has been reduced and become more penetrable. It forms a less opaque and consuming dimension of human work and desire. From the beginnings of settlement, the horse and cart, the train and telegraph, transected the space of the countryside. The telephone, automobile, and radio compressed it. Television, cellular phones, faxes, satellite communications, and the Internet have now collapsed it. Having lost its expanse and integrity, space is no longer the primary determinant of locality, an abiding framer of human experience, or an elemental claimant of human time and energy. Space no longer defines or governs place as it once did. Everywhere becomes everywhere else, which is (so to speak) no place in particular. Like space, time also has lost its role as a fundamental and fixed determinant of experience and, thus, as a creator of locality.

The farm is merely a site where a family temporarily resides and survives. It is the outpost around which they synchronize their individual comings and goings, and where they watch television and use their computers. Once the compelling gathering point of generations and the focus of their energies, sacrifices, hopes, and destinies, the farm has become a mere coordinate in a transitory world. It no longer pegs its members to a fixed place and time. It has been transformed into yet another depot in the countryside through which people and goods pass on their way from city to country and back.

The younger generations' inner worlds are as transformed as the landscape around them. The young people value the individual in ways that their parents and grandparents, so attached to the discipline of family and land, never did. The newer generations indulge their sentiments and nurse their feelings more. They are softer. They would not sacrifice their happiness, nor that of their spouses or children, for the farm. They assert their authority less; they are less prone to act out their anger. Politeness, caring, and the law take control of and civilize a countryside once filled with epithets and fistfights. Police and psychologists march in lockstep, controlling external and internal environments. The police offer relief; psychologists promise therapy; together they contain anger. Even the ministers' sermons in the countryside no longer brim with fire and threat, but instead ooze with love and understanding. The progressive mollification of farm protest—from the aggressive Holiday movement of the 1930s, which involved direct and armed conflict, to the accusing but pleading and begging 1980s farm-protest group Ground Swell—chart the taming of person, group, and the minds and ways of the countryside.

Nothing restrains the forces of the outside world. Unresisted and undeflected, they intrude on the countryside in unprecedented ways. Opinions, images, ideals, sensibilities, and even strangers themselves enter the rural mind as if it were without barrier. Seducing and beguiling, they arrive with everything that suggests the easy attainability of a pleasant world. The agents of change enter the rural community without knocking, and, trafficking in the contraband of wishes and daydreams, they steal minds and hearts.

In sum, the rural sons and daughters of ethnic farm families have come to resemble their urban counterparts in their attitudes about happiness and comfort. This is true in the ways they value opportunities and careers, companionship and love. While detailed attitude studies are yet to be undertaken, ethnic farm-family sons and daughters appear to be indistinguishable from the nation at large in their patterns of travel, leisure activities, and discretionary spending.

Everywhere in the countryside, the cloth of the old way is rent. This is the same story told in one form or another across the nation and throughout the world. In *Hoe God verdween uit Jorwerd* (How God Disappeared from Jorwerd), the Dutch writer Geert Mak describes the contemporary passing of a way of life in a Frieschlander village in the northern Netherlands. He describes a community that for centuries lived by and organized itself around the arduous tilling of the soil and the raising of animals. It regulated individuality, sexuality, child-rearing, and the place of the elderly. Defining the horizon of experience and imagination, the community imposed its ways as though they were the norms of everyday life and the very conditions for survival. Writing in the 1990s, Mak describes the rapid disappearance of this world over the last thirty years.

Southwestern Minnesota resembles northern Holland. Small farms and self-standing towns are rapidly disappearing. With them go the people and the experience they nurtured. In a mere two decades, these unique ways of life have vanished. Minnesota, whatever it is to become in the days ahead, will have to do so without farm and village. In one way or another, it will become a virtual entity in a world of virtual places.

The power of virtual places and imagined Minnesota prevents most commentators from recognizing the implications of the policies they advocate. So deeply embedded in imagined Minnesota is the family farm that observers have begun to speak of farmers without agriculture. Fond of seeing horizons broken by the outlines of silos and groves and yet frustrated by the complexities of agriculture, one *Star Tribune* editorial encouraged Minnesotans to acknowledge that "[e]ven farmers would benefit from a rural policy that is less focused on agriculture."[46] And, when offering up a prescription for the future of Minnesota, the same editorial envisioned a rural Minnesota that is culturally, economically, ethnically, and ecologically like everywhere else:

> [A shared vision for western Minnesota] should make provision for the infrastructure that is crucial to economic health—education, transportation, water and sewer, health care, telecommunications. It should encourage stewardship of the area's natural resources, and development of their tourism potential. It should include welcoming more racial and ethnic diversity.[47]

Southwestern Minnesota's simultaneous decline and transformation are not unique. Agricultural regions elsewhere in the state and the nation have experienced the same eclipse of family farming and the small town. The earlier collapse of mining and timbering had similar consequences for towns and ethnic communities of central and northern Minnesota. Only where the lure of lakes has attracted fresh populations has demographic decline been averted.

Ironically, the core of the metropolis also experiences the same transformation as older industries and populations flee the center and new populations crowd into the center and the suburbs. Demographic decline, the loss of retail businesses and jobs, and failed communities define one half of the metropolitan experience, while turnover and turbulence define the other half. Overrun by franchises, inhabited by mobile populations, and increasingly built up around class stratification, the metropolis struggles and suffers in ways parallel to the countryside as it seeks community, tradition, leadership, and renovation.

Surely this metamorphosis fostered by decline and nurtured by mobility signals the end of Minnesota's older forms of social cohesion. Growing disparities between rural and urban income, employment, poverty, and quality of life also point to a state that is cracking, coming undone, and breaking up.[48] Perhaps its fragmented and ideological politics—which put in office the extremes of Senators Wellstone and Grams, and Governor Ventura—best testifies to fragmentation. Insiders may not be off the mark when they say that Minnesota's political parties are irreparably shattered.

HERE WE RETURN to the principal paradox of this essay. The dramatic transformation we have sketched does not spell the imminent end of Minnesota as a cultural construct. In fact, at least for the short term, the more removed the abstract cerebral Minnesota becomes from its diverse and conflicting body, the more vital and important Minnesota the idea becomes.

Minnesota—abstract, contrived, and even entirely artificial—offers an identity, a set of icons, images, and stereotypes that support a vast range of public discussions. It provides Keillor and Hollywood with material to spin radio-wave and celluloid yarns sufficiently distinctive yet vaguely familiar enough to keep audiences in their seats and tuned in—to applaud the twists and turns of what they already know. It allows Minnesotans to know and say who they are when they encounter Iowans, South Dakotans, or even people from far away. It supports politicians, bureaucrats, philanthropists, and others who wish to enter the public discourse riding, so to speak, their favorite stalking-horse.

Minnesota, however artificial and abstract it might be, constitutes an identity in a complex, intrusive, and overbearing world. And, on reflection, this is no small thing. The presumption of actually being a place and having a culture allows residents, and those who identify with the state, a way to take measure of who they are and what they value in a world often beyond their understanding and control. Aside from furnishing a certain "northern snobbery," this identity also provides a sense of self and community. It brings a sense of moral entitlement to one's judgment of what others could and should be. It does this at the very time when other values and certainties have fallen into doubt. It forms a platform of presumption. Secure and decent in heart, Minnesota is energetic, rich, and progressive enough to obtain the best things democratic industrial society has to offer. Even if a bit pretentious and hypocritical, the progressive beliefs at the heart of Minnesota make for a good place to live. The state is both big and small enough to be considered home. It gives citizens a place to talk about, favorably compare against, and identify with. This is no small thing in this jumbled era of so much travel and interaction.

Minnesota culture (a banner to wave, a joke to tell, a movie to see, a jersey to buy, a trademark to register) prospers as an ideal in direct relation to the degree it is divorced from the fate of its diverse regions and rich peoples.[49] The more Minnesota becomes an abstract Totem Pole (or May Pole), the more easily metaphors, morals, events, aspirations, and sentiments ceremoniously parade around it. In other words, the culture prospers by virtue of its virtuality. As actual places in the state quit being themselves and become everywhere else, Minnesota, by being none of them, becomes the ideal representative of all of them.

Minnesota was born to be disincarnate. It did not arise out of parents, neighborhoods, ethnic communities, or fixed places. Its matrix was ideas. It grew around notions and images of region, state, and nation. Education and teachings, ideals and ideologies, created it. Commerce, literature, and media nurture it.

Minnesota culture exists as a conglomerate. It is formed by remembered events and places—from Fort Snelling to New Ulm's statue of Hermann the German—that evoke shared recollections. It is expressed by a range of common experiences—having once gone to a Minneapolis Lakers basketball game to having played hockey with magazines for shinguards. It arises out of and is kept alive by familiar arguments, whose twists and turns are as well known as the emotions they evoke are predictable. As an ideal, Minnesota remains constantly under construction. Politicians, citizens, and state and national commentators, reacting to events or merely carrying on their tired discussions, continually make and remake Minnesota.

Like many regions, Minnesota has at its center a certain moral core. As suggested earlier, we take that core to be the idea of the North Star State and all the metaphors (be they pure, white, or cold) that suggest Minnesota truly is the virtuous republic to the north. The state keeps claiming to be a good and decent place to live. *Minnesota Milestones*, adopted in 1991 as the master plan for quality life in the state, proclaimed, "We Minnesotans like our state. We believe Minnesota is a good place to raise a family . . . and enjoy life."[50]

What finally explains Minnesota's vitality as a culture lies in its ingestible artificiality. It serves as an intellectual comestible in an era when man truly does not live by bread alone. Minnesota provides a way to feel, think, and talk—as we all must—about life in a changing society and nation. It allows us to create a village and community with which we are familiar and at home. There we can fasten our sentiments and identity and focus our mind and values while separating ourselves from the complexity, magnitude, impurity, and sense of helplessness that go with the nation and the world at large.

Similar to such diverse regions as Bavaria and the American West, Minnesota mediates between locality and nation.[51] A relatively rich and malleable ideal, it offers a sense of embodiment and moral place for all in the state who need to find conceptual ground between the polarities of locality and nation. It sustains everyday conversations between home and world, self and society. Minnesota not only facilitates amicable conversations with outsiders, but also provides a universally needed "snobbery." It cannot get much better than being a Minnesotan in Minnesota.[52]

The increasing importance of Minnesota coincides with larger transformations. As localities lose their boundaries, individuals are ever more removed from necessity and concrete community. They live more by mind than body. They become increasingly distant from actual places while television, the Internet, careers, education, vacations, and second homes connect them to multiple distant points in society at large. Their autonomy, as a grove of experience, memory, and meaning, is breached. Various forms of media homogenize ideas, feelings, and language, and place no longer defines mind or morals.

Nationality, the quintessential identity of modern times, drowns in complexity, divisions, and corruption. It pales in the limelight in which it stands. Balkanized by region, race, wealth, religion, and gender, the nation offers only moral and cognitive dissonance. Its nuances and machinations exceed coherence, its girth is too great to embrace. The venality of its managers and its failure to surmount obstacles in these ordinary days deny it the power and the drama it deserves.

As locality sinks and nation provides no sure summit, Minnesota momentarily towers above them. It provides a realm large enough for ambitions, while small enough to gather sentiments. It serves as middle ground between disintegrating local communities and a faltering nation. Minnesota advances as a moral and emotional identity. How long it will remain vital and move its users to laud it with spirited exaggeration invites conjecture. Surely Minnesota as an ideal is hardy enough to outlast a downturn in the economy. It can even survive the descending spiral of state politics, for after all, we, like everyone else, profess our own goodness not as a result of politics but in inverse proportion to the machinations of our politicians. As long as the state is perceived to embody and respond to the will of its people, Minnesota will keep its grip on hearts and minds.

What is uncertain is how much decline, turnover, and turbulence Minnesota can withstand. Will it, at a delayed pace, follow the fate of its own farms and villages, communities, and neighborhoods? Will it too both dissolve within and be overrun from without, unable to follow the widening and quickening gyre of ever-distant but more imposing market and world? At one and the same time Minnesota's fate might lie in its smallest village and the nation at large. If the state fails to cohere in fact and as an ideal, its audience will look elsewhere for more enduring and pacifying republics.

None of this, however, means abstract Minnesota will die when its community does. In this case, body and spirit will not end their earthly existence at the same time. In fact, their mutual deaths could be separated by generations. Indeed, like a dying star, the North Star State may burn brightest with its last embers. Surely, already a popular and profitable stereotype, Minnesota will echo the symbols and images media commentators and political caricaturists have affixed to the state long after all substantive meaning has been drained from them. In the end, Minnesota the idea, like many new forms of community, may prove more durable than many traditional communities.[53] Thus, Minnesota's very abstractness may account for its potential longevity in an increasingly abstract age.

But all this delivers us to the threshold of more speculation than this essay can bear. We dare not stray to reflections on the fate of regions and nations, republics and empires, because all that is finally at issue here is the fate of Minnesota culture. In the meantime, we Minnesotans—at least those of us not against sugar and fun—are better off eating our cake and having it too. After all, a feast today assures felicitous memories tomorrow. And being part of Minnesota is a pleasant way of being at home in an increasingly epicurean world.

Notes

The authors gratefully thank Eugen Weber, John Adams, Will Craig, Elizabeth Raymond, and others.

1. On the three biomes of Minnesota, see John R. Tester, *Minnesota's Natural Heritage: An Ecological Perspective* (Minneapolis: University of Minnesota Press, 1995), 6–7.

2. William E. Lass, *Minnesota: A History* (New York: W. W. Norton and Co., 1983), 6.

3. See John Joseph Flynn, "Minnesota's Sense of Place: Creation through Images," Ph.D. thesis, University of Minnesota, 1992, 140–144.

4. "Minnesota: A State That Works," *Time* (13 August 1973): 34.

5. "Minnesota Continues to be a Magnetic Presence in the Midwest," *Star Tribune*, 31 December 1998, 1B, 6B; Daniel J. Elazar, "A Model of Moralism in Government," in *Minnesota in a Century of Change*, ed. Clifford E. Clark Jr. (St. Paul: Minnesota Historical Society Press, 1989), 354–355. See James R. Shortridge, *The Middle West: Its Meaning in American Culture* (Lawrence, Kans.: University Press of Kansas, 1989), 114–117; and "Minnesota: A State That Works," 24.

6. "Minnesota Ties as Nation's Healthiest State," *Star Tribune*, 7 August 1990, 1B (online version).

7. On the state's leadership in the nation, see "Minnesota: The Successful Society," in Neal R. Peirce, *The Great Plains States of America* (New York: W. W. Norton and Co., 1973), 110, 150; and David S. Boyer and David Brill, "Minnesota, Where Water Is the Magic Word," *National Geographic* 149 (2) (February 1976): 217.

8. On the role of moralism in distinguishing Minnesota politics, see Elazar, "A Model of Moralism in Government," 354–356.

9. "State of the State, a Statistical View," *Star Tribune*, 16 January 1996, 1A (online version). On balance, see Shortridge, *The Middle West*, 114–117.

10. "Minnesota Tops Livability Study," *Star Tribune*, 10 April 1998, 1 (online

version); "Minnesota Trails N.H. on Livable-States List," *Star Tribune*, 7 October 1991, 3B (online version); "Minnesota is No. 3 on 'Most Livable' List," *Star Tribune*, 9 March 1992, 6B (online version); "Minnesota Just Short of Bronze," *Star Tribune*, 1 June 1994, 6B (online version); "Rochester Grabs Another No. 1," *Star Tribune*, 21 August 1996, 1B (online version).

11. Maude L. Lindquist and James W. Clark, *Minnesota: The Story of a Great State* (New York: Charles Scribner's Sons, 1950), 3.

12. Boyer and Brill, "Minnesota, Where Water is the Magic Word," 217; and John Fraser Hart's section in Tom L. McKnight, *Regional Geography of the United States and Canada* (Englewood Cliffs, N.J.: Prentice Hall, 1992), 294.

13. "Is Quality of Life Falling?" *Star Tribune*, 28 June 1996, 1B.

14 See Annette Atkins, "Minnesota: Left of Center and Out of Place," in *Heart Land: Comparative Histories of the Midwestern States*, ed. James H. Madison (Bloomington, Ind.: Indiana University Press, 1988), 26.

15. Wy Spano on the television program *Almanac*, broadcast 20 August 1999.

16. See "Minnesota: A State That Works," 34; and Elazar, "A Model of Moralism in Government," 354–355.

17. Even the famous *Time* article warned about Minnesota complacency: "Minnesota: A State That Works," 31; see also "Are We Simply Smug?" *Star Tribune*, 27 June 1990, 1A (online version); and Atkins, "Minnesota: Left of Center and Out of Place," 27, 29.

18. See "Man Who Once Praised Minnesota Now Chides It," *Star Tribune*, 16 January 1991, 7B (online version); and Doug Grow, "For Many, the State is No Longer the Land of 10,000 Dreams," *Star Tribune*, 26 July 1992, 3B (online version).

19. On the imagined community of the nation, see Benedict Anderson, *Imagined Communities* (London: Verso, 1983), 15–16.

20. See Rhoda R. Gilman, *The Story of Minnesota's Past* (St. Paul: Minnesota Historical Society, 1991), 217.

21. On the connection between the print medium and the imagined community of the nation, see Anderson, *Imagined Communities*, 38–49.

22. On the role of commerce and mass media in creating and fostering Minnesota's regionalism, see Karal Ann Marling, "Culture and Leisure: 'The Good Life in Minnesota,'" in *Minnesota in a Century of Change*, ed. Clark, 546–549.

23. "Minnesota: A State That Works," 24. See also Atkins, "Minnesota: Left of Center and Out of Place," 26.

24. See Anne R. Kaplan, Marjorie A. Hoover, and Willard B. Moore, *The Minnesota Ethnic Food Book* (St. Paul: Minnesota Historical Society Press, 1986), 6. "California cuisine" has set the precedent. On food as a symbol of identity, see Barbara G. Shortridge and James R. Shortridge, "Food and American Culture," in *The Taste of American Place*, ed. Barbara G. Shortridge and James R. Shortridge (Lanham, Md.: Rowman & Littlefield, 1998), 6–7.

25. See George Moses, *Minnesota in Focus* (Minneapolis: University of Minnesota Press, 1974), 11–12.

26. On caucus attendance, see David Brauer, "Can the DFL Heal Itself?" *Minnesota Monthly* (November 1999): 103.

27. Nick Coleman, "Where's Our Minnesota Mojo Gone?" *St. Paul Pioneer Press*, 22 August 1999 (online version).

28. Joseph A. Amato and John Meyer, *The Decline of Rural Minnesota* (Marshall, Minn.: Crossings Press, 1993), 23.

29. Ibid., 40–41.

30. Joseph A. Amato, "New Peoples and New Orders: The Metamorphosis of Contemporary Rural Minnesota," posted at <http://www.farmfoundation.org/1999NPPEC>.

31. Barbara Lukermann et al., *Trade Centers of the Upper Midwest: Three Case Studies Examining Changes from 1960 to 1989* (Minneapolis: Center for Urban and Regional Affairs, University of Minnesota, 1991), 8–13.

32. Thomas L. Anding et al., *Trade Centers of the Upper Midwest: Changes from 1960 to 1989* (Minneapolis: Center for Urban and Regional Affairs, University of Minnesota, 1991), 40.

33. This is apparent in the recent county population and household estimates posted by the State Demographic Center at Minnesota Planning <http://www.mnplan.state.mn.us>. See also its *Minnesota Milestones 1998: Measures that Matter* (St. Paul: Minnesota Planning, 1998), 55.

34. "Twin Cities Population Growth Leads Upper Midwest," *Independent* (Marshall, Minn.), 10 March 2000, 14A.

35. Ibid.

36. Joseph A. Amato, "Harvest of Risk," *St. Paul Pioneer Press*, 27 June 1999, 20A.

37. See Joseph A. Amato and John Radzilowski, *Community of Strangers: Change, Turnover, Turbulence, and the Transformation of a Midwestern Country Town* (Marshall, Minn.: Crossings Press, 1999), 58–63.

38. See Joseph A. Amato et al., *To Call It Home: The New Immigrants of Southwestern Minnesota* (Marshall, Minn.: Crossings Press, 1997), 39–40.

39. See Yi-Fu Tuan, *Topophilia* (Englewood Cliffs, N.J.: Prentice-Hall, 1974), 238.

40. See Amato and Meyer, *The Decline of Rural Minnesota*, 13–16.

41. The hierarchy and the prospect of decline is outlined in Lukermann et al., *Trade Centers of the Upper Midwest*, 9–10, 39–41.

42. For some, this growing resemblance of small towns to bedroom communities is not just a symptom of decline. The lead DFLer (Democratic-Farmer-Labor Party) on the House Agriculture Finance Committee and the chairman of the Right to Be Rural Coalition recently accused advocates of corporate agriculture of seeking "[to turn] rural towns into 'bedroom communities.'" See "Public Forum," *Independent*, 18 August 1999, 4A.

43. See William Cronon, *Nature's Metropolis: Chicago and the Great West* (New York: W. W. Norton and Co., 1991), 17–19.

44. See Joseph A. Amato, *Servants of the Land* (Marshall, Minn.: Crossings Press, 1990), 47–50.

45. Ibid., 38–44.

46. As reprinted in the *Independent*, 7 September 1999, 4A.

47. Ibid.

48. "Urban Areas Top Quality-of-Life Study," *Star Tribune*, 18 June 1993, 3B (online version); "Most Seniors Living Well, Study Says. But Older Minnesotans Living Outstate Fare Worse than Average," *Star Tribune*, 1 April 1993 (online version); John Tichy and William J. Craig, *What the 1990 Census Says about Minnesota: Income and Poverty* (Minneapolis: Center for Urban and Regional Affairs, University of Minnesota, 1995), 16, 102–105; and *Minnesota Milestones 1998*, 56–57.

49. Minnesota is described as a trademark in Gilman, *The Story of Minnesota's Past*, 217.

50. *Minnesota Milestones 1998*, 7.

51. In the case of German identity, the creation of *Heimat* brought nation and locality together. See Alon Confino, *The Nation as a Local Metaphor* (Chapel Hill, N.C.: University of North Carolina Press, 1997), 98–99, 188–189.

52. "Minnesota: A State That Works," 24.

53. On the durability of new forms of community, see Victor Turner, *The Ritual Process* (Chicago: Aldine Publishing, 1972), 202–203.

DAVID A. LANEGRAN

Minnesota: Nature's Playground

MINNESOTANS HAVE FUN. We see our state as a place filled with opportunities for adventure, relaxation, and "edutainment." Frequently referred to as "the theater of seasons," the state's changing weather multiplies the varied landscapes by four. Each lake, valley, hilltop, forest, bog, and field has four distinct personalities created by the weather. In the winter, Minnesota gets very cold and normally has considerable snowfall. By contrast, the summers are hot with sudden storms. The change from summer to winter produces a fantastically colorful landscape through which pass hundreds of thousands of migratory birds. The spring, although not as colorful as fall, is characterized by racing streams, a northerly migration of birds, and vegetation bursting with life. Minnesotans have developed special ways to play in all landscapes in all seasons. An army of hunters, several thousand strong, fills the forests and fields every fall. In the subzero dead of winter perfectly normal people sit on overturned pails, staring at holes they have bored in the ice, waiting for a fish to swim by and take their bait. In the summer, a huge fleet of pleasure boats is launched to carry people in circles around the lakes. Special vehicles are purchased to carry us off the roads into the depths of swamps so we can get away from it all. Are we different from other Americans? "You betcha"—we have learned to enjoy our time in Minnesota.

Walking on the Water

In Minnesota we all can walk on water. In fact, we drive trucks on it. For at least three months, and in most years five months, the 10,000-plus lakes, the rivers, and the ponds of Minnesota are covered with a layer of ice strong enough to support mini-settlements of ice-fishing houses. Minnesotans have fished through the ice for decades. It is possible that the first people to develop the

DAVID A. LANEGRAN *is John S. Holl Professor of Geography at Macalester College.*

technology were commercial fishermen who strung their nets under the ice. Perhaps the first ice-fishermen were dairy farmers with time on their hands during the winter. However it began, ice fishing is a signature event in Minnesota. Each winter there are ice-fishing contests attracting thousands of entrants. One wonders what the fish think when one morning the lake is suddenly full of dangling hooks and the noise of happy people and thousands of footsteps crunching on the ice. It is not too surprising that the contestants usually catch very young and small fish.

For several years various entrepreneurs have tried to promote stock-car races on the frozen lakes, but have met with limited success. Parka-clad spectators peering through clouds of their condensed breath and cars spinning around on ice lack the appeal of NASCAR racing on sun-drenched raceways in the South. Perhaps racing on frozen lakes is too similar to the normal winter commute on icy, snow-filled streets to be amusing.

Why Don't We Stay Inside and Curl Up by the Fire?

This is not the place to trace the development of recreation and sport in modern American culture, but a few generalizations about that process may help explain some of our behavior. During the last half of the twentieth century Minnesota has gradually evolved from a landscape of work toward a landscape of play. During those five decades the average income and amount of leisure time available to individuals and families gradually expanded. With increased time and money, Minnesotans, like all Americans, followed the admonishments of advertisers and began to develop ways to fill their leisure time and spend their money. In this regard Minnesotans are like all citizens of wealthy countries. However, there are a few pieces of conventional wisdom and some scholarly observations that may be useful in understanding why the special recreational landscape of Minnesota has been developed.

Most Minnesotans will tell visitors that the best way to survive in Minnesota is to be active. Do not fight the environment; find a way to enjoy it. If days are cold and snowy, take up winter camping, cross-country skiing, skating, or any one of innumerable winter sports. If the weather is hot and humid, go swimming, enjoy the breeze on a golf course, or get the wind blowing through your hair on a powerboat racing around in circles on a lake. This attitude may spring from the early agriculturalists' bouts with cabin fever, a specific form of madness associated with being confined to a small room during the harshest times of winter.

Not everyone believes that intense activity is the best way to deal with the changes in the weather. Indoor recreation enthusiasts, those who curl up with a good book in front of a roaring fire as winter descends, balance outdoor aficionados. These "couch potatoes" prefer drinking a cold beer or iced tea in a shady spot to playing a round of golf or game of tennis during the heat of summer. In fact, the nonactive may outnumber the outdoors enthusiasts in the state, if we consider the fact that, along with other Americans whose lifestyles have become sedentary, a large fraction of adult Minnesotans are overweight.

Conventional wisdom aside, scholars have recognized special aspects of Minnesota culture. John Rooney and Richard Pillsbury have placed Minnesota in the "sports for sports' sake" region.[1] In this portion of the United States, schools and recreation programs offer almost everyone a chance to participate in the sport of their choice. High-school athletics are supported as recreational outlets for participants and spectators. Although most towns support basketball for high-school boys and girls, very few elite basketball players are produced in the region. In addition, Rooney and Richardson describe this region as a "bastion of girls' high school athletics." The "sports for sports' sake" region is vast. Its eastern border begins west of Green Bay and runs south through central Wisconsin to the Mississippi River and follows the Mississippi south to southern Missouri, but excludes St. Louis. The southern border runs west from Memphis through Arkansas along the northern Oklahoma border to the Rocky Mountains in southern Colorado. There it runs northward along the Rocky Mountain front through eastern Colorado, Wyoming, and Montana and along the Rocky Mountains to the Canadian border (it also includes Alaska). The region contains only three cities that support major-league teams in baseball, basketball, football, or hockey.

Just as in other states, recreation and sports have been embedded into the school culture of Minnesota for many reasons. Participation in sports teaches leadership and aids personal development. It also promotes community spirit, both within the schools and in the larger community that supports the schools. Minnesotans expect their children to participate in sports; therefore schools offer a variety of activities that runs the seasonal gamut and appeals to all.

While everyone is encouraged to participate, recreation in Minnesota is undoubtedly gendered. Males dominate the popular images of hunting. In fact, the most frequent justification for hunting is the camaraderie of the hunting camp. Fishing is harder to categorize. Males are most frequently portrayed, but advertising images also depict happy families in fishing boats. Increased gender equality is also apparent in other landscapes. Ladies' days at golf courses have essentially disappeared, and young men and women are seen on ski slopes in approximately equal numbers. There seems to be a trend toward more equal participation in tennis, jogging, and biking. While Minnesota shares many attributes with the other parts of the "sports for sports' sake" cultural region, there are several special recreational landscapes that warrant further investigation.

Classification of Landscapes

The meaning of places is determined by complex interactions among the physical environment, buildings and other modifications humans have added to the landscape, and interpretations made by individuals of the landscape. Children are experts at transforming humdrum landscapes into enchanted places. In Minnesota nature helps children by changing golf courses into snowy slopes perfect for skiing or sliding. Snowplows create great banks of snow that are perfect for playing "King of the Hill." This works for adults as well. A high retaining wall can become a perfect face for rock climbers, harvested cornfields become hunting grounds, and cutover timberlands become spiritual retreats.

Writers such as Leo Marx, Yi-Fu Tuan, and Roderick Nash have described a gradient in landscape values that ranges from urban through rural and pastoral to wilderness.[2] The values attached to these landscapes have varied over time. Tuan argues that in the late eighteenth century the "Jeffersonian ideas categorized the city as profane, the pastoral or middle landscape as Edenic and the wilderness as also profane." But by the late twentieth century, values had shifted. The center of large urban areas and the landscapes of urban sprawl were still profane, while the middle landscape and threatened wilderness became Edenic. Wilderness has become an ecological ideal and no longer thought of as a profane place to be conquered and transformed into a cultivated area. The pastoral areas between the city and the wilderness consist of a variety of places. Some are agricultural; others are locations where mining or lumbering occurs. And others may be resorts and small towns. These diverse places have distinctive landscapes that are the physical expression of the environmental processes and human activities found within those areas. The landscapes can be thought of as the cultural footprint on the land. According to the above-mentioned authors, Americans have differing opinions about these landscapes. Some places are thought to be beautiful or romantic and are highly valued. Others are considered ugly and dangerous and are to be avoided. As will be discussed later in this essay, the values about landscapes held by Minnesota residents vary by social class and geographic location.

It is possible to classify recreational landscapes according to a set of gradients that, while separate, have strong relationships. At one end we have the landscape of home, which is comfortable and predictable, but affords few opportunities for recreation and physical activity. At the other end are the dangerous landscapes that are filled with risk and demand mental and physical preparation. The wilderness is both dangerous for the average or unskilled individual and safe for those who are well prepared. It can be a place for personal testing or quiet communion with nature.

Another gradient of landscapes is the degree to which they are modified by human activity. Frequently called the cultural landscape, the built environment reflects the values, needs, and desires of humans. Built recreational environments range from backyard swing sets and jungle gyms, to ball courts, gymnasiums, and swimming pools, to area stadiums and golf courses. The reservoirs constructed behind dams are probably the largest recreational landscapes that have been created by direct human activity.

In addition to built recreational landscapes are those places that, while not actually built or cultivated by humans, are heavily managed. Minnesota's lakes, marshes, streams, rivers, and forests are all controlled areas. Water bodies are regularly stocked with fish, streams are managed for trout habitat, forests are harvested for timber, and marshes are drained or sometimes flooded for waterfowl. At the extreme are landscapes that are protected from human activity. What we call wilderness in Minnesota exists because as a community we have decided to limit the depredations of human economic activity. Thus we can see at least two gradients in the landscape: one based on the degree to which humans have altered the place and the other based on the degree of danger or amount of special knowledge needed to survive in the place.

Rituals of Place in the Recreational Landscapes

Rooney points out that Minnesotans would rather participate in sports than watch them. High-school sports and amateur leagues are used to define communities to a remarkable degree. Towns of all sizes boast baseball and softball fields, basketball courts, football fields, hockey arenas, and ice rinks. Brilliant lights on high poles pierce the dark humid nights each summer as the "town ball" leagues pit the local townsmen and farmers against those down the road. Agriculturists take pride in maintaining immaculate turf playing fields. The crowds are small but enthusiastic. In the fall, town ball yields to football leagues tailored to the size of the school. Some schools field teams with only nine players, and there are four levels of regular eleven-man teams. All through the harvest seasons the teams compete for the right to play in Minneapolis's

Hubert H. Humphrey Metrodome for the state championship. Although not as football-crazed as Texans, Minnesotans still promote the sport.

We all work together while we play against each other. Both boys' and girls' athletics are used to enact ritually the regional struggles between various parts of the state. The title "state champion," whether for volleyball, swimming, dance teams, football, or wrestling, is an ardently pursued prize. Each year it is suburbs against the city, the north battling the south, and the metropolitan area versus the rest of Minnesota. Hockey teams from Baudette and International Falls, wrestling teams from Caledonia and Blue Earth, basketball teams from Litchfield and Minneapolis North, cross-country and track teams from Mounds View and Stillwater struggle before hometown and community fans for statewide bragging rights. The images and myths spun around the adolescent athletics hark back to older times when parents and other relatives competed. Regional images are also honed through sports. Hockey players from the north are reputed to have skated to school in bitterly cold temperatures on frozen rivers with the howling of wolves ringing in their ears. Wrestlers from the south are said to possess iron grips and bulging arm and shoulder muscles earned by hand-milking herds of Holsteins before catching the school bus. Football players with a blue-collar work ethic are extolled along with prized basketball players who learned their moves on the tough playgrounds of the inner city. When all the state tournaments are over, the round of play practice and competition begins again with a new cohort to replace the graduates.

Once upon a time young people played games and sports without the interference of adults. Today, in order to produce athletes, parents and communities have combined to create landscapes and lifestyles organized around recreational activities. Communities have built athletic fields and ice arenas to provide spaces for children to learn, practice, and compete. Elaborate systems of leagues have been created to ensure that children get the proper training and competition. Baseball, soccer, and hockey are probably the most extreme examples of this phenomenon. Modeled after baseball's "Little League," other sports established similar layers of competition. In some cases the parents have actually defied the weather and now both hockey and soccer players compete year-round. Because "ice time" in the indoor arenas is limited, games are scheduled at all times of the day. Hockey parents (usually moms) ferry the boys and girls to various venues in vans filled with the paraphernalia of pads, sticks, skates, and uniforms. Minnesota even hosts an international soccer tournament each summer.

Along with the leagues, games, and practices have come a host of specialized camps for budding athletes. There are goalie camps, power-skating camps, and "big-men" basketball camps, among others. The specialized athletic camps compete with the more traditional summer camps of the YWCA, YMCA, Scouts, and churches.

The Lake Cabin Up North

In Minnesota there is a generic place called "up north" or "at the cabin." Approximately 5.6 percent of the households in Minnesota own about 132,000 seasonally occupied properties in the state. The actual location of the family's lake place may or may not be north of its primary residence. It may be a very simple structure without indoor plumbing, or it may be a five-bedroom, three-bath house. No matter; it is still "the cabin." Having a "summer home" is too pretentious for Minnesotans. That is what the bosses of the railroads and the mill owners had. Real Minnesotans have cabins. This fascination with a cabin on a lake may be traceable back to the Scandinavian culture of many of the immigrants; today many of the families in Sweden and Norway own second homes, although many are farmhouses rather than lakeshore properties. Whatever the reason, twentieth-century Minnesotans love lake cabins.

At first the cabins were built on lakes close to towns or on lakes that could be reached from the Twin Cities by trains. The glacial moraine region of central Minnesota is pocked with hundreds of ideal lakes. They have sandy bottoms with a sharp slope down to the lakeside. The best lakes have good populations of fish. The mixed forests of the transition zone between the prairies of the south and west and the pine forests of the north are perfect places for cabins. They were not all log cabins in the pines, but the first cabins were primitive. Water had to be pumped by hand, and outdoor privies were standard. Baths were taken in the lake, and all the cooking was done on wood stoves. But working while everyone else played made homemakers unhappy, and whenever possible the cabin was improved. Electricity for lights and appliances, propane for stoves or furnaces, and indoor plumbing were added over the years. In fact, shortly after the midpoint of the century, the suburban lawn was introduced to the vernacular cabin landscape design.

The Minnesota Fleet

Unlike other navies, the Minnesota fleet has more captains than crew. The crafts are generally small and carry arms only during the waterfowl hunting season. The fleet is large and consists of 793,107 bottoms not including canoes, duckboats, riceboats, or seaplanes. The fleet grows about 1 percent a year.[3] At first, fishing boats designed by local Scandinavian builders, such as Lund or Larson, were rowed or pushed by small outboard motors made by other Scandinavian firms such as Evinrude and Johnson. Neither the boats nor motors had to be big, because families were not in a hurry and most lakes were not large. However, once waterskiing was invented in Lake City, Minnesota, life at the cabin was altered forever.

The peaceful mornings and evenings that had been spent in quiet conversation and contemplation of the ways of nature (especially fish) were shattered by the roaring ski boats pulling a new form of athlete, the water-skier. After a short time, lakeshore owner organizations and townships adopted rules to confine waterskiing—and, more recently, jet skis (sort of a motorcycle for use on water)—to certain hours of the day and to certain lakes. New water sports have made lake cabins even more popular with the young and athletic. Fishing has not disappeared, but the concept of a primitive fishing cabin has.

With the prosperity of the last three decades of the twentieth century, the number of developed lakeshore properties has skyrocketed. The wealthy newcomers have changed the culture of the north. There is now a huge market for a wide range of consumer goods, higher-quality roads, entertainment facilities such as golf courses and restaurants, and services needed by the summer population to maintain its suburban lifestyle.

Canoeing

The many lakes of Minneapolis are great places for romantic canoe rides. On warm Wednesday nights a small flotilla assembles off the shore near the Lake Harriet band shell to languish in the sounds of pop tunes wafting out over the water. The state's rivers have become popular places for downstream travel in rented canoes, usually in the spring when the water is high. More recently the kayak has become popular for those who like to skim over the water without a partner.

For most Minnesotans, canoeing and the Boundary Waters Canoe Area Wilderness are inseparable. The BWCAW is located in northeastern Minnesota. Established as a special management area within the Superior National Forest, the area is managed by the Department of the Interior for three primary purposes: wilderness and recreational activities, watershed management, and the protection of threatened and endangered species. The BWCAW is not a huge area (about one million acres) but it has over 1,200 miles of convoluted canoe routes. The two hundred thousand people who get permits to canoe it each year are spaced out in what amounts to long lines with significant intervals. Thus, even though it is regarded as the most heavily used wilderness area in the United States, canoe parties can still feel alone and refresh their souls.[4] Although we canoe an all sorts of water bodies, the archetypal trip is one to the Boundary Waters where cold lakes, granite outcrops, islands, and dense forests define the wilderness experience.

Hunting

In 1999, slightly over 8 percent of the state's population—359,690 Minnesotans—bought licenses to hunt white-tailed deer and took to the woods. They hunted in all sections of the state, from the cornfields of the south to the bogs and aspen forests of the north. It is not possible to know how many were afield at any one time, but it is safe to assume that the vast majority were out on the opening day of the season. In the forested sections of the state all outdoor activities are limited during "The Season." Hunters are required to wear blaze-orange clothing, and bikers, walkers, dogs, and horses are advised to wear bright clothes as well. While not frequent, accidental shooting deaths occur each season.

Rituals are important in hunting. Hunting companions are selected with great care. While solitary hunters are common, hunting is most often done in intergenerational groups. Boys and a growing number of girls are apprenticed into the sport after passing firearms safety classes. Hunting shacks, like lake cabins, come in all styles and sizes. Most are spartan and decorated with antlers, old furniture, ample larders, and tables for playing cards. The hunting camps are egalitarian places where all are expected to contribute to the success of the hunt. However, expertise is respected, as some butcher, some cook, and others tell "Sven and Ole" jokes.

During the fall in northern Minnesota most men are not expected to be available on weekends for several weeks before the hunting season begins because they are preparing their camp and deer stands. During the season they are in the woods, and after the season they are talking about the activities of the earlier weekends. There are actually several different deer seasons. Hunters using bows get the first chance at the deer herd; those using firearms, mostly rifles but some shotguns, follow them. Finally the traditionalists who use old-fashioned "black powder," percussion rifles, try their hand. Those interested in hunting moose need a special permit and follow greater restrictions. Fat and sleepy bears on their way to hibernation are also hunted. When the season finally draws to a close in late November or early December, the annual population of deer, moose, and bears has been reduced, but the populations of all three animals continue to expand in response to favorable environmental conditions.

Big game hunting with firearms for deer, moose, and bear is only one form of this popular sport. In the agricultural landscapes of the southern part of the state, the pheasant hunters take the fields. Some take up positions on the edges of fields of corn, soybeans, or prairie, and others in the party walk through the fields driving the wary birds toward them. Heavy birds, the pheasants are reluctant flyers and prefer to elude their pursuers by running through the vegetation or remaining concealed. Thus, good bird dogs are invaluable companions to the hunters. The dogs flush the birds, then locate and retrieve them after they have been shot. Pheasant hunting can be an idyllic walk through the sunny autumn landscape in the company of friends and loyal canine companions. Small-town social organizations hold special hunters' pancake breakfasts to raise money, but there is usually no expectation that hunters will pay for permission to hunt private land. Similar to the pheasant hunters in the fields, hunters in the forests pursue woodcock, partridge, and grouse.

Duck and goose hunting, on the other hand, is best on cold rainy days when the birds fly low and stay close to the marshes. Although some try to sneak up on ducks resting on small bodies of water—called "jump-shooting"—most hunters conceal themselves and their dogs in blinds or camouflaged boats behind strings of decoys. They take to their stations well before dawn, and when the sun rises they attempt to call the birds into shooting range. Their quiet solitary pastime is generally cold and uncomfortable. But when the fast-flying waterfowl come into range, pumping adrenaline raises the temperature of hunters, both human and canine. The dogs, whether Chesapeakes or Labradors, are born to swim and joyfully plunge into the icy water after downed birds.

The most solitary of the bird hunters are the approximately forty thousand who seek wild turkeys. This is a relatively new sport, growing rapidly in response to the population explosion of the once nearly extinct birds. The Department of Natural Resources, in cooperation with sportsmen's clubs, has restocked wild birds in woodlots and farm fields in the southern and central parts of the state. Turkey hunters dress like trees, cover their faces with camouflage paint, and, in the wee hours of the morning while the birds are roosting, take up their hiding places. When the sun finally rises they attempt to call tom turkeys to them by imitating the seductive calls of lonesome hens.

Turkeys are not the only wild birds that are increasing as a result of landscape management by humans. The population of Giant Canada geese is exploding. These birds were thought extinct until a small flock was discovered living permanently on a reservoir in Rochester that was kept ice-free year-round by warm water discharged from a local power plant. These birds were local favorites and fed by the townsfolk. Once the DNR realized the birds were living in Rochester, conservation agents captured young birds and relocated them to new breeding grounds each summer for several years. The relocation program was a stunning success. It turns out that geese love parks, and they especially love the suburbs. They like the warm water of urban parks and thrive on the lush grass of golf courses and cemeteries. Now the bird has become something of a problem. Although not quite as numerous as pigeons, the birds soil the jogging trails and golf links. Guardian ganders frequently challenge golf carts and slow-moving cars. The burgeoning numbers of offspring of the urban geese created the need for yet another relocation program. Each year city park rangers rounded up the goslings before they could fly and shipped them off to game reserves in other states. Minnesota has exported so many geese there are no more places willing to take surplus birds. The large number of resident geese has made a special hunting season necessary.

Fishing

There is nothing in Minnesota quite like "the opener," or the opening weekend of fishing. While all sorts of fish are popular with anglers, the state's premier fish is the walleye pike. This native fish can grow very large, but most of those caught are less than five pounds. The fish are said to have soft lips, and one must be careful when they nibble bait. If one is overly eager the fish will get away. In most years the governor participates in a media event during the opener. The Friday night before opening weekend the northward-bound lanes of all the roads are jammed with pickup trucks and sport utility vehicles pulling boat trailers.

This sort of fishing is very social. There are no solitary fishermen on the opener. Even though it is seldom a warm weekend, it is considered the beginning of summer. For several years the weekend coincided with Mother's Day. This presents a dilemma that some have attempted to solve with the "take a mother fishing weekend." While it is a time for bonding and relaxation, the fishing opener is occasionally marred by drownings and traffic accidents.

Trout fishing has several openers, but unlike the walleye opener there are no traffic jams, drownings, or accidents. Trout streams are found in southeastern Minnesota along the limestone bluffs of the Mississippi and also along the north shore of Lake Superior. These two beautiful but sharply contrasting landscapes attract fly fishermen, who prefer to work the streams by themselves. Because there are no "stream cabins," trout fishermen stay in motels or, even better, pitch tents in the parks or public land close to the streams. The spring nights are cool, and so they pack themselves in layers of sleeping bags and blankets. Shortly after sunrise the crisp smell of campfires made with dry oak fills the misty valleys. After a few cups of scalding coffee the men and women don their thigh-high boots and wade into the cold water. It only seems that they are lashing the water with their fly rods when, in fact, they are carefully positioning their flies so the wily trout strike without thinking. Most trout fishermen do not keep all they catch. Many use barbless hooks and prefer to return their catch to the streams.

Minnesota landscapes are managed for trout. Although a sizable natural or native population exists, trout are also stocked in some streams. The DNR has several programs designed to maintain the fast-flowing clear streams of the limestone bluffs. The banks of streams are stabilized and logs or low barriers of rocks are installed so that they jut out into the stream. These structures, called wing dams, force the stream into narrow channels where the water picks up speed. The faster-flowing water is able to scour the streambed and create holes, which provide an environment more conducive to trout.

Family Feuds—Private Recreation on Public Land

The public owns much of the land in Minnesota. The state and federal governments own approximately 23.5 percent of the entire state. The vast majority of public land is in the northern forest zone, where the U.S. Department of Agriculture Forest Service, the U.S. Fish and Wildlife Service, and the National Park Service combined hold 6.5 percent. Another 5.5 percent came to the counties as tax-forfeited lands. The Minnesota DNR owns 10.31 percent, and various other state departments own 0.06 percent. The vast majority of the land is northwest of Duluth.[5]

The presence of so much public land in northern Minnesota has created a major controversy over the proper use of the land and the denizens of the forest. It is a clash between those who want to use the land for a variety of recreational purposes and those who view it as a commercial resource. The population living in the rest of the state has two sometimes conflicting views of the region. There are those who believe the land should be managed for sports such as hunting, snowmobiling, and fishing. Others view it as a preserve for wild animals such as moose, deer, and otter, or a place for contemplative individuals to interact with the wilderness and thereby find a deeper meaning in life. To provide for their needs is the BWCAW as well as a large section of the area designated the Voyageurs National Park, both located along the Canadian border. The most persistent controversy involves the use of the forest outside the special protected areas. Pulp and paper companies' desire to harvest timber clashes with the views of environmentalists such as the Minnesota Center for Environmental Advocacy, who believe that too much timber is being cut too quickly to maintain the necessary habitats for animal life and water quality.

The Singing Wilderness: BWCAW

Superior National Forest was established in northern Minnesota through several administrative processes between 1905 and the present. Shortly after World War I, when the highway system was developed in this part of the state, camping and outdoor recreation in the national forest began to become popular. By 1919, about 12,750 people had visited the forest. Competition between the new outdoor enthusiasts and the timber companies working in the forest soon developed. The two decades between 1920 and 1940 were filled with controversy between those interested in developing hydropower and those interested in recreation. In the late 1920s the secretary of agriculture, William M. Jardine, issued a proclamation creating a "primitive area." In 1958 the present name was established. Although we call it a wilderness, it is not a virgin forest. It has been largely cut over and experienced various forms of sparse settlements. Today the BWCAW is a roadless area, and air travel below 4,000 feet is forbidden. The use of motors in the area is severely restricted, but those who want to use motorized fishing boats and snowmobiles in the area believe the landscape should be made available to a wider fraction of the population and not just limited to the canoeist.

For many canoeists the BWCAW is already too crowded. Some feel that the wilderness experience begins only after they have paddled a full day without seeing another human. The YMCA and Scout camps using the area have developed special traditions and cultures based on the wilderness experience; for example, some camps use only handcrafted wooden canoes that reflect the fragility of the wilderness. But no matter what material is used for canoes, all the camps extol the virtues of the simple life and teach campers to care for the environment.

Infernal Machines

While canoeists are quiet and fishers and hunters—whether after waterfowl, deer, wild turkeys, or small game—are expected to be silent while in pursuit, during the past few years a new machine has posed problems for the landscape.

A class of motorized vehicles with four or six wheels designed to travel off roads has become increasingly popular in the rural regions of the state—the All-Terrain Vehicle, or ATV. While some hunters use these to get to and from their "stands," recreational-use ATVs have caused a major conflict on public land.

In Minnesota, ATV registrations have exploded 803 percent since 1984, going from 12,235 to today's 110,449. Hunters are angry because the ATV riders break trails through the forest, disturbing their hunt. It is legal to drive an ATV off a state trail, but ATV opponents contend the machines are tearing up public lands, creating noise problems, and frustrating those who are looking for solitude in the woods. ATV advocates argue they have an equal right to use public lands. They further contend that their license fees should be used to make more trails for them on the public land. In response, the DNR attempted to classify state forest lands into three groups for the purpose of managing off-road vehicle use: managed, limited, and closed. In the managed forest (90 percent of the total), all roads and trails would be open to ATVs. They also suggested that off-trail riding should be banned in the remaining 10 percent. Legislators rejected their proposal. The debate between the riders and the environmentalists is not over, but it appears that new a form of recreational landscape will be created in the forest.

Right to Hunt

Tension over the use of the publicly owned forest also generated an intense debate in the late 1990s over the right to hunt. As a result, the Minnesota legislature passed a law guaranteeing residents of Minnesota the right to hunt and fish, despite the protests of various groups of animal rights advocates. In addition, Minnesota's residents and political leaders have been engaged in a lengthy debate on the management of the wolf and deer populations in the northern part of the state. Deer hunters encourage the Division of Forestry and other sections of the DNR to create a landscape that will support a large number of deer so the hunters may harvest them.

The Great State Get-together

Lovers of solitude avoid one of the state's most famous recreation landscapes: the 360-acre Minnesota State Fair grounds. The twelve-day-long fair is one of the nation's largest and best-attended agricultural, educational, and entertainment events, in recent years attracting over 1.6 million people annually. The fair's agricultural and creative competitions draw over 35,000 entries each year. Livestock, fine arts, crafts, school projects, baked goods, fruit, vegetables, bee and honey products, flowers, butter, and cheese are all brought to the fair. But that is not all. In addition to the exciting carnival rides, six stages provide over 500 free performances during the exposition. The grandstand, originally built to showcase horse races, now features pop, rock, and country music artists as well as comedians. It is also a great place to shop, browse, or learn. Over four million square feet of exhibit space contain booths housing manufacturers, retailers, educational institutions, artisans, politicians, news media, and a wide variety of government agencies.

Best of all, the fair is a great place to eat! It boasts the Midwest's largest collection of food vendors, with more than three hundred culinary concessionaires. Everything from ethnic foods to traditional favorites like mini donuts, fried cheese curds, and frosty malts, along with twenty-five different foods-on-a-stick, all can be found at the fair. There are so many cauldrons and vats of hot grease bubbling that some say that the air of the fair grounds gets saturated with fat molecules after a couple of days, allowing a person to gain weight by just walking around at the fair and inhaling the ambient atmospheric calories.

The fair is the last great ritual of summer. It ends with Labor Day and the start of school. For the rest of the year the fair grounds are essentially idle, although a few buildings are used for special events. The hippodrome hosts horse shows and sporting events. In June the many streets of the grounds are converted into parking lots for the fancy cars entered in the "Back to the Fifties" car show. Brilliantly painted hot rods and dream machines create one of the most festive landscapes imaginable.

Historical and Cultural Landscapes

There is another sort of recreational landscape developing in Minnesota and the rest of the United States. These are the historic sites and places that have been determined to have some message for the present and future generations. In recent years, people have flocked to places such as Historic Fort Snelling, where historical interpreters show visitors what life was like in 1827. The National Park Service manages a rebuilt fur-trade depot at the Grand Portage National Monument site, where a great rendezvous took place each year between traders and voyageurs who wintered in the boreal forests northwest of Lake Superior and fur-company managing partners from Montreal who came west across the Great Lakes in huge cargo canoes. There are also living history farms and lumber camps, which employ reenactors to illustrate working and living conditions in the nineteenth century.

In Minneapolis, the milling district at the Falls of St. Anthony has been declared a historic district. Here visitors can go on a walking tour or engage a guide for a lively interpretation of the ruins and rebuilt structures. Forestville State Park in southeastern Minnesota contains a fully stocked country store from the 1890s, but little is for sale there. There are few sites associated with the pre-European populations that are open for viewing. Access to most of them is restricted to protect the pictoglyphs and mounds. One of the most interesting of these sites is the Pipestone National Monument in southwestern Minnesota. There visitors can visit not only outcrops of the sacred calumet stone, but also see the traditional quarries and watch Native Americans produce artwork with the freshly cut stone. These places provide opportunities for "edutainment" — a mixture of education and entertainment attracting cultural tourists.

Theater of Seasons

The bounds of this essay prohibit a view of all the landscapes and activities developed by Minnesotans over the years to keep themselves amused. The ever-changing landscape constantly calls to us. In the long summer days, golf courses, lakes, forests, and trails pull us out of the air-conditioned comfort of our apartments and homes. Every town in the state takes a weekend to transform itself into a playground. There are Polka Days, Corn Days, Pumpkin Festivals, and a variety of celebrations named after some local claim to fame. The streets are converted to shopping and socializing spaces, and for a day the town is the recreational center of the area. The brilliant change in colors of fall draw even the most obstinate "couch potato" out for a walk. During the short winter days the crystal fields of winter have a more limited appeal. The sidewalks are treacherous for the elderly and the cold can kill. But nonetheless, bike paths are brushed free of snow for joggers and walkers. The parks are crisscrossed with ski trails. Most families have a few snowbirds who head for Arizona or Florida each winter, frequently reminded of the fun they are missing back home. With the coming of spring the snowbirds return, and the cycle of preparation for the intense summer begins again.

Conclusion

Are we different? More adventurous? More willing to come to terms with the environment? The Minnesota navy plies the lakes and rivers; the woods and fields are full of hunters. Temporary villages appear on the lakes each winter, and St. Paulites insist on celebrating the Winter Carnival during January's coldest weeks. We try our hand at every conceivable sport, even if we are not particularly good at any of them. We probably are not all that unusual. We have just learned to have fun in the landscape and enjoy our time in Minnesota.

Notes

1. John F. Rooney Jr., and Richard Pillsbury, "Sports Regions of America," *American Demographics* 12 (1992): 30–37.

2. Leo Marx, *The Machine in the Garden: Technology and the Pastoral Ideal in America* (New York: Oxford University Press, 1964); Yi-Fu Tuan, *Topophilia: A Study of Environmental Perception, Attitudes, and Values* (New York: Columbia University Press, 1990); Roderick Nash, *Wilderness and the American Mind* (New Haven, Conn.: Yale University Press, 1967).

3. Minnesota Department of Natural Resources Boat and Water Safety sections, "Minnesota Boat Registration 1959–1999," unpublished, 3 December 1999.

4. See web site at <http://www.gis.umn.edu/snf/info/brochures/bwguide.html>.

5. Minnesota State Planning Agency, *Minnesota Public Lands, 1983* (St. Paul: Minnesota State Planning Agency, 1983), 5.

JOHN S. ADAMS

Minnesota: A Work in Progress
Shaping the Landscape and the People

THINK OF MINNESOTA as a remote place on the North American continent—halfway between the equator and the North Pole, and midway between the Atlantic and the Pacific. Its location is remote from areas of older settlement, yet it is centrally located, and it knows about and interacts with much of the continent.

Minnesota's farmers, business people, teachers, political leaders, and journalists have traditionally cultivated a sophisticated awareness of political events and trends in both the national and international arenas. Livelihoods depended on knowing what was happening in the world, and staying one step ahead of better-located competitors. At the same time, Minnesota's geographic isolation has until recent years perpetuated a distinctive Upper Midwest culture. Minnesota's location at the center of the continent has resulted in positive as well as negative consequences; but as demographic, economic, and cultural forces move over the state, reshaping land and life, it is not always clear which is which.

Minnesota Enjoys a Good Location

In the early days of settlement and economic life, Minnesota—over 410 miles northwest of Chicago, and 1,250 miles from New York—needed to be smarter and better informed to compete effectively with such older, established Eastern business centers as New York, Boston, and Philadelphia. With a location at the northwestern edge of the North American Manufacturing Belt, and at a marginal location for the profitable export of bulky grain and lumber products to national and world markets, remote events such as modest shifts in commodity prices or transportation costs brought about relatively large

JOHN S. ADAMS *is professor of geography, planning, and public affairs in the department of geography at the University of Minnesota.*

consequences for Minnesota's producers.[1] In order to succeed, they had to monitor national and world events—and they did.

Nineteenth-century Minnesota business leaders were well educated for their time. Mostly from New England, of British and Irish stock, they maintained old-school and family ties—which they used to good advantage in acquiring the latest technologies, raising investment capital, marketing products, and monitoring government policy. When they reached the Minnesota territory, they also reached the end of the pine forests that lay just beyond the western shores of Lake Superior. Many remained, deploying their fortunes and business acumen in new pursuits, while a few moved on to exploit the forests of the Pacific Northwest. Meanwhile, as timber companies and lumber operations advanced westward from New England across the Great Lakes region during the early decades of the nineteenth century, a frontier of permanent agricultural settlement advanced west of the Appalachian Mountains across Ohio, Indiana, Illinois, and eventually into Wisconsin, Iowa, and what was to become the state of Minnesota.

Minnesota Enjoys a Bad Location

Even though Minnesota's remote location offered a few advantages, it also imposed handicaps. Relatively isolated and off the beaten path during the heyday of pre–World War I immigration, Minnesota and the Twin Cities of Minneapolis and St. Paul had a locational disadvantage compared with North American industrial centers that lay closer to the European origins of immigrants in attracting people and resources.

By the end of the 1890s, agricultural areas of America's northern heartland were as populated as they were to become. Agricultural settlement west of the ninety-eighth meridian into the central Dakotas and Montana declined sharply as annual rainfall decreased from Minnesota's average of twenty to thirty inches while at the same time increasing in unpredictability. The edges of the northern pine region, with their poor acidic soils and short frost-free growing season (80–120 days), offered little that was attractive to permanent agricultural settlers.

Today's Upper Midwest region consists of the states of Minnesota, North Dakota, South Dakota, Montana, the northern counties of Iowa, parts of northwestern Wisconsin, and Michigan's Upper Peninsula (figure 1). Historic banking, business, and railroad links, reinforced by migration flows, unified this region throughout the twentieth century, with the Twin Cities emerging to dominance as its economic and cultural capital. As a regional metropolis, the Twin Cities compete with Chicago, 410 miles to the southeast; Kansas City

Figure 1: Minnesota in the Upper Midwest

Source: Cartography Laboratory, Department of Geography, University of Minnesota.

(440 miles) and Denver (920 miles) to the southwest; and Seattle (1,670 miles) and Portland (1,730 miles) to the west. Since the United States was settled mainly from east to west, the older established urban areas could maintain a disproportionate prominence over areas to the west by their control of investments, business management, and transportation systems—i.e., roads, canals, and railroads.

The Minneapolis–St. Paul metropolis has dominated Minnesota demographically, politically, and economically, but for much of the state's history, Duluth has been Minnesota's second major commercial and industrial center, and the financial, business, and cultural capital of the northeastern part of the state. Once high-grade and easily accessible iron ore was discovered, north (in the Mesabi and Vermilion Ranges) and west (in the Cuyuna Range) of Duluth, the city quickly flourished (along with the city of Superior, Wisconsin, across the mouth of the St. Louis River) as a Great Lakes port and management center for business activity supporting the iron industry, including at one time a small blast furnace and steel-production facility. In addition, the Port of Duluth provided an outlet for grain from the Red River Valley.

When the Great Lakes–St. Lawrence Seaway opened for traffic to the Atlantic Ocean in 1959, grain and ore traffic increased. Grain for export had previously been shipped from Duluth-Superior to Buffalo, New York, transferred from there to rail for Baltimore, and then loaded on oceangoing vessels for export. With the opening of the Seaway, direct overseas shipment from Duluth-Superior became possible. The impact of the Seaway on the iron economy was different; commerce could flow in both directions along the waterway, thus permitting low-cost iron ore imports from abroad. Hence the competitive pressures on Minnesota ore increased at the same time that the best ore deposits were shrinking. On the positive side, the opening of the Seaway meant more competition among transportation modes, with the result that the iron and steel operations on the Great Lakes were stabilized, and Minnesota and Duluth maintained some of their markets. But hopes that the Seaway would enhance Duluth as a general cargo port, bringing imports into the northern heartland, went unfulfilled—rendered unviable by the area's sparse population.

Despite Duluth's far northern location and difficult climate, it is likely that the city would have become larger and more prominent if a greater share of nearby mining properties, mining activity, and transportation businesses had been owned and controlled by local residents rather than by financial, iron, and steel interests in Pittsburgh and New York. Earnings that might have been returned to the region and reinvested in northeastern Minnesota left the state, and Duluth's economic potential was never fully realized. The city counted a population of only 85,000 in the 1990 census after losing more than 10 percent. of its residents in the 1980s, with some of the decline due to a flight to the suburbs. The two-county metropolitan area contained many of the iron-mining communities and a total population of 241,000; but even with a large area included in the count, the Duluth-Superior area contained less than 10 percent of the population of the greater Twin Cities area. Yet Duluth and its region maintained significant political clout in state politics even as its population and economy were increasingly overshadowed by the Twin Cities—largely as a consequence of the fact that, for many years after 1920, the Minnesota legislature failed to reapportion itself following each decennial census. The 1962 U.S. Supreme Court decision *Baker* v. *Carr*, requiring that all legislative districts have approximately equal populations, necessarily ended this neglect—which further diminished Duluth's prominence.

In the case of Chicago versus the Twin Cities, the larger and earlier-established Chicago used its locational advantage of proximity to Eastern and European markets, along with its early control over railroad freight tariffs, to out-compete the Twin Cities throughout much of Wisconsin, Iowa, and

Nebraska. By manipulating railroad freight rates, Chicago railroad interests were able to monopolize freight movements and wholesale trade markets up to the eastern edges of the Twin Cities. On the other hand, Twin Cities railroad interests were able to capture the markets west of the Twin Cities to the Rocky Mountains.

Had the Twin Cities been closer to Chicago, they might have been overwhelmed by their larger rival as were Milwaukee, Wisconsin (90 miles north of Chicago on Lake Michigan) or Des Moines, Iowa (335 miles to the south), Iowa's capital and largest city. The Twin Cities were just distant enough from Chicago, with sufficient tributary region to the west and north and a sufficient number of wealthy, canny, and aggressive business leaders, to succeed where many other Chicago competitors fell by the wayside.[2]

Nature Shapes the Land

If geographic location on the North American continent yielded certain advantages and disadvantages during the settlement and economic development of Minnesota, the state's physical environment and natural resources—an essentially flat terrain shaped by the action of glaciers that advanced over the area and finally retreated during the last Ice Age—bestowed certain economic opportunities while curtailing or precluding others.

The last ice sheets withdrew across Minnesota's 84,000 square miles between ten and eleven thousand years ago, leaving behind a surface of moraines and till plains with an elevation that generally varies between 1,000 and 1,500 feet above sea level.[3] Because the retreat of the last major ice was relatively recent, the state's drainage system is immature; thousands of lakes and wetlands persist throughout the region, as in other recently glaciated places around the Great Lakes—Wisconsin, Michigan, Manitoba, and Ontario.

Minnesota covers a large area. At its admission to the union in 1858 it was the largest state in the country. The distance from Minnesota's southeast corner to its northwest corner, about 630 miles, is roughly equal to the distance from Washington, D.C. to southern Maine. Because of its large size—roughly equal to the island of Great Britain—weather and growing seasons differ from one part of the state to another. Three major air masses influence Minnesota's weather at different times of the year. From the north comes cold, dry Canadian air; from the west, warm, dry Pacific Ocean air that drops much of its moisture as it passes over the Rocky Mountains; and from the southeast comes warm, moist air from the Gulf of Mexico. Local weather, which changes every three or four days, depends on which air mass dominates.

Minnesota's vegetation at the time of permanent European settlement consisted of three broad zones (see figure 2). Forests of pine, spruce, fir, and bog conifers (such as tamarack), interspersed with bogs and swamps, dominated the northeast third of the state. From the northwest corner of the state east of the Red River Valley to the rugged Driftless Area in the extreme southeastern corner (untouched in the last glacial ice advance) lay a broad band of hardwood forest, mainly oak, maple, and basswood, interrupted by patches of prairie. Finally, prairie—interrupted by gallery forests of elm, ash, cottonwood, and willow along the flood plains of major river valleys—covered the southwestern third of the state.

Soils for agriculture varied from rich, dark, and fertile beneath the prairies in the southwest to rocky, thin, and acidic in the northeast by Lake Superior and in the Arrowhead Region north of the lake. Precipitation varied from abundant and predictable in the northeast to sparse and variable in the southwest. The frost-free growing season was longest in the south, declining to under a hundred days in the far north. The combination of soil, precipitation, and growing season meant that south-central and southeastern Minnesota were the most attractive sites for European-style agriculture, while farming of any kind remained relatively unprofitable or risky in areas north and northeast of the Twin Cities. By 1900 agricultural settlement corresponded closely with the profitability of farming. The size, prosperity, and density of towns serving and supported by agricultural settlement reflected the density of agricultural population and the prosperity of farming.

Minneapolis and St. Paul lay within the deciduous hardwood forest zone that roughly divided the state on a southeast-to-northwest line. The cities traditionally enjoyed convenient access—first by water, then by trails and railroads—to the densely settled parts of the state, and later to the iron ranges in northwestern Minnesota. The different subregions of the state contributed in complementary ways to the state's economy. It was through the Twin Cities that the parts were connected with the outside world.

Diverse Peoples, Different Agendas

As Yankee lumbermen and merchants pushed their way westward into Minnesota's pine forests, and permanent agricultural settlers entered the southeast part of the state from Wisconsin and Iowa, native Indian peoples who had first lived there were steadily displaced. Prior to the onslaught of businessmen and farmers, the region around the Great Lakes had been occupied by various tribes of the Algonquian language group. In the Lake

Figure 2: Minnesota Vegetation at the Time of European Settlement

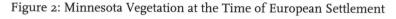

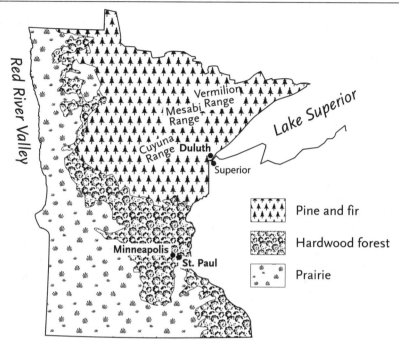

Source: Cartography Laboratory, Department of Geography, University of Minnesota.

Superior region, the Ojibwe tribe (known as the Chippewas in the southwestern part of their region, and as the Mississaugas in the southeast) had been doing business with French fur traders since the seventeenth century. West of the Algonquian areas lay the Dakota or Sioux Indian lands, separated by a sharp and often hostile boundary between the two distinctive Indian languages and cultures.[4]

As the timber harvest moved relentlessly westward into northeastern Minnesota, and the agricultural frontier rolled into the southeastern part of the state, the Ojibwe Indians shifted west ahead of the Europeans, and in turn pushed the Dakota Indians out of the woodlands and onto the prairies farther west. By the 1820s the boundary between the two Indian cultures lay across Minnesota along the western edge of the hardwood forest belt; clashes between tribes and friction between Indians and white settlers became common.

While the Indians were being displaced and permanent agriculture made its imprint on the area, business leaders and land speculators began shaping the towns, transplanting a New England-style, town-meeting tradition into city governance. An emphasis on citizen participation (although Indians and women still lacked the vote) was exemplified by the charter of Minneapolis, which provided for four separately elected government boards: for schools, the public library, city parks, and general city government.

In the leading cities of St. Paul and Minneapolis, Yankee leadership recognized early the need for city planning, and the local business oligarchy acted decisively—by today's standards high-handedly—on behalf of what it saw as the community's long-term interests. Perhaps the most noteworthy example is the securing, through public acquisition, of lands around the lakes in and near both cities and along river embankments to be set aside as parks for public use—routinely ignoring public objections that such expenditures of tax money were excessive and unnecessary. The foresight of this initiative has been vindicated in countless ways, not the least of which is the way that the splendid natural and residential environments near the lakes have retained thousands of upper-middle-class business and professional elites whose counterparts in most other American cities long ago abandoned city life for the distant suburbs.

If the vanguard of businessmen and farmers came from older settled areas of the eastern United States, by the 1870s the overwhelming share of newcomers were immigrants, principally from Germany and Scandinavia. As they emigrated to North America, the frontier of settlement had moved well beyond the Appalachians and had reached the Upper Midwest. Minnesota received such large numbers of German and Scandinavian immigrants in the 1860s, 1870s, and 1880s simply because the frontier of settlement reached Minnesota at precisely the moment that the bulk of emigrants from Europe were coming from northwestern parts of the continent.

Between 1890 and World War I the modernization frontier moved across eastern, southeastern, and southern Europe. By the time the millions of resulting emigrants reached the United States, the frontier of agricultural settlement in the Upper Midwest had passed beyond Minnesota to the Dakotas, then petered out. Some Poles and Russians made it to the Dakotas, and some Ukrainians settled in the prairie provinces of western Canada, but most immigrants after 1890 found economic opportunity in the industrial cities and mining areas in states to the east of Minnesota.

A few later European immigrants found manufacturing jobs in St. Paul and Minneapolis, and significant numbers settled on Minnesota's northeastern iron ranges. But unlike most U.S. Manufacturing Belt states east of Minnesota and north of the Ohio River, Minnesota was initially settled only once—

between 1830 and 1930, mainly by persons of northwestern European stock, together with some transplanted Easterners. They arrived with a purpose and stayed, and together gave the state its traditional culture as they reshaped the terrain, exploited resources, established a Lutheran and Catholic religious environment, and pursued economic and civic life in ways that created a distinctive cultural island at the center of North America that only recently has begun to resemble much of the rest of the country.

Government Surveys, Communication Routes, and the Settlement System

If one flies over Minnesota—whether in winter or summer—one cannot fail to notice the chessboard layout of property boundaries and land-use patterns. Minnesota's land east of the Mississippi River was part of the old Northwest Territory, a vast public domain north of the Ohio River and west of the Appalachians to the Mississippi River, formerly owned or claimed by eastern states (mainly Virginia) but ceded to the federal government under the jurisdiction of the Congress of the Confederacy. Minnesota's land west of the Mississippi was part of the Louisiana Territory purchased from France in 1803. As Minnesota achieved territorial status in 1849 and statehood nine years later, government surveyors began mapping and subdividing the land so that individual parcels could be legally identified and ownership conveyed to railroad companies, farm settlers, and others.

The basic unit of land was the "congressional township," a parcel six miles on a side, and subdivided into 36 square "sections," each a square mile, or 640 acres, in area. Each section was in turn subdivided into four square "quarter sections" of 160 acres, which became the typical farm plot in Minnesota as the federal government distributed land to farm families for permanent agricultural settlement.

The federal government also granted land to railroad companies, which in turn sold it to raise capital for railroad construction. Once a proposed route was established by consultation between the government and the railroad company, the company received alternate sections of land within a band six miles wide on either side of the planned rail line, with the government retaining the remainder of the sections. The idea was that the state would get rail service, the railroad would get customers, and farmers would get land near the railroad for the easy marketing of their produce.

Minnesota's earliest rail lines branched out overland from river ports along the Mississippi River, following river valleys or overland trails that had been laid out and used by Indians and fur traders prior to permanent European settlement. Early railroads connected the trading centers. Where lines intersected, towns emerged. Elsewhere, the railroad companies established towns every six to ten miles as rail lines penetrated what would become newly settled agricultural areas. The combination of railroads and agricultural settlement provided the geographical framework for the emergence of trade centers throughout Minnesota in the nineteenth century. Over time the network of trade centers evolved into a well-defined hierarchy, with the Twin Cities metropolis as the state (and regional) capital.

Immigration, Settlement, and Minnesota's Local Cultures

Successive waves of entrepreneurs and permanent settlers populated Minnesota's farms and towns once native peoples were pushed farther westward or confined to reservations, usually on isolated northern lands. French fur traders had operated in the area for many decades prior to the nineteenth century, but their agenda was commerce, not permanent occupation of the land. When the fur business waned, they moved on.

Mid-nineteenth century bonanza wheat farmers established farms and built farmsteads on a speculative basis for later sale to farm operators eager to capitalize on the booming cash market for the commodity. By the late 1890s, the map of Minnesota's rural and urban settlement patterns had assumed roughly the form it would have in the next century (see figure 3). Farms covered nearly all the land west and south of the northeastern cutover region. In northern and northeastern parts of the state, small dairy and grain operations struggled for survival against long winters, cool summers, and infertile soil. Towns serving and supported by agriculture were closely spaced and prosperous in the south and southeast, but were widely spaced farther to the west, and struggled mightily in the north.

As Minnesota's eighty-seven counties filled with immigrant farm settlers between the 1860s and 1890s, each county assumed a slightly different ethnic character that was often reinforced by chain migration, whereby those arriving first recruited fellow townsfolk and church members from their homeland. So it was that counties or parts of counties developed distinctive flavors as Belgian Catholic, Swedish Lutheran, Bavarian Catholic, Swiss Mennonite, Norwegian Lutheran, or Irish Catholic—still visible in the churches they built, in the cemeteries they filled, and in the names on Main Street businesses and professional offices.

Before World War I and well into the 1920s Minnesota's local rural communities in most ways remained culturally isolated from one another and from outside influences. Many elderly used languages brought from Europe. Occasionally foreign-language newspapers delivered news from the old country, plus domestic news of special interest to the group. Surplus grain and animal products were sold through dealers in nearby towns. After World War I, second- and third-generation farm populations increasingly linked up with mainstream urban American culture. Farm prosperity promoted travel, trade, and migration off the farm to urban schooling and employment.

During much of the twentieth century, most Minnesotans maintained a personal or professional concern with the state's farm economy. If residents did not live on a farm, they had relatives who did, or were in a business that sold to farmers, or bought products from them. These links with the land, combined with northwestern European religious and cultural traditions, provided a solid foundation for the socially conservative and economically liberal sentiments that long characterized Minnesota politics—best exemplified by the passions of Minnesota's greatest political leader, Hubert H. Humphrey. Minnesota's social conservatism is rooted in Lutheran and Catholic backgrounds. In the late twentieth century almost two-thirds of Minnesotans claimed affiliation with a religious denomination, with 80 percent of that group about evenly split between Catholic and Lutheran. The state's economic liberalism derives in part from progressive religious convictions, but perhaps is more an offshoot of Scandinavian socialist traditions of mutual aid and support. Farm purchasing and marketing co-ops, housing co-ops, and retail co-ops continue as a successful tradition in Minnesota and the Twin Cities to the present day.

But as Minnesota came into increasing economic dependence on national and international markets for agricultural products, the farm stage was set for trouble from two directions—economic vulnerability and waning political influence. When prices plummeted during periodic farm crises from the early 1890s through the Depression, Minnesota's independently minded farmers often reacted violently to the idea that their welfare depended on forces beyond their control. Until the last third of the twentieth century, by which time their numbers and political influence had diminished to insignificance, the populism of northern prairie farmers and farm-related businesses in Minnesota and the Upper Midwest was a formidable political force.

In an earlier time, when 95 percent of Minnesota's population was northwestern European stock, most residents probably felt they were part of the majority mainstream culture group. Questions of identity turned on differences between Norwegian Lutheran and German Lutheran, or between Irish Catholic and German Catholic, with political debate centering on capital/

farmer/labor and rural/urban/mining interests. Today's greater ethnic diversity in Minnesota's cities and small towns triggers questions of identity that take novel forms. Politics that had been shaped by territorial and economic interests have been partly replaced by a new politics of ethnic solidarity.

Now that most of the state's population is comfortably middle class and urban-focused (even if living in the countryside), political fragmentation is based on identities delineated by economic position, ethnicity, ideology, and residential location—for example, African Americans, immigrants, Latinos, wealthy Indians, poor Indians, Asian Americans, central city residents, suburban commuters, abortion foes, environmentalists, and so forth. The 1990s saw a vigorous national debate erupt over how the Census Bureau should count and classify various immigrant and minority groups. As Minnesota becomes less a cultural island and comes to mirror the population profiles typical of other regions of the United States, the same identity politics infect the state— "it's not *who* you are, but *what* you are."

Minnesota's Links with World Events

From the American Civil War until World War I, Upper Midwest farmers and manufacturers operated on generally favorable terms with markets at home and abroad. Protestant Yankee business and banking leadership provided commercial and financial ties with the outside world, while farmers and laborers of immigrant stock worked hard and lived close to home.

The opening of the Panama Canal in 1914 changed things. Grain from the Dakotas and Montana now had a Pacific Ocean outlet to national and international markets, thereby undermining the Twin Cities' monopoly market for cheap grain from northern prairies, an arrangement that had favored Minneapolis millers for years. As the prices that Minneapolis paid for raw materials rose, and as railroad freight rates were revised to Minnesota's disadvantage, grain milling began a slow shift to Buffalo and Kansas City while northern prairie grain producers saw their incomes rise; this was bad for millers' profits but good for Twin Cities wholesalers and producers of consumer goods.

The Depression years hurt farmers and city businesses alike. As the bottom dropped out of commodity prices, farmers and retail merchants suffered. When retail business waned, wholesaling and manufacturing declined. The downward spiral endured until the end of the 1930s when World War II expanded demand for food, fiber, and ore from Minnesota's iron ranges.

After 1945, national growth and regional economic transition reshaped the

Figure 3: Population Distribution in Minnesota

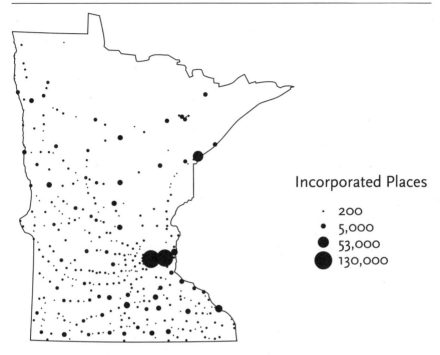

Incorporated Places

· 200
• 5,000
● 53,000
⬤ 130,000

Source: Cartography Laboratory, Department of Geography, University of Minnesota.

economic and settlement geographies of Minnesota and the Upper Midwest. Farms had become completely mechanized and consolidated; much of the rural population left for urban employment opportunities in business and industry. The state's deposits of high-grade iron ore had been heavily depleted during the war, and foreign iron ore began entering the U.S. market at bargain prices. Chemical engineers and material scientists at the University of Minnesota invented a method for beneficiating low-iron-content taconite to produce a uniform, marble-sized pellet of more than 60 percent iron that found a strong and steady market in Great Lakes–area iron and steel mills, thereby giving Minnesota's mining industry a renewed lease on life.

Later decades saw an increasing number of Minnesota and Twin Cities companies move beyond a local and regional focus to national and international ambitions. Many persons who had grown up in Minnesota migrated to schools and jobs elsewhere, while the Sun Belt beckoned retirees, if not permanently then at least for the winter months. A vigorous Twin Cities economy attracted domestic and foreign migrants. Local radio and television became increasingly national in its ownership and content. By the end of the 1990s, the forces of globalization affecting all parts of the world had succeeded in changing much of the character of the state. A place once caricatured as a distinctive cultural island in America's northern heartland was increasingly understood by outsiders and residents alike as simply a colorful and occasionally amusing variation on national and global themes.

A Distinctive Local Culture, Waning in Places

It is probable that in the last half of the twentieth century there was more personal wealth owned and controlled in Minnesota on a per-capita basis than in all but a half-dozen or so other states; in foundation wealth and philanthropy Minnesota was also among the nation's leaders on a per-capita basis. Much of the locally owned wealth was originated and retained by privately held companies that reinvested earnings rather than paying out dividends to satisfy stockholders. The result has been some of the nation's largest and most profitable privately held companies.

A significant number of Minnesota companies have tried to do good while doing well. During years when leading local companies were closely and privately held, with their founders continuing to influence company policies, corporate philanthropy flourished. In ways that parallel the tradition of the cooperative in agriculture, corporate Minnesota shared its income and wealth with the state's schools and cultural institutions—art, music, theater, and dance; children's and science museums; public radio and television; international people-to-people and world-affairs programs; neighborhood rehabilitation efforts; benevolent societies—and demonstrated a commitment to the idea and practice of corporate social responsibility.

Early fortunes gained from grain and lumber milling, railroads, iron mining, manufacturing, banking, and later ones built on printing, publishing, and the hotel and hospitality industry, have supported independent philanthropic foundations (e.g., McKnight, Northwest Area, Bush, General Mills, Minneapolis, Saint Paul) as well as corporate foundations (e.g., Target/Dayton Hudson, Blandin, Carlson Companies, Star Tribune) to a degree that is unusual in the United States. Although public rhetoric can enhance divisiveness by dwelling on the fact of increasing racial and ethnic diversity (in a place exceptionally homogeneous by national standards), there continues to be a sense of community cohesiveness as philanthropies join with churches and civic organizations to help Minnesota and the Twin Cities work together on common community-development agendas.

There was a time before World War II when who you were depended on where you worshipped, how you took care of your property, how you treated your neighbor, and the level of your contribution to the community. Against these measures, the generation that came of age in the 1980s and 1990s differs in nearly all respects from Minnesota's earlier generations. To begin with, many of them come from other states and from non-European backgrounds. Those with roots in Minnesota have grown up immersed in a commercialized popular culture no different from that saturating the cultural environment of the rest of the country. If Minnesota's young people differentiate themselves today, it is along ethnic, racial, and social-class lines rather than by means of their Minnesota culture. National media shape speech, tastes, values, ambitions, and behaviors, while migration to and from Minnesota means countless bridges linking a cultural island with—indeed, making it part of—the national mainstream. To be sure, there is plenty that remains distinctively Minnesotan, but it is found more in working-class neighborhoods, in Minnesota's smaller cities and towns, in the agricultural countryside, and on the Iron Range than in popular media or the upper-middle-class suburbs of the Twin Cities.

The Twin Cities area, except for parts of their downtown cores, have increasingly become like other large metropolitan areas in America. They are shaped by the same corporate- and media-driven, materialistic atmosphere that affects all other parts of the country. Even though Minnesota's marriage rates, home-ownership rates, church-membership rates, and family orientation are among the highest in the country, as incomes continue to rise, values, tastes, speech patterns, accents, driving habits, entertainment tastes, and food preferences converge toward national norms. In this light, the 1998 election of Jesse Ventura—a former professional wrestler and popular iconoclastic radio talk-show host—as governor of Minnesota shocked many older natives, but came as no surprise to voters under the age of forty. If former Minneapolis mayor and U.S. senator Hubert Humphrey were running for either of those offices today on a platform of economic liberalism and social conservatism he probably would be soundly defeated, and possibly laughed out of town, so much has the state changed.

Redistribution of Minnesota's Population and Economic Activity following World War II

During the first century of Minnesota's settlement and economic development the population dispersed, a transportation infrastructure was put in place, and towns and cities emerged to support an economy based largely on resource extraction—mainly agriculture, forestry, and mining. Following World War II, the economy of Minnesota and the Twin Cities area—and, for that matter, of most of the Midwest—saw the accelerating transformation of economic structures and redistribution of economic activity as resource-based industries (agriculture, mining, forest products) and manufacturing were increasingly supplemented by a broad array of expanding business and personal-service industries, transportation, retail trade, recreation and leisure industries, professional services, and government. The transformation was driven by technological, demographic, and social forces, can be measured in diverse ways, and has affected rural and urban parts of the state differently.[5]

As agriculture was mechanized, production expanded, prices dropped, profit margins narrowed, and farms consolidated with correspondingly fewer workers needed. In the 1950s, outmigration from Minnesota's rural areas totaled 278,000—almost 10 percent of the state's 1950 population of three million. Minnesota's cities and towns absorbed 180,000 of these, while the remainder left the state for jobs mainly in the cities of the Northeast or the West Coast. With its best ore deposits depleted, Minnesota's iron-mining industry languished; the small resurgence made possible by the taconite industry required many fewer workers on Minnesota's Iron Range. Pine forests harvested before 1915 now contained deciduous hardwoods mixed with second- and third-growth scrub pine of limited commercial value. New, capital-intensive technologies were deployed to manufacture building materials from the hardwoods, but labor requirements were modest.

By the time of the 1990 census, three out of every four Americans lived in urban areas—places of 2,500 persons or more. The rest lived in small towns, in houses along country roads, or on dispersed farmsteads. Minnesota's population was 62 percent urban in 1960, 70 percent urban in 1990.[6] As metropolitan populations expanded in size and dispersed into postwar suburbs, the work week shortened over the three intervening decades from 38.6 to 34.4 hours for goods-producing workers, and hourly earnings adjusted for inflation rose. Retailing pursued consumer purchasing power into the suburbs and automobile-oriented suburban shopping centers appeared in the midst of households with the time, money, and mobility to shop not just for necessities, but increasingly for recreation.

Professional services like education, law, and medicine began expanding in the 1950s as children of the postwar baby-boom era entered school. The number of births began rising in 1944 and peaked nationally in 1959–1961 (a year or two later in Minnesota). As the numbers of children increased more schoolteachers were needed along with trainers of teachers, and trainers of the trainers. In the 1960s, more than half the white-collar jobs created in the

United States were in education, and Minnesota and the Twin Cities participated fully in that trend. Moreover, rates of high-school completion rose steadily after World War II, with college-going rates rising as well. The census of 1960 reported that 44 percent of Minnesota's population age twenty-five and older had completed high school (versus a U.S. average of 41 percent); but by the end of the 1960s and through later decades 75 to 80 percent of eighteen-year-olds were finishing secondary school on time, 50 to 60 percent of those graduates entered post-secondary institutions, and about half of those entering completed a college or university degree.[7] Minnesota's education industry expanded briskly after 1960, and the education and training it provided supported the transformed economy of the postwar decades. As the education industry expanded, cities and towns with colleges and universities saw their employment bases and populations rise steadily.

Banking and brokerage services, legal services, insurance, and the medical industry flourished together, each providing lucrative business for the others. As service industries boomed, places that were home to these activities—such as the Twin Cities—saw their fortunes improve. Outside Minneapolis–St. Paul, the world-renowned Mayo Clinic and its associated hospitals helped elevate the city of Rochester and its medical industry to the status of one of Minnesota's largest and most important metropolitan centers. The city had a population of 41,000 in 1960, having grown by 36 percent in the previous decade. By 1990 it had reached 71,000 and was still growing steadily as its principal industry continued to prosper.

Government remained a modest industry in America until the Depression years of the 1930s, accounting for only about one dollar in seven of gross domestic product (GDP), of which four-fifths was spending by state and local governments. The country emerged from World War II with a much enlarged federal government, but state and local governments were not far behind. With the Cold War military buildup, expansion of public education, highway building and maintenance, the building and managing of suburbia, and the rebuilding of core areas of the central cities during the urban-renewal programs of the 1950s and 1960s, total government budgets as a share of GDP expanded through the 1950s, reaching a peak of a quarter of GDP at the end of the 1950s and early 1960s.[8] Of course as the government industry expanded, Washington, D.C., state capitals, and county seats expanded their job bases and their populations.

In Minnesota, state and local government expanded faster than elsewhere in the country. Largely this was due to the state's system of personal income tax, which was steeply progressive. Many other states relied instead on retail sales taxes, excise taxes, or personal and corporate income taxes that were less progressive or that levied a flat percentage on taxable incomes. By contrast, Minnesota's tax structure meant that as incomes rose with higher productivity in the 1940s and 1950s, and later with the war-induced inflation of the late 1960s, state revenues rose at a much faster rate. The state then used these extra revenues to expand its own programs and to increase aid to local governments, including public-school districts.

Thus Minnesota's economy after World War II grew steadily while its profile changed from one emphasizing resource-based industries and goods manufacturing toward enterprises focused on transportation, communications, and utilities; wholesale and retail trade; business and personal services; finance, insurance, and real estate; professional services; recreation; education; and government. Meanwhile, the state's population grew from three million in 1950 to five million in 2000, while redistributing from farms and rural areas to urban centers, and from high-density central city areas into low-density suburbs. At the close of World War II, seven of ten persons in the Twin Cities area—which then had a population of 1.2 million—lived inside the fifty-five square miles of the city of Minneapolis or the fifty-three square miles of St. Paul. Fifty years later, the built-up portions of the Twin Cities metropolitan area sprawled over an area of perhaps 6,000 square miles, with only one in five residents living in the two central cities. People abandoned old jobs and followed new jobs to locations where they were available. Many types of retail trade, service, and recreation jobs were simultaneously pursuing consumer purchasing power into new suburban areas, and into expanding regional centers with their economies anchored in government, education, professional services, and modern automobile-oriented retailing.

Minnesota's Leading Companies Today

There are more than two hundred publicly-owned companies in Minnesota, with 35 of them boasting market values exceeding $1 billion.[9] The goods and services these companies produce and sell exemplify contemporary trends in the national economy, while at the same time dramatizing differences between the state's economy at the end of World War II and today. Of the top one hundred ranked by annual revenues, twenty-nine are retail or service companies, thirty-four are manufacturers, nine are health-care or medical organizations, ten are financial institutions, thirteen are information-technology companies, and five are telecommunications or energy companies. The top five Minnesota firms in each of these six categories taken together account for 81 percent of sales, nearly 86 percent of profits, and 87 percent of the market value of all the top one hundred publicly held Minnesota companies combined.[10]

There are different ways to measure the importance of Minnesota-based companies—by annual revenue, by return on assets, by return on equity, or by return on revenue. Other possible indices include measures of corporate citizenship and indicators of responsibility toward society or the environment. Notwithstanding the measures used, these leading companies reflect what the state's economy has become and is becoming at the dawn of the twenty-first century. Most business leadership is centered in the greater Twin Cities area, but eleven of the top one hundred companies are headquartered elsewhere in Minnesota.

A debate persists over "old economy" (i.e., resource-based industries, goods manufacturing) versus "new economy" (i.e., information, technology-intensive, and financial services industries) directions for Minnesota business. Some venerable Minnesota companies with significant name recognition—Pillsbury, Honeywell, and Norwest Corporation, for example—merged with or were acquired by companies elsewhere. Conversely, Minnesota-based companies such as Medtronic vigorously acquire businesses headquartered beyond the state's borders. The state's business future depends on competing successfully with tenacious competitors around the country and around the world. Venture capital moves toward promising ideas and the prospect of quick returns in fast-growing parts of the country, so an average-size state such as Minnesota must work harder and smarter to retain and expand its slice of the economic pie.

For any state, the keys to retaining and expanding its slice include heavy spending on basic research, building and maintaining high-tech business incubators, and establishing sizable high-tech venture-capital funds that will invest in promising regional companies. In addition, a state needs one or more well-supported world-class research universities to serve as magnets for national and international faculty and student talent, and for companies that crave new scientific and technological ideas as soon as they become available. After talented newcomers are attracted to the campuses of these institutions, many remain in the vicinity to provide the human capital without which all the other ingredients for business success will languish. Today's vigorous centers of scientific and technical innovation—such as Seattle, the Bay Area of northern California, Austin, Texas, the Boston-Cambridge area, and North Carolina's Research Triangle Park—all are characterized by this combination of leading centers of scientific research and technological advance and supporting business and financial infrastructures.

Remodeling the Landscapes of Production and Consumption

Flat terrain, abundant lakes, a taste for low-density residential environments with home ownership, and state and federal tax policies promoting home ownership combine to make rural and urban Minnesota a land of widely spaced single-family farmsteads, urban-oriented households on residential lots of one, two, five, and ten acres, and sprawling suburbs. City neighborhoods continue to lose population—the state's average household size, which stood at 3.4 in 1960 (compared to a U.S. average for the same year of 3.3), dropped to 2.58 in 1990 (compared to a national average of 2.63). Because state population is rising while average household size declines, the number of households and housing units in Minnesota has steadily risen at a rate faster than population growth. The fastest growth in population and housing is in the two dozen or so counties located within an hour's drive of the Twin Cities and its built-up suburbs, but other fast-growing centers like Rochester, St. Cloud, and Mankato, plus a host of smaller regional centers, experience similar growth and sprawl, albeit at a much reduced scale.

In Minnesota, and the rest of the United States, federal income-tax laws permit households to deduct mortgage-loan interest and real-estate taxes from taxable incomes. Moreover, states that (like Minnesota) levy a state income tax also normally permit deductability of mortgage-loan interest and real-estate taxes. With the progressive rate structures of the federal and state tax codes, whereby higher increments of taxable income are subjected to successively higher marginal tax rates, the more expensive the house one buys, and the higher one's taxable income, the greater the tax relief or subsidy to which a household is entitled. It is no surprise, therefore, that new construction in the suburbs of Minnesota's cities and nearby countryside is characterized by ever larger and more extravagant houses. Because federal and state government pay much of the cost (by means of tax deductions), it makes economic sense for middle- and upper-middle-class households to indulge their housing tastes to the maximum extent possible.

As new housing estates sprawl into suburban and exurban areas around Minnesota cities, population and purchasing power are relocated from older, built-up central cities to the suburban edges. The radial and circumferential interstate highways built between and through American metropolitan areas from the late 1950s to the 1970s facilitated the opening up of agricultural lands for auto-oriented urban development. As suburbs expanded and population relocated outward, business followed—not just retail stores and shops for everyday needs, but also manufacturing and warehousing desiring single-story facilities with convenient car and truck access for employees, deliveries, and shipping. Today, the majority of jobs and population in the greater Twin Cities area are located outside the central cities of Minneapolis and St. Paul. In fact, in the metropolitan area of almost three million persons, the two central cities account for only 28 percent of the total. Central-city employment as a share of the metropolitan total declined from 43 percent in 1980 to 31 percent by 2000. Meanwhile the developing suburban areas got 84 percent of new metropolitan area jobs in the 1980s and 1990s.

But while suburbia sprawls to accommodate traditional households with traditional (if increasingly extravagant) tastes, a range of alternative household types have put pressure on city and suburban housing markets across Minnesota. One is the elderly household of one or two persons. With their longer lives and substantial purchasing power the elderly are free to leave the family home for a retirement center, an extended-care facility, or a downtown condominium close to shopping, restaurants, medical care, and other destinations within easy walking distance when they prefer not to drive.

A second form of alternative household is the single working person living alone in rented or owned quarters, but delaying, perhaps indefinitely, a family life with partner, spouse, or children. Single-person households in the United States account for about one-fourth of all households, and the share has been rising. A third element in the urban housing landscape is gay and lesbian individuals and couples living in or close to city centers where diversity in population composition and lifestyle often is more readily accommodated and supported.

As families tend toward smaller size and as nonfamily households proliferate, the character of Minnesota towns and cities departs from the traditional pre–World War II profile. The 1990 census counted 1.648 million households in Minnesota. Of this total, family households (i.e., two or more related persons) comprised 69 percent of the total, while single-person and other nonfamily households comprised 31 percent. Married-couple households (with or without children) accounted for 57 percent of all households.[11] Thus family life remains strong for many Minnesotans, and traditional families remain a plurality of households throughout the state, but they are no longer as prominent as they once were.

The waning of the traditional nuclear family has been matched by a flourishing material culture that has drawn most Minnesota women into the paid work force outside the home and away from childbearing, child rearing, and homemaking as their dominant career. Although a substantial proportion— perhaps a majority—of university-educated and professional women pursue careers for reasons of personal fulfillment, commitment to public service, or for the challenges and stimulation thereby provided, when a representative sample of Minnesota's working women were asked, "Why are you working outside the home?" the first response of Minnesota women is, "For the money." The extra income provides the ticket to the goods and services that most Americans feel they cannot (or should not) live without, whether it be new electronic entertainment and communication devices, a second (or third) car, a larger wardrobe, travel and entertainment, or restaurant food rather than dinner prepared at home.

For many decades, Minnesota households earned above-average wages and salaries but were slow to adopt the consumption trends originating elsewhere, principally in New York and California. In the 1960s and 1970s, market researchers discovered that, accounting for its disposable incomes and wealth positions, Minnesota was "understored." The retail chain stores responded by flooding the downtowns and shopping malls with the same array of shopping opportunities present in almost every other metropolitan area of the United States.

The "malling of Minnesota" (and the United States) reached its pinnacle with the Mall of America in Bloomington, a second-tier suburb south of Minneapolis near the international airport—a hub for Northwest Airlines. The MOA, an extravagant cathedral of material consumption—with over four hundred retail stores, shops, restaurants, bars, and theaters—is the largest shopping mall in the nation, and dramatizes how the values, tastes, and ambitions of the Minnesota of the 1990s depart from those of the earnest, hardworking, and thrifty "understored" society of the 1950s. To be sure, entire planeloads of tourist shoppers descend on the MOA each weekend from Japan, France, the United Kingdom, other international departure points, and places around the United States; but a substantial share of the 40 million annual visitors come from Minnesota and surrounding states.[12]

Watching shopping-entertainment malls expand and proliferate across the state, one gets the impression that everyone must be well off. Some are—such as the members of Indian tribes operating profitable casinos. The small Mdewakanton Sioux community operates two casinos in the suburbs southwest of Minneapolis, with each registered member pocketing income of a half million dollars per year.[13] At another extreme, Ojibwe Indians on the Red Lake Reservation in remote northern Minnesota are too distant from population centers, recreation sites, and job centers to establish a profitable casino business, so they live lives of dreary poverty and unemployment. Perversely, most of the business at the Ojibwe casino comes from tribal members—who can ill afford to lose what little they have.

Other groups struggling to obtain a foothold on the lower rungs of the economic ladder include African immigrants, recently arrived Latinos, and unskilled workers transplanted from moribund mill towns throughout the Great Lakes Rust Belt. The fact that urban prosperity is vivid makes the plight of those left behind and running to catch up all the more poignant. In an earlier day, Minnesota's rich and poor also looked and felt different from one another, but they lived closer together and perhaps had greater familiarity with how each other lived.

As retail trade and services displace agriculture and manufacturing as leading sectors of the new Minnesota economy, the commercial-industrial landscape of Minnesota towns and cities reflects the shifts. Formerly "high order" activities such as antique shops, hobby shops, gourmet food stores, and specialty clothing, confined to downtowns of large cities in an earlier day, are now common features of suburban malls and the main streets of small towns—a response to higher incomes and elevated consumer tastes. Meanwhile, "low order" everyday retailing—groceries, household needs, and casual clothing, for example—have consolidated into huge hypermarkets such as Wal-Mart and Target Greatland, drawing customers from fifty to a hundred miles away.[14]

But giant retail centers are not alone in their peculiar forms of gigantism. Suburban high schools with enrollments in the thousands are common even though research demonstrates that five hundred is an optimal size for learning and healthy social development. Regional hospitals with hundreds of beds and thousands of staff can offer a maximum range of services and procedures, but like the Wal-Marts and oversize high schools, the larger the facility and service area, the greater the traffic volumes and vehicle miles traveled to distribute the goods and services. Benefits for some mean new costs of noise, pollution, and congestion for others.

Life of the Mind and Spirit

As commercial-industrial life reshapes Minnesota's landscapes and built environments, profound change is underway in schools and in patterns and places of worship. When Minnesota culture was more homogeneous, there was a shared agreement that the schools should teach basic skills and instill the myths on which the American experiment was built. The public schools were Protestant in orientation, reflecting the beliefs and religious practices of the founding fathers and mothers. The parochial schools—mostly Roman Catholic and a few Lutheran—shared the task of skill development and Americanization, with the added duty of instilling and protecting the faith of their young charges.

The U.S. tradition of locally run public-school districts produced 8,087 districts in Minnesota by 1918, a number that dropped to 2,581 by 1959 as rural population decline and transportation improvements prompted district consolidation. Some large cities obtained legislative charters to create special districts—St. Paul and Minneapolis, most notably—which then grew without subdividing as the cities' population expanded.

When suburban areas around the Twin Cities flourished following World War II, formerly rural school districts serving those areas expanded to accommodate the children of young suburban families, creating a mosaic of independent districts within the sprawling metropolitan region. Some districts were prosperous and served mainly children of upper-middle-class and professional families. Others reflected the resources, tastes, and concerns of households positioned elsewhere on the socioeconomic spectrum. The type and quality of schooling that pupils received varied depending on where they lived. With growth in metropolitan population and outward expansion of suburban development, disparity of opportunity among school districts intensified.

Inside Minneapolis and St. Paul, racial and economic segregation developed among school attendance areas. For example, in 1960 the Minneapolis school district (covering fifty-five square miles) contained about one hundred neighborhood elementary schools (kindergarten through sixth or eighth grade), so almost all pupils were able to walk to a neighborhood school. At the same time, the cities of Minneapolis and St. Paul contained most of the older, cheaper housing stock in the expanding Twin Cities area. In that year, the metropolitan-area population of 1.5 million was only 1.8 percent nonwhite (mainly lower-income African-Americans), but those minority households were highly concentrated in just two small inner-city neighborhoods adjacent to downtown Minneapolis, and a third just west of downtown St. Paul. Meanwhile, the cities' upper-income and wealthy families occupied exclusive neighborhoods near the lakes, along the creeks, or on properties overlooking the Mississippi River valley, with their children attending school together.

The result was racial and economic segregation of children in the schools based on segregation of housing by value. It was this situation that prompted courts in the Twin Cities, like those elsewhere in the United States, to mandate busing of pupils to achieve racial balance in the schools. This court action motivated some households to relocate to suburban housing beyond the reach of the central-city school districts—which of course aggravated racial and socioeconomic disparities between the districts at the core and those serving the suburban periphery.[15]

So, too, as teaching nuns abandoned the classroom for other pursuits and American bishops declined to expand the Catholic school system into middle-class suburbs, parochial schools waned. Disputes roiled over curriculum content and teaching methods, and a beleaguered generation of newly minted school-teachers entered the profession from the late 1950s to the 1970s, often less well educated and inadequately trained for the requirements of changing times.

Higher education expanded rapidly beginning in the late 1940s and 1950s, stimulated in part by the GI Bill—the federal support program for college-bound veterans that paid tuition, fees, and subsistence as they earned degrees. Postsecondary schooling had been restricted to the few during the first half of the century, but by the 1950s and 1960s the doors to Minnesota colleges and universities were increasingly open to all who had completed secondary school, and about four out of five eighteen-year-olds had done so, one of the highest ratios in the nation. Minnesota's legislature and taxpayers endorsed with enthusiasm the demand for higher education by supporting and expanding five separate postsecondary systems. First is the University of Minnesota, the state's flagship research and doctoral institution with campuses in Minneapolis, St. Paul, Duluth, Morris, and Crookston. Second is a system of seven state universities that had their origins as teacher-training schools. Third is a system of publicly supported community colleges—two-year institutions that feature a mix of vocational courses and a general collegiate transfer curriculum that provided the foundation for a four-year degree. Fourth is a system of vocational-technical colleges with training programs of six months to two years intended to match the needs of local and statewide economies. Finally is the Minnesota private college system of about twenty schools, almost all of them religious in origin or affiliation. In all, over eighty colleges and universities provide postsecondary education and training, one of the most developed systems of higher education in the United States; there is a campus within easy commuting reach of nearly all high-school graduates in the state. But maintaining the system is difficult. Minnesota has a population of just under five million persons—average in size among states, but spread over a much larger than average area. The result is more college campuses per capita than almost any other state.

Despite heavy investment in schooling at all levels, there is disquiet in many quarters about whether schools at any level are doing the job that the society and the economy require. Gaps persist between what schools teach, what students choose to study, what basic inquiry yields, and what the economy needs in the way of higher education, job training, and applied research. In Minnesota and around the country, mechanisms to close these breaches do not appear to exist at present. The fact that each state system of higher education and each private school enjoys a measure of independence in resolving these issues is a positive sign. If answers were supplied and imposed by a national higher education ministry the situation would probably be far more troublesome.

Divergence among the needs of society, inertia in colleges and universities, and the type and quality of their products is only one way to view the problem. Some roots of the problem lie in the society at large, and specifically in problems facing elementary- and secondary-school systems. Most available curriculum is academic rather than vocational, based on the generally accepted presumption that the schools should prepare all pupils for college or university. For pupils uninterested in or lacking skills for an academic, college-oriented curriculum, the junior and senior high schools have little else to offer; not surprisingly, dropout rates are high across the country, often exceeding 25 to 30 percent among immigrant and minority pupils in central-city high schools. Part of the dropout rate can be traced to the difficulty of providing the individualized instruction that today's pupils seem to require and expect, in addition to the lack of support from home. But perhaps a larger, more troublesome issue is the pervasive contempt among American educators for training young people to make things or to fix things, a bias that some have termed the "British Disease." Simply put, vocational and technical education in the United States is held in low esteem. It is seldom presented by parents, teachers, and counselors as a worthy and rewarding educational path for junior and senior high-school pupils. In fact, to the extent that high-school teachers are fully informed of such career paths, which is extremely rare, they and the school boards that employ them usually discourage pupils in their charge from aiming in these directions.

Minnesota has more than twenty-five technical colleges, but they are poorly supported financially or politically. Admission is restricted to persons aged eighteen or over who hold the equivalent of a high-school diploma. At one time, local public-school systems in Minnesota operated vocational high schools or vocational tracks within broad-based high-school programs. In Minnesota and across the country, serious questions persist about how to link school systems with the demands of a complex, global economy, and how to prepare high-school pupils as well as college and university students with the general education, technical training, social skills, and civic awareness they need to enter the work force and society smoothly and productively. On balance, higher education in America and in Minnesota seems to work satisfactorily by some measures, while falling short on others. But a disturbing fraction of young people reach the age of eighteen lacking what they need to succeed. They are casualties of school systems weakly adapted to today's needs, causing the economy and the society to suffer.

There are other ways for Minnesotans to stimulate the mind and revive the spirit, and the state's numerous colleges and universities do part of the job. High levels of education, combined with the state's income and wealth position, mean demand for resources to support the arts—music, drama, painting, sculpture, dance, creative writing, and more. Churches, synagogues, and mosques are full and well supported by old residents together with immigrant newcomers to the state, including 43,000 Muslims and 15,000 Hindus.[16]

For many Minnesotans, religious affiliation and involvement is supplemented or replaced by efforts in good-government organizations, political parties, service clubs, neighborhood-improvement organizations, and community-service activities. For many, spirits are revived by regular weekend renewal at "the lake," and the state has more than ten thousand of them. In fact, Minnesota has so much open space and lakeshore per capita that its abundance, modest cost, and convenient access mean that regular retreats to nature are a characteristic feature of Minnesota life. On the other hand, the growing populations and expanded enthusiasm for outdoor recreation of all types mean additional pressure on limited natural resources and serious disagreements over how to use the state's forests, lakes, and natural areas. Those who desire a quiet wilderness experience disdain the noise of motor boats. Those seeking to preserve pristine wilderness areas come into conflict with business interests who see the forests as timber to be harvested, or mineral deposits as development opportunities.[17]

Recent Migrations to and from Minnesota

As old-time residents reshape forms of livelihood, spending patterns, leisure-time pursuits, and forms of intellectual and spiritual renewal, their numbers are augmented by streams of newcomers. Whereas early residents almost exclusively traced their origins to Great Britain, Ireland, and northwestern Europe, almost all immigrants in the 1990s originated elsewhere. Soviet Jews came in small but steady numbers, aided by Jewish congregations in the Twin Cities. Trouble in the Balkans following the dismemberment of Yugoslavia brought refugees to Minnesota. After the Vietnam War ended in the mid-1970s, refugees from Southeast Asia arrived in increasing numbers, often sponsored by church groups. Initial successes attracted later arrivals. Especially significant are the Hmong, a mountain people from Indochina who had worked with the American military during the war, and thus found themselves in trouble when the war ended. Through chain migration and family reunification the Twin Cities now contains the second-largest Hmong population in the United States.

African immigration to Minnesota and especially Minneapolis accelerated following civil wars in Somalia, Eritrea, and Ethiopia. With an experience paralleling the Hmong, family reunification and linked immigration brought to the Twin Cities the nation's largest Somali immigrant group. During the Central American civil wars of the 1980s, people displaced by the violence and political upheaval found their way to Minnesota cities and towns, joining Latinos with origins in Texas and Mexico who had first come to Minnesota as migrant farmworkers following fruit and vegetable harvests northwards. Eventually, increasing numbers stayed in Minnesota.

Other recent newcomers are midwestern residents seeking economic opportunity in Minnesota and the Twin Cities, which in the 1990s was the fastest-growing major metropolitan area in the Midwest. Some have returned to Minnesota from West Coast and Sun Belt locations where they lived and worked before deciding that Minnesota was a better option than they realized. Of course, some residents do leave. Young people head for Colorado, California, Oregon, and Washington state, or move east for school and work. Retired "snowbird" couples divide their year between Minnesota in the summer and Arizona, south Texas, or Florida in the winter. Other retirees sell houses in the city, town, or farm, and move permanently to the peace and tranquility of their place on a northern lake.

New Meanings for Civic Life

As Minnesota's values and behaviors converge toward national averages, we see traditional human-service professions increasingly monetized and often self-serving. Jobs formerly performed in the spirit of community service and compensated by modest stipends, job security, and the high esteem of community members—law, medicine, clergy, teaching, government—are now often distracted and occasionally corrupted by financial goals and competitive career ambitions. Government and education have become large and mature industries with elected officials and educators referring to students and citizens as "customers" without a trace of irony.

Philanthropy becomes a business with professional staffs establishing "track records" with an eye toward better-compensated positions in larger organizations. Foundations, despite having greater independence of action than any other contemporary institution, increasingly pursue agendas that too often display a trendy orientation toward short-term rather than long-term outcomes, instead of working to reform basic structures of society.

Political parties become distorted into vehicles for building careers for party professionals, and in the process drift away from concerns of ordinary citizens and become less relevant to political debate and the electoral process. Good-government groups like the Minneapolis-based Citizens League struggle to democratize their memberships only to discover that new members and young people are seldom inclined to long-term strategic analysis. It is hard for inexperienced members to accomplish in public life what they are discouraged from in a daily life of just-in-time production, and a consumption climate of instant gratification—which is to say, planning for a long-term future.

Across Minnesota and across the land it is plain that the important questions continue to be asked: What is good? What is true? What is beautiful? Who are we? Where are we headed? Old institutions provided answers that served Minnesota's citizens well for a long time. But at the turn of the century, with the unifying bonds of war, depression, and ties to the farm a distant experience or a vague memory, there is a need for reshaping institutions based on new institutional designs. Our schools, which served us well, are just one example of institutions that are groping to invent new ways to do new jobs.

Despite troubling trends toward some form of cultural convergence, Minnesota's cities and countryside remain different and agreeable places, still displaying evidence of deep roots in a conservative culture, and reflecting a distinctive mix of Scandinavian cooperative thinking with practical New England town hall sensibilities. It handled the twentieth century reasonably well, and seems poised to confront the twenty-first with a large measure of competence and confidence.

Notes

1. John R. Borchert, *America's Northern Heartland* (Minneapolis, Minn.: University of Minnesota Press, 1987).

2. William Cronon, *Nature's Metropolis: Chicago and the Great West* (New York: W. W. Norton & Co., 1991).

3. George M. Schwartz and George A. Thiel, *Minnesota's Rocks and Waters: A Geological Story* (Minneapolis, Minn.: University of Minnesota Press, 1973). The relationship between the state's geological history and its subsequent ecological development is beautifully illustrated and explained in John R. Tester, *Minnesota's Natural Heritage* (Minneapolis, Minn.: University of Minnesota Press, 1995).

4. Theodore C. Blegen, *Minnesota: A History of the State* (Minneapolis, Minn.: University of Minnesota Press, 1963). The most comprehensive account of immigration and settlement in Minnesota is June Drenning Holmquist, ed., *They Chose Minnesota:*

A Survey of the State's Ethnic Groups (St. Paul, Minn.: Minnesota Historical Society Press, 1981).

5. James M. Henderson and Ann O. Krueger, *National Growth and Economic Change in the Upper Midwest* (Minneapolis, Minn.: University of Minnesota Press, 1965).

6. Census data come from several sources: U.S. Bureau of the Census, *County and City Data Book, 1962: A Statistical Abstract Supplement* (Washington, D.C.: U.S. Government Printing Office, 1962); *County and City Data Book, 1994: A Statistical Abstract Supplement*, 12th ed. (Washington, D.C.: U.S. Government Printing Office, 1994); and *Statistical Abstract of the United States, 1993*, 113th ed. (Washington, D.C.: U.S. Government Printing Office, 1993).

7. *County and City Data Book, 1962*, Table 2.

8. *Statistical Abstract of the United States, 1993*, Table 690.

9. Patrick Kennedy et al., "ST 100: The 9th Annual Star Tribune 100," *Star Tribune*, 19 March 2000, D1, D8–12.

10. Ibid., D1.

11. *Statistical Abstract of the United States, 1993*, Table 69.

12. *Minnesota Almanac 2000*, ed. Chris McDermid (Taylors Falls, Minn.: John L. Brekke & Sons, 1999), 230.

13. Pat Doyle, "The Casino Payoff: Gambling Creating Disparity of Wealth Among Tribes," *Star Tribune*, 4 November 1997.

14. Trade centers and trade areas of the Upper Midwest constitute a hierarchy, with the Minneapolis–St. Paul metropolis at the pinnacle. Over the years, the retail trade and service functions performed by these centers have changed as transportation has improved. Regional shopping centers attract consumer dollars that formerly supported small town Main Street merchants, yet the locations and relative sizes of Minnesota's cities, towns, villages, and hamlets have remained surprisingly constant. See John R. Borchert and Russell B. Adams, *Trade Centers and Trade Areas of the Upper Midwest*, Urban Report No. 3 (Minneapolis, Minn.: Upper Midwest Economic Study, University of Minnesota, 1963); Thomas L. Anding et al., *Trade Centers of the Upper Midwest: Changes from 1960 to 1969* (Minneapolis, Minn.: Center for Urban and Regional Affairs, University of Minnesota, 1990); and William Casey, *Trade Centers of the Upper Midwest: 1999 Update* (Minneapolis, Minn.: Center for Urban and Regional Affairs, University of Minnesota, 1999). The 1999 study results and its definition of today's hierarchy of Minnesota's Regional Centers are used by the Minnesota Department of Transportation as a basis for long-range highway planning for the state.

15. The history of St. Paul's voluntary desegregation policy and busing plan, and the Minneapolis program following a 1972 federal district court order, is summarized in Council of Metropolitan Area Leagues of Women Voters, *Metropolitan School Desegregation and Integration* (St. Paul, Minn.: Council of Metropolitan Area Leagues of Women Voters, 1991); and *Linking Commitment to Desegregation with Choices for Quality Schools* (Minneapolis, Minn.: Citizens League, 1979).

16. Clark Morphew, "Controversy over House Chaplaincy Doesn't Reflect America," *St. Paul Pioneer Press*, 26 February 2000, 9E.

17. Kevin Proescholdt, Rip Rapson, and Miron L. Heinselman, *Troubled Waters: The Fight for the Boundary Waters Canoe Area Wilderness* (St. Cloud, Minn.: North Star Press of St. Cloud, Inc., 1995).

THOMAS D. PEACOCK & DONALD R. DAY

Nations Within a Nation:
The Dakota and Ojibwe of Minnesota

IN 1967, WHILE TAKING a mandatory course in Minnesota history in seventh grade, Don Day asked the teacher why he never mentioned American Indians in his lectures. The teacher told Don, and the class, that "Indians did not contribute to the social, political, or cultural development of the state of Minnesota." Although Don knew the teacher was wrong, he did not have the courage to stand up to him. The cognitive dissonance Don felt that day many years ago still exists within many American Indian students' daily lives. Today, many American Indians are still struggling to exist in two worlds: the professional, fast-paced, technological world of high finance and instant communication, and the traditional world of their ancestors, which involves native languages, sweat lodges, pipe ceremonies, spirit names, fasting, and other traditional customs. Although we have come far in our teacher-training efforts, we still have far to go to better understand the indigenous people of this country.

Tribal nations called Minnesota home for many thousands of years before the arrival of Europeans in the region. To indigenous people, the land on which they live and the communities of which they are a part have deep meaning. Home is more than a city or state of residence. It is the whole of a place—its lakes and woods, animals, sounds, spirit, and cycles. It is the sacred place of ancestors. This deeper meaning is why tribal people have such a deep and abiding veneration for this land many know as Turtle Island, or North America. In this sacred land, all things are interrelated. All things are part of the great circle that is life:

> Everything the Power of the World does is done in a circle. The sky is round,
> and I have heard the earth is round like a ball, and so are all the stars. The wind,
> in its greatest power, whirls. Birds make their nests in circles, for theirs is the

THOMAS D. PEACOCK *is associate professor in the department of education at the University of Minnesota, Duluth.* DONALD R. DAY *is assistant professor in the department of education at the University of Minnesota, Duluth.*

same religion as ours. The sun goes forth and goes down again in a circle. The moon does the same, and both are round. Even the seasons form a great circle in their changing, and always come back again to where they were. The life cycle of a man is a circle from childhood to childhood, so it is in everything where power moves. Our teepees were round like the nests of birds, and they were always in a circle, the nation's hoop, a nest of many nests, where the Great Spirit meant for us to hatch our children.[1]

—Black Elk, Oglala Lakota holy man

Misconceptions abound about the indigenous people of North America. Foremost is the mistaken notion that all "Indians" are alike. There are, in fact, over five hundred unique tribal groups, each with its own history, culture, language, and beliefs. Another common misconception is that the indigenous people have disappeared, that their cultures have died and the people been assimilated into a larger American culture. Most tribal nations, however, still possess sovereignty as a result of treaties with the United States and continue to maintain their identities, cultures, and communities.

For many hundreds of years, two different tribal nations, with different languages and cultures, have lived in the area now known as Minnesota (a Dakota word for "sky-tinted water"). The Dakota ("friends" or "allies"), also called the Sioux (from *Nadouessioux*, a French corruption of the Ojibwe word *Naudoway*, or "enemy"), preceded the Ojibwe. The Ojibwe migrated into Minnesota soon after contact with the French, acquiring firearms as a result of the fur trade, which were used to push the woodland Dakota from Greater Minnesota to the southern prairie.

The Dakota and Ojibwe Peoples

All stories have a beginning, and this one goes back to the time of creation. While Western culture promotes the idea that ancient people migrated to the Americas nearly twelve thousand years ago over a land bridge across the Bering Sea, which now separates Siberia and Alaska, the indigenous people of this continent have their own stories of how they came to be here. In the Ojibwe story of creation, the Creator made the people here. The Creator had a vision in which he saw all the things of the universe—stars and star clusters, galaxies, moons, planets, and Earth. On Earth he saw oceans, lakes, rivers, streams, ponds, meadows, grasses, flowers, mountains, deserts, and forests filled with many different kinds of trees, plants, and animals.[2]

After he had visions of these things, he brought into existence all that he had dreamed. He created the materials in which all physical things are based— wind, rocks, water, and fire. With these materials he created all the wonders of the universe—the galaxies, suns, moon, planets, and the great voids between worlds. Then he created the earth and all the things of the earth, and to each of these things he gave its own soul-spirit.[3]

He created plants and put them on the earth in the places where they would be most useful to other plants, animals, and people, and he gave each of them a purpose—growing, healing, and beauty. Next he created our elder brothers the animals—the fish, the four-legged creatures, the birds, and those that walk on two legs. Each was created for a reason, given unique powers and a place in the world. Last in the order of creation were people.

THE EARLY PEOPLE OF MINNESOTA

Much of Minnesota was covered with a sheet of ice several miles thick nearly twelve thousand years ago during the last glacial period. With the retreat of the ice came the return of plants, trees, grasses, and flowers. Our elder brothers the four-legged and the birds called this home. Then the people of other nations, the Cheyenne, Blackfeet, Fox, and Menominee, lived there. The Dakota, and later the Ojibwe, then settled the area.

The Dakota people were once the primary tribal nation in what is now Minnesota, calling all of Minnesota and western Wisconsin their homelands. The seven bands of the Dakota formed a political alliance called the Oceti Sakowin, or Seven Fires.[4] The Yankton and Yantonai (Dwellers at the End Village and Little Dwellers at the End) spoke a dialect of the language called Nakota. The Teton (Dwellers of the Plains) spoke and continue to speak the Lakota dialect.

The four other bands—the Mdewakanton (Dwellers of the Spirit Lake), Sisseton, Wahpeton, and Wahpekute bands of Isanyanti, or eastern Dakota— once lived along the shores of Mille Lacs in central Minnesota, where the mounds of their earth lodges can be seen today.[5] These bands were expelled from that area in the early eighteenth century by advancing Ojibwe, and they were forced to settle in the prairie lands of southern Minnesota. Fearing disruption in the lucrative fur-trade industry, the U.S. government negotiated a treaty between the two tribes, leaving the Dakota with the land south of the Minnesota River. This treaty with the Ojibwe, negotiated at Prairie du Chen in 1826, established a geographical boundary between the Dakota and Ojibwe people.[6]

The ancestors of the Ojibwe were the Lenni Lenape (the Grandfathers, known today as the Delaware), who migrated across this great continent from the west to the east.[7] The epic story of that journey is known as the Wallum Olum. Recorded on bark tablets and song sticks (sticks with songs, historical

American Indian Population by County in Minnesota, 1990

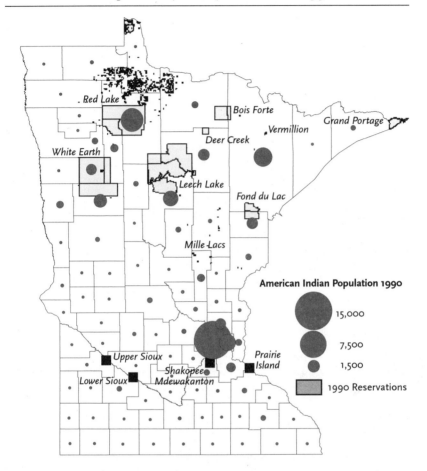

Total American Indian population for Minnesota in 1990: 49,909 (1.1%). The eleven reservations and communities in the state are shaded and labeled (Deer Creek and Vermilion are part of the Bois Forte Reservation). Source: U.S. Bureau of the Census, tape STF-1A, 1990. Map by Laura Hansen, University of Minnesota.

events, and pictographs inscribed on them), this written record is the oldest recorded account of people in North America, dating before 1600 B.C. The Ojibwe lived on and near the Atlantic Ocean nearly six hundred years ago near the mouth of the St. Lawrence River.[8] Basil Johnston suggests that they lived there for so long that most forgot that their true origins lay in the West.[9] The westward migration began as a journey as one people with the Ottawa (*Odawa*, or "traders") and Potawatomi (Keepers of the Perpetual Fire). Separation of the three peoples came at the Straits of Michilimacinac (where Lake Michigan converges with Lake Huron). At that point some Ojibwe proceeded north and became the First Nation Ojibwe of Canada and the ancestors of present-day Ojibwe of the Grand Portage Reservation. Another group went south and west to what is now Minnesota.

The Taking of Dakota and Ojibwe Land

The coming of Europeans to the continent forever altered tribal life. Treaties between the indigenous nations and the United States were used to acquire land for white settlement. In these treaties, large tracts of Minnesota land passed from tribal to white hands. The indigenous people were forced to move onto reservations, which represented but a fraction of their traditional homelands. Between 1826 and 1871 (the treaty period) six treaties and agreements with the Dakota nation, and sixteen treaties, agreements, and major pieces of legislation affecting the Ojibwe, were used to take native land.[10] As a result of these treaties, tribes retained limited sovereignty (rights of self-governance and nationhood) and rights to hunt, fish, and gather (treaty rights) on lands they ceded. Even after the treaty period ended in 1871, the federal government passed numerous congressional acts and executive orders and the Supreme Court ruled on a variety of court cases that reaffirmed the U.S. government's special relationship with American Indian tribes.[11] This relationship, although constantly challenged by conservative antitreaty organizations, still exists.

Dakota Communities and Ojibwe Reservations

The majority (over thirty thousand) of the indigenous people in Minnesota now live in the urban areas of Minneapolis, St. Paul, Duluth, and Bemidji, where they have established their own supportive educational, human services, and cultural programs. The Phillips neighborhood in Minneapolis has the largest concentration of American Indian people in the state of Minnesota. Approximately 17 percent of the city of Bemidji is comprised of American Indians, and many make their home in the central hillside area of Duluth.

Four Dakota communities were created through treaties, legislation, and federal proclamation. The Lower Sioux and Upper Sioux communities, located along the Minnesota River in southwestern Minnesota, once encompassed an area 150 miles long and 10 miles wide on either side of the river, but were reduced to less than half that size, and only the southern side of the river, by subsequent treaty.[12]

The Dakota Conflict

An uprising of Dakota in 1862 because of starvation and overcrowding resulted in the death of over 1,200 whites and Dakota, and led the federal government to abrogate its treaties with the Dakota and force their removal from Minnesota. The Prairie Island and Shakopee-Mdewakanton communities, considered "friendly" by the U.S. government because they had not participated in the uprising, were given back some of their lands in 1866.

The Dakota Conflict resulted in the hanging of 38 Dakota men on December 26, 1862, in Mankato, Minnesota. This is the largest mass execution of Americans the U.S. government ever condoned. Abraham Lincoln gave the orders to have the Dakota executed, but granted pardons to 269 other Dakota warriors. The major result of the Dakota Conflict was the dispersal of the majority of Dakota people out of Minnesota to Nebraska and South Dakota, among other areas.

Establishment of the Dakota Communities and Ojibwe Reservations

All of the Ojibwe reservations were established by treaties and are considered separate and distinct nations by the U.S. government. The seven Ojibwe reservations are Grand Portage, Bois Forte, Red Lake, White Earth, Leech Lake, Fond du Lac, and Mille Lacs. An outline of Dakota and Ojibwe communities is as follows:

Reservation	Treaty	Approx. Land (acres)	Population
Mille Lacs	1837	10,500	1,300
Fond du Lac	1854	24,000	1,100
Grand Portage	1854	56,000	500
Leech Lake	1855	29,600	4,700
Red Lake	1863	637,000	5,400
Bois Forte	1866	42,000	500
White Earth	1867	67,000	4,500
Shakopee-Mdewakanton	1887–1893	650	250
Prairie Island	1887–1893	534	—
Lower Sioux	1888–1934*	1,743	612
Upper Sioux	1938 Proclamation	746	150

*Congressional Acts of 1888, 1889, 1890, and Indian Reorganization Act of 1934.
Source: American Indian Learner Outcome Team, *American Indian History, Culture and Language* (St. Paul: Minnesota Department of Children, Families and Learning, 1995), 43.

Federal Indian Policy: 1887–1953

One of the most important pieces of legislation passed by Congress regarding American Indians was the General Allotment Act of 1887, also known as the Dawes Severalty Act, or simply the Dawes Act.[13] Although the author of this act, Senator Henry Dawes of Massachusetts, may have had the best intentions for American Indians when he proposed the legislation, this act turned out to be one of the most damaging pieces of legislation ever inflicted upon American Indians. The Dawes Act authorized the federal government to survey Indian lands, divide them into small tracts, and assign ownership of the pieces to individual American Indians.[14] As a result of the Dawes Act, land occupied by American Indians for centuries was broken up and parceled out, with the vast remaining amounts of land sold to non-Indian people.[15] With the passage of the Dawes Act, American Indians lost the majority of their homelands.

The history of the United States is filled with pendulum swings regarding American Indians. At times, government officials wanted American Indians to be fully assimilated into American society; at other times, government officials believed that American Indians were uniquely diverse and could add strength to a multicultural country. The Indian Reorganization Act of 1934 recognized, for the first time, the communal cultures of American Indians everywhere, including Minnesota. The most important consequence of the act was the establishment of modern tribal governments. In the 1950s, government officials acted in the belief that American Indians were in the way, that their cultures were inferior, and that the best resolution was to assimilate them as quickly and efficiently as possible.[16] This was the mentality of many policymakers when Congress passed House Concurrent Resolution 108 and Public Law 83–280 in 1953. House Concurrent Resolution 108 sought to cancel the federal government's trust responsibility with American Indian tribes as had been specified in most treaties. Public Law 83–280 conferred upon certain designated states full criminal and civic jurisdiction over Indian reservations. Individual states were given the authority to deal with American Indian tribes as state leaders wished rather than having to abide by the federal government's protectionist policies.[17] The 1950s highlighted a long history of government officials breaking treaty after treaty with American Indians.

The Education of Minnesota's Indigenous People

Before the arrival of Europeans, the purpose of education was twofold: to teach practical life skills to young people, and to enhance the soul and encourage spiritual growth. Each was important and relied upon the other to balance the life journey. To possess only the skills of living without knowledge of the spirit would be to live a life without purpose, depth, or meaning. To focus solely upon inner growth would be to ignore the customary skills of survival necessary in earlier times. Traditionally, Ojibwe education was in three phases.[18] The first phase lasted until a child was about seven years old, during which the child was cared for and nurtured by grandmothers, aunts, and elders. The second phase began when the young boys went with their fathers, uncles, and older cousins to learn the ways of men in providing sustenance by hunting and fishing. At this time, the young girls went with their mothers, grandmothers, aunts, and older cousins to learn the ways of women in providing for the home and tending a garden. The third phase of education was the search for wisdom, which would consume the rest of an individual's life. The search for wisdom was a quest to know the whole story of things—to know things in their simplicity and in their complexity, and to know the many layers of meaning.

The coming of Europeans to North America touched the core of nearly every aspect of the Dakota and Ojibwe cultures: language, family and social structure, customs, values, insights, spiritual beliefs and practices, and institutional and governmental structures. Tribal people still suffer from the effects of the undeniable oppression of that period and its accompanying internalized dysfunction. This dysfunction still manifests itself in high student dropout rates (around 40 percent) and low scholastic achievement, a mistrust of formal schooling, high rates of adolescent pregnancy, poverty, and high rates of crime throughout Indian country.[19]

FORMAL EDUCATION OF TRIBAL PEOPLE

With the arrival of the early French traders came Jesuit and Franciscan missionaries. It was their purpose to convert people they believed were pagan, devoid of any knowledge of God, to Christianity. The formal education of Dakota and Ojibwe children was initially done in immigrant homes and churches. Many of the first formally educated Indians were half-breed children— from intermarriages of white and Dakota or Ojibwe people—many of whom were educated at home. Soon, however, church missions and schools were opened in Indian communities throughout Minnesota. Although these schools were operated by Christian missionaries, they were paid for by the federal government.

The federal role in Indian education grew markedly with the passage of the Indian Civilization Act of 1824, which provided federal funding for formalized schooling of Indians. Mission schools were soon complemented by federal manual (trade) and boarding schools. By 1838, the federal government was operating six manual and eighty-seven boarding schools for American Indian students.[20] Dakota and Ojibwe people were being sent to off-reservation boarding schools in Pipestone, Minnesota; Flandreau, South Dakota; and Carlisle, Pennsylvania. The use of education to remove the tribal cultures and traditions from the lives of young Indian people, coupled with the banning of their religious practices, resulted in the loss of languages and parenting skills and contributed to low self-esteem in generations of Indian people.

MISSIONARY SCHOOLS AND BOARDING SCHOOLS

When Europeans first arrived in North America and made contact with American Indians, they gave little consideration to aboriginal cultures, heritages, or lifestyles. Europeans had two main views regarding American Indians during their initial contacts: (1) American Indians were a race doomed to extinction because they could not or would not adapt to an "advanced" European lifestyle, and (2) American Indians were simply a product of their environment and would assimilate European-American values if they had enough opportunities to be exposed to "superior" influences of white society.[21]

The primary purpose of mission schools was to "Christianize" American Indians into becoming "American."[22] Many federal policymakers supported the belief that unless American Indians converted to Christianity and acquired European-American values, white and Indian cultures would forever be incompatible.[23] Missionary schools have been cited as the main means used to eliminate American Indian cultures so that the assimilation of American Indians into the larger society would take place more efficiently.[24]

When the federal government began to dominate the education of American Indians in the late 1800s, the need for missionary schools was significantly reduced.[25] The main objective of federal policymakers was to convert the American Indian into their image of the ideal self-reliant American individual.[26] Boarding schools were created to separate American Indian children from their parents and their "inferior" cultures.[27] In both the nineteenth and twentieth centuries, the federal government implemented a forced assimilation policy by which young American Indian boys and girls were forcibly removed from their homes and sent to boarding schools across the country.[28] Assimilation in those schools took two major forms: industrial training and the inculcation of values. Half of each student's day in boarding school was devoted to some form of manual or industrial training.[29]

SELF-DETERMINATION THROUGH EDUCATION

With the passage of the Indian Reorganization Act in 1934, American Indian parents had a greater voice in their children's education. The act modified the curriculum—providing teachers with special training in American Indian cultures and traditions—and acknowledged the traditional and religious backgrounds of American Indian people.[30]

As Americans became more tolerant of cultural pluralism in the 1960s, there came a resurgence of ethnic pride in Minnesota's Dakota and Ojibwe communities. A cultural and spiritual awakening spread throughout Indian country. As more Indian people went into higher education, Indian studies departments developed in the colleges and universities of Minnesota that had significant American Indian student populations. With the enactment of the Indian Education Act in 1972 and the funding appropriated for its implementation, a new cadre of American Indian school employees entered the public schools as home school coordinators, Indian youth advocates, social worker aides, language and culture teachers, and tutors. For the first time in many schools, Indian students had an Indian adult to advocate for them in school matters. Indian associations and clubs were formed in many schools, and efforts were made to add tribal culture, language, and history to the curriculum. Perhaps most importantly, the Indian Education Act empowered Indian parents by mandating the creation of American Indian parent committees in all schools having Indian education programs.

This new attention to the educational conditions of American Indians in public schools sometimes led to conflict between reservation communities and nearby public-school personnel. Many Indian students continued to score lower than their non-Indian student peers on standardized achievement tests, had higher dropout rates, were more likely to be referred for special educational services, and were more likely to be targeted for both in-school and out-of-school suspension. American Indian parent committees often demanded changes in the way schools provided education to their children and requested that districts hire American Indian teachers and administrators. Parent committees also sought representation on local school boards and pushed for a curriculum that was inclusive of tribal culture and history. Frustrated with the unwillingness or inability of local school officials to respond to their demands, some parents pulled their children out of school and set up all-Indian schools. What began as a student walkout with little funding and few books is now the Bug-O-Nay-Ge-Shig School, located on the Leech Lake Reservation in the town of Cass Lake, one of the largest tribal schools in Indian country. Similarly,

Indian parents in the Onamia school district set up their own tribal school on the Mille Lacs Reservation.

Urban schools like the Heart of the Earth Survival School in Minneapolis and the Red School House in St. Paul began under the leadership of urban Indian parents and the American Indian Movement, a nonviolent activist group. Tribal schools, operating under the auspices of local tribal governments, were founded at Cass Lake (Bug-O-Nay-Ge-Shig School), White Earth (Circle of Life School), Mille Lacs (Nay Ah Shing School), and Fond du Lac (Fond du Lac Ojibwe School and the Little Black Bear School). These schools combine conventional academics with a solid tribal curriculum.

Tribal colleges were founded to serve unique functions in Indian communities by providing certificate programs that allow graduates to enter the work force after two years, regular two-year transfer programs, and a host of language and cultural programs. More importantly, tribal colleges provide the kind of support many Indian students need to succeed in higher education, such as personalized financial aid services, culturally sensitive Indian faculty, staff, and administrators, and a focus on serving the local community. Minnesota's tribal colleges include the Fond du Lac Tribal and Community College in Cloquet, the Leech Lake Tribal College in Cass Lake, and the White Earth Reservation Tribal College in White Earth.

The important point in all these recent developments is that tribal people have gained significant control of and input into the educational decision-making process, and the result is that Indian people have more and better choices. Minnesota's American Indian students from preschool through postsecondary school have a range of options, including local Head Start programs, K–12 tribal schools, tribal colleges, and four-year colleges and universities.

Traditional Tribal Economies

For many hundreds of years, the Dakota and Ojibwe of Minnesota lived in bands of 300 to 400 people. Each group used the resources of its area. Both the Dakota and Ojibwe relied extensively on the forests, rivers, and lakes for food, materials for clothing, tools, housing, and transportation. In the spring the maple trees were tapped and gardens were planted. In the summer the gardens were tended, and blueberries, strawberries, raspberries, and cranberries were harvested. The women and girls boiled down the berries and spread them in the sun to dry for use during the long winter months. Fishing, which was done year-round, was especially productive in the summertime. When the weather cooled in the fall, the Dakota and Ojibwe began preparing for the cold winter ahead by stocking up on food and building and reinforcing housing shelters. The Ojibwe were, and still are, famous for the harvesting of wild rice from the lakes and rivers of northern Minnesota. Once processed, wild rice could be stored and used years later. During the winter, the men spent much of their time hunting and trapping. They used snowshoes and sleds for travel. Later on, with the advent of the fur trade, the men and women of the Dakota and Ojibwe worked hard trapping and processing the furs of beavers, mink, rabbits, bears, and other animals to trade for goods the Europeans possessed, such as knives, pots and pans, and salt and other food items. Although there were some lean times and an occasional dispute between the Dakota and Ojibwe, the tribes lived in relative accord with each other. To a great extent, American Indians did not pursue technological advances or the domination of the land, choosing instead to live a spiritual existence in harmony with nature.

Contemporary Tribal Economies

With the arrival of European Americans in Minnesota and elsewhere, American Indians became one of the most economically depressed groups in the country. This status still holds today. With shrinking land bases due to treaty negotiations and wars, American Indian resources became more and more limited. Even though government policy changes afforded American Indian tribes a greater measure of economic self-determination in the 1960s, their business development initiatives were relatively unsuccessful. Like African Americans after the Civil War, American Indians in the 1970s and 1980s were systematically denied loans to begin businesses or invest in capital ventures. With no financial assistance and limited resources, economic enterprises often ended in failure.

In addition to a lack of access to capital, Indian reservations are often limited by geographical location. In the early 1990s, Grand Metropolitan of Minneapolis was interested in developing a food-processing plant on the Leech Lake Reservation, but withdrew because of the transportation costs of shipping materials and goods to and from the reservation, which is located approximately two hundred miles north of Minneapolis.[31]

A major roadblock in developing successful American Indian businesses and enterprises is the lack of educated, qualified, and committed American Indian personnel to administer them. People who are born and raised in a community are often more committed to that community than people who are hired from the outside. Realizing this, tribes have begun to dedicate significant sums of money for scholarships, grants, and loans to their tribal members so they can acquire the education and training needed to make good employees, administrators, and businesspeople.

The Dakota and Ojibwe have tried many economic development initiatives over the years. Although some of the economic initiatives had some success (logging, wild-rice harvesting, commercial fishing, and tourism), most did not succeed, because of untrained personnel or a lack of resources—both natural and financial.

Indian Gaming and Casinos

Without a doubt, the most significant development in the history of economic stability within Indian tribes in Minnesota and nationally is the evolution of Indian gaming and casinos. Before the passage of the Indian Gaming Regulatory Act of 1988, unemployment rates on Indian reservations in Minnesota were extremely high. According to Marge Anderson, former chief executive officer for the Mille Lacs Band of Ojibwe, unemployment on the Mille Lacs Reservation was approximately 60 percent in 1991, but has shrunk to much more tolerable levels since then.[32] Although the unemployment rates on Indian reservations still exceed the state and national averages, the rates have decreased significantly where casinos are located.

Gaming and casinos are controversial. Economic, moral, philosophical, and social arguments can be, and have been, made about the impact of gaming on society. Despite these arguments, many states, including Minnesota, have legalized gaming. Thirteen out of the first seventeen gaming compacts in the United States were signed in Minnesota. In Minnesota there are eighteen casinos, which employ approximately eleven thousand people, 75 percent of them non-Indian.[33] Indians and non-Indians employed at casinos pay all taxes required by state and federal law, including income and FICA taxes. Nationally, Indian gaming is a business now valued at $9.6 billion annually. In Minnesota in the early 1990s, Indian gaming paid wages of $80 million a year and earned revenues of about $900 million a year.[34]

The economic benefits of gaming and casinos in Minnesota have been incredible. Within the past ten years, Minnesota's Indian reservations with casinos have made tremendous economic strides in developing their infrastructures, establishing businesses, providing educational, social, and health-care services to their members, and supporting a variety of social, cultural, and educational endeavors in their respective communities. Marge Anderson, in an address to the Minnesota legislature on April 9, 1998, stated:

Prior to 1991, the only employment on the reservation was within the tribal government or for a government program. Even then, salaries were barely at or above minimum wage. Most of the homes on the reservation were broken down, and many were unfit for habitation. Our children attended school in a building unfit for learning, and our water supply system was plagued with pollution. Life on the Mille Lacs Reservation was one of extreme hardship and despair. Today, you would never recognize our community as the same reservation. . . . Never again will a child live in substandard housing as most of us did. Never again will a child be denied quality, state-of-the-art health service as many of us were. Never again will a child be afraid to drink the water as we all were. Never again will a child go to bed hungry as too many of us did.[35]

The Dakota and Ojibwe are two of many tribes across the country that are benefiting from tribal gaming. After decades and decades of oppression, the Dakota and Ojibwe are slowly recovering from the neglect and hopelessness that engulfed them for so many generations. They are building new houses, roads, schools, and community centers as well as creating new businesses and investing in their tribal education initiatives. Now more than ever, the Dakota and Ojibwe people are taxpayers as well as recipients of government assistance where Indian gaming operations are located. Local governments and the state are enjoying increased tax revenues, which contribute significantly to the overall economy of Minnesota and the nation.

The positive aspects of Indian gaming are significant to the great majority of Indian and non-Indian people throughout the state. For some, however, there is a dark side to this "new buffalo." Gambling-related problems have increased exponentially along with legalized gambling. Problem gambling is identified as a behavior in which a person suffers some loss of control over his or her gambling activities, with negative consequences.[36] Gambling problems range from minor (the gambler loses more money than he or she can afford to) to serious (the gambler loses his or her home, family, and friends).

A major downside to Indian gaming is the misconception that all Indians are now rich. Although some American Indian tribes in Minnesota and nationally have done extremely well financially, most tribal members do not receive profit shares from their tribe's gaming efforts. The three largest tribes in the state of Minnesota—Red Lake, Leech Lake, and White Earth—all have casinos. None of their members receives per capita payments from their gaming enterprises. These tribes are benefiting from Indian gaming profits by hiring tribal members who are unemployed or underemployed. Although a job at $7–$10 per hour may seem minimal to many, it is significant to a family with a history of unemployment. As stated earlier, gaming profits are being used for tribal infrastructure development, education, and tribal business initiatives that benefit everyone.

The stereotypical notion that gaming has brought great wealth to all Indians also influences the views and decisions of legislators and corporations regarding Indian tribes. Too often, those seeking funding for social, health, or tribal education programs are denied because legislators and corporate leaders think they should simply go to their tribal representatives and secure whatever funds they need from their tribal councils. In 1998, Carl Pohlad, the billionaire owner of the Minnesota Twins baseball team, recommended (with significant support from a variety of legislators) that Minnesota's Indian tribes should buy the Twins a new stadium costing many hundreds of millions of dollars using their Indian gaming profits.[37] Fortunately, the majority of Minnesota's state legislators are aware that Indian tribes are still trying to put together their own infrastructures with Indian gaming revenues. Consequently, the suggestion that the tribes should build the Twins a new stadium subsided.

The rationale for supporting tribal gaming is twofold: the revenues will help the tribes and surrounding communities become self-sufficient, and the tribes should have a right to govern their own lands. Except for a minority of compulsive gamblers, Indian gaming in Minnesota has been a boon to Indians and non-Indians alike since its legalization a decade ago.

Political Activism

Indian gaming is the first successful enterprise Indian tribes have had to "kick start" their economies since the arrival of Europeans in Minnesota. Because tribes now have some revenues that are owned and managed by the tribes themselves, which they are investing wisely, they are becoming more significant players educationally, socially, culturally, and politically in Minnesota. Although American Indian tribes are treated as sovereign nations by the United States, their actual relationship with the federal government could be viewed more as semi-sovereign because of their huge dependence on government assistance for social, health, and educational programs.

In the late 1960s and early 1970s, when American Indians began entering institutions of higher education in significant numbers, many began to study the treaties their people had signed with the U.S. government and realized the concessions they had been granted for signing away their lands. Today, Indian tribes are confronting the state and federal governments in court in order to legally fish, hunt, trap, and initiate gaming enterprises on behalf of their people. Almost all court cases are being won by the tribes, because the concession agreements are clearly articulated in the treaties and have been approved and incorporated by the Constitution. It is ironic that education, a tool intended to eliminate tribal cultures and heritages and thus assimilate American Indians into the mainstream of American society, is, in actuality, helping to preserve them.[38]

The relationship between Minnesota's Indian tribes and the Minnesota legislature can be described as one of highs and lows. For many years, most Minnesota legislators treated Indian tribes as second-class groups. In the 1970s, however, Indian tribes began to develop positive relationships with many Minnesota legislators. To a great extent, these positive relationships still exist. With the advent of Indian gaming revenues and the expansion of Indian treaty rights, this relationship is more important than ever. Considering the great financial impact Indian gaming and treaty rights have had on all aspects of Minnesota's economy, it is prudent for both the Minnesota legislature and the tribes to have a close working relationship.

In a backlash against the fighting between Democrats and Republicans in Minnesota, the people elected a Reform Party candidate to the governorship in 1998—a former pro wrestler named Jesse Ventura. The people of Minnesota are relatively split about their views of Governor Ventura. He has made remarks offensive to many, including about American Indians. Governor Ventura also stated that if American Indian tribes wanted to consider themselves sovereign nations, they should not ask the government for financial assistance. On the other hand, he is developing a special relationship with some Indian tribes by inviting tribal council members along on some of his education endeavors. For Indian tribes in Minnesota, Jesse Ventura's tenure as governor should be an interesting and closely watched one.

A Remarkable Renaissance

American Indians in Minnesota are living in exciting times. Tribal people have the financial seeds of prosperity planted and the knowledge to use them wisely for the betterment of all humanity. One of Minnesota's most influential American Indian leaders was Marge Anderson. Her words reflect the thoughts and beliefs of most American Indian leaders in Minnesota:

> Our culture teaches us that the things of greatest worth in this world are our Elders, our children, our natural resources, and our sovereignty. These are what we strive to protect, at all costs. Every decision which we make as a Nation, especially every decision relating to economic development, must be based upon cultural beliefs, and result in the protection of these precious gifts. At Mille Lacs, we always look seven generations ahead. We know that if we do not keep the protection of our resources and the needs of future

generations at the center of each decision we make, even the most seemingly certain of economic plans will surely fail.[39]

Not only is there a renaissance in the way tribal officials are leading American Indians into the twenty-first century, but there is also a renaissance forming in the classrooms, where American Indian students are acquiring the knowledge and skills necessary for the economic, social, political, and cultural preservation of their people. This movement is creating a new type of warrior, who carries not bows and arrows but books and degrees. Through education, the American Indian warriors who are emerging today will be the salvation of their people tomorrow.

Contemporary American Indian men and women in Minnesota live in two worlds. Many are members of Christian churches, and English is the primary language spoken at home. Many American Indians have felt ambivalent about their heritage at some point in their lifetimes, but at the same time they are proud to be American Indians, and contemporary American Indians do not believe that attaining an education will force them to lose their "Indianness."

Throughout Minnesota, tribal members are returning to the sweat lodge ceremonies, pipe ceremonies, and big-drum societies of the past. Dakota and Ojibwe languages, once near extinction, are being taught in homes and schools. The Dakota and Ojibwe people in Minnesota have learned that they do not have to give up their Indian identities to live and prosper in modern society. With so much conflict, violence, and turmoil in the world, American Indians are finding peace and strength in the ways of their ancestors.

Notes

1. John Neihardt, *Black Elk Speaks: Being the Life Story of a Holy Man of the Oglala Sioux* (Lincoln: University of Nebraska Press, 1998), 194–196.

2. Basil Johnston, *Ojibway Heritage* (Lincoln: University of Nebraska Press, 1976). In Ojibwe culture, there is no distinction between male and female when referring to the Creator. For efficiency purposes, we use "he," although "she" is just as appropriate.

3. Ibid.

4. American Indian Learner Outcome Team, *American Indian History, Culture and Language* (St. Paul: Minnesota Department of Children, Families and Learning, 1995), 43.

5. Ibid.

6. Elizabeth Ebbott, *Indians in Minnesota* (Minneapolis: University of Minnesota Press, 1985).

7. Thomas Peacock, ed., *A Forever Story: The People and Community of the Fond*

du Lac Reservation (Cloquet, Minn.: Fond du Lac Band of Lake Superior Chippewa, 1998).

8. William W. Warren, *History of the Ojibway People* (St. Paul: Minnesota Historical Society Press, 1984).

9. Johnston, *Ojibway Heritage.*

10. Ebbott, *Indians in Minnesota.*

11. John W. Tippeconnic III, "The Education of American Indians: Policy, Practice and Future Directions," in Donald E. Green and Thomas V. Tonnesen, eds., *American Indians: Social Justice and Public Policy* (Milwaukee: University of Wisconsin System, Institute on Race and Ethnicity, 1991), 180–202.

12. Ebbott, *Indians in Minnesota.*

13. Adams, "Fundamental Considerations."

14. Ibid.

15. Jeffrey Wollack, "Protagonism Emergent: Indians in Higher Education," *Native Americas: the Akwe:kon's Journal of Indigenous Issues* 14 (4) (Winter 1997) 12–23.

16. Wollack, "Protagonism Emergent."

17. Stephen L. Pevar, *The Rights of Indians and Tribes: The Basic ACLU Guide to Indian and Tribal Rights*, American Civil Liberties Union Handbook, 2d ed. (Carbondale: Southern Illinois University Press, 1992).

18. Johnston, *Ojibway Heritage.*

19. Linda Cleary and Thomas Peacock, *Collected Wisdom: American Indian Education* (Needham Heights, Mass.: Allyn and Bacon, 1998). On student dropout rates, see Quality Education for Minorities Project, *Education that Works: An Action Plan for the Education of Minorities* (Cambridge: Massachusetts Institute of Technology, January 1990).

20. Jon Reyhner and Jeanne Eder, "A History of Indian Education," in Jon Reyhner, ed., *Teaching the American Indian Students* (Norman: University of Oklahoma Press, 1989).

21. Linda Skinner, "Teaching through Traditions: Incorporating Native Languages and Cultures into Curricula" (commissioned paper) (Washington, D.C.: Indian Nations At-Risk Task Force, Office of Educational Research and Improvement, U.S. Department of Education, 1991).

22. Tippeconnic, "The Education of American Indians."

23. Wilber J. Scott, "Attachment to Indian Culture and the Difficult Situation: A Study of American Indian College Students," *Youth & Society* 17 (4) (1986): 381–394.

24. Marjane Ambler, "Without Racism, Indian Students Could Be both Indian and Students," *Tribal College Journal* 8 (4) (Spring 1997): 8–11.

25. Bobby Wright, "American Indian and Alaska Native Higher Education: Toward a New Century of Academic Achievement and Cultural Integrity" (commissioned paper) (Washington, D.C.: Indian Nations At-Risk Task Force, U.S. Department of Education, 1991).

26. David W. Adams, "Fundamental Considerations: The Deep Meaning of

Native American Schooling, 1880–1900," *Harvard Educational Review* 58 (1) (1988): 1–28.

27. Paul Boyer, "Higher Education and Native American Society," *Tribal College Journal* 1 (1) (1989): 3–17.

28. Tippeconnic, "The Education of American Indians."

29. Adams, "Fundamental Considerations."

30. Judith E. Fries, *The American Indian in Higher Education: 1975–76 to 1984–85* (Washington, D.C.: U.S. Department of Education, Center for Educational Statistics, 1987).

31. David Fettig, "Articles on American Indian Economic Development," unpublished paper, The Federal Reserve Bank, Minneapolis, Minn., 1992.

32. Marge Anderson, "Economic Development in Indian Country," statement to the Minnesota legislature, 9 April 1998, St. Paul, Minn.

33. A list of tribal gaming operations by state is available from the National Indian Gaming Commission in Washington, D.C. For employment statistics, see the National Indian Gaming Association web site at <http://indiangaming.org/info/pr/statistics.html>.

34. Fettig, "Articles on American Indian Economic Development."

35. Anderson, "Economic Development in Indian Country."

36. Henry R. Lesieur and Sheila Blume, "The South Oaks Gambling Screen (SOGS): A New Instrument for the Identification of Pathological Gamblers," *American Journal of Psychiatry* 144 (9) (1987): 1184–1188.

37. Gregory Borchard, "Casinos' Windfalls Is Due the Tribes," *Minnesota Daily*, 22 January 1998.

38. Paul W. Day, "The U.S. Federal Trust Responsibility with American Indians," a speech presented at the Fifth Annual Minnesota Indian Education Association Conference, Duluth, Minn. (November 1989).

39. Anderson, "Economic Development in Indian Country."

RICHARD M. CHAPMAN

Mixing New and Old Wine in Minnesota: Spirituality, Ecumenism, and Religious Traditions in Ferment

OUT OF MINNESOTA'S PAST comes a creation story that strikes a discordant note with present-day religious trends. In the cosmology of the Ojibwe, who migrated to the Minnesota region prior to the area's first European settlers, one story tells that humankind began when the Creator sent singer-birds to Mother Earth carrying life-seeds to the four cardinal directions, spreading the beauty and magnificence of life across her surface. The Creator then breathed upon the four corners of Mother Earth through a sacred shell, forming man, and lowered him to earth. Finally, the Creator commanded the original man to name all the plants, animals, and landforms found upon the earth. In this way all of creation was infused with sacred meaning and possessed both physical and spiritual properties.[1]

Like the Ojibwe, Minnesotans from the indigenous past down to the present have characteristically defined themselves and their differences with others according to their sacred stories, ritual practices, and spiritual beliefs. Religion has thus constituted a defining feature of the state's people, characterized notably by large contingents of Lutherans and Catholics. Indeed, in the century just past, the state's people might boast of an exceptional religious identity, consistently returning figures significantly above the national average in measures of church membership and participation in religious organizations. A recent survey determined that, excepting the Southern states, Minnesotans trailed behind only the Dakotas (with which they share much geographically and culturally) in having the smallest percentage of respondents claiming no religious identity whatsoever.[2]

Nevertheless, unlike the Ojibwe, Minnesotans today increasingly dwell in two distinct and separate worlds—one sacred and private, the other secular and

RICHARD M. CHAPMAN *is assistant professor of history at Concordia College in Moorhead, Minnesota.*

public. Little different from American society as a whole, but sharply contrasting the seamlessness of an Ojibwe cosmological order, contemporary religious ways in Minnesota reveal a fundamental paradox: religion is simultaneously all-encompassing and nowhere to be found. Sociological surveys consistently reveal that most Americans believe in a Supreme Being, but they also indicate that far fewer worship regularly—and even for these, matters of faith seem of little import in day-to-day living and working. Many, even most, continue to pray, but are more likely to place faith in the wonders of science and the magic of technology; prayer and sacrifice may be approached as last resorts.[3] At the same time, one observes in contemporary Minnesota the resurgence of personal forms of religious seeking, the continued growth and diversification of faith-based institutions and enterprises, and the zealous insertion of faith into politics, all despite the overwhelmingly secularist bent of public life. Religion may often be trivialized in popular culture and the media, yet it stubbornly maintains its grip in multiple societal footholds.[4] Certainly the resilient shaping power of religion in American culture and society seems assured into the future.

If religion's social significance lies today somewhere between the poles of all and nothing, how did it arrive at this point? Understanding the path from the past to the present situation appears especially important in a state like Minnesota, whose claims to religious exceptionalism would suppose a less ambiguous, more distinct positioning of religion in everyday life. One might think to explain religion's anomalous status as a natural result of the diversification of Minnesota's population over time, but as a place characterized by a rich heritage of cultures and peoples, the state has long displayed considerable diversity—far more, indeed, than the enduring image of the state as a northern-European enclave has admitted. But for over a half-century following statehood in 1858, Minnesota's residents were not particularly conscious of such differences.

Until the period around World War I, Minnesotans typically dwelt in functionally isolated settlements—on farms, in small towns and villages, and in urban neighborhoods, where they could reasonably suppose or maintain the illusion that everyone thought, worshipped, and believed much as they did. The key social pivots occurred as economic changes, urban migration, the rise of higher education, and great national events reconstituted the state's communities and brought formerly separated peoples together, a process of change by exposure to difference that continues down to the present.

The new, broadened "publics" in the workplace, in educational institutions, and in citizens' associations have ramified in ways that illuminate religion's current paradoxical role in Minnesota. First, they helped to foster a secular, democratic pluralism engendering a shared public culture that could, ideally, mediate among diverse religious, ethnic, and cultural groups in the state in order to find common ground. Second, they encouraged both a formal ecclesiastical and functional ecumenism that built connecting bridges among the state's diverse religious constituencies, sometimes eroding existing differences of theology, liturgical practice, and religious identity. Finally, they gave encouragement over time to a kind of mix-and-match approach to personal faith that allowed creative and novel adaptations, an intermingling of religious and spiritual traditions that defies conventional denominational categorizations.

Minnesota's Religious "Islands"

Over thirty years ago historian Robert Wiebe described the nineteenth-century United States as a collection of separated "island communities."[5] His characterization aptly captures the static cultural, social, and geographical landscape of Minnesota's early ethnic communities and their residents' inner-directed frame of reference, both of which persisted into the early twentieth century. Religious observance and identity of a marked ethnic flavor came close to the heart—or perhaps one should say the soul—of these island settlements. After all, most of the state's settlers held to a Catholicism or Lutheranism tinged by distinct national or regional histories in Europe, and they interwove their beliefs, rituals, and practices in the communities they fashioned. A Polish traveler to Winona in 1874 conveyed some of the spirit of this world in remembering a wonderfully effervescent experience worshipping there:

> The music remembered from childhood, and the Latin liturgy, transported me into a kind of hypnosis. So also did the garb of the priest, with his head gray as a dove, the heads of the worshippers, bowing in humility, and the sermon, delivered in a tongue almost never heard. Politics and half-American customs and religious views that had become a part of me,—all these fled at once from my mind. In the company of these children I too became a child.[6]

Ethnic religion in the popular imagination of the state is closely associated with the history of Norwegian and Swedish immigrants who settled the Upper Midwest in large numbers beginning in the mid-nineteenth century and continuing into the twentieth.[7] Together with smaller numbers of Finns, Danes, and Protestant Germans, they created in Minnesota a strong Lutheran presence by the early twentieth century. Throughout the twentieth century Minnesota's Lutherans always accounted for around 25 percent of the state's population; according to a 1990 social survey on religious identification, over one-third of Minnesotans currently identify themselves as Lutherans.[8]

In the past, however, the Lutherans in Minnesota hardly constituted a unified kingdom. National-ethnic differences and theological disputes divided them and subsequently led to the formation of numerous distinctive Lutheran church bodies. Indeed, disputes attending the formation of the Evangelical Lutheran Church of America in the late 1980s, and the move to establish theological and liturgical concord and a common ministry with mainline Protestants in the late 1990s, illustrate ongoing debates surrounding Lutheran identity and practice. Today, however, disagreements are at best only remotely attached to the ethnic identities of earlier generations.

In their separate locales, Lutheran immigrant groups, through their own religious organizations, built up successful local communities around the state. Religious enterprises—whether churches, schools, temperance societies, ladies' auxiliaries, or missions—anchored much of this community life. They frequently formed the conduit of ethnic life and group identity and mediated participation in the wider spheres of business, government, and education.

Divisions, indeed separation, among groups of Lutherans probably enhanced community participation by expanding the range of religious choices available. Education provides an excellent case for the links among Lutheran religious values, group diversity, and institution-building. Lutheran tradition placed a premium on both religious and liberal education, and clergy were in short supply in young frontier settlements. In response, the establishment of institutions of higher education among Minnesota's Lutherans was channeled through synodical variety. A diverse group of Lutheran liberal-arts colleges with distinctive traditions resulted: Gustavus Adolphus, Augsburg, St. Olaf, and two Concordias—one of mixed theological Norwegian heritage in Moorhead, the other, in St. Paul, belonging to the German Missouri Synod.

Catholicism in the region dated to the arrival of Jesuit missionaries who accompanied fellow French traders and trappers in the preterritorial period. This important early influence, together with the Irish presence in St. Paul's formative years, confounds the state's Scandinavian Lutheran image, dramatized nowadays in the imposing architecture of St. Paul's cathedral overlooking the urban landscape of the state's capital city. Paralleling the Scandinavian movement to Minnesota territory after 1850, Roman Catholics from southern Germany and Central Europe came to the region and created strong and distinctive rural settlements. By the early twentieth century Stearns County in central Minnesota had a higher proportion of Catholics, a stunning 60 percent, than any other county in the nation; throughout the twentieth century, Catholics consistently accounted for around 30 percent of Minnesota's religious pie, often outdistancing the state's Lutherans in survey counts.[9]

Like their immigrant Lutheran counterparts, Minnesota's Catholics erected strong community institutions and, boasting their own robust tradition of scholarship, built St. John's University and the College of St. Benedict as centers of faith and learning in the state's Catholic heartland near St. Cloud. Paralleling Lutheran religious diversity, Catholic orders and dioceses in Minnesota created several additional liberal-arts colleges around the state—St. Catherine, St. Thomas, St. Mary's, and St. Scholastica among them. Other ethnic Minnesotans, pursuing their own distinctive traditions and communal needs, developed island communities along similar lines.

Minnesota's Jewish population, at first primarily adherents of Reform Judaism hailing from Central Europe, settled early in St. Paul, and then in Minneapolis beginning in the late 1860s. The state's Jews, like its Lutherans and Catholics, diversified considerably after 1880 when Orthodox Jews from Eastern Europe, fleeing exclusion and increasing persecution, settled in Minnesota. They built a rich communal life of synagogues, auxiliaries, workers' unions, and philanthropies. Jewish *landslayt*—hometowners and folk coming from the same region in the Old Country—established their own national organizations. Between 1880 and 1905, for example, the number of synagogues and temples in Minneapolis grew from one to a dozen, reflecting the national and regional origins of the growing Jewish immigrant population. In small-town Minnesota, Jews struggled against obstacles of geography and demography to keep religious rituals and practices alive.[10]

Black Minnesotans in numbers first came to St. Paul during and immediately following the Civil War. They adapted African American faith traditions in several congregations, notably African Methodist Episcopal, Baptist, Episcopal, and Catholic. In the first half of the twentieth century, Pilgrim Baptist and St. James A.M.E. churches became important social and religious centers in the St. Paul black community. Other Minnesotans of varying ethnic traditions in the past constituted communities and organized identities around a number of institutional posts, including nationally based Orthodox congregations, Maronite Catholicism, the Mennonite Church, and Eastern Rite Catholic traditions. A tiny Muslim presence dated from the early twentieth century.[11]

Ojibwe and Dakota peoples in the later nineteenth century struggled to maintain vestiges of traditional ways, or sought solace and meaning in Christian religions to compensate for the destruction of their worlds. Some Ojibwe turned to Catholicism or responded positively to the religious message of

Protestant preachers and teachers who assaulted traditional spiritual values and rituals within cultures already beset by the loss of traditional lands, hunger, and demoralization.

Amplifying this complexity is the rich diversity within denominational communities that further confounds popular expectations of Minnesota's people. Not confined to Scandinavians, Lutherans in Minnesota numbered Baltic peoples, Slovaks, and even some Czechs and Poles. Among the Scandinavians were dissenters from Old World state churches who formed Baptist, Covenant, and other free churches. Besides the Irish and Germans, Minnesota's Catholics encompassed Poles, Italians, Slovenes, Czechs, Slovaks, Hungarians, Romanians, and others.[12] One is struck by the succession of community-building stories, replete with sacrifice, faith, and hard work, that characterized waves of Minnesota settlers. Each group gathered spiritual and human resources into vital institutions, organizations, and efforts that undergirded successful and functionally autonomous settlements.

Native-born Yankees marked one disquieting element in Minnesota's nineteenth-century cultural and religious landscape of island settlements. Arriving in the region by the mid-nineteenth century, these New Englanders and settlers from upstate New York established their cultural presence, political influence, and business leadership throughout the state, rather than building up strong geographic centers. Heirs of a revivalist evangelical Protestantism that spawned millennial fervor and numerous reform movements earlier in the century, Yankees characteristically aimed to achieve a broader social and political influence and not local independence. They thus challenged the isolationism of autonomous local settlements. Their faith in democratic institutions and an independent citizenry led to the creation of a large public university along with denominational colleges—Carleton, Hamline, and Macalester—which overlapped the educational priorities and community-building spirit of other Minnesota newcomers. They planted Methodist, Episcopalian, Presbyterian, and Congregational churches throughout the state. Benjamin Henry Whipple, the first Episcopal bishop in Minnesota, spearheaded missionary efforts to the state's Native American peoples.

Conflict, Comity, Cooperation

As ideological devotees of a restive evangelical Protestantism, Minnesota's Yankees built religious institutions and programs premised on wider community engagement. Writing to Minnesota Methodist circuit preacher and reformer Edward Eggleston in 1859, churchman Noah Lathrop appealed for the best kind of conference delegates. They would, he argued, "do what I think right on the various questions now before us[,] especially they must be sound on the slavery question, and have stamina enough [to] put it through if they can."[13] The Congregational Conference of the Minnesota Territory in 1856 took positions representative of the concerns of old-guard Protestant denominations in the state during the latter half of the century. "Strong anti-slavery resolutions were passed, as well as a resolution deprecating the spread of the vice of intemperance, and pledging the churches to the most unremitting efforts against both of these evils."[14] Missionary enterprises, revivals, temperance movements, social activism, and various charitable endeavors all expressed the zealous impulse for religious transformation and social reform that characterized the Anglo-Protestant presence in Minnesota. A half-century later, morally earnest Yankee reformers in the state turned Progressive causes like women's suffrage and temperance into a secular gospel.[15] In the campaign against alcohol, they found allies among many Scandinavian religious pietists as well as others with Old World temperance traditions. Such reform activities, in making common political cause across ethnic groups, began to reduce the social distance separating Minnesota's local religious communities.

Politics and political campaigns obviously played an important part in dividing and uniting Minnesotans of varying communities, religious persuasions, and social identities. Significantly, participation in politics could connect isolated, local community concerns with a wider public sphere. Scandinavians in particular followed this route in making their mark on Minnesota's developing political culture. Alongside Anglo-Americans, Scandinavians found early success as political candidates and officeholders in the state. Remarking on the link between Lutheranism and the Republican party in Minnesota's political history, scholar John E. Haynes observed, "In the campaign literature of progressive Republicans, one is struck by the frequency with which candidates made sure that a Lutheran church was pictured on brochures. One is tempted to see progressive Republicanism as a sort of secularized Scandinavian Lutheranism: earnest, moralistic, well meaning, and moderate."[16] Mirroring national patterns, Minnesota Catholics on the whole were less than comfortable with the sanctimonious moralism of Yankee and Lutheran Republican political initiatives and became strong supporters of the state's Democratic party.

Other personalities and forces also eroded the relative independence of isolated religious groups in Minnesota. Archbishop John Ireland, a towering figure in the history of Minnesota Catholicism, resolutely advocated the adoption of the English language by the state's ethnic Catholics as the guarantor of a strong, influential, and triumphant Catholic presence into the future. Ireland's vision of an American Catholic Church, assisted in its implementation by clerical leadership in the local church hierarchy, met hostile resistance from the state's ethnic Catholics that peaked in the German language controversy in Stearns County during the political hysteria of World War I. Over time, Americanization, played out through common educational experiences and a shared consumer ethic, contributed to greater similarity among disparate ethnic Catholics in Minnesota. Later movements within the Catholic Church—liturgical renewal, rural-life programs, and the Second Vatican Council—gave further impetus to commonality. So, too, the significant portion of Minnesota Catholics residing on the land and engaged in agriculture meant that Catholics and non-Catholics alike shared a common rural experience. Hard, often unrequited toil on the land, punctuated repeatedly by the economics of diminishing returns in the twentieth century, hammered out the anvil chorus of a common attachment to the soil and a rural way of life.

A watershed in the movement for Americanization, World War I also laid the basis for joint planning and cooperation among voluntary charitable and social-service organizations. Initiated by Minnesota's business leadership, the War Chest (as it was originally called) aimed to achieve efficiency through a single annual fundraising campaign and to bolster collective support and voluntarism in support of the war effort. Long known as the Community Fund (now the United Way), it established a working relationship among organizations from multiple religious and sectarian perspectives. Through their religious organizations Minnesota's immigrants had long cared for their own as a central communal virtue; the Community Fund brought together those traditions on a broader, nonsectarian basis. In 1918, Minneapolis's Community Fund invited the Associated Jewish Charities to become a partner, a notable exception to the social and economic exclusion of Jews practiced in the city.[17] Around the state the Community Fund functioned as a form of secular ecumenism based on philanthropic cooperation, on the principle that what was good for one was good for all.

Historically, the confluence of religious traditions in the state led equally to conflict and cooperation. To apply one historian's words to the state as a whole, religion has figured in the creation of a "civic culture" in Minnesota, by providing a "repertoire of public ritual . . . by molding the mentalities and morals of their members, by encouraging or discouraging civic activism, and by supporting or opposing nativism, racism, progressivism . . . ."[18] Some jostling and group competition predictably followed as isolated groups experienced increased exposure to one another. Moreover, in a now familiar pattern, newcomers found that the dominant Protestant Euro-Americans in Minnesota frequently took exception to their differences. Thus, the state's Protestant majority sometimes recoiled at those who threatened to dilute the dominant religious culture of the state. In this way they presided over public institutions and adopted social patterns that determined the inclusion or exclusion of new arrivals.

Anti-Semitism in the state can be traced back to the political speeches of Populist figure Ignatius Donnelly in the late nineteenth century. The cultural climate continued to be very uncomfortable for the state's Jewish residents as anti-Semitism crescendoed in the late 1930s, reputedly making Minneapolis, where most of the state's Jews resided, the nation's "capitol [*sic*] of anti-Semitism."[19] Jews were not admitted into the city's social and recreational clubs until the 1950s. As social, economic, and educational exclusion receded in the years following World War II, Minnesota's Jews were often at the center of political struggles and legal efforts in communities around the state to maintain religious neutrality in public-school rituals and celebrations. Such actions frequently brought controversy and roiled Protestant constituencies that sought expression of their majority religious preferences in concerts and graduation ceremonies. As late as 1988 one northwestern Minnesota school superintendent remarked on the issue, "This is a 'one-religion' school district with thirteen Lutheran churches within its boundaries, so people have to find something else to argue about."[20] In the 1990s Minnesota continued to be targeted occasionally by anti-Semitic appeals, which together with the memory of exclusionary policies, led most of the state's Jewish citizens to feel threatened in their minority status.[21]

Through the twentieth century, Lutherans, native Protestants, and Catholics dominated the religious landscape in Minnesota, typically carving out separate spaces in local communities or regions in the state. Accommodation between them never came easily. Radio personality and essayist Garrison Keillor has humorously, yet faithfully, described the perennial religious division of Protestant and Catholic in small-town Minnesota communities. "Our Prairie Home Cemetery is divided into Catholic and Us; they have their gate and we have ours, and a low iron fence with spikes separates the two. After service, while our elders stroll among the stones, we boys practice jumping the fence. . . . When you clear the fence, then you have to jump right back over or else."[22] Longtime residents of Minnesota's small towns and communities describe a bifurcated social and physical geography cleaved along religious lines, Catholics on one side, Lutherans on the other.

In some locales sectarian disagreements surfaced where religious outreach programs competed, limiting their effectiveness. Beginning in the 1920s, Catholic dioceses and Protestants through programs of the Home Missions Council, and, later, the National Council of Churches, established separate ministries for the state's Hispanic migrant population. Beyond traditional evangelism, these efforts additionally set up community centers, health clinics, educational programming, and childcare. HMC staff in Ortonville, Minnesota, bemoaned "Catholic propaganda" as undercutting Protestant efforts among the state's migrant population. Reflecting a certain anti-Catholic strain, this perception stemmed also from definite programmatic differences in the Catholic migrant ministry as well as the greater Spanish language facility of their priests and workers. For example, another Protestant missionary objected that their Catholic rivals in this work became overly involved in political and economic affairs. Some Minnesotans expressed nativist views in questioning the very existence of such migrant ministries and programs. Similar obstacles hindered the education of Hispanic youths in the region. One Red River Valley teacher reported in the late 1950s "that she discouraged local migrant children from attending because she was unwilling to go into the basement of the school to find books for them."[23]

Apart from overt hostility and discrimination, the state's ethnic and religious minorities have, not surprisingly, experienced estrangement at times, a feeling of not fully belonging. A Mexican American resident of St. Paul's East Side who lived away from the community's nucleus on the West Side recalled in the 1930s: "I was darker and I felt that in order to be American, you had to be white, you had to speak English well . . . Even though I couldn't speak Spanish well, I still had an accent and I could tell it. . . . So, I was embarrassed that I was a Mexican American."[24] Forty years later a Spanish-speaking resident of Minneapolis who had just moved to St. Paul reported nearly identical sentiments. "I don't feel strange about speaking my language. . . . In Minneapolis, I never dared."[25] In the same period one reporter described "an invisible barrier" dividing "the permanent residents of the Red River Valley and their migrant neighbors."[26]

More recent immigrants to the region voiced similar feelings. In 1979, a Palestinian Muslim resident of Minneapolis described her children's difficulty "living in the suburbs where everyone is blond and blue-eyed and Protestant. . . . Their names are different, their religion, their background at home, their food." While experiencing overall social acceptance, a Sudanese Muslim family living in the Red River Valley expressed similar sentiments twenty years later, especially as its children encountered the traditions of the dominant Christian culture at Christmas.[27]

Despite persistent religious differences and the all-too-real alienation felt by some, the dissolution of Minnesota's island communities between 1900 and 1950 paved the way for greater understanding and cooperation—if not always acceptance—among the state's rich traditions of faith. The result came close to a civil religion, a collective faith in a single "[Minnesota] Way of Life," to apply sociologist Will Herberg's phrase to the state.[28] Civil religion held forth the democratic promise of overcoming religious and social differences in order to work out common solutions to common problems of political and economic life. Sociologists of religion Barry Kosmin and Seymour Lachman, in describing Minnesota's religious culture, have asserted that "Lutherans take pride in their civic virtues and their strong sense of community which their religion promotes."[29] Certainly Lutheranism has made a signal contribution to the state's repository of civic virtue, inasmuch as classical Lutheran theology gives considerable scope to learning and secular know-how in public life alongside a commitment to serve one's neighbor as the natural response to grace. But both New England Protestants and the Catholic Church also helped to shape the state's communal ethos in fundamental ways, the former through a strong heritage of reformist activism and ecumenical initiatives, the latter through its firm commitment to universal economic justice and advocacy on behalf of workers and the dispossessed. Similarly, the Jewish population of the Twin Cities gained national recognition for the dynamism of its community-service organizations in comparison to similarly sized Jewish urban settlements in the nation. Moreover, the story of nearly all of the state's ethnic settlements is a story of avid, associational life in which religious institutions and communities figured prominently.

Minnesota's heritage of lively island communities, consistently disposed and actively organized to seek the care and comfort of their own people, may explain much about the state's enviable record of community activism, voluntarism, charitable giving, and nonprofit organizations, long noted by scholars of the philanthropic sector. The results of political scientist Robert Putnam's mapping of "social capital" in the United States are thus not very surprising. He identified the Upper Midwest region around Minnesota and the Dakotas as the area with the highest stock of community trust, reciprocity, social participation, and mutualism in the nation as a whole.[30] Distinctly prophetic injunctions associated with social justice, communal service, and helping one's neighbor are certainly deeply embedded in the state's patterns of both corporate and individual generosity. They are apparent as well in the careers of several notable Minnesota political figures whose faith commitments injected vigor into their public careers. Republican governors J. A. O. Preus,

Luther Youngdahl, and (more recently) Al Quie made religious faith a defining feature of their public service. The biographies of national leaders such as Hubert Humphrey (Methodist as a child and later a Congregationalist) and Walter Mondale (the son of a Methodist preacher, reared in small-town southern Minnesota) highlight solid ethical values in the making of public policies predicated on civil rights, economic justice, and responsibility to the state's most vulnerable citizens.

Not a reflex only of its religious islands and their heritage of giving, the state's rich philanthropic tradition is a product of the merging of many cultural and environmental impulses. Minnesota's history of insurgent and maverick politics and grassroots movements—from populism to farmer-labor politics and labor radicalism—has contributed unmistakably to the state's patterns of open, honest government and citizen involvement. These essential political traditions manifested secular faiths in political transformation and social change quite different in form and content from traditional religious faiths, but they have been no less vital to Minnesota's ethos.

A term like "minnesotization" might well convey the coming together of the state's ethnic-religious traditions during the first half of the twentieth century. In forging a shared civic faith, that process came to stress three tenets incumbent on community members. These tenets required active participation in the life of a formal religious institution; a commitment to ethical involvement and cooperation in building the commonweal; and the polite acknowledgment and allowance of religious difference especially within the faith traditions privileged by their numerical dominance. This brand of generally tolerant, community-oriented, public ecumenism is carried forward in perceptions like those of Patrick Henry, director of the Institute for Ecumenical and Cultural Research at St. John's University in Collegeville. Responding a decade ago to a conference focused on interfaith dialogue, Henry observed, "Minnesota . . . has a tradition of open politics and widespread active religious life that lends itself to thoughtful consideration of [religious and ideological differences]. . . . on balance a remarkable civility infuses debate . . . rooted in the state's history and culture, and does not reflect a religious indifference."[31] One must remember, despite Henry's sanguine outlook, that things have not always been so in the state: intergroup civility and cooperation depended upon interactions and negotiations over time, and especially upon the indispensable tools of dialogue made available by an organized ecumenical presence in the state. Religion's unique place in Minnesota originated in this confluence of religious communities in the state's public life; but minnesotization, while giving credence to broadly shared social values, ethical principles, and an ever-present

Deity, simultaneously muted the distinctive attributes of particular religious traditions and ritual identities. As we shall now see, Henry's perception seems more clearly linked to the distant past in Minnesota than to contemporary religious realities in the state.

Coming Together, Coming Apart

During the second half of the twentieth century, the defining principles of a civil religion in Minnesota became less certain even as they threatened to unravel. Three distinct but ultimately interrelated factors may account for the changed religious-political atmosphere in the state. First, as sociologist Robert Wuthnow and others have learned, the erosion of institutional and denominational faith traditions, whether as cause or effect, occurred alongside more fluid, less predictable patterns of personal spiritual practices and religious identities.[32] Second, the revival of new evangelicals and religious conservatives, a national as much as a Minnesota phenomenon, complicated the religious-political nexus in the state, particularly as regards the state's tradition of civil, quiescent, pragmatic discourse that evolved earlier in the century. Finally, the arrival of new peoples from Southeast Asia, the Middle East, and Latin America, beginning in the 1970s, transformed in dramatic fashion the cultural and religious fabric of the state. They recreated at least in part the island communities that typified the state at the turn of the twentieth century.

Ecumenism, in the strictly religious sense of the term, ironically fostered conditions that began to undermine seldom-questioned denominational and church affiliations among Minnesotans. Preaching closer cooperation, religious fellowship, and communal dialogue, the ecumenical movement in Minnesota at first paralleled and accented the embracing of a civil religion. With the establishment of the Minnesota Council of Churches in 1947, ecumenism in the state looked ahead beyond the mid-century mark with considerable optimism and renewed momentum. In the 1960s, key Lutheran bodies and Eastern Orthodox congregations joined the MCC. At the same time, Minnesota Catholics commenced cooperation in MCC-sponsored programs as pronouncements of the Second Vatican Council supported ecumenical objectives in urging a wider Christian fellowship.[33] In this same period the Jewish Community Relations Council of Minneapolis and Saint Paul, ably led by Samuel Scheiner from 1939 until 1974, actively promoted dialogue and greater understanding between the area's Jews and Christians. The local Minneapolis chapter of the National Conference of Christians and Jews gained recognition in 1949 for having done more than any other chapter in the country in improving social relations.[34]

While seeking theological dialogue and ecclesiastical concord, ecumenism partially detracted from the clarity of older religious distinctions of ethnicity, liturgical practice, and theology. Especially hard hit, Minnesota's mainline Protestant churches were largely stagnant or grew only slowly in the second half of the twentieth century, growth often stemming from church merger rather than organic increase. American Baptists, the United Church of Christ, Disciples of Christ, the Episcopal Church, Presbyterians, and Methodists combined saw their church membership increase only 22 percent between 1957 and 1990. Indeed, of these, American Baptists, Disciples, and Episcopalians actually experienced a net membership loss during this period.[35]

Beginning with comity agreements governing church planting on the nineteenth-century Minnesota frontier, the Protestant establishment churches had donned the ecumenical mantle the earliest. In part, mainline Protestants were victims of their own success, having had the largest cultural impact on the nation as a whole—although in Minnesota, historically, their numbers were small by comparison to the Lutherans and Catholics. But even here, ecumenical impulses generated opposition. Traditional Catholics in Minnesota who wished to preserve existing ritual structures and the Latin mass greeted the liturgical reforms of Vatican II with suspicion or outright rejection. Similarly, when Minnesota's Lutherans, with the exception of the Missouri Synod, culminated a century of ecumenical conciliation by joining the Evangelical Lutheran Church in America in the late 1980s, some Lutheran congregations chose independence, fearing the dilution of theological doctrines and the potential loss of autonomy.

Amidst membership declines in some quarters and growing ecumenical ferment, conservative and evangelical churches grew healthily following 1960. Held back by the strong nucleus of Lutherans and Catholics, these groups nonetheless grew palpably in Minnesota; individuals and churches among the state's Lutherans and Catholics also found theological, social, and political alliance with the rising conservative tide. The charismatic renewal in particular made powerful inroads among both Lutherans and Catholics in the 1970s, fostering spiritual affinity with Pentecostal and holiness traditions that bespoke an experiential rather than an official ecumenism. Minnesotans who claimed the language "born again" to describe their religious experience underscored the growth of a conservative, evangelical movement in the state. In 1986, the Minnesota Poll found that 20 percent of respondents so identified themselves; ten years later, an even higher proportion of those polled, 25 percent, reported a born-again religious conversion, a figure comparable to national findings.[36] Significantly, new groups participated in the evangelical surge. For instance, while the majority of Minnesota's Hispanics remained nominally Catholic, increasing numbers who settled out of the migrant stream joined conservative religious movements, evangelized through Pentecostal and Assembly of God churches where Spanish-language services and less structured liturgies seemed to offer greater cultural and religious autonomy.[37]

Traditional church structures and denominations seemingly exert less pull now than previously in Minnesota, true also in the nation as a whole. The bland, undifferentiated character of a generic civil religion that accompanied the acculturation of immigrant groups (*à la* Herberg) seemed to have generated its own dialectical reversal. Indeed, accumulated snippets of impressions, stories, and experiences reveal a sharpened tendency among Minnesotans to exert personal autonomy and eclecticism in their spiritual searching. New religious constituencies—compounded of individual social, political, and theological convictions, and often valorizing personal experience—now vie with, and overlap, denominationally based determinants of religious life. Consistent again with national patterns, perhaps also a reflex of their penchant for intellectual independence and functional pragmatism as well as growing ecumenical sensitivities, Minnesotans flavored their religious beliefs and practices with new verve and spice. Selectivity in adherence to formal church teachings marked, perhaps, the single outstanding hallmark of this proclivity. In 1983, the Institute for Ecumenical and Cultural Research, based in Collegeville, published *Faith and Ferment*, reporting the findings of a major survey of religious beliefs and practices in Minnesota. The study found that nearly half (48 percent) of all respondents believed that it was sometimes necessary to obey one's own conscience above church dictates, while over half (51 percent) felt that "people have the right to ignore or disobey church laws on the basis of their Christian beliefs."[38] Among Minnesota's Catholics, a recent poll found that 84 percent maintained that "a person can be a good Christian and not go to church," the same proportion of non-Catholics who share this view.[39]

Popular writers like Kathleen Norris opened up new vistas in the exploration of alternative religious observances, which some Minnesotans took up.[40] Raised in the Presbyterian Church, Norris discovered the rich and meaningful ritual forms of classic Benedictine monasticism, whose disciplines of prayer, meditation, and work she found deeply fulfilling and well suited to the stark topological bleakness of the northern Great Plains. Experiences shaped by charismatic renewal, personal religion, and nondenominational fellowships and prayer study groups also illustrated novel forms of religious cohesion. At its extreme, one senses the potential of an entirely privatized, personal religion with little if any meaningful connection to the corporate existence of a congregation, church body, or social-political life of any kind. "Sheilaism," the term coined by Robert Bellah and his associates to indicate private religion, is hard to measure among Minnesotans but may be gauged indirectly in survey responses, such as the 13 percent of respondents who identified their religion recently as generically "Protestant" or "Christian," answered "none," or refused to answer at all.[41] At the same time, as historian and theologian Martin Marty has recently reminded us, the natural dynamic of spiritual growth and vital personal faith necessitates that individuals add to their received traditions "the stories of their own lives."[42] In the blooming of multiple religious flowers, both within and without the state's dominant faith traditions, Minnesota appears more experimental and eclectic in its current spirituality than in the past.

Despite the diffusion of variegated spiritual pathways, the *Faith and Ferment* study first identified the emergence of two religious clusters in Minnesota transcending traditional denominational markers. Though limited by its focus on the Christian faith, the study nonetheless suggested the social salience of two distinctive religious tracks, developing in parallel fashion in the state. A conservative style gave prominence to the personal experience of religious conversion, held a high view of biblical authority, shunned worldly engagement, and maintained a restricted view of the church along with more definite ethical boundaries. A liberal style expressed greater accommodation to contemporary currents and more fluidity regarding doctrine, authority, and personal morality.[43]

The emergence of two religious styles in Minnesota reflected as well the social-religious foundations for a new politics. In particular, the growth of new evangelical churches and the widening appeal of conservative theological perspectives sowed seeds of discontent that altered Minnesota's political culture beginning in the mid-1970s. The election of Jimmy Carter, a self-described born-again Christian, in 1976, together with a gathering conservative opposition to the political transformations and social movements spawned by the 1960s as well as to secular and scientific-educational challenges to religious authority, brought into focus a new political consciousness. For the new conservatives, mainline churches and the ecumenical program they espoused were complicit in these scandalous affronts to an old-time, bedrock religion.[44]

By itself, the strong interchange of religion and politics in Minnesota was hardly a new development. The moralistic tone of Minnesota political life is legendary to the point of feckless stereotype. Mainline Protestants in Minnesota, increasingly joined by the immigrant churches of the Lutherans and Catholics, had long supported social and political engagement, favoring moderate to progressive political positions. What appeared strikingly novel was the degree to which religious convictions in Minnesota became politicized after 1975 and the intensity of the political passions stoked in the process.

The volatile political climate of the 1960s and 1970s, and the state's changing demographic profile in the 1970s and beyond, set the context for renewed theological debate, church activism, ethical deliberation, and the reinterpretation of mission. Regnant public issues—racism and discrimination, chauvinism toward women and minorities, economic injustice, sexual politics in society and the family, peace and justice at home, U.S. policy toward the developing countries—directly touched the life of religious communities, which took them up with new vigor and assertiveness. Many mainline religious constituencies embraced a liberal social agenda and moved to include the disfranchised in a religious "beloved community" as well as in the larger society.

Responding to a profound sense of communal declension and the threat of heterodoxy, evangelical and conservative cadres and citizens began to organize politically. By the late 1970s they stood poised to seize control of the conservative wing of Minnesota's Independent-Republican Party and to contribute to important electoral victories at the polls. Quickly tagged the "New Right," the movement's constituents, one analyst observed, believed "that the activity and authority of God in the world has been obscured by the teaching of secular humanism; that pluralism has eroded the absolute value of Christian principles and Americanism; that the family, the unit divinely ordained and above all other human institutions, is under Satanic attack."[45]

From the mid-1970s on, a long train of public and legislative debates steamed through the state, creating a vituperative, acrimonious religious politics in its passing. Abortion in particular, but also such issues as male-female roles and the family, homosexuality, minority rights, school prayer, and public-school curricula deeply divided Minnesota's religious communities, leading public discourse away from the tradition of civil religion to teeter at times on the edge of incivility. The attachment of fixed religious commitments to ideological positions on the Right and the Left frequently pushed political discourse to the margins. Minnesota's heritage of earnest, moralistic politics thus lived on. However, through the exaggeration of religion in Minnesota's public life and the visible polarization of its communities and peoples engendered by a divisive brand of religious politics, the state witnessed the demise of some of the state's other civic virtues: tolerance, acceptance, compromise, evenhandedness, and pragmatic discourse. In this way, religion's unique place in Minnesota exists now at the intersection of an increasingly untenable expression of particularistic public religion and a teeming personal, yet still communal, quest for spiritual experience and renewal. Indeed, this recent incarnation of religious politics may readily be seen as a compensatory response to a lost world of island communities where religious values were certain, clearly defined, and seldom contested.

As the twentieth century closed, Minnesota's demographic profile looked far more heterogeneous than it had fifty or a hundred years earlier. New population groups chipped away at the state's traditional identity as a northern-European heartland. More significantly, new immigrants to the state further bewildered citizens who looked back wistfully to the order and clarity of the island past. Since 1960, refugees fleeing war and political turmoil around the globe, as well as immigrants seeking opportunities and an improved quality of life, arrived in Minnesota in ever-larger numbers. Koreans, Chinese, Southeast Asians numbering Laotians, Cambodians, and Hmong, Central Americans from El Salvador and Guatemala, Lebanese and Afghans, Somalis, Bosnians, and Croats have transformed the state's cultural texture. Longer present in Minnesota than these groups, migrant Tejanos and native Mexicans employed as seasonal farm workers increasingly settled out of the migrant stream in Minnesota communities after World War II and, along with Central American peoples, added to the growth of the state's diverse Hispanic population.

Paralleling this growth, longer-standing minority groups in the state experienced significant demographic increases during the same period. From a starting point of 15,500 in 1960, Minnesota's Native American population stood at nearly 50,000 in 1990. Predominantly Ojibwe in heritage, this magnification followed a larger demographic and cultural revival among native peoples nationally. Similarly, the population of the state's African Americans, shaped by natural growth and in-migration, reached nearly 95,000 in 1990, almost three times the figure two decades earlier. The number of Hispanics in the state more than doubled between 1970 and 1990, equaling almost 54,000 by the latter date.[46]

The newcomers added to a growing mix of languages, customs, traditions, and religious beliefs in the state's communities. Following a well-worn Minnesota pattern, these groups typically organized self-help and claimed cultural identity and fellowship by means of religious organizations and rituals. The Chinese and Vietnamese along with Cambodians and Laotians contributed to a small but growing Buddhist element in the state, while the Muslim presence grew through adherents arriving from Lebanon, Afghanistan, Iran, and Bosnia. Among the Iranians settling in the state were followers of the Baháʼí religion as well as Muslims, Jews, and Christians. According to one newspaper account, the number of Muslims in the state reached 15,000 in the early 1990s.[47]

Koreans, Chinese, and Southeast Asians, too, shaped by missionary activity in the homeland as well as by sponsoring churches and religious social services, brought another dimension to the diversity of Christian witness in the state while simultaneously building church fellowships that preserved language and ethnic patterns. The spiritualism of the Hmong, expressed through shamans, well-defined clan systems, animal sacrifices, and a complex evocation of spirit-world forces in everyday life, perplexed average Minnesotans who cared to notice. The Hmong interpretation of epilepsy, that "the spirit catches you and you fall down," while seemingly consistent with older Pentecostal traditions or more recent charismatic movements, truly marked a strange parvenu in Minnesota's menu of religious expressions. More acceptable if less known to homegrown Minnesotans, many Hmong, whether in Indochina or their new homes, converted to Protestant or Catholic Christianity.[48]

Adding to the heritage of Black Protestantism, prophetic protest, and church-based community life, many African Americans in the state took up the quest for forgotten roots during the ethnic revivals that surged in the wake of the 1960s political movements. The celebration of Kwanzaa, a spiritual and ritual invocation of severed connections with old Africa, as an alternative to Christmas, the central festival of white Christianity, gave significant expression to this trend. Similarly, the Christianity of reservation churches, urban congregations, outreach programs, and missions identified the Native American struggle for meaning, identity, and collective voice. In the 1980s, congregations like the United Church of Christ's All Nations Indian Church in south Minneapolis consciously blended Christian and Native American traditions. Meanwhile, a new spirit recovered traditional stories, rituals, and ways. Eddie Benton-Banai, a member of the American Indian Movement in Minnesota, explained in the 1970s that "spiritualism is the tradition of the tie that binds us down to our ancestors."[49] Among the state's growing Hispanic population, established residents and newcomers coalesced around Catholic parish churches that structured vibrant communities, notably Our Lady of Guadalupe Church on St. Paul's Lower West Side, the site of the state's first significant gathered Hispanic presence.[50]

More important than the actual numbers of newcomers has been the perception of change that the newcomers created, best reflected in the reactions of native Minnesotans. As one commentator recently described the change, "It's not a world that some old-timers—many Minnesotans—are comfortable with. When we talk about [Minneapolis] as the Garden of Eden and say we're being invaded by serpents from Gary and weeds from East St. Louis, we're telling ourselves a pack of lies."[51]

Some responses activated well-established traditions of hospitality and benevolence. Minnesotans representing the state's dominant faiths—organized through local congregations, sectarian social services, start-up ministries, national denominations, and para-church initiatives—reached out to refugees, aliens, and sojourners, supplying resources, sponsorship, cultural mediation, companionship, and welcome. As sponsors of refugees fleeing civil war and political violence, Minnesota congregations and laypersons demonstrated spiritual and political solidarity with the struggle of Central American peoples to achieve justice and peace during the 1980s. Among the first sanctuary churches in the country, St. Luke Presbyterian in Minnetonka dramatized its commitment by helping to create a national movement that sheltered illegal refugees deemed ineligible for political asylum by the Reagan administration.[52] Responding to the plight of Southeast Asians, local churches and nonprofit religious agencies, working through government channels, sponsored thousands of families, giving Minnesota one of the largest settlements of Southeast Asian peoples in the country. One participant, a lawyer who first became involved in the sanctuary movement in Minnesota, found his legal work in support of asylum cases to be "rewarding for me psychologically, emotionally, and spiritually."[53]

A darker picture, however, shaded the reception with which native Minnesotans greeted many of these newcomers. Hostility, violence, and social separation expressed the range of antipathies directed at those whose language, religious practice, tradition, and behavior singled them out as different. In the worst cases hostility between different groups erupted in violence. In the summer of 1979 a melee broke out when fifty white young people assaulted five Vietnamese teens at a St. Cloud city park. Around the same time, the Chinese Christian Fellowship of Lauderdale experienced repeated vandalism and disruption of services at their worship site, a former school building.[54] Interethnic tensions and violence surfaced in many of the state's growing multicultural urban neighborhoods; incidents of hate crimes increased during the 1990s. Fires at minority houses of worship in the Twin Cities had the markings of religious bigotry, yet could not be irrefutably confirmed as such. Transitions in the ethnic-religious mix of the state, together with the perceptual changes accompanying them, clearly recreated an earlier pattern of diverse and separate communities. Together with a divisive political environment, the expansion of the religious horizon represented by the sacred traditions of new immigrants, Native Americans, and Eastern mysticism challenged Minnesotans with new opportunities for ecumenical exchange, spiritual inspiration, and a new civil *via media* at the dawn of the twenty-first century.

In the end, searching out the religious direction of Minnesota and its people is far more daunting today than it was fifty years ago because of the multiplicity of religious and spiritual avenues Minnesotans are increasingly willing to search. On the one hand, Minnesotans are probably less religious today—in the sense of pious fealty to the preachments and practices of a particular tradition—than one hundred years ago. On the other, Minnesotans may now be more spiritually discerning in seeking, wherever it may be found, deep inner fulfillment that can link life's daily material conditions and struggles to a source of transcendent meaning. Discerning the future is, at best, a tenuous enterprise, but introducing another story associated with the Ojibwe may serve to bring this excursion through religious Minnesota full circle. Passed down through generations, the story of the "shaking tent" ceremony tells of an Ojibwe conjuror in the region of Ontario, who gathered his people around the outside of the tent. Seated within, he spoke to them while pounding his drum, calling down visitors from heaven. The visitors came, showing at the opening of the tent as bright silk cloth—red, blue, and white—which the people had never before seen, thus foretelling the coming of the English traders.[55] If Minnesota's religious lodge could likewise be shaken today, it would bring down a multicolored raiment, telling of a rich future of diverse religious searching—like Joseph's coat, one garment of many hues.

Notes

The author wishes to thank Carroll Engelhardt, Ann Kavanaugh, Joy Lintelman, and David Sandgren for helpful comments, encouragement, and suggestions on early drafts of this essay. Likewise, fellow essayists in this volume offered excellent criticism and friendly advice, much of it followed, which significantly improved the essay.

1. A version of this story of the Anishinabe is found in Edward Benton-Banai, *The Mishomis Book: The Voice of the Ojibway* (St. Paul: Red School House, 1988), chaps. 1 and 2.

2. Barry A. Kosmin and Seymour P. Lachman, *One Nation Under God: Religion in Contemporary American Society* (New York: Harmony Books, 1993), 88–89. New Jersey, at 5.5 percent, is virtually the equivalent of Minnesota in this "no religion" category. Various surveys of religious groups in the United States in 1906, 1936, and 1980 showed Minnesotans maintaining formal religious affiliations at a rate higher than the national average: 41 percent to 39 percent in 1906, 48 percent to 42 percent in 1936, 55 percent to 43 percent in 1980. See Census Bureau, *Religious Bodies: 1906, Part 1* (Washington, D.C.: Government Printing Office, 1910), 25, 46; Census Bureau, *Religious Bodies: 1936, Volume 1* (Washington, D.C.: Government Printing Office, 1941),

17, 61; and Bernard Quinn et al., *Churches and Church Membership in the United States, 1980: An Enumeration by Region, State, and County* (Atlanta: Glenmary Research Center, 1982), 1, 150. Population comparisons from U.S. Census for 1910, 1940, and 1980.

3. Kosmin and Lachman, *One Nation Under God*, 46–48.

4. Stephen L. Carter explored the societal limitations of "disbelief"—a defining characteristic of our legal and political institutions and public discourse, he argues— in *The Culture of Disbelief: How American Law and Politics Trivialize Religious Devotion* (New York: Basic Books, 1993).

5. See *The Search for Order: 1877–1920* (New York: Hill and Wang, 1967), xiii, chap. 3.

6. Frank Renkiewicz, "The Poles," in *They Chose Minnesota: A Survey of the State's Ethnic Groups*, ed. June Drenning Holmquist (St. Paul: Minnesota Historical Society Press, 1981), 369.

7. The following section builds on my earlier essay, "Religious Belief and Behavior" in *Minnesota in a Century of Change: The State and Its People Since 1900*, ed. Clifford E. Clark Jr. (St. Paul: Minnesota Historical Society Press, 1989), 507–538.

8. Kosmin and Lachman, *One Nation Under God*, 88–89.

9. *Religious Bodies, 1906, Part 1*, 327, 329; U.S. Census for 1910; *Religious Bodies, 1936, Volume 1*, 232–233; Quinn et al., *Churches and Church Membership in the United States*, 156.

10. Richard M. Chapman, "'To Do These Mitzvahs': Jewish Philanthropy and Social Service in Minneapolis, 1900–1950," Ph.D. dissertation, University of Minnesota, 1993; Linda Mack Schloff, "Jewish Religious Life in Four Market Towns," *Minnesota History* (Spring 1988): 3–14.

11. See Chapman, "Religious Belief"; Holmquist, *They Chose Minnesota*, passim.

12. Holmquist, *They Chose Minnesota*, passim.

13. Noah Lathrop to Edward Eggleston, 24 June 1859, Edward Eggleston Papers, Minnesota Historical Society Collections, St. Paul.

14. *Pioneer and Democrat*, 15 November 1856, in Works Projects Administration, Minnesota, Papers, Minnesota Historical Society Collections; see section on "temperance."

15. Here and below see Daniel J. Elazar, "Model of Moral Government," and John E. Haynes, "Reformers, Radicals, Conservatives," in Clark, *Minnesota in a Century of Change*, 354–356, 362–364.

16. Haynes, "Reformers, Radicals, Conservatives," 381; see also 360.

17. Chapman, "To Do These Mitzvahs," chap. 2.

18. Kathleen Neils Conzen, "Forum: The Place of Religion in Urban and Community Studies," *Religion and American Culture* 6 (2) (Summer 1996): 113.

19. Carey McWilliams, "Minneapolis: The Curious Twin," *Common Ground* (Autumn 1946): 61–65.

20. Quoted in Bruce J. Dierenfield, "Rooting Out Religion: Church-State Controversies in Minnesota Public Schools Since 1950," *Minnesota History* (Winter 1993): 311.

21. *Star Tribune*, 20 March 1999, 7B; 16 July 1997, 1B; 19 October 1996, 8B; 11 February 1994, 1A (online versions).

22. Garrison Keillor, *Lake Wobegon Days* (New York: Viking, 1985), 119–120.

23. Dennis Nodín Valdés, *Al Norte: Agricultural Workers in the Great Lakes Region, 1917–1970* (Austin: University of Texas Press, 1991), 109–110, 152–157.

24. Frank Guzman, quoted in Susan M. Diebold, "The Mexicans," in Holmquist, *They Chose Minnesota*, 95.

25. Diebold, "The Mexicans," 103.

26. Ibid.

27. Deborah L. Miller, "The Middle Easterners," in Holmquist, *They Chose Minnesota*, 522; *Fargo Forum*, 7 January 2000, A10.

28. Will Herberg, *Protestant-Catholic-Jew: An Essay in American Religious Sociology* (Garden City, N.Y.: Doubleday, 1955; reprint, Garden City, N.Y.: Anchor Books, 1960), 75 (page citation is to the reprint edition).

29. Kosmin and Lachman, *One Nation Under God*, 60.

30. Robert D. Putnam, "What's Happened to Civic Engagement in America and How Can We Fix It?" lecture presented at Fourteenth Annual Faith, Reason, and World Affairs Symposium, Concordia College, Moorhead, Minn., 26 September 1999.

31. Patrick G. Henry, "A Minnesota Response," in *Attitudes of Religions and Ideologies Toward the Outsider: The Other, Religions in Dialogue Volume 1*, ed. Leonard Swidler and Paul Mojzes (Lewiston, N.Y.: Edwin Mellen Press, 1995), 180.

32. Robert Wuthnow, *The Restructuring of American Religion: Society and Faith Since World War II* (Princeton: Princeton University Press, 1988), esp. chap. 5; R. Stephen Warner, "The Place of the Congregation in the Contemporary American Religious Configuration" in *American Congregations*, vol. 2: *New Perspectives in the Study of Congregations*, ed. James P. Wind and James W. Lewis (Chicago: University of Chicago Press, 1994), 54–99; Martin E. Marty, *A Nation of Behavers* (Chicago: University of Chicago Press, 1976).

33. Chapman, "Religious Belief," 528–529.

34. Laura E. Weber, "'Gentiles Preferred': Minneapolis Jews and Unemployment, 1920–1950," *Minnesota History* 52 (Spring 1991): 173–174, 179, 182.

35. National Council of Churches of Christ, *Churches and Church Membership in the United States* (New York: NCCC, 1957), tables 50–51; Martin B. Bradley et al., *Churches and Church Membership in the United States, 1990: An Enumeration by Region, State and County* (Atlanta: Glenmary Research Center, 1992), 209–219.

36. *Minneapolis Star and Tribune*, 10 January 1986, 1A; *Star Tribune*, 28 December 1996, 5B (online version). A 1993 Minnesota Poll reported a response of 23 percent, referenced in *Star Tribune*, 3 March 1996, 1A (online version).

37. Diebold, "The Mexicans," 96–103; Valdés, *Al Norte*, 184–185.

38. Joan D. Chittister and Martin E. Marty, *Faith and Ferment: An Interdisciplinary Study of Christian Beliefs and Practices* (Minneapolis/Collegeville: jointly published by Augsburg Publishing House and the Liturgical Press, 1983), 95, 157.

39. *Star Tribune*, 14 September 1996, 9B (online version).

40. See Kathleen Norris, *Dakota: A Spiritual Geography* (Boston: Houghton Mifflin, 1993) and *The Cloister Walk* (New York: Riverhead Books, 1996); "Methodist Woman Starting Monastery in Benedictine Tradition in Minnesota," *Fargo Forum*, 29 August 1999, A4.

41. Robert N. Bellah et al., *Habits of the Heart: Individualism and Commitment in American Life* (Berkeley: University of California Press, 1996, first published 1985), 220–221. The authors refer to a particular woman, Sheila Larson, whose religion she named after herself, suggesting the "logical possibility of over 220 million American religions, one for each of us"; Kosmin and Lachman, *One Nation Under God*, 92.

42. Quoted in *Star Tribune*, 29 April 1998, 3A (online version).

43. Chittister and Marty, *Faith and Ferment*, 258–263.

44. Here and below see Chapman, "Religious Belief," 527–532.

45. Chittister and Marty, *Faith and Ferment*, 147.

46. See Holmquist, *They Chose Minnesota*, 32, 74, 94; U.S. Census for 1990.

47. Miller, "The Middle Easterners," 524; *Star Tribune*, 8 August 1992, 2E (online version).

48. See Sarah R. Mason, "The Indochinese," in Holmquist, *They Chose Minnesota*, 580–592; Anne Fadiman, *The Spirit Catches You and You Fall Down: A Hmong Child, Her American Doctors, and The Collision of Two Cultures* (New York: Farrar, Straus, and Giroux, 1997); Paja Thao, *I Am a Shaman: A Hmong Life Story with Ethnographic Commentary* (Minneapolis: Southeast Asian Refugee Studies Project, Center for Urban and Regional Affairs, University of Minnesota, 1989).

49. *Minneapolis Star and Tribune*, 8 June 1986, 1F; Benton-Banai is quoted in Martin E. Marty, *Pilgrims in Their Own Land: 500 Years of Religion in America* (New York: Penguin Books, 1984), 438; David Beaulieu, "A Place Among Nations: Experiences of Indian Peoples," in Clark, *Minnesota in a Century of Change*, 425–426.

50. Diebold, "The Mexicans," 96.

51. *Star Tribune*, 8 October 1994, 1B (online version).

52. *Minneapolis Star and Tribune*, 22 October 1985, 1B; *Star Tribune*, 16 January 1997, 1A (online version).

53. Mason, "The Indochinese," 582; quote is found in *Star Tribune*, 4 July 1993, 1B (online version).

54. Mason, "The Indochinese," 585; Sarah R. Mason, "The Chinese," in Holmquist, *They Chose Minnesota*, 542.

55. Norval Morriseau, "Visitors From Heaven," in *Native American Testimony* (New York: Penguin Books, 1992), 10–12.

JOHN E. BRANDL

Policy and Politics in Minnesota

IN A FEW GENERATIONS GOVERNMENT in Minnesota has gone from conservative to radical to liberal to cautious to receiving leadership from a wrestler who says he stunned the world.[1] Governance in Minnesota has been distinctive and often innovative, influenced by sturdy settlers, geographic isolation, prosperity, and brilliant leaders. Lately, residents of the state, like other Americans, have grown increasingly skeptical of claims of governmental beneficence. Once smug, Minnesotans no longer see their state as immune from the array of social, racial, and environmental problems that beset the rest of the United States, and they are far from convinced that government can set things straight.

Four themes emerge. One, the two major political parties, formerly vibrant, are no longer either innovators or compromisers, but rather enclaves of the like-minded obdurate. Two, governors innovate. Three, many important ideas advanced by governors come not from executive branch colleagues nor from the political parties nor from legislators but from policy entrepreneurs outside government. And four, policies that thrive over time tend to be those that are built upon a robust theory of how the world of public affairs works; that is, rather than merely depending on spending or good intentions they in some systematic way orient individuals to accomplish the desired public purpose.

The Parties

At times during the twentieth century each of three different political parties saw salad days in Minnesota. All have since fallen on hard times and there are signs that a new party may have future success. The century ended with the Republicans controlling the state's House of Representatives and the Democrats the Senate. The governor had run under the banner of the new Reform Party,

JOHN E. BRANDL *is dean of the Hubert H. Humphrey Institute of Public Affairs at the University of Minnesota.*

but that party has no easily described agenda, holds no other elective offices in Minnesota, has since changed its name to the Independence Party, and has disaffiliated from the national Reform Party. For now, rather than having three-party rule the state could more aptly be thought of as being governed by two weak parties and a celebrity.

For nearly half of the last century the Democratic Party in Minnesota was all but irrelevant. In 1922, Anna Dickie Olesen, the Democratic candidate for the U.S. Senate, could console herself that her 18 percent of the votes nearly tripled the number received by her party's candidate for governor. In 1930, the Democrats' gubernatorial candidate had support from less than 4 percent of the electorate. As late as 1940 Democrats received only one-tenth of the votes cast for governor and one-fifth of those cast for senator. The Republicans were so dominant that in the late teens of the century when the radical Nonpartisan League started to run candidates for office it did so not as a separate party nor even as a faction within the Democratic Party, but rather as a Republican bloc. Soon the incompatibility of the staid Republicans and the roughhouse league (which all along dallied with socialists) was apparent, and by the 1920s it had become a full-fledged party—the Farmer-Laborites—that was running candidates for major offices.

Through most of the 1920s and 1930s and into the 1940s, Farmer-Labor was the state's second party, and sometimes the first. The leading scholar of Minnesota radicalism, Richard M. Valelly, contends that by the 1930s, the time of the Great Depression, the Farmer-Labor Party "was easily the most successful . . . of all the cases of state-level radicalism" in America.[2] For eight years of that decade the Farmer-Laborites occupied the governor's office and for nearly half the decade both of Minnesota's U.S. Senate seats. The party's gifted and charismatic Floyd B. Olson was elected governor in 1930, and when reelected in 1932 and 1934 he brought scores of Farmer-Laborites into the legislature. There ensued a brief Farmer-Labor heyday. "I am not a liberal," Olson declared. "I am a radical."[3] Passed into law were a mortgage moratorium, a state income tax, and labor legislation banning yellow-dog contracts. Still, many in his party thought Olson too moderate, for he never seriously tried to enact such planks of the Farmer-Labor platform as the socialization of much of the state's transportation, mining, and manufacturing. Over the course of a few years after Olson's sudden death in 1936 at age forty-five, the Farmer-Labor Party fell apart. Too radical for its constituency, led by politically unskilled ideologues, and outmaneuvered by the Republicans, it was finished as a significant force by the early 1940s.

Helping along the Farmer-Laborites' self-immolation was the Republican Harold Stassen, who was elected governor in 1938 at age thirty-one. Previously the Republicans had tried to ignore or destroy the political Left even when, as with the Nonpartisan League, it operated within the GOP. Stassen co-opted the Farmer-Laborites, and in doing so invented a moderate form of Republicanism that extended such of its rival's policies as the mortgage moratorium, and even embraced anti-loan-shark legislation that the Farmer-Laborites had favored but had not been able to pass.

In 1944, prodded by Franklin Delano Roosevelt and fully aware of their decades of impotence, the Democrats acceded to a merger with the Farmer-Laborites. This union was engineered by the Democrat Hubert H. Humphrey, who was elected mayor of Minneapolis the following year. By 1948, after a bitter fight, Humphrey and his allies had forced those Farmer-Laborites of the extreme Left, including Marxists and other radical socialists, out of the new Democratic-Farmer-Labor Party. In the summer of that year at the national Democratic convention, Humphrey gave what admirers still remember as his finest speech. Though privately fearful that driving the conservative Southern Democrats from the party (which happened!) could mean the end of his political career, he courageously and successfully argued for inclusion of a civil-rights plank in the Democrats' platform. That fall Humphrey was elected to the U.S. Senate under the DFL banner. Thus began the career of Minnesota's most successful and influential politician.

Working independently, Harold Stassen and Hubert Humphrey created a broad political center that dominated Minnesota politics for the next several decades, each drawing his party away from intemperate partisanship. Both were brilliant, indefatigable, nonideological, and convinced of the nobility of public service. They were internationalists in a state much of whose political leadership had opposed participation in both the world wars. Stassen and Humphrey drew to government service scores of the state's most able young people, many of whom became outstanding politicians in their own right. Among Republicans the most illustrious of these was Elmer L. Andersen, who has combined public service (state senator, governor, chairman of the board of regents of the University of Minnesota) with a highly successful business career. In Minnesota, as elsewhere, fewer Republicans than Democrats make a life of politics. More of Humphrey's associates than Stassen's have had distinguished careers in public life: Congressman and Senator Eugene McCarthy; Senator, Vice President, and Ambassador Walter Mondale; Governor and Agriculture Secretary Orville Freeman; Federal District and Circuit Court Judge Gerald Heaney; State Senator, Congressman, and Minneapolis Mayor Donald Fraser; Ambassador Geri Joseph; Minneapolis Mayor Arthur Naftalin. Still only in his mid-thirties after having been elected governor three times,

Stassen resigned the job after the 1942 election and entered the navy. By war's end, the wunderkind may have considered Minnesota too small a stage. He tried for the 1948 nomination for president that the Republicans ultimately gave to Thomas Dewey. Stassen has always remained eager to run for office, although never again did he do so successfully. Had he returned to run against Humphrey in 1948, the state's ensuing political history and that of the two men might have been quite different—at the time Stassen was much the more accomplished, eminent, and electorally successful. For the three decades between his election to the Senate and his death in 1978, Humphrey was the state's most prominent politician. His talent, integrity, exuberance, compassion, and phenomenal memory (it seems that thousands of Minnesotans remember him greeting them by name years after their last having met) endeared him even to many who found his big government enthusiasms unappealing.

Still, the Republican Party dominated state politics until the early 1970s. Before 1972 the Democrats had never controlled both houses of the legislature. Indeed, throughout the century the Republicans had always held the Senate. (Between 1913 and 1973 legislators were officially undesignated by party, yet they caucused as conservatives and liberals, which, many people believed, betrayed their party colors.) When Orville Freeman was elected governor in 1954 he was the first Democrat to hold that office in forty years.

Stassen's conception of the Republican Party as broad, moderate, and co-opting of the Left prevailed long after he moved from the state. Thus, the three-term Republican governor Luther Youngdahl (1947–1951) was not only—like Stassen—Scandinavian, stolid, and moralistic; he too saw social responsibilities for government, and he advanced public housing, education, care for the mentally ill and disabled, and race relations. Later, when Minnesota Republicans were ashamed of President Nixon and of a mind to dissociate themselves from what they saw as harshly conservative policies of the national party, they for a time changed their name to the Independent-Republican Party.

After the early 1970s, however, the parties grew more dissimilar. Each moved away from the centrist conception that held sway in previous decades, and legislative veterans tell of less cordial personal relations. Several factors contributed to this development. Skillful leadership, along with the reintroduction of party designation of legislators and the Watergate debacle's nationwide effect, gave the Democrats 3-to-1 majorities in both houses in the mid-1970s. With such predominance, they could and did ignore and isolate legislative Republicans. Party practices contributed to intellectual isolation. Each of these two parties has usually attracted tens of thousands of citizens to its biennial caucuses, at which issues are discussed and delegates elected to later conventions. Since the 1970s, as an effort to ensure proportional representation of different interests, the Democrats have resorted to "walking sub-caucuses," which involve the various subsets of a caucus (e.g., those who favor banning pari-mutuel betting, or protecting the northern wilderness, or increasing education funding, or endorsing a particular candidate for governor) physically gathering in different parts of the room. Discussions take place and each sub-caucus elects its share of the caucus's allotted number of delegates to the next convention. In this way, accommodation and even discourse between persons with serious disagreements are made unnecessary; indeed, of course, each of the sub-caucuses tends to elect its most hot-blooded and least conciliatory members as delegates. No issue illustrates the phenomenon better than abortion. Although the arrangement gives even a tiny contingent of pro-lifers a chance to elect a delegate, over time the sub-caucuses of pro-life Democrats have dwindled in size. They feel unwelcome in the party, and both they and their adversaries have been trained in intransigence. The party is organized so as to favor obstinacy in those who aspire to a leadership role in it or who wish its endorsement for election to public office.

Recent decennial redistrictings have sometimes exacerbated the problem. Some politicians see it in their interest to divide the state so as to leave few swing districts. Incumbents generally feel safer in districts drawn so as to pare off neighborhoods of unfriendly voters. But in safe districts, as in sub-caucuses, the dominant party hardly tends to nominate its most open-minded or inventive members for elective office.

The very size of state government has contributed to the increasing distinctness of the parties. Immense increases in appropriations have not only been a response to interest groups; they have encouraged further lobbying by those groups. In the time of Stassen or Youngdahl, particularly as legislators were elected without party designation, not as much was at stake for legislators, parties, or citizens when the legislature was in session. But the annual general fund budget of the state grew from $500 million to $11.5 billion over the last third of the century, an increase of 10 percent per year compounded annually. Even after adjusting for inflation, the state is spending nearly four times as much per Minnesotan this year as it did in 1967.[4] With so much money on the table, interest groups have proliferated; each is disposed to set explicit conditions under which it will support a candidate. Democrats, the party of government, are the more affected by this practice. Also, many of them need a job. Prior to the early 1970s the legislature was dominated by economically comfortable, rural Republicans. Since then many more legislators have come to rely on their elected position for their livelihood. This can get them into difficulty. On one occasion in the 1980s, a legislator who sponsored one of the year's most important bills had successfully taken the bill through committee and prepared it for consideration by the whole House. Some angry lobbyists took him aside and indicated that if he persisted with the bill he could expect to lose their endorsement in his next campaign. He voted against his own bill, perhaps because he could not imagine leaving the legislature for another line of work. Thus has the Democratic-Farmer-Labor Party of Minnesota, famed for its creativity in the days of Humphrey, Wendell Anderson, and Arthur Naftalin, become conservative; it lacks inventiveness. The party's base, the recipients of appropriations, identify progress not with reform but with increased spending on the existing programs that provide them with salaries and raises.

Republicans in Minnesota as elsewhere came to be associated with cuts in spending and taxes. And when, as has happened once a decade for the last thirty years, Republicans have achieved control of the House of Representatives for a term, their frustration at not being able to enact their agenda in the face of an opposing Senate (which has remained Democratic since 1973) has sometimes resulted in personal denigration of their adversaries and attacks on the very governmental institution in which they serve. This has not been conducive to cooperative policy-making.

By the 1998 election Minnesotans had become so disillusioned with the major parties—even when scions of Humphrey, Mondale, and Freeman all were running for governor—that they elected to the office the former professional wrestler Jesse (The Body) Ventura. Ventura's outrageous personal conduct seemed a mark of appealing authenticity to citizens disenchanted with the carefulness, lack of candor, and deference to interest groups many had come to see as characterizing career politicians.

At the end of the century the other two top elected officials in the state are arguably the country's most conservative senator, Rod Grams, and the most liberal, Paul Wellstone. It remains to be seen whether other Jesse Venturas will be able to exploit the propensity of the parties to put forward their extremes for public office.

Governors as Innovators

By election day in 2002 it will have been twenty-four years since Minnesota elected a governor who came to the office as the choice of either the Democratic or the Republican Party. The decline of the political parties—and of the legislature—is demonstrated by the fact that typically in recent decades it has been not the parties or the legislature but independent-minded governors, often in defiance of their respective parties, who have brought innovative public policy to the state.

With few exceptions, the last instances of major legislative innovation occurred around 1970. When the Republican Harold LeVander was governor (1967–1971), conservatives controlled the legislature. Wyman Spano, one of the state's most respected lobbyists and political commentators, has written that LeVander "had a very definite sense of his responsibility to become governor but not a sense of what particularly he was supposed to do once he had the job."[5] Leading legislators at the time were full of ideas and worked cooperatively with LeVander's talented chief of staff, David Durenberger. Guiding the legislature was Senator Gordon Rosenmeier, chairman of the powerful committee on committees. For decades after his time, lore in the Senate had it that Rosenmeier was that body's most able and influential member ever. He and his colleagues "saw themselves as running the Senate, and through it, the state," said Royce Hanson in his book on the legislature.[6] The 1967 legislature enacted a metropolitan governance structure, including a metropolitan council that exists to this day for the seven-county Twin Cities region. Also, legislators put in place a taxing and spending pattern that was completed a few years later during Wendell Anderson's time as governor (1971–1976), when it came to be known as the Minnesota Miracle. The notion was that increased state taxes (the legislature introduced a state sales tax over LeVander's objection) permitted state aid to cities and schools. This apparently simple idea changed the relationship between the state and local governments, for with big money now flowing from St. Paul, policy-making for local governments and for education came more and more to be made not by city councils and local school boards but at the Capitol.

Working with the conservative legislature, Wendell Anderson greatly extended the Minnesota Miracle policy. This remarkable achievement entailed a substantial expansion of the income tax in order to put the state in the position of paying 70 percent of school expenditures, thus enabling local governments and school districts to reduce property taxes. Also created by the conservative legislature in cooperation with Anderson in his first term was the metropolitan area's fiscal disparities law, an ingenious tax base sharing arrangement that mathematically pools, then redistributes, not property taxes but part of the growth in the area's commercial and industrial property tax base. The arrangement stipulates that communities with rapidly growing amounts of business property do not have available to them all of that property to tax. For property tax purposes the amount unavailable to them is offered to less property-wealthy communities. Whatever tax rate a local government applies to the property physically within its jurisdiction also applies to its part of the shared base. The scheme accomplishes a combination of redistribution, local control, tax discipline, and constraint on competition among local governments for new businesses. The tax base sharing legislation was sponsored by a suburban legislator, Representative Charles Weaver, but much of the work of devising and passing the fiscal and metropolitan legislation was accomplished by senior rural members, part of the club of legislators who, even though their districts were not directly affected by the legislation, saw themselves as having responsibility for the whole state.

To this day the legislation of the late 1960s and early 1970s shapes the governance of the metropolitan area as well as the fiscal relationship between the state and its local units of government. As we shall see later, it also has had important implications, only dimly recognized at the time, for the size and role of government in Minnesota.

The high point of legislative ascendancy in policy-making that occurred just before and after 1970 came about for a number of reasons—the acquiescence of one governor (with a deft assistant), the skill of another (as he faced a legislature controlled by people not of his political persuasion), and the ability of unusually talented legislators with a Burkean understanding of their role.

After his second year as governor, Anderson worked with a legislature both houses of which were controlled by the Democrats. Since it had never before happened that the Democrats held the legislature and the governorship at the same time, and since a plethora of Great Society legislation had just passed in Washington, a great number of bills were ready to be taken up. Anderson led the legislature through a session of policy-making still unsurpassed in the sheer amount of major legislation enacted. *Minnesota Politics and Government*, the new standard work on politics in the state, describes this achievement as follows:

> Anderson, flanked by his tough and able chief of staff, Tom Kelm, and the DFL-dominated legislature, passed an incredible array of legislation they had favored for years but could never get enacted: money for education and the disabled, an open-meeting law, a prohibition on corporate farming, an anti-strikebreaking law, and the Public Employees Bargaining Act, which guaranteed strong unions among Minnesota's public employees. The Equal Rights Amendment (for women) to the federal Constitution was ratified easily. Party designation for all subsequent legislatures was approved. A new state zoo was authorized. The next year added campaign-finance reform, no-fault auto insurance, the creation of a Housing Finance Agency, and elimination of income taxes for the working poor.[7]

In early 1976, like the Farmer-Laborites forty years earlier, the Democrats appeared ready for many years of rule. They had Hubert Humphrey in the U.S. Senate, a popular and highly successful governor, vast majorities in the legislature, and in the fall of that year their other U.S. senator, Walter Mondale, was elected vice president. Then Wendell Anderson committed political suicide. After the fall 1976 elections he resigned the governorship, which gave that job to Lieutenant Governor Rudy Perpich. Thereupon, Perpich appointed Anderson to Mondale's seat in the U.S. Senate. No one in Minnesota politics has ever made a worse miscalculation. Not only was Anderson unable to keep the Senate seat when he came up for election in 1978 (and unable ever again to win an election), but the voters' fury boiled over on Perpich and the legislature. The governorship was won by Republican Congressman Al Quie, and the Democrats lost thirty-two House seats to the Republicans in that one election. The problems for the Democrats went on and on. Humphrey died in 1978 and the Republicans took his Senate seat in the fall. The formidable Martin Olav Sabo, Speaker of the Minnesota House of Representatives, was elected to Congress, which ended his masterful leadership at the state capitol. Shortly thereafter, Nick Coleman, the beloved leader of the Democrats in the Minnesota Senate, died. Never since have the Democrats in the legislature been as ably led. Never since has Minnesota had the distinguished representation in the U.S. Senate it had for the combined total of forty-seven years that Humphrey, McCarthy, and Mondale, all national leaders, served there. However, after a few years the state did move into a new period of gubernatorial leadership and innovation.

Every Minnesota governor since Wendell Anderson has come into office determined to improve elementary and secondary education and convinced that integral to that ambition is an increase in state spending. The basic policy of the state, the Minnesota Miracle—high state taxes that enable St. Paul to send large amounts of aid to local governments and school districts—has prevailed for thirty years. Eventually each governor has come to see the relationship between education spending and educational achievement as weak and thus has come to see the Minnesota Miracle as fundamentally flawed. To illustrate: over a three-decade period in the late twentieth century, real education spending per child in Minnesota tripled. That is, after adjusting for inflation, at the end of that time on average the state was spending three times as much on each child as it had on the child's parents thirty years earlier when that older generation was in school.[8] No one claims that there has been a corresponding improvement in the educational level of children. Each governor eventually has concluded that parental choice is a necessary alternative to bureaucratic provision of education by government, and some form of parental control of education spending is preferable to the state's merely turning money over to districts.[9] That is the main shift in policy thinking of recent years in Minnesota, one embodied in five first-in-the-nation policies enacted between 1985 and 1997. With one exception, the policy changes have been led not by the legislature or the political parties, but by governors.

Governor Al Quie (1979–1983) was hampered and ultimately done in by a national economic downturn that nearly coincided with his four years in office. Democrats held majorities in both houses of the legislature during most of his term, and they were successful in attributing budget shortfalls caused by economic conditions to Quie's management of government. Quie takes considerable pride in having achieved, during his term in office, indexing of the income tax, an institutionalizing of frugality.

Two men, Democrat Rudy Perpich and Republican Arne Carlson, dominated state politics from 1982 to 1998; each served as governor for eight years during that period. Each came to the job without the backing of his party— a sign of the weakening of both the Democrats and the Republicans—which freed both governors to be more inventive than if they had been more beholden to interests supporting the status quo in their respective parties. Each was the son of poor immigrant parents who valued education. Each, earlier in life, had decided that choosing schools other than those designated by the government for him or his family had had a beneficial effect. Each made his biggest contribution in the field of elementary and secondary education, the most important responsibility of state government and, at 30 percent of the total, by far the largest appropriation item in the budget.[10]

After Perpich lost his 1978 race, he went to Europe to work for the computer company Control Data. He returned in 1982, took on the DFL's endorsed gubernatorial candidate in the primary, and defeated him. Without money or organization, but with energy, shrewdness, and charisma, he was elected governor in the fall. Eight years later, Arne Carlson won an even more surprising victory. In September of 1990, he not only lost the primary to the Republican Party's endorsed candidate; he carried only one of the state's eighty-seven counties. In October it was learned that some years earlier the winner of that primary had allegedly been swimming nude in the presence of teenage girls. The state Supreme Court allowed the Republicans to replace his name on the ballot with Carlson's, and after a two-week race the loser of the primary election won the general election and became governor.[11]

In 1985, Perpich proposed that students be permitted to cross district lines and attend public school in the district of their choice. The associations representing teachers, administrators, and school boards fiercely opposed this open enrollment bill and prevented its passage. Permitted to pass almost as a consolation prize was a bill that authorized high-school juniors and seniors to attend college at public expense and receive both high-school and college credit. This foot-in-the-door move started to develop a constituency for public-school choice as families throughout the state exercised the opportunity to decide where their children might best learn. Remarkably, particularly given the united opposition of the public school associations, the college-credit legislation passed despite the absence of support from any broadly based interest groups. Perpich's proposal benefited greatly from the support and skill of the (Republican) majority leader in the House, Connie Levi.

Two years later the major breakthrough came. Open enrollment passed and was signed into law, though with the loophole that districts could opt out. The next year the loophole was removed. The 1987 legislature also passed, and Perpich signed, a bill that authorized school districts to contract with public or private providers of education for children who were doing poorly in school or had dropped out.

Thus, by the time Perpich left office in 1991 he had signed into law three new policies expanding parental choice in education, including the country's first statewide choice plan. He had done this despite the active opposition of the lobbies usually thought to be the most powerful in the state, and without countervailing interest groups supporting the legislation.

The fourth of the five new education policies of the 1980s and 1990s required the single most impressive instance of legislative skill and leadership in memory. Arne Carlson owed his election to the education interest groups, particularly the two teachers' unions. They ordinarily support Democrats but were so furious with Perpich that they urged their members to vote for Carlson in 1990. For a time, Carlson listened to them. For example, his first commissioner of education moved to that job from his position as chief lobbyist for the Minnesota Education Association, the state's largest teachers' union. In 1991, the assistant majority leader, Senator Ember Reichgott, reintroduced legislation permitting the formation of charter schools.[12] Reichgott was ambitious for higher office. Still, she and her ally in the House, Representative Becky Kelso, defied the education interests and, without the support of their political party, worked the legislation into law. They had to water it down to do so. The law limited the number of charters to eight in the whole state; a majority of the board members of a charter school had to be teachers; and no other entity than a school board could issue a charter. Still, once passed in Minnesota the idea caught on and was improved upon in dozens of other states, and Minnesota has since loosened those early restrictions.

The last in the string of education reforms—education tax credits—was an achievement of Arne Carlson. After a few years in office he had come to view the effort education interest groups put into improving their own working conditions as a diversion from improving the education of children and had begun to press for extending the school-choice policies of the state. After unsuccessfully supporting a voucher trial, he started working for education tax credits—which amount to much the same thing as vouchers but have a more appealing ring to them. He faced opposition to vouchers from the Right, from religious groups who feared that with vouchers would come state-government strings on their schools. Carlson's policy adviser, Tim Sullivan, recognized the equivalence of vouchers and tax credits, and the political appeal of the latter. In 1997, knowing that sympathetic Republicans had enough strength in the House to prevent override of a veto of major legislation, Carlson insisted on passage of tax credit legislation as a condition for signing any education appropriation, and he prevailed. The legislation opened to low-income people the possibility of choosing public or private schools, although at the latter only expenses other than tuition are eligible for credits.

Neither of the political parties had a role in the invention of any of the five reforms or in the efforts at passage in the legislature. Only in the cases of Levi, Reichgott, and Kelso was the leadership of individual legislators crucial. But in almost all of the reforms no one else played a role half as important as the governor's. Perpich and Carlson each eventually came to link his own policy preference with a passion that came from personal experience with the schools. Each devoted single-minded effort to the passage of education reforms. With five major policies having been enacted in the period from the mid-1980s to the mid-1990s, a general direction of policy seems set.

Over the years Minnesota appears to be replacing its central policy, the Minnesota Miracle. It is moving away from a policy of allocating state funds to local bureaus, and toward a policy of government funding for individual choice. Although I have illustrated that new direction using the state's largest responsibility, elementary and secondary education, I claim for it more sweeping application. For example, for nearly two decades the state has been holding back, although sometimes grudgingly, on appropriations to colleges and universities and has been providing some grants and loans directly to needy students, who take that government money to the public or private institution of their choice. Direct aid to institutions remains a much larger state appropriation than is aid to students, but the new direction has been an explicit part of policy-making since the current student-aid policy was enacted in 1983. If and as the state encounters rough economic times in the future, the new direction can be expected to be invoked in support of student choice, accountability, and concentration of aid on the needy. This policy change is sweeping in an even broader sense—as not only a description and analysis of state policy for education, but also a prediction of a direction of policy for state services in general.

Governor Jesse Ventura has been an innovator not in policies espoused but as a campaigner, both before and after he was elected in 1998. The celebrity as politician, he was well known to the citizenry as a wrestler and talk-show host even though he had little campaign money to spend. On election day he surprised everyone by drawing to the polls large numbers of first-time, previously disaffected voters. In office he has appeared regularly on national news and talk shows, wisecracking with the best of them. Thus has he received valuable publicity without paying for it and set popularity records in the polls. In his first year in office he put forward three policy proposals: a huge tax rebate, a light rail line from downtown Minneapolis to the Twin Cities airport and the Mall of America, and the elimination of one house of the legislature. The rebate, made possible by the prosperous economy and the frugality of Arne Carlson, easily passed the legislature. Ventura shrewdly arranged for it to happen automatically. Taxpayers received hundreds, even thousands, of dollars in the mail on the basis of the tax forms they had filed the previous year. Rebates of this magnitude had never happened before, and Ventura got the credit. His proposal for light rail is highly controversial, but it has been approved by the legislature. However, a study by Ventura's own Department of Transportation predicts that if built the proposed line would attract few riders and calculates its costs as far outweighing its benefits. The proposal for a unicameral legislature is tailor-made to receive Ventura's support: it is simple, it would save the taxpayers money, and it would get rid of politicians. Still, he has not been able to convince the legislature of its value, or to create strong public support. None of Ventura's proposals is complicated. ("Government's not brain surgery," he says.) And none would have great influence on any major problem facing the state. Ventura's celebrity itself, not any policy position, is his political cachet.

Ventura revels in the celebrity-worship he evokes, and he multiplies his appeal to many by thumbing his nose at establishment individuals and institutions. He reflects a society fed up with its government, comfortable enough to think that most of what it wants it can get without government, and disposed to see government not as consequential and difficult but as irrelevant and entertaining.

Where Policy Innovations in Minnesota Come From

In 1872 Walter Bagehot set out to determine why the British "excel all other nations." His startling conclusion was that England's success could be attributed not to natural resources, climate, geography, genetics, or religion but to what he called "a polity of discussion," a practice of requiring that important issues are widely and openly debated.[13] Had he not made that breathtaking claim I would be hesitant about suggesting the same for Minnesota in the twentieth century.

For many decades Minnesota has had an unusually rich civic culture. Its origins go back over a century to the massive immigration of Easterners and Europeans. At that time, and still today, the Twin Cities, the state's only large metropolitan area, was many hundreds of miles from any other metropolis. Minnesota's businesses and its government could not be managed from elsewhere. Elsewhere was too far away; Minnesotans were on their own.

The capitol is in St. Paul, which is contiguous to Minneapolis, the region's economic center. The University of Minnesota, the state's only comprehensive university, also lies in the Twin Cities. People of influence in one sector of society have always been personally familiar with leaders of other sectors; they live and work nearby. Up to the present day a large number of people work for firms founded and based locally—General Mills, Honeywell, Minnesota Mining and Manufacturing (3M), Cargill, Pillsbury, and many others, especially Dayton's. Dayton's was the national leader in organizing the Five Percent Club—firms that donate 5 percent of their profits to charity. A tradition of business leaders accepting civic responsibility persisted for a long while. The Twin Cities were their home as well as the home of their businesses. Until recently it was not uncommon for the state's leading businesspersons to participate in local civic organizations. Lately the firms have become multinationals with most of their revenues generated elsewhere, and management has shifted from the founding families to transients who might have lived in San Francisco or Atlanta last year and will be moving on to Boston or Dallas next. Minnesota has a weaker claim on the loyalties of such persons than it had on their predecessors. Instead of participating in broad-based civic groups, today's executive is active in the Minnesota Business Partnership, an organization consisting of the CEOs of the state's hundred largest firms.

Concentration of a high fraction of the state's population in one metropolitan area has had the effect of diminishing the parochialism of some politicians. A rural legislator who represents several counties and dozens of cities and school districts always has an outer office full of people from the home district waiting for an opportunity to make the case for a new school or tax break or road. The urban legislator who represents only part of one city is more free to choose which issues to advocate, more anonymous, less pressured to understand the job as advancing parochial interests, more free to ask what is best for the whole state.

Still, generating a culture of discourse requires more than any of the forces just mentioned. Other places in America have loyal local firms as well as a concentration of business, government, and educational entities. The Minnesota difference lies in the existence of policy entrepreneurs who influence government from outside with their ideas. Throughout America one can find honorable examples of this—for example, the League of Women Voters or Common Cause. Minnesota went a step further, as we will see in a moment. To have an effect, ideas need to be publicized, and for decades that was greatly aided in Minnesota by the visionary John Cowles, publisher, before the papers were merged, of the *Minneapolis Star* and the *Minneapolis Tribune*. The papers did much to stimulate a civic climate that was open to ideas. Cowles hired outstanding reporters and gave them free rein. Today, when public affairs are typically reported as athletic contests—who hit whom—many Minnesotans look back to a golden age of journalism, in the 1950s and 1960s.

A unique Minnesota institution, the Citizens League, came into being during that time, helped along by the newspapers taking its work seriously. Over the last forty years many of the state's important policy innovations have originated in the league. The Citizens League stands against the prevailing conception of politics and policy-making in America. Interest group liberalism has become the generally accepted way Americans understand politics. Interest groups come together in the political marketplace and, as in private markets, competition between rival groups is expected to yield compromise and mutual satisfaction. Of course, there is much to recommend that practice; in our time prosperity, freedom, and the peaceful resolution of disputes have made the combination of representative democracy and market capitalism the aspiration of nearly every country in the world. Still, competition in politics has not yielded as rich an array of innovations as has competition in private markets. Government requires more than competition. James Madison, an inventor of the idea that competition in politics can discipline self-interest, also believed in the indispensability of public spiritedness. Politicians do not "do every mischief they possibly can," he said. "I go on this great republican principle, that the people will have virtue and intelligence. . . . To suppose that any form of government will secure liberty or happiness without any virtue in the people is a chimerical idea."[14] Perhaps Madison could take for granted that the virtue, i.e., public spiritedness, he believed essential to the successful operation of this country would be nurtured in families, neighborhoods, schools, and churches. Two hundred years later, that would appear to be a less safe assumption.

The central ethic of the Citizens League is this: One participates as a seeker of the public good, not as an agent of this or that interest group. The league is open to anyone. It has roughly 2,500 dues-paying individual members; also, scores of private firms make annual donations. The latter number is dwindling as businesses apparently are coming to define their interests more narrowly than in the past. The league is becoming more dependent on individual membership fees. The organization's main work goes on in its study committees, of which there have been hundreds over the decades. Each year the board picks several issues—for example, metropolitan governance, welfare, higher education, or transit. A study committee is formed for each, which typically meets weekly for some months before issuing a report analyzing the issue and offering recommendations. The league has always had a tiny staff of superbly competent people, but its lay members accomplish the great bulk of the work of the study committees. Any member can join any committee, although sometimes if the board determines that a member has a vested interest in the issue it will deny participation on a committee to that person. At league meetings one does not hear "at the bank we think . . ." or "the university's position on that is . . ." Of course, the very influence of the league attracts to its committees those with an ax to grind and makes perfect compliance with the ethic a will-o'-the-wisp. However, the ethic broadly characterizes league practice, with several results. Public spiritedness is not only expected but fostered. People are drawn to membership out of a desire to be part of an organization with such an aspiration. Also, the size, influence, and reputation of the league provide cover for politicians who take up league proposals. And importantly, the league procedure and ethic yield innovative public policies.

Almost all of the innovations mentioned earlier had their beginnings in the Citizens League. Consider the following excerpts from league reports dating from 1967 to 1990: "We recommend that the 1967 Legislature create a Metropolitan Council. . . ."[15] "In coming years as the tax base of the area grows, give each locality access to a part of the growth of the tax base in the entire area, regardless of how much of that growth actually occurs within its own boundaries."[16] "Local use of the property tax should be reduced. Specifically, most of the locally-collected property tax for schools should be replaced by state-collected taxes."[17] "Public educational dollars should follow parents' choices about which schools or educational services should be utilized."[18] "The state should . . . stay on its innovative course by authorizing (not mandating), in

Minneapolis and St. Paul, 'chartered' public schools. . . ."[19] "This fiscal arrangement [the Minnesota Miracle] created a cycle of increased local property taxes, followed by state legislative action to reduce property taxes with sales and income tax revenues. The pattern is problematic. . . . Although the relationship between the state and local units of government cemented in 1971 with the 'Minnesota Miracle' may have been appropriate at the time a new foundation is now necessary."[20]

That brief collection of quotations serves as a running prophecy of future state policy; in each case the prophecy was fulfilled within a few years by government action. The league invented the state's basic policy, the Minnesota Miracle. Now, having concluded that that policy is a failure, it is constructing policies that are replacing it. The Citizens League both reflects and cultivates the civic culture of Minnesota. Of course, not all policy innovation occurs within league meetings, and there are important areas of public affairs—health policy, for example—on which the league has had little influence. But the league may very well have no peers elsewhere in America in its combination of disinterestedness, quality analysis, and influence.

The most influential Minnesotan of recent decades, Ted Kolderie, was executive director of the league from 1967 to 1980, but since that time he has been an independent policy entrepreneur, devoting his life to studying policy, discussing it with others, and devising alternative ways of accomplishing the public's work. It is hard to find a major policy reform in the last third of a century in which Kolderie did not have a hand. He was one of the inventors of the Minnesota Miracle, and for two decades he has been working on the fiscal and education policies that are replacing it. Along with Kolderie, other Citizens League executive directors—Ray Black, Verne Johnson, Curt Johnson, and Lyle Wray—have created and sustained this great organization and, through it, formed public affairs in the area and state for nearly half a century.

Kolderie credits the cream of a generation of Minnesota lawyers with institutionalizing public spiritedness in the civic affairs of the region. David Graven, Bill Frenzel, Wayne Popham, Richard Fitzgerald, Greer Lockhart, James Hetland, William Johnstone, and many others brought their lawyerly thinking not only to the causes of their clients but to the issues of the day. The very structure of a Citizens League committee's activity follows the lawyer's procedure of finding facts, applying appropriate law (or policy or values), and arriving at recommendations for action. Some businesspersons have participated in civic affairs in this public-spirited way. Even when he was CEO of Cray Research, at the time the maker of the world's most powerful computers, John Rollwagen chaired the league committee that first proposed the formation of charter schools. Roger Hale is only slightly more engaged in public affairs in retirement than he was as CEO of the manufacturing firm Tennant. For several decades leading firms hired such persons as Thomas Swain, chief of staff for then-governor Elmer L. Andersen and later executive vice president of the St. Paul Companies; Dennis Dunne, vice president of Northwest Bancorporation; Leonard Ramberg, vice president of Northwestern National Bank; Peter Vanderpoel, director of the state planning agency and later director of communications for Northern States Power; Charles Neerland and Peter Heegaard, each of whom was an official at Northwestern Bank as well as Citizens League president; James Hetland, University of Minnesota law professor, first chairman of the Metropolitan Council, and vice president of First Bank Systems; and the inimitable Wayne Thompson, a career city manager who joined Dayton's and became that firm's chief link to governmental affairs. These individuals were hired not as public-relations officers, nor only as distributors of funds to charities, but to bring ideas to civic life. However, it is troubling that in this most prosperous time fewer firms are encouraging their executives to engage in work that contributes to the public good. Fewer leading professionals and businesspersons than in the past participate in public affairs other than as agents for their clients' or firms' interests. If fewer dramatic policy changes have emerged from the league in recent years, it may be because even in Minnesota people are moving away from civic participation and toward special interest politics on the one hand and cocooning at home on the other. More ominous is the possibility that contemporary life with its ease of communications and transportation is leading to a destruction of the local and a corresponding sense of inability to affect public affairs.

Still, some policy entrepreneurs continue to come forward. Joe Nathan is a former public-school teacher now directing the Center for School Change at the University of Minnesota's Humphrey Institute. He has been a leading developer of education policies that substitute for the bureaucratic organization of the schools, which he sees as the downfall of the public-school system. His brains and the influence his ideas have had with governors and legislators made him a central actor in four of the five education reforms described above. In their book, *Transforming Public Policy: Dynamics of Policy Entrepreneurship and Innovation*, Nancy Roberts and Paula King use education policy change in Minnesota as the defining example of policy entrepreneurship by persons outside government.

George Latimer has served both as mayor of St. Paul and president of the Citizens League, the latter during a time when the league is extending its reach beyond public policy to ask what will be necessary to guarantee a vibrant private economy in the future. Paul Ellwood and Walter McLure invented and constructed the theory behind health maintenance organizations. Joe Graba, Dan Loritz, and John Cairns have served in government but have had perhaps as much influence in later years contributing their thinking to the design of policy.

Typically the state's policy entrepreneurs have concentrated on devising new policy, not organizing political support, and most have done so without strong affiliations with political parties or ideologically based groups. In recent years Mitchell Pearlstein has become one of the state's most influential individuals by forming an aggressively conservative think tank and linking it with entities that do political organizing and lobbying. Pearlstein is uncommonly able, but the kind of work he does is similar to that done by many others across the country. Similarly, as in other places in America, the state is still served by many able politicians. Outstanding legislators of recent years include, in the Senate, Roger Moe and Gene Merriam; in the House, Ann Wynia and Dave Bishop; and in Congress, Tim Penny and Vin Weber. And, of course, interest groups ordinarily have preponderant influence on policy. But the archetype of Minnesota's distinctive contribution to policy-making is Kolderie—intelligent, knowledgeable, inventive, persistent, unaligned with political organizations— a seeker of the public interest and a designer of policy. In Minnesota, individuals with ideas, but without organizational heft behind them, can still have influence because of the habit of discourse in the state.

Which Policies Work?

Policy entrepreneurs occupy a niche between academicians and politicians. They attempt to design policies that work by systematically fostering behavior that brings about the desired public purpose. Before developing this point it is helpful to dwell for a moment on the kinds of research conducted in academia and the ways in which politicians go about their work.

The dominant research project in the social sciences is the attempt to explain the formation and operation of human institutions, the practices and rules that influence human behavior. The goal is to create a system of equations in which both institutional change and individual behavior are fully predicted. If such a project were ever successful, it would mean that there is no room for individual human agency, no place for independent behavior by people. Humans could understand but not influence their institutions of governance. So the great bulk of academic research in this field is not suited to help individuals who wish to bring about change. There is a strain of evaluative policy research that is more relevant, but most of it consists of analyses and evaluations seeking to determine what practices would be efficacious if implemented; for example, what school curriculum or road surface or medical treatment would, if tried, succeed. At first blush that would seem to be the most needed form of research. However, the governance problem is not to determine what works. The governance problem is to get people to do what works, somehow to orient free people to accomplish not only their private objectives but public purposes as well. So, much academic research is not directly relevant to persons wishing to change public policy.

Politicians also change policy, of course, but typically they do so by bringing about compromise. Compromise is essential and proper. It can be sufficient when it is merely a matter of dividing funds among different groups. But when the question is not who gets what, but what they will do with the money—when there is an expectation that a service will be produced—compromise can be unhelpful. Competing interests (for example, teachers' unions, agricultural organizations, or environmental groups) come forward to demand their portion. If the recipients of the funds are satisfied with the share a compromise allocates to them, politicians might not be inclined to look further. I once chaired Minnesota's Legislative Audit Commission, which is composed of senior representatives and senators. The commission oversees the legislature's very accomplished group of policy analysts whose task it is to evaluate state programs designated by the commission. On one occasion, upon hearing that the staff had produced a report critical of the implementation of a program, a representative said, "What the _____ are they doing? They work for us, right? Then what the____ are they doing trashing a good DFL program?" Legislators have more on their plate than seeing to it that government programs are operated well. Thus, whether there is a correspondence between spending and results is rarely the preoccupation of legislators.

The recognition that policy-making should be understood not as allocating budgets but as designing arrangements that accomplish public purposes came only slowly to Minnesota, but it did happen here before catching on elsewhere in America. After the Minnesota Miracle had operated for a few years, property taxes started to rise again. Since the state government was reimbursing individual property taxpayers for the taxes they were paying to cities and school districts, those local governments were pushing up their taxes. In some cases local authorities explicitly told taxpayers that they need not mind tax increases because much of the increase would be picked up by state government. And all governors (until the present) came to see that merely allocating funds did not guarantee results. They were supposed to be proud of the Minnesota Miracle. It had put a lot of money into the schools and had accomplished some equalization of spending between rich and poor districts. But they also noticed those rising property taxes, and they saw that students were not doing appreciably better.

A 1980 Citizens League report provided a way of understanding what was happening and laid out a broad agenda for reforming government. "The essential function of government," the report said, "is *deciding.*"[21] Not allocating money, not operating programs, but deciding. Central to that function is the arrangement of incentives so that individuals, while meeting their own objectives, accomplish public purposes as well. The report contrasted that idea with the view, long dominant in the United States, that if government concludes that something should be done, then government itself should undertake to do it. (Unspoken and unexamined is the assumption that benevolent government can be expected to accomplish its intended public purposes.) By the thinking of the 1980 Citizens League report, the Minnesota Miracle's allocation of money to local governments and schools was flawed because the incentives it created effectively undermined its effectiveness by pushing up property taxes. Also, the education of children might or might not require monopoly government schools; the issue is not whether government funds and operates the service but whether children learn. Similarly, in another area of government policy, regulation of businesses might be better accomplished by using financial incentives rather than government monitoring to make it in the interest of a company not to gouge customers or pollute the environment. The major recent change in the policy thinking of Minnesotans is the growing acceptance of the idea that policy is not self-implementing but depends on institutionalizing incentives to carry it out. Policy that relies on increasing appropriations or wishful thinking or the spontaneous goodwill of government employees or the exhortations of politicians can be expected to fail. To make the case that a policy should be tried is to put forward a plausible theory that if the policy action is taken, then people will be inclined (by systematic reward or penalty or inspiration) to behave in ways that achieve public good.

Conclusion

Governor Ventura's election is something of a diversion from the direction just described. He has an interesting, not to say undeveloped, understanding of how government can achieve its purposes. When asked during the campaign how he would bring the legislature around on issues, he flexed his muscles. When as governor he signed a bill giving a large budget increase to the schools, he pulled himself to his full height, pushed out his chest, jabbed an index finger outward, and declared that now if the schools did not do a better job, "they'll have to deal with me."

The populace finds this wildly entertaining. A July 1999 poll bestowed on Ventura a higher approval rating than that achieved by any other Minnesota governor whose popularity was investigated in this way.[22] For many Minnesotans he appears to be something of a surrogate complainer about the state of government and the complexity of the world. He talks back for them (it is no accident that before the election he was a radio talk-show host). To him, politicians who decline to vote to put on the ballot his constitutional amendment that would eliminate one house of the legislature are "gutless cowards." He repeatedly declares that he does not and will not meet with lobbyists. His message is clear and popular even though not explicitly articulated: The legislature is a nuisance. He has a direct link with the people. They are smart enough to know what is good for them and do not need either politicians or lobbyists to mediate for them.

Much about contemporary life bolsters his position. Corruption, incompetence, and inefficiency have hardly been foreign to government. A citizenry more highly educated and knowledgeable than in the past deserves to be treated accordingly. The nastiness of popular culture fosters a perception that persons in positions of authority are incompetent. Modern technology permits easier communication of views. Finally, there is the age-old American mistrust of government. And so it is possible that Ventura is a harbinger. Perhaps the future of politics holds more celebrities and amateurs, and the future of government includes less representation, more direct democracy.

Do not bet on it, though. Ventura has not yet been tested. The main achievement of his first year and a half in office has been to return to taxpayers a surplus that had accrued because of a booming economy and the frugality of his predecessor. The argument for representative government is not that people are stupid but that they are selfish. Representation is part of the American complex of checks and balances—a system that George Washington compared to the saucer into which one pours tea for cooling. Some day citizens and politicians in Minnesota will notice that the serious challenges—slums, inadequate education, a fragile environment, despair on the farms, and many more—remain. Then they will have to ask themselves once again how best to confront the fact that people usually do not achieve public purposes spontaneously. I am betting on a revival of civic life that, while accommodating flash in public leaders, relies on serious public discourse.

Notes

1. I do not refer directly to my own role in the events described here, but I did participate in many of them, as a legislator for twelve years, an official adviser to Governors Wendell Anderson and Arne Carlson, an unofficial adviser to Governors Al Quie and Rudy Perpich, a columnist for the Minneapolis *Star Tribune,* and an active member of the Citizens League. I will only briefly summarize the operation of the state government and the political history of Minnesota. Several fine book-length treatments of the subjects exist. See especially Richard M. Valelly, *Radicalism in the States: The Minnesota Farmer-Labor Party and the American Political Economy* (Chicago: University of Chicago Press, 1989); G. Theodore Mitau, *Politics in Minnesota* (Minneapolis: University of Minnesota Press, 1970); Royce Hanson, *Tribune of the People: The Minnesota Legislature and Its Leadership* (Minneapolis: University of Minnesota Press, 1989); and Daniel J. Elazar, Virginia Gray, and Wyman Spano, *Minnesota Politics and Government* (Lincoln: University of Nebraska Press, 1999).

2. Valelly, *Radicalism in the States,* 49.

3. Mitau, *Politics in Minnesota,* 15.

4. General Fund: Historical Expenditures, Minnesota Department of Finance, <http://www.finance.state.mn.us/sbs/pdf/HISTEXP2.pdf>; *Fiscal Facts for Minnesotans: The Green Book* (St. Paul: Minnesota Taxpayers Association, 1967), 2; and *Faces of the Future* (St. Paul: Minnesota Planning, State Demographic Center, May 1998), 4.

5. Elazar, Gray, and Spano, *Minnesota Politics and Government,* 122. On page xxix, Spano is credited with authorship of the chapter in which the quoted passage appears.

6. Hanson, *Tribune of the People,* 103.

7. Elazar, Gray, and Spano, *Minnesota Politics and Government,* 124.

8. Allen Odden, "Linkages Among School Reform, School Organization and School Finance," Finance Center of the Consortium for Policy Research in Education, University of Southern California, Los Angeles, 19 February 1993.

9. Even at the time of the birth of the Minnesota Miracle one can find hints of the later rejection of it. As governor, Wendell Anderson supported education choice. An education tax credit was passed into law in 1971. It was declared unconstitutional in 1974 by the Minnesota Supreme Court (*Minnesota Civil Liberties Union* v. *State of Minnesota*) because its benefits were limited to those attending private schools. Later the U.S. Supreme Court (*Mueller* v. *Allen* [1983]) let stand a Minnesota tax deduction for education expenses because, after having been modified, it applied to public as well as private school expenses.

10. Gregory C. Knopff, ed., "A Fiscal Review of the 1999 Legislative Session," Office of Senate Counsel and Research, Minnesota State Senate, St. Paul, Minn., December 1999, 72.

11. Chief Justice A. M. Keith made the decision that permitted Carlson's name to appear on the general election ballot as the Republican candidate. (Perpich was the Democratic candidate.) The elegant and charismatic Keith is the only person in the

state's history to be elected to all three branches of government. After serving as state senator and lieutenant governor (and after a spectacular but unsuccessful attempt while in the latter office to run against the incumbent governor), he practiced law for many years before being appointed to the Supreme Court by his good friend Rudy Perpich. Following Keith's ruling, Perpich shunned him ever after.

12. A charter school is one operated by an entity other than a school district. It negotiates a charter or contract with a district—or with the state government or other state-authorized entity—to educate students. The charter typically lays out conditions, e.g., levels of student achievement, that must be attained in order for the school to continue operation. The charter school receives public funds but is permitted to operate without some of the regulations governing ordinary public schools. Charter-school proponents note that they are a form of public school; they receive their charter from a government, or governmentally designated, entity, cannot engage in religious schooling, and must admit anyone who applies.

13. Walter Bagehot, *Physics and Politics* (Westford, Conn.: Greenwood Press, 1973), 145, 146.

14. Gaillard Hunt, ed., *The Writings of James Madison*, vol. 5 (New York: G. P. Putnam's Sons, 1904), 223.

15. Citizens League, "A Metropolitan Council for the Twin Cities Area," Minneapolis, Minn., 9 February 1967, 3.

16. Citizens League, "Breaking the Tyranny of the Local Property Tax," Minneapolis, Minn., 20 March 1969, 2.

17. Citizens League, "New Formulas for Revenue Sharing in Minnesota," Minneapolis, Minn., 1 September 1970, 4.

18. Citizens League, "Rebuilding Education to Make it Work," Minneapolis, Minn., 4 May 1982, 33.

19. Citizens League, "Chartered Schools = Choices for Educators + Quality for All Students," Minneapolis, Minn., 17 November 1988, i.

20. Citizens League, "Remaking the Minnesota Miracle: Facing New Fiscal Realities," Minneapolis, Minn., 8 October 1990, 4.

21. Citizens League, "Issues of the '80s: Enlarging Our Capacity to Adapt," Minneapolis, Minn., 27 August 1980, vi.

22. Robert Whereatt, "Minnesota Poll: Ventura's Job Approval Drops, But Only Slightly, in New Poll," *Star Tribune*, 2 March 2000, <http://www.startribune.com>.

The Irresistible Force Meets the Immovable Object: Minnesota's Moralistic Political Culture Confronts Jesse Ventura

WHAT MAKES MINNESOTA TICK, politically speaking? In the late 1980s one of the major political parties dumped its gubernatorial nominee because he (allegedly) swam nude with teenage girls eleven years earlier. The charge was never conclusively proven, and there was no suggestion that any physical contact had taken place. But the very thought of such impropriety drove the leading gubernatorial candidate from the stage.

In 1993 there were two major legislative scandals. A group of solons accepted the hospitality of the city of Duluth and attended, many with their families, an annual winter weekend in that port city. In addition, the Speaker of the House played golf in San Diego on the day before the opening there of the annual convention of the National Conference of State Legislators. In spite of Duluth's mean January temperature of 2.2 degrees—very mean indeed—the 1993 trip led quickly to a total ban on lobbyists or interest groups providing anything of value to legislators. As for the Speaker, after her golf game she returned to Minnesota where she quickly resigned her post—protesting (to no avail) that she had not missed any meetings because the NCSL conference had not formally started.

Minnesotans actually believe that what happened at a private party eleven years earlier is a relevant criterion for evaluating a gubernatorial candidate. They actually believe that going to Duluth in the middle of January is a legislative junket, not a punishment. (One must like ice fishing, snowmobiling, or skiing to understand this.) And they really believe that golfing is improper when accomplished on the same trip as a serious legislative conference.

Indeed, Minnesota's politics is set apart in many ways. Democrats are

VIRGINIA GRAY, *formerly professor of political science at the University of Minnesota, is Robert Watson Winston Distinguished Professor of Political Science at the University of North Carolina at Chapel Hill.* WYMAN SPANO *is a partner in Spano & Janacek, and publisher and co-editor of* Politics in Minnesota.

known as the Democratic-Farmer-Labor Party, and Republicans used to be called the Independent-Republican Party. The Reform Party of Minnesota, an outgrowth of Ross Perot's 1992 and 1996 presidential campaigns, continues to exist in Minnesota but in diminished form; Governor Jesse Ventura and most of the party's members left the national party in early 2000 and adopted the name "Independence Party." These things do not happen in other states. And, from a different perspective, no state scores as consistently high as Minnesota on so many policy and innovation rankings.[1] No other state scores as well, either, on measures of desirable social outcomes, like low crime and incarceration rates and high comparative education test scores.

The Moralistic Political Culture

Part of the explanation for Minnesota's uniqueness lies in its political culture. The notion of political culture was advanced by Daniel Elazar in his 1966 work *American Federalism: A View from the States*, a work recently recognized for its lasting contribution to the study of federalism.[2] Elazar theorized that the United States shared a general political culture that is a synthesis of three major subcultures: the individualistic, the moralistic, and the traditionalistic. The values of each subculture were brought to this country by the early settlers and spread unevenly across the country as various ethnic and religious groups moved westward. These migration streams deposited their political values much as the Ice Age shaped the land's geology. Today's political differences can be traced back to the political values and perspectives of the earliest settlers.

In Elazar's schema, the moralistic subculture emphasizes the commonwealth. In this view, the role of government is to advance the common good or the public interest. Thus, government is a positive force in the lives of citizens. Politics revolves around issues, and politicians run for office on the basis of issues. Corruption is not tolerated because government service is seen as public service, not as business. The administrative bureaucracy is viewed favorably and as a means to achieving the public good. Politics is a matter of concern to all citizens; it is therefore a citizen's duty to participate in elections.

The moralistic view was brought to the New World by the Puritans; their Yankee descendants transported these values as they moved westward across the upper Great Lakes into the Midwest and across the Northwest. In Minnesota, later waves of Scandinavians with similar values reinforced this moralism. Present-day examples of moralistic subcultures are Minnesota, Vermont, and Washington.

In distinct contrast is the individualist subculture, which emphasizes the marketplace. Government is simply another facet of the marketplace, with a necessary but very limited role. Politicians run for office out of material motivations; bureaucracy and especially the civil service are viewed negatively as a deterrent to the spoils system. Corruption in office is tolerated because politics is understood, by the citizenry, to be a dirty business in which some thievery is always going on. Political competition tends to be partisan and oriented toward gaining office. Illinois, with its long tradition of financial scandals and history of machine politics and vote fraud, provides a good example of the individualistic culture at work. Other examples are New York and Nevada.

The third subculture, the traditionalistic, is found in the South. The purpose of government under this philosophy is to maintain the existing social and economic hierarchy. One result of traditionalistic values is that a large number of southern officeholders are related to other officeholders within a state. Government is a family business, and ordinary citizens are not expected to participate in political affairs—indeed, their participation is often actively discouraged.

Contemporary migration patterns between regions may either reinforce or override the cultural base laid by the first settlers. A sudden population influx, such as has happened in Florida over the last three decades, can transform the political culture.

Elazar's theory has a great deal of intuitive appeal to many scholars of state politics; it has been tested by a variety of researchers and held up fairly well. Even those who do not subscribe to his thesis would grant that state boundaries do make a difference in citizens' values and attitudes. Today's cultural differences are not as distinct as when Elazar wrote in 1966, but nonetheless, Minnesota does stand out from other states in identifiable ways consistent with the moralistic label.

Moralism's Impact on Political Participation

We start our examination with Minnesotans' proclivity for participation. They are habitual voters, as one would expect in a moralistic state. Since mid-century, Minnesota's voter turnout has consistently been about 20 percent above the national average, usually ranking among the top five states. State law makes the act of voting easy by allowing registration at the polls, which only a few other states do. Moreover, surveys show that Minnesotans participate in a broad range of community activities at a higher rate than the national average.

The 1998 gubernatorial election showed dramatically the significance of high voter turnout and the state laws facilitating it. Minnesota's turnout was 60.4 percent, the highest nonpresidential turnout since 1982; national turnout was 36 percent. A critical factor fueling that high turnout was same-day registration: 15.7 percent of Minnesota voters registered at the polls, the highest figure since 1974, when same-day registration was first instituted in the state. This ability to mobilize new voters at the last minute greatly benefited gubernatorial candidate Jesse Ventura. His election is not such a surprise in light of the structural features facilitating it—features one would expect in a moralistic culture.

Minnesota ranks high in terms of another form of participation—joining interest groups. In 1997 it ranked fifth in the number of groups registered to lobby in the legislature (now over 1,200).[3] As in other states, the total number grows every year. Beyond this, Minnesota's lobbying community is remarkably fluid, with new organizations constantly being created and old ones dying or temporarily disappearing.

While organized interests enjoy strength of numbers, national rankings show the overall influence of Minnesota's interest group system as weak in its impact relative to other political actors; in fact, Minnesota ranked among the bottom four states in the strength of interest groups, according to a national survey in 1998.[4] Despite the relative lack of clout possessed by lobbyists who represent traditional groups, lobbyists working in other states often marvel at the strength, in Minnesota, of a group of lobbyists often ignored or barely tolerated in other legislatures—the "do-gooders" and the "hobbyists." The former term refers to persons who represent organizations but have few if any resources other than themselves and the purity of their ideas, while the latter refers to unpaid people representing no one other than themselves.

One reason the system of interest-group representation in Minnesota is relatively weaker arises from the state's tight regulation of lobbyists and the interests they represent. Whereas most states only began to require the registration of lobbying groups after Watergate, Minnesota has done so since the early 1960s. Minnesota law closely regulates the electoral efforts of interest groups and their associated political action committees: legislators are restricted in the proportion of total campaign dollars they can accept from PACs, lobbyists, and big donors. And in 1994, after the "Phonegate" incident (in which members of the legislature used government phones for personal business), the legislature enacted the "no cup of coffee" rule: effectively, legislators cannot accept anything of value from lobbyists. (Fittingly, this and other ethics legislation was authored by Senator John Marty, son of renowned church historian Martin Marty.) Since 1990, legislators have not been allowed to hold campaign fund-raisers during the legislative session. Corruption and the perception of corruption are taken seriously in this moralistic political culture.

Public Policy in a Moralistic Culture

Consistent with but (as we shall see presently) not necessarily coincident with the moralistic label, Minnesota is the epitome of a high-tax and high-spending state. It is a high-tax state in part because it is relatively affluent (although its tax effort goes well beyond that predicted by its wealth), and in part because its citizens believe in public services. In a 1995 survey, 75 percent of respondents said that they got their money's worth from their state and local taxes.[5] Unsurprisingly, when a state raises a lot of tax revenue, it spends a lot too; usually Minnesota ranks among the top ten states on general expenditures. Government is thought to be a positive instrument working for the common good.

What does Minnesota spend its money on? The state has been innovative in a number of areas. It was the first to ban smoking in restaurants, the first to allow schoolchildren choice among public schools, and the first to enact pay equity based on comparable worth for male and female state employees. The state was a leader in the reform of criminal-sentencing guidelines in the 1970s; in implementing welfare-to-work and waste-recycling programs in the 1980s; and in guaranteeing health care, fostering charter schools, and suing tobacco companies in the 1990s. State bureaucracy embraced innovative management principles before the now hackneyed "Total Quality Management" had spread beyond business-school classrooms; it tried enterprise government before "reinventing government" was invented. The state has gone further, faster, toward providing health insurance for all citizens, surpassing all states except Hawaii.

In an analysis of Minnesota's record of policy innovation, several features exemplify the moralistic influence. One is the prevailing view among public officials that "pretty good" is not good enough. For example, in 1991 Minnesota's health-care system was in good shape by national standards, but as Senator Linda Berglin observed, "being a little better than the mess in the rest of the country isn't good enough."[6] Lawmakers went on to establish MinnesotaCare, a subsidized health-insurance program serving over 100,000 low-income citizens. Passage of the bill involved a bipartisan effort in which the Republican governor and the DFL speaker both went on the House floor to round up votes.

The view that "pretty good is not good enough" extends to the structure of government itself. Minnesotans love to tinker with government, or at least talk

188 VIRGINIA GRAY & WYMAN SPANO

about it. In the mid-1980s there was a serious effort to reduce the size of the legislature (the Minnesota Senate is the nation's largest, at sixty-seven members). This reform was defeated, but out of it grew a sustained effort to transform the two-house legislature into one house. The argument that "only one state has ever done this; it must not be a good idea" did not pass muster in the policy debate, which has continued for fifteen years.

A second feature of the policy process is that Minnesota has an unusual number of policy entrepreneurs, including private individuals, public-affairs organizations, think tanks (such as the Citizens League), and public officials. For example, open enrollment (letting students pick the public schools they wish to attend) was the brainchild of a group of nine individuals, mostly outside of government and education, who caucused frequently to discuss their ideas of reform. No one in Minnesota thought it odd that nine people with no particular constituency and no ax to grind other than making a better education system contributed the most important ideas to the education policy debate. Public policy is everybody's business.

How the Moralistic Culture Shapes the Electoral System

Minnesota's system for finding, nominating, and electing candidates for various state offices is a triumph of the moralistic culture. The state's elections stand out from those in all other states in that Minnesota's are less influenced by special interest money. In Minnesota, in 1982, 85 percent of the money spent on state-level political campaigns came from nonpublic sources. By 1996, private contributions as a percentage of overall spending on campaigns for state office had fallen to 39 percent. Said another way, Minnesota taxpayers pay nearly two-thirds of the cost of the state's election campaigns.[7]

Like many states and the national government, Minnesota began campaign finance reform with taxpayer checkoffs. Unlike others, however, Minnesota went to alternative revenue sources when checkoff participation dropped. In 1977 Minnesota reached its zenith on checkoffs, when 27 percent of the taxpayers used the system. By 1998 that participation rate had fallen to 9 percent—a harbinger of antipathy toward the major parties.

A 1992 innovation, still unique to Minnesota, allowed for a $50 single taxpayer ($100 joint taxpayer) rebate for political contributions to state-level candidates. The idea, of course, was to reward small contributors and to entice them to participate in politics.

All of this "public" money (we include the rebated money as public) exists inside a campaign-financing scheme that has effectively provided an answer to the question bedeviling candidates everywhere: how much is enough? Candidates for state office in Minnesota face a spending limit, an amount that grows larger each election with inflation and that, most activists agree, is large enough to win a contested race. The rare candidate who decides not to remain within the spending limits is punished by not receiving public funds, while his or her opponent—assuming the opponent had agreed to abide by the limits at the start of the campaign—not only receives public funds but is released from having to abide by the limits. The net effect of this system is, quite simply, that for state-office candidates in Minnesota, money does not matter much. Legislative candidates, even candidates for statewide office, are rarely evaluated on the basis of their ability to raise money. Any candidate in a remotely competitive district can usually raise enough to get close to the spending limits. Elections simply have not been decided by money.

If money has not mattered, what has mattered? Political parties have mattered significantly in elections. Minnesota is one of eleven states in which political parties endorse candidates prior to the state's primary election. Minnesota is also one of only four states where that preprimary endorsement is entirely unofficial—in other words, the party's stand on a particular candidate has no impact on whether or not that candidate gets on the primary ballot, nor does the ballot reflect in any way which candidate received the party's blessing. Despite this unofficial status, party endorsement has been aggressively sought by candidates.

The party endorsement process in Minnesota begins in a way not surprising in a moralistic state. Each party holds precinct caucuses, open meetings all over the state where those willing to say they belong to the party elect their leaders and representatives to conventions at which candidates will be endorsed. How many people participate in these caucuses has been a subject of great controversy over the years. Anecdotal evidence tends to reinforce the claims of longtime party regulars that there were large crowds during the 1960s and 1970s, with considerably more than 100,000 people involved statewide. The authors found that in 1996, approximately 61,000 people attended the DFL and Republican caucuses in Minnesota. In 2000 the Republican Party had about 25,000 precinct caucus attendees; the DFL Party, using a new weekend caucus system which proved to be unpopular, only 11,000.[8] The declining numbers of precinct caucus attendees provided ammunition to the growing group of Minnesotans who asserted that the party endorsement system had lost its credibility.

The "success" of preprimary endorsements (i.e., when the party's endorsed candidate survives the primary and is the party's eventual candidate in the general election) has fluctuated significantly in recent times, particularly endorsements for governor. Of the ten candidates endorsed by the major parties in the five gubernatorial elections from 1960 through 1978, only one failed to win the primary election, and all five governors elected during this time had been endorsed by their party. From 1982 through 1998, however, the picture was quite different. In those five elections, only five of the ten endorsed gubernatorial candidates made it to the general election—and only two of those five actually became governor.

Preprimary endorsements work much better at the legislative level, however. More than 95 percent of Minnesota's current legislators have been endorsed by either the Republican or DFL Party. This seeming contradiction between statewide and legislative district endorsement can perhaps best be explained by the reality that volunteers are still important, even decisive, in local contests, while statewide races are staffed almost exclusively by paid personnel.

One of the hallmarks of Elazar's moralistic culture is the apparent tendency for the electorate to punish those engaged in political activity when it appears their motivation has ceased to center on the good of the whole commonwealth and instead becomes focused on the interests of the individual officeholder or party. From the public's perspective, by the early 1990s both of Minnesota's major political parties had crossed over the line. There was nearly universal agreement that the parties had become too extreme, and that candidates seeking party endorsement were forced into long reaches to the left (or right) in order to attract support from the increasingly extreme activists. In 1994, for example, both parties endorsed gubernatorial candidates who simply could not win against any sort of reasonable alternative.

In 1998, the parties continued to besmirch their increasingly troubled reputations. The Republican Party endorsed a candidate, Norm Coleman, mayor of St. Paul, who had switched parties less than a year earlier. In the DFL, on the other hand, the party's endorsed candidate, Hennepin County Attorney Mike Freeman, was defeated in the primary election by Attorney General Hubert H. Humphrey III. Another primary-election candidate was Ted Mondale, a former state senator. The three came to be known as the "my three sons" candidates, in honor of their famous fathers—former Governor and Secretary of Agriculture Orville Freeman, and Hubert Humphrey and Walter Mondale, both of whom had served as U.S. senator and vice president. The presence of these three candidates in a single election imparted to the DFL Party an aura of family careerism that seemed further to rankle Minnesotans' moralistic tendencies.

Moralism at the Local Level

Elazar's political-culture theory makes clear that having a moralistic political culture—with politics focused on the common good, and not on the individual politician's or party's benefit—is not synonymous with a liberal politics; it simply means that whatever is done has to be done for the benefit of all. Utah, for example, is a state whose generally moralistic culture is almost as widespread as Minnesota's, yet which is recognized as politically conservative. For reasons probably relating to weather and settlement patterns, however, Minnesota does have a long tradition of governmental activism, particularly at the local level. When combined with the moralistic culture's emphasis on the common good, Minnesota's local governments are almost communitarian in their orientation.

The scope of Minnesota's local government activism is astounding, especially to persons involved in local government in other states, where activity levels are considerably lower. Tucked in the northeast corner of the state, Minnesota's smallest county, with 4,100 residents, owns and manages a combined hospital and nursing home. The reason, of course, is simply that no private entity was willing or financially able to establish such a facility, and the county board thought it was necessary. In the opposite (southwest) corner of the state, the city of Worthington reports to Minnesota's state auditor eleven different publicly owned enterprises, including a city-owned hospital and nursing home, a liquor store, a golf course, an auditorium, a municipally owned electric power company, and an airport. Perusal of the state auditor's reports on cities unearths ninety-two with "cultural and recreational" enterprises—swimming pools, boat docks, ice rinks, community centers, and so forth.[9]

Nor is this local-government responsiveness and activism limited to nonmetro areas or years gone by. The metropolitan counties participate in a massive regional park system that, combined with the city and state park systems, makes the Twin Cities enormously attractive to families who enjoy outdoor recreation. Both Minneapolis and St. Paul have very active neighborhood organizations—reputedly the most active in the United States—with real power to influence issues like development, housing availability, and the like. Many of the suburban communities have city recreational or government/community centers that see such widespread patterns of use that their role in real community-building cannot be doubted. One suburban city manager told one of the authors that 60 percent of the citizens of his city over sixty-five years of age were in the beautiful civic center at least once a month, participating in senior programs.[10] The city's web site lists forty-three weekly or biweekly activities for seniors, from balloon volleyball to yoga.

All of this community-building behavior is, of course, expensive. Minnesota began equalizing its school spending in 1971, becoming one of the few states to accomplish that task without court-ordered help. Through the 1970s and 1980s Minnesota also moved toward equalization of other local-government expenditures. Eventually, the proposition came to be accepted in significant portions of the state's political mainstream that "fairness" was to be defined as meaning that students and citizens throughout Minnesota had the right to expect the highest quality, active educational and general governmental services, regardless of the wealth of the local community.

Minnesotans from both political parties tend to agree with the egalitarian thrust of that statement as it pertains to education. The equalization of other local-government services has been much more controversial, however. Despite the controversy, the state has paid an ever-growing share of local government expenses in Minnesota. In small cities (those under 2,500 people) the state provides an average of 32 percent of the budget, while only 26 percent comes from taxes. (The remainder comes from municipal fees, city-owned enterprise income, and so forth.) In large cities, the state provides, on average, 25 percent of the budget, while taxes make up 38 percent.[11] The result: Minnesota ranks fourth in the nation in per-capita local-government total expenditures, while ranking twenty-third in per-capita local-government tax revenue.[12]

Looking to the state for improving the quality of life in Minnesota is not limited to local-government operating expenditures. Minnesota ranks third among the states in per-capita legislative appropriations to state art agencies. At $2.76 per person, the Minnesota contribution is more than twice the $1.30 national average.[13] And the state legislature has increasingly participated in providing local governments and nonprofit organizations with capital funds. The largest portion of the funds from the biennial bonding (or capital budget) bill in Minnesota has always been dedicated to the construction and maintenance of state-owned buildings, but the number and variety of non-state-owned capital projects has grown exponentially.

An example of state/local activism funded through capital expenditures is the Mighty Ducks Ice Arena Grant Program, coordinated by the Minnesota Amateur Sports Commission. (The moniker "Mighty Ducks" came from a movie of the same name, about youth hockey, which was filmed in Minnesota.) Since the program's first year, in 1995, the state has provided more than $17 million, mostly in capital grants, to sixty-one ice arenas throughout the state. The $17 million was matched by $123 million in local government and/or private dollars. According to the Minnesota Amateur Sports Commission web site, there are approximately 11.4 million visits to the sixty-one arenas annually.

How Governor Ventura Differs from the Moralistic Culture

When the 1998 Minnesota gubernatorial campaign arrived at its surprising conclusion, it appeared that Minnesota had chosen as its governor someone who would challenge, perhaps dismantle, the state's political culture. Certainly the campaign itself, and what was known about Jesse Ventura, the victor, made such an upheaval entirely plausible. As a candidate, Ventura was a stylistic contrast to past generations of Minnesota political leaders; in that sense he seemed clearly outside the moralistic culture. It was somewhat less evident, however, whether he challenged the substance of that culture.

Certainly one aspect of Minnesota style that Ventura challenged, and that figured prominently in the campaign, had to do with the long-held tenet in Minnesota politics that candidates had to appear to be serious about and knowledgeable concerning what government had done and should (and should not) do to address people's concerns. The presumed necessity of this appearance of knowledge was probably the result of a combination of moralism and the generally conservative, staid demeanor of previous Minnesota public figures. True to this pattern, in the early part of the 1998 campaign one of the DFL primary candidates, Ted Mondale, put out a lengthy hardcover book detailing his policy proposals. Mondale's was a classic Minnesota-culture gesture. Candidates were supposed to be specific about what they believed, and specific about what their opponents had done that they did not like.

Jesse Ventura did not have a book about his policy proposals, nor was his web site filled with policy-wonkish detail. During the series of debates between Ventura and the two major-party gubernatorial hopefuls who had made it to the general election—St. Paul Mayor Norm Coleman and Attorney General Hubert H. (Skip) Humphrey III—Coleman and Humphrey would argue over a policy or program, to be followed by Ventura admitting he did not know the details. Political professionals thought the tactic fatal for Ventura. Minnesotans, it was presumed, liked politicians who knew what they were doing. But as the nine debates wore on, it became clear that Ventura had found a perfect tactic to highlight his status as a nonprofessional in the political world. Ventura managed to make the possession of knowledge about government into a negative for his opponents, especially since they constantly disagreed over whatever policy or program they were discussing.

Jesse Ventura won the governorship on November 3, 1998, with 37 percent of the vote. Republican Norm Coleman had 34 percent and Democrat Skip Humphrey 29 percent. A delightful short analysis of the election, *We Shocked the World! A Case Study of Jesse Ventura's Election As Governor of Minnesota*, by

St. Cloud State University professors Stephen Frank and Steven Wagner, reveals that Ventura won by using the features of Minnesota's moralistic culture to his advantage. We mentioned previously the fact that 15.7 percent of the voters registered to vote on election day; Ventura won 75 percent of those first-time and long-absent voters.[14] Without same-day registration, Ventura would have come in third. But, obviously, same-day registrants were not all of the Ventura story.

From the authors' perspective, Ventura's victory grew out of his brilliant campaign that, essentially, allowed the public to vote against political parties and politicians in general. Ventura's message was effectively delivered in thousands of ways, and the overall thrust of the message was quite clear: "I'm not one of them." Political analysts who offered public predictions about the campaign (including one of the authors of this essay) missed predicting Ventura's victory because they missed the most salient fact of the campaign, namely, that the election had little to do with the candidates' stands on various issues. Frank and Wagner's analysis of an election-day poll conducted under their supervision shows that Ventura had substantial leads over Humphrey and Coleman when the answer to the question "Why did you vote for the candidate you voted for?" had anything to do with the candidate's character, personality, or personal characteristics. But when people offered policy reasons for voting for a candidate—such as a position on education, abortion, crime, or the budget surplus—Ventura received almost no votes. For Ventura voters, the issues simply did not matter.[15]

What was known about Ventura's stand on issues when the campaign ended was slight, but there were some issues he addressed that had also been addressed by the other two candidates, including:

· support for returning the entire budget surplus to taxpayers;
· support for gay rights;
· opposition to laws restricting birth control and abortion;
· opposition to gun control, but support for training requirements
    and waiting periods;
· opposition to Minnesota's high per-vehicle charges for license plates;
· opposition to high taxes on lake cabins;
· opposition to Minnesota's fee on personal water craft;
· advocacy for a unicameral legislature;
· ambiguous support for the legalization of prostitution;
· support for the legalization of marijuana for medicinal use and
    for the growing of industrial hemp.

Ventura was perceived to oppose higher-education student aid because of his oft-repeated comment to students: "if you're smart enough to go to college, you're smart enough to figure out how to pay for it." At the same time, however, he did not specifically say that he was opposed to such aid. He was also perceived as being opposed to state payment for child care, since he often denigrated state involvement in the activity and spoke instead about the need to get grandmothers or friends to do child care. Again, however, he was not specifically quoted as saying such aid should be terminated.

In the campaign, then, Ventura challenged the moralistic culture stylistically. He left many signs that he would also do so substantively. What has happened since the election? Will Ventura redo Minnesota's political culture, or is he conforming to its basic precepts?

By any standard, Jesse Ventura's governing style is unique and unprecedented in Minnesota's political culture. In his previous careers he was a pro-wrestling "bad boy" and a radio "shock jock." In other words, he was an entertainer who earned his living insulting others, either physically or verbally. He knows how to incite a crowd and bring it to its feet; he knows how to intimidate opponents over the airwaves with verbal insults. His whole performance is so testosterone-driven that it is hard to imagine he is now in the same profession as Michael Dukakis and Jimmy Carter. His prior history carries over into his conduct in the state's highest office.

Minnesota is a state where professional comedians have learned that humor must be politically correct; jokes about ethnic groups or any marginalized group are not thought to be funny. Governor Ventura has ignored that cultural norm; in fact, he seems to go out of his way to attack other political actors. He has called legislators "gutless cowards"; called one Christian Coalition lobbyist a "fat load"; and termed local-government officials from nonmetro areas "stupid" and "thick as a brick."

The governor's syntax has not always been so colorful, but it could rarely be considered Minnesota-sensitive. Near the end of his first year in office, the governor was the keynote speaker at a conference of government policy analysts; instead of praising them for their legitimate accomplishments (arguably, they've done the best job in the nation), he used the occasion to blast them. They should get off their duffs, be innovative—but not spend any money, he said. Press relations follow much the same pattern. If the governor is irritated by reporters, he sometimes simply refuses to hold press conferences or give interviews; if he is asked a question that he does not want to answer, he sometimes ends the interview abruptly and stalks out angrily.

But perhaps even further outside the norms of the moralistic culture is the governor's penchant for insulting ordinary citizens, much of which he did in a *Playboy* interview in November of 1999 but also on various national TV talk shows and on his weekly radio call-in show, *Lunch with the Governor*. To list a few, he has insulted the Irish (they were so drunk they laid out crooked streets in St. Paul), callers on his radio show (one person was termed a "puke," another was called ignorant), fat people (they have no willpower), single mothers (they should have thought about how to raise the child before they hopped into bed), women (sexual harassment is not a big deal; he wants to be reincarnated as a 38DD bra), religious adherents (organized religion is a crutch for weak-minded people), and most cruelly, suicide victims (also weak-minded people whom he doesn't respect). There was substantial public backlash against his insults, especially on behalf of suicide victims, churchgoers, and women. But the governor just said he was being honest—which some people said they found refreshing.[16]

In addition to his running attacks on various groups, the governor's style of dress, demeanor, and behavior have challenged the mores of the moralistic culture. His inauguration party was a clue to what was to come: he held an informal party at the Target Center sports arena, rode in on a Harley, mounted the stage to the screaming adulation of the crowd, wearing a fringed leather jacket, a pink feather boa, skull-and-crossbones earrings, and a "do-rag" on his head, yelling "Let's party, Minnesota"—which he then proceeded to do for hours. Not a scene that anyone would have imagined in the staid North Star State.

Lastly, the governor's relentless pursuit of private financial gain while in office has gone against the grain of Minnesota's moralism. In Minnesota, the tenet that government is for the common good meant that public officials were not permitted to profit from their public service in any way. Governor Ventura violated this precept, but in a way never before imagined. He was never accused of graft, bribery, or misuse of any public funds; nonetheless, he has "cashed in" on the governorship of Minnesota through shrewd use of his celebrity status. In the summer of 1999, for example, he appeared in the World Wrestling Federation's "SummerSlam," a pay-per-view event that featured Minnesota's governor as the referee. His well-advertised and publicized appearance earned him, it is estimated, between $1 and $3 million, although he contributed a small percentage of it to charity.[17] Despite wrestling's high ratings on cable television, many Minnesotans seemed to be shocked at the sexist, obscene, and violent nature of "SummerSlam" and at the fact that their governor was participating.

Governor Ventura has written (or, more accurately, has had ghost-written for him) a popular book about his personal history, including his sexual exploits. Entitled *I Ain't Got Time to Bleed*, the book spent thirteen weeks on the

New York Times's best-seller list. A second book, tentatively titled *I Stand Alone*, is in the works.

Ventura has been very conscious of his copyrighted persona while governor, and he has worked hard to keep his name in the public eye while preventing others from taking advantage of his image. He makes frequent trips out of the state to appear on late-night or Sunday morning talk shows; these interviews are light on policy substance and heavy on personal philosophy. They are, in short, designed to add to his value. Jesse action figures and T-shirts, which figured prominently in the campaign, remain popular items. The governor does not personally gain from the sale of these items; the proceeds are split between his political committee and charities he has created. Yet the lengths to which Governor Ventura's lawyers will go to protect his commercial image was demonstrated in the summer of 1999 when a Minnesota state senate committee secretary with a very small handmade-greeting-card business received a letter from Ventura's lawyers demanding she desist selling cards with the governor's caricature on them. Ventura is a rarity, nationally but especially in Minnesota: a governor who has found a way to make money, substantial money, while being head of state.

How have Minnesotans reacted to their governor's style? Ventura's job-approval rating started out at an impressive 73 percent in January of 1999. It fell to 54 percent approval after the *Playboy* interview in the fall of 1999; afterwards the governor toned down his personal remarks and focused more on public policy. By early 2000 his approval rating had rebounded to nearly 70 percent, although it fell somewhat during the 2000 legislative session.[18] Minnesotans seem to separate personal style and behavior from job performance, much the way the American people did in their reaction to the misdeeds of President Bill Clinton, whose poll numbers held up remarkably well during the impeachment crisis.

While Ventura has run roughshod over some parts of Minnesota's political culture from a stylistic perspective, in other ways he is a surprising conformer. Many have commented that Ventura's cabinet is among the best in recent memory. He was lauded editorially for finding and hiring well-qualified people who were Republicans and Democrats, and some without any previous political experience (although he was criticized for appointing few minorities). Thus, while Ventura himself campaigned with disdain for opponents who discussed the intricacies of programs and policies, he surrounded himself with high-quality policy (not political) wonks. In this way, he conformed to the Minnesota political culture; spoils and cronyism are frowned upon when governors are making the few appointments they have to make in a moralistic state. Even gubernatorial appointments are to be given to the best qualified, not to the best connected. Ventura has managed to be the ultimate outsider who uses insiders to his own advantage.

One of the most important hallmarks of a moralistic political culture is widespread civic involvement. Minnesotans are more civically active than residents of other states, and candidate Ventura benefited from that. His main policy proposal thus far, the unicameral legislature, was justified in just those terms; he argued that one house would be more accountable, open, and accessible to the people. The idea never caught on, however, and it failed to receive significant legislative support.

Part of Ventura's difficulty in convincing legislators to send a unicameral constitutional amendment to the people lies in his constant battering of the legislative branch and of various intermediary institutions, like political parties, the media, and interest groups and their lobbyists. He seems to have no conception of a role for Minnesota's parties, or for their national equivalents, except as a foil against which to organize a third party. He makes clear that organized interests are not welcome in his office, and, although some of his principal staff were once lobbyists, he refuses to meet with any lobbyists. Thus, he dismisses those vehicles by which the people have actual, democratic power and substitutes for them his own judgment of "what's best for Minnesota," his most frequent answer both during and after the campaign when asked what he would do when faced with one or another policy option.

Jesse May Have Shocked the World, But Will He Change the Culture?

Will Governor Ventura damage Minnesotans' propensity to participate in government? In the end, we think not, but he may damage Minnesota's civic openness and leave significant scars on the body politic. One of the reasons so many citizens are so active in Minnesota is that the government has been responsive to them. Governmental responsiveness works best when citizens band together in groups or political parties. It is not possible for government to respond to each individual citizen, so citizens must gather their interests into coherent groupings (what political scientists call the aggregation of interests). Governor Ventura, however, defines organized interests and the two major parties as despicable.

Ventura's distrust of political parties doesn't stop with Republicans and Democrats. He had a long-running feud with the Perot wing of the national Reform Party; eventually, in early 2000, Ventura left the national party and spearheaded the formation of the Independence Party in Minnesota. Governor

Ventura does not seem to engage in any extensive, or even minimal, party-building activity, however, and most of the state's political observers do not expect any Independence Party legislative candidates to be elected in 2000. Citizen distrust of political parties and interest groups existed before Governor Ventura was elected, of course, but the constant refrain of antiparty, antigroup themes from his bully pulpit can add significantly to that distrust.

We estimate that Governor Ventura will not, however, have a long-term impact on the role of political parties and interest groups in moralistic Minnesota. Interest groups, as noted, already had relatively little clout. The fact that this governor chooses not to deal with interest groups will not make them more powerful, at least in the short term, and it is difficult to make them less powerful. Yet it is hard to imagine that Minnesota's long-standing propensity for organizing many groups and actively petitioning its government will go away because of the governor's attitude toward them.

We also do not believe that Governor Ventura will be able significantly to diminish the key role that Minnesota's political parties play in the state's elections. As previously discussed, Minnesota's moralistic election system is based on a combination of strong political parties and substantial public financing of campaigns. Governor Ventura attacks the parties but does not concomitantly attack the widespread use of public funds. (Indeed, Ventura's campaign for governor was largely publicly financed.) Leaving public financing in place means that state-level candidate credibility cannot be purchased privately in Minnesota; it must be earned by means of a candidate's working to achieve significant name identification with the public. Name identification can be earned by previous public service, by party support, or by previous celebrity status—the route Ventura used. His path is an unusual one, however; and it is hard to imagine that a series of celebrities would seek office in Minnesota, thus obviating the need for political parties.

Neither do we believe that Governor Ventura will have a long-term impact on the public's view of Minnesota's media. Seen from a national perspective, Minnesota must be considered to enjoy one of the best situations in the country relative to media coverage of public affairs. The *St. Paul Pioneer Press*, a Knight Ridder publication, and the *Star Tribune*, based in Minneapolis and owned by the McClatchy chain, compete vigorously but decently. Both provide extensive daily public-affairs coverage. The two papers have six full-time reporters covering the legislature and often more when it is in session. The governor is not impressed, however. In April of 2000, the *Pioneer Press* won a Pulitzer Prize for uncovering a major academic-cheating scandal about the University of Minnesota's men's basketball team. When the story first appeared in March of

1999, Governor Ventura called the reporting "despicable." When told that the paper had won a Pulitzer for its efforts, Governor Ventura remarked, "That's terrific. 'Cause I heard the *National Enquirer* won it a year earlier." Despite such remarks, it is our guess that the media, especially the print media, will survive the Ventura years continuing to play an important informational role in the state's policy discussions. This is not to say that the role of print media in the Internet age will not continue to evolve; rather it is to suggest that Governor Ventura's opinion of the media will not contribute significantly to that evolution.

It is also difficult to imagine that Governor Ventura will permanently change Minnesotans' attitude toward elected officials—that is, departing from the expectation that the elected officials' sole focus will be the good of all. With his various money-making schemes, Ventura is a good example of someone from the individualistic culture, where making money is, to some extent, the point of the exercise. Ventura's problem is simply that he operates in a culture firmly moralistic in tone. In the 2000 legislative session a bill was introduced applying the same strict standards regarding outside activity now operative for most state employees specifically to the governor. The bill did not pass in 2000, but eventually it will. On this subject, the moralistic way will prevail.

In terms of governmental activism, especially at the local level, Governor Ventura does seem to be firmly committed to curtailing how much government can respond to petitioners. In his first budget Ventura lopped off all the operating funds going to nonprofit organizations, although he did relent in the end and most of the funding was restored. He similarly ignored local governments and arts groups in his first bonding-bill proposal in 2000. The governor's rhetoric around bonding makes clear that he believes it wrong for the state to participate in a "local" construction project, like an ice arena or community center building. If the governor is able to shut down the Minnesota legislature's ability to respond to petitioners of all kinds, then he may well be able to carve away at the number of people who think of the state's governmental apparatus as their own. Such a change would alter Minnesota's local government-activist bent. Yet the governor is not alone in seeking a diminution of the state's role in financing local government projects; Republicans, too, are attempting to do that. Generally, however, Republican legislators are not nearly as absolutist about a rejection of "local" projects as the governor's rhetoric indicates he is.

A difficulty in predicting Governor Ventura's impact on policy—and on the political culture—stems from his bravado; that is, it is difficult to figure out what he means from what he says, or to predict his policy position from his rhetoric. In his first State of the State message, the governor proclaimed to Minnesota's citizens that "the free ride is over" in all areas. Yet after his first legislative session was over, Ventura approved the largest student aid bill in Minnesota history. The same happened with child care. Indeed, not only did the governor approve the largest child-care bill in Minnesota history, he also approved an administrative transfer of $60 million in additional child-care money.

The difficulty in ascertaining the governor's position on specific issues was highlighted toward the end of the 2000 legislative session when an attempt was made by his staff to fashion a compromise on what came to be known as the "women's right to know" bill, a statute that would have required a twenty-four-hour waiting period and mandated that women seeking the procedure read an informational brochure prescribed by law before they could receive an abortion. Those supporting the bill thought they had an agreement with the governor's staff on the measure; he vetoed it, however, prompting the Speaker of the House to suggest that he was considering no further agreements with the governor unless those agreements were in writing. Similar problems occurred at the end of the 1999 session. Various commissioners—operating under the assumption that when the governor told them they were "in charge" they were, in fact, in charge—struck agreements with the legislature on certain spending items, only to have the governor undo their work entirely by means of the line-item veto. Commissioners themselves were surprised, and even chagrined, especially because the governor placed next to each of his vetoes a little hand-stamped pig to symbolize that he was cutting pork.

Will Jesse Ventura wean Minnesota from its activist, moralistic ways? He will change it; certainly he has already changed the state's national image. But the Minnesota culture will grind on, whether Governor Ventura approves or not. Ventura will not whip government, but he will rein it in, just as his predecessor, Arne Carlson, did before him. In the end, Minnesota will remain staunchly moralistic—and intermittently activist.

Notes

1. See, for example, Michael Mintrom, "Policy Entrepreneurs and the Diffusion of Innovation," *American Journal of Political Science* 41 (July 1997): 738–770; or Kathleen O'Leary Morgan and Scott Morgan, eds., *State Rankings, 2000: A Statistical View of the 50 United States* (Lawrence, Kans.: Morgan Quitno Press, 2000), iv, which has ranked Minnesota first on its "most livable state" index for the past four years.

2. Daniel J. Elazar, *American Federalism: A View from the States* (New York: Thomas Y. Crowell, 1966).

3. Virginia Gray and David Lowery, "The Stability and Expression of Density Dependence in State Communities of Organized Interests," paper presented at the annual meeting of the American Political Science Association, Atlanta, Ga., 2–5 September 1999, Table 1.

4. Clive Thomas and Ronald Hrebenar, "Interest Groups in the States," in *Politics*

in the American States, 7th ed., ed. Virginia Gray, Russell Hanson, and Herbert Jacob (Washington, D.C.: CQ Press, 1999), 137.

5. Cited in Daniel J. Elazar, Virginia Gray, and Wyman Spano, *Minnesota Politics and Government* (Lincoln: University of Nebraska Press, 1999), 167.

6. Robin Toner, "Health Care in Minnesota: Model for U.S. or Novelty?" *New York Times,* 9 October 1993, 9.

7. Elazar, Gray, and Spano, *Minnesota Politics and Government,* 82.

8. Dane Smith, "Low Turnout, But DFL Caucuses Work," *Star Tribune,* 13 March 2000, 3B.

9. Compiled from Office of the [Minnesota] State Auditor, *Revenues, Expenditures, and Debts of Minnesota Cities under 2,500 in Population, December 31, 1995* (St. Paul, Minn.: Office of the State Auditor, 30 June 1997); and idem, *Revenues, Expenditures, and Debts of Minnesota Cities over 2,500 in Population, December 31, 1995* (St. Paul, Minn.: Office of the State Auditor, 30 June 1997).

10. Spano interview with Jerry Splinter, city manager, City of Coon Rapids, Minnesota, 11 July 2000.

11. *Revenues, Expenditures, and Debts.*

12. Morgan and Morgan, *State Rankings,* 2000, 330, 328.

13. Ibid., 156.

14. Stephen I. Frank and Steven C. Wagner, *We Shocked the World! A Case Study of Jesse Ventura's Election as Governor of Minnesota* (Fort Worth, Tex.: Harcourt College Publishers, 1999), 29.

15. Ibid., 22.

16. These comments come from a variety of sources. Ventura's drunken Irish comment was made during a 23 February 1999 appearance on *The David Letterman Show.* The caller denounced as "puke" had called into a 24 March 2000 Ventura appearance on "Garage Logic," a daily talk show hosted by Joe Soucheray on KSTP 1500 AM. Ventura's comments about fat people, single mothers, women, organized religion, and suicide victims are drawn from his interview in *Playboy,* printed in the November and December 1999 issues. Ventura's personal assessment of his honesty is found in Robert Whereatt, Conrad deFiebre, and Dane Smith, "'My Fault is Honesty': Governor Stands by *Playboy* Interview Amid Criticism," *Star Tribune,* 1 October 1999.

17. At a press conference on 14 July 1999, Ventura announced the event and noted that his appearance fee of $100,000 would be donated to charity. Dane Smith, "Ventura Will Rule the Ring as Guest Referee," *Star Tribune,* 15 July 1999, 1. Speculation that Ventura's percentage of the revenue from the "Summer-Slam" event would amount to somewhere between $1 and $3 million was reported in a number of published sources. See, for example, Dan Barreiro, "WWF Isn't So Bad if the Price is Right," *Star Tribune,* 23 August 1999, 3C.

18. Dennis J. McGrath, "Ventura's Job Approval on Rebound," *Star Tribune,* 13 January 2000, 1.

MICHAEL O'KEEFE

Social Services:
Minnesota as Innovator

MINNESOTA HAS LONG HAD a reputation for a strong commitment to activist government and innovative social-welfare programs. State government over the years has been viewed as a positive instrument for the betterment of society, a perspective that Minnesota shares with many of the northern European countries whose sons and daughters settled this state. Minnesotans have long balanced a strong belief in personal responsibility with a recognition of the necessary role of government. The local community, individuals, and private organizations have always had a critical role to play, but so does government. In Minnesota, the public and private sectors work together and complement each other more strongly than in many other states.

These values—private responsibility combined with action for the common good through government—have had an impact on the national stage as well, through the leadership of Minnesotans like Hubert Humphrey, Eugene McCarthy, Walter Mondale, and the many fellow citizens they drew to Washington. Humphrey, elected to the U.S. Senate in 1948, was an enthusiastic old-fashioned liberal. He was concerned about injustices and inequities in society and convinced that government can be an instrument for good. He pursued his goals tirelessly through many years in Congress, as vice president to President Lyndon Johnson, and as the Democrats' presidential candidate in 1968.

Eugene McCarthy, who also had gone to Washington as a senator, was a more intellectual, almost ascetic practitioner of liberal political philosophy. In the late 1960s, he emerged as a spokesperson for those opposing the increasing involvement of the United States in the Vietnam War, challenging Johnson in the primary and sparking the president's decision not to run again. Walter Mondale, who had replaced Hubert Humphrey in the Senate in 1964, continued the tradition of liberal Minnesota leadership in that body. He became vice

MICHAEL O'KEEFE *is Commissioner of the Minnesota Department of Human Services.*

president to President Jimmy Carter and, like Humphrey, ran unsuccessfully for the presidency.

The very visible liberal views of these and other leaders have helped create a strong image of Minnesota as a liberal state, quite in keeping with the Scandinavian heritage of many of its people. The work of Minnesota policymakers at home has reinforced that perception. Over the past several decades, Minnesota has been a source of innovative social-policy thinking and experimentation. Its political leaders have tackled tough policy questions, sometimes successfully, other times less so, and are nearly always ready to ask the basic questions and challenge conventional thinking. Minnesotans are willing to try innovative policies, though cautiously, after thoughtful debate and often first as pilot programs.

One area in which Minnesota has been an innovator is welfare reform. In 1996, the U.S. Congress enacted major reforms in the federal programs that provide support to low-income families with children. Ten years before that, however, Minnesota policymakers had begun their own discussions of how to fix a welfare program that most agreed had serious shortcomings. Over the following years, the legislature created a series of programs, moving, within the constraints of federal law, toward significant reform of welfare.

In early 1992, the Minnesota legislature approved a pilot program for testing in a limited number of Minnesota counties. That program, the Minnesota Family Investment Program, was successful in moving families off welfare and toward self-sufficiency. The MFIP was the only state welfare-reform initiative that increased work among participants while at the same time raising family income and reducing poverty. The program served as one of the prototypes federal policymakers looked to as they crafted their changes in the federal Aid to Families with Dependent Children program. It was eventually expanded statewide as Minnesota's current program of support for low-income families.

Minnesota has also been a leader in health care from its earliest days. As the clinic established by the Mayo brothers in the early 1900s grew, so did Minnesota's reputation as a national—and later international—center for high-quality health care. Managed care was pioneered in the state in the 1940s. Both the concept and the name of the health-management organization originated in Minnesota. In 1988, it became the first state to subsidize a health-insurance program to cover uninsured children. And, as with welfare, this program helped shape a federal program designed to stimulate states to ensure that low-income children have access to health care.

Minnesota's investments in health care are among the highest in the nation. The vast majority of Minnesotans have health-insurance coverage, an estimated 95 percent compared with a national average of 84 percent of the population. Roughly half a million lower-income citizens of the state, close to 11 percent of the total population, have health coverage subsidized by state or federal programs. These investments have produced results. People in the state live longer, on average, than people in all other states but Hawaii—an unusual pairing of states, to be sure.

In these and other areas, Minnesota has been an innovator in social policy, testing new approaches to welfare, health care, and education. Many of these have been adapted by other states or have formed the seeds of federal legislative initiatives. Minnesota has played this role over decades, under the political leadership of both Democrats (in Minnesota, the Democratic-Farmer-Labor Party, or DFL) and Republicans.

Why has Minnesota been such a source of new ideas in social policy? Its contributions over many years suggest that the reasons go deep and are not an accident of one era or the contributions of a single extraordinary leader. A commitment to social welfare, and a willingness for the government to play a significant role in ensuring that welfare, are clearly strong elements of the culture of Minnesota. Welfare has roots in the early peoples who settled the state, nourished and maintained by subsequent generations.

The outside observer might ask, reasonably, whether Minnesota really deserves its image as the liberal innovator in social policy. Minnesota is by no means alone among states as an innovator. And a few other states, once they embrace reform, have been more daring in their innovations.

These questions will be addressed in this essay. They cannot, of course, be answered definitively, given the many factors and circumstances that have shaped the political and social culture of this, as any other, state. It is possible, however, to look more closely at the nature of Minnesota's commitment to social welfare and to speculate about those characteristics of the people and place that, coming together, created that commitment.

Innovation in Minnesota: Welfare Reform

Welfare reform is both the most far-reaching and the most recent of significant reforms in social policy in Minnesota. The federal program that defined welfare in the United States for more than half of the twentieth century began in 1937 with the creation by Congress of the Aid to Dependent Children program. This program directed financial assistance to needy families caring for children who had been deprived of the support of one or both parents because of death, abandonment, or physical or mental incapacity. Originally, only children were eligible for the program. In 1950, support was extended to the caretaker of the child as well. Thirteen years later, in 1963, as part of the federal "War on

Poverty," the program shifted its focus to families with children, becoming the Aid to Families with Dependent Children program. In 1970, unemployed fathers were made eligible for support through AFDC, and in 1979 unemployed mothers were added, creating a generous program of support for a wide range of low-income families.

With these expansions, the program became a safety net for the very poor families of this country. The various changes, however, also left the program with multiple—and sometimes conflicting—goals. For some, its purpose was to reduce poverty, for others, to reduce dependency and costs to the federal and state governments. The conflict between these goals has been the central conundrum of welfare reform. Reforms have either increased work or increased income, but seldom both.

The changes in AFDC made in the late 1970s did not resolve this conflict. In fact, even as AFDC expanded its reach, criticisms about its effects were growing as well. By the early 1980s, policymakers were increasingly concerned about the long-term dependence of some families on welfare and the lack of incentives for recipients to seek or accept employment. Stories of "welfare queens," single mothers who allegedly chose to have large families because of the increased AFDC checks that resulted, made frequent appearances in the media. The program did not encourage work, since it required a reduction in benefits by one dollar for every increase of a dollar earned by the participant beyond a fixed limit that varied by family size. When other costs of working—child care, transportation, clothing—were taken into account, a person was clearly worse off working at a low-wage job than staying on welfare.

Given Minnesota's image, one would expect that concerns about the negative social impact of the program would have pushed welfare reform onto the state's agenda. That was not the case. The benefits in Minnesota's welfare program have been consistently more generous than in most other states. That generosity has created a persistent sense among some that Minnesota is a magnet for low-income people who migrate here for welfare and health benefits.

This sense was at the heart of a conflict over welfare in the 1986 Minnesota legislature; the state's engagement with welfare reform began in earnest as a result of that dispute. Convinced that overly generous benefits were drawing low-income families to the state, the Republican-controlled House of Representatives took action to slash welfare benefits by a substantial 30 percent. The DFL-controlled Senate, on the other hand, firmly rejected the cuts. The stalemate set off a process that, over eight years, would result in Minnesota's creative approach to welfare reform.

In an attempt to get past the stalemate between the Minnesota House and Senate, then-governor Rudy Perpich created a bipartisan welfare-reform commission. The governor charged the commission with looking at welfare in Minnesota, whether it was too generous relative to other states as well as other issues. He asked the group to sort out differing views, seeking where possible common ground on which to make changes.

The commission was composed of government officials from the legislature, state agencies, and counties, as well as leaders of nonprofit organizations. The eighty-seven counties in Minnesota, ranging in population from 4,200 to over one million, administer welfare programs under the supervision of the state. Nonprofit job training and social-service organizations play an important role in Minnesota, doing some of the actual delivery of publicly supported services under contract with counties or the state as well as providing additional services with funds provided by private foundation grants. Recognizing the important role of those agencies that actually administer the program, the commission was co-chaired by a county commissioner (the elected official who sets policy for a county) and the head of one of the largest nonprofit social-services agencies in Minnesota.

The early conversations of the group were polarized and contentious. Minnesotans, however, have a pragmatic "let's get the job done" streak. They are also uncomfortable with conflict and more willing than not to step back from an argument to look at the facts. And this is what the commission did, plunging itself into a fact-finding and knowledge-building effort.

The group began by reviewing the facts about welfare reform in Minnesota, taking testimony from experts and meeting with service providers, welfare recipients, and citizens. Interestingly, the commission found little evidence that Minnesota was a "magnet" for welfare families. It determined that about 60 percent of recipients used welfare as a source of temporary support until they could get back on their feet. The remaining 40 percent were long-term users of welfare. Only a small fraction of these had significant handicaps— limited intellectual capacity, physical disabilities, or mental illness—preventing them from holding jobs. Most were able-bodied but lacking the education, job skills, or motivation to stand on their own.

Within about six months of the beginning of its work, the commission had reached a consensus on the shortcomings of AFDC and had identified a variety of potential reforms. In its report to the governor, the group called for abandoning AFDC altogether, replacing it with a welfare program that would provide greater incentives to recipients to get a job than to remain on public support. The commission also reached a realistic, if politically difficult, conclusion: substantial reform of welfare would cost significantly more at the start than the current program, although true reform could be expected to create impressive savings down the road. The commission's most significant contribution was probably the consensus that the goal for an improved welfare program should be to increase family income rather than simply decrease case loads. The focus was shifted firmly toward moving families to self-sufficiency rather than simply getting them off welfare.

Minnesota's image as an innovator in social-welfare programs would suggest the rapid adoption of these recommendations. That did not happen. Responding to the commission's report, the legislature enacted a limited reform program in its 1987 session, one constrained both by disagreements among legislators and by requirements imposed by the federal welfare program. In its reform efforts, the state sought exceptions to many of those requirements, but without success.

Undiscouraged, state policymakers continued their efforts to create a welfare program that reflected the recommendations of the welfare-reform commission. This work resulted in the initial design of what would become Minnesota's current welfare program. By 1988, the outlines of the MFIP had been developed. That year, the legislature authorized state officials to seek congressional action to allow Minnesota to launch a test of this program. Those efforts continued over the next few years, as did the refinement of the program's design as a result of ongoing conversations with community groups, recipients, and legislators.

In 1991, the governor asked the legislature for money and authority to begin field trials in early 1993. Again, the legislature could not reach agreement and authorized only modest money to continue planning for the pilot. Finally, a year later, the legislature approved the pilot, to begin in April of 1994 in seven counties. By then, federal policy had shifted and the state had the flexibility it needed from that direction as well. The conflict over the effects of welfare in 1986 had stimulated eight years of policy development, discussion, and argument finally resulting in a design for a program of public support for poor families that would become an exemplar of effective reform.

Initial results of the evaluation of the MFIP trials were encouraging, indicating that significantly more MFIP families held jobs than those receiving traditional assistance. The evaluation found that 40 percent more long-term urban recipients of the MFIP were working than in the control group. Those employed had a 27 percent increase in earnings, and poverty within the MFIP group had been reduced by 16 percent compared to the control group.

The most recent and final follow-up evaluation of the MFIP pilot shows dramatic improvement in the stability of families in the program. Among two-parent families, there was a 40 percent increase in marriage rates, a decline in domestic abuse by 18 percent, and improved school performance among children. These results were achieved over a three-year period in comparison to families on AFDC. Unique among states in its welfare programs, Minnesota seems to have corrected, dramatically, the tendencies of the old welfare system to break up families.

As noted, federal welfare reform was signed into law by the president in 1996. Eight months later, in April of 1997, then-Governor Arne Carlson signed Minnesota legislation that expanded the MFIP statewide. By July of 1998, all welfare recipients in Minnesota had moved off AFDC and onto the new program.

The goal articulated by the 1986 commission remains the central focus of the program: to reduce both welfare dependency and poverty. Parents are expected to work. Cash benefits are reduced when the participant has earned income, but only 64 percent of earnings are deducted from the cash payment until the family reaches an income of 120 percent of the federal poverty level, at which time they leave the program. Low-paying or part-time jobs therefore increase the family's income, not reduce it. And other benefits, such as child care and subsidized health insurance, continue, although with decreasing subsidies depending upon the earned income. For those who need it, employment training and counseling are provided. A training and job-search plan is required of participants, and those who do not follow through on that plan face a reduction in their monthly cash payments. The statewide program has one very significant provision that was not in the pilot program: a limit of eligibility for benefits from the program of five years. This limit reflects a similar limit on eligibility for federal welfare dollars.

A unique element of welfare reform in Minnesota is the significant participation of private philanthropy in the implementation of the program. In early 1997, the McKnight Foundation, a Minneapolis-based philanthropy, committed $20 million over two years toward helping ensure the success of welfare reform in Minnesota. The foundation committed an additional $6 million early in 2000, making by far the largest private commitment to the implementation of welfare reform in the nation. The foundation, created by William L. McKnight, one of the principal builders of the 3M corporation, has from its inception dedicated a significant portion of its giving to programs that serve the needs of low-income people.

Staff members of the foundation had been among the many who worked closely with state officials as they refined the design of the MFIP over several years. Having watched the pilot closely, they concluded that only with effective cooperation at the local level would the program succeed for the hardest-to-employ welfare recipients. Counties, whose employees work directly with recipients, need to be at the table. But so do employers who will be expected to hire workers, some of whom will require additional counseling and training in the workplace. Nonprofits need to be part of the local effort as well, given both the work they do for the counties and the additional services they provide low-income people—services that can be critical for someone's success at getting and keeping a job.

Convinced of the need for collaboration at the local level, the foundation offered the bulk of the $20 million to local communities if they would form partnerships between these different players and, as partners, develop their plans for implementing the MFIP. The foundation limited eligibility for its grants to partnerships that serve five hundred or more welfare recipients, encouraging smaller counties to work together, particularly when they had common employment markets.

The McKnight Foundation ended up funding twenty-two partnerships across the state, involving eighty-six of the eighty-seven counties. Its support has made an important contribution to the ongoing success of Minnesota's welfare reform. Most government money is highly targeted and limited in its uses by detailed statutes and regulations. Private money, on the other hand, can be as flexible as the donor allows. The purpose of the McKnight funding was to support the planning and joint efforts of the partnerships and to meet the needs of welfare recipients where state and federal dollars were limited or could not be used. Transportation has been an important use of those funds, as have additional counseling, job training, and child care.

So far, welfare reform in Minnesota has been successful but by no means totally so. In a spirit of full disclosure, it should be noted that the evaluation and refinement of the program continue. Significant challenges remain.

The program has resulted in both increased employment and increasing earnings among participants. Late in 1999, the state earned a federal bonus for both the wage levels of working participants and their persistence in employment. In spite of those results, however, many recipients are not self-sufficient, working but not yet earning enough to exit the program. They continue to draw reduced cash payments, using up their lifetime eligibility limit of sixty months.

The Department of Human Services, which administers the program, estimates that as many as 7,500 families could use up their eligibility by mid-2003. These families make up about 17 percent of all who are now in the program. Some of these families will undoubtedly receive exemptions or extensions of their limit on welfare. Like many states, Minnesota makes exceptions to the time limit on benefits for people with serious disabilities or mental illness or who are caring for a seriously ill or disabled child. And the federal program makes exceptions to its limit on support for up to 20 percent of a state's caseload.

In this first year and a half of the new program, the emphasis has been on getting the participant into the workforce as soon as possible and then shifting attention to another, unemployed, recipient. As the program matures, other challenges are emerging. Welfare workers will need to pay increased attention to participants who are employed but at very low wages, developing strategies to help them enhance their job skills and increase their earnings. And as those most ready for employment get into jobs, those remaining will be individuals with multiple barriers to employment: limited basic education, few job skills, little or no experience with the acceptable behaviors of the workplace, and chemical or alcohol dependency.

As noted, Minnesota's program is unusual in that it has been shown to increase both employment and overall earnings of participants. Minnesota is not at the top, however, in the speed with which participants become employed or the percentage who are employed full-time. A recent analysis comparing Minnesota's and Wisconsin's programs criticized Minnesota for lower job-placement rates. Wisconsin puts significantly more pressure on welfare recipients to get into the workforce, requiring work, approved training, or job-search activities as a condition for payments and insisting that participants find work within two years. Given these requirements, it is not surprising that overall employment rates in Wisconsin are higher than in Minnesota.

Minnesota's primary explanation for differences in outcomes compared with Wisconsin is that it is emphasizing long-term self-sufficiency as the goal, not aiming to achieve the highest possible immediate employment rates. Some Minnesota policymakers, however, are not satisfied with this explanation and have proposed increasing the sanctions for those not cooperating with the program. Currently, cash payments are reduced first by 10 percent and then by 30 percent if a recipient refuses to cooperate with the program. Critics would raise the maximum sanction to a full 100 percent reduction. They contend that a 30 percent reduction in cash payments, while other benefits such as food stamps, child care, and health insurance remain, is an insufficient incentive for the truly recalcitrant.

Those who oppose imposing a total sanction worry about the impact on children in sanctioned families and the potential for increased homelessness.

They also note that variations in how counties administer the program will create serious inequities. Some counties, they insist, make extensive use of the training and counseling opportunities in the program, while others do not. Given this, sanctions may well be imposed unevenly across the state or even within large counties, given the discretion welfare workers exercise.

This review of how Minnesota has dealt with welfare reform suggests several observations about the state as an innovator in social-welfare programs. In spite of the widespread impression that Minnesota's center of political gravity is firmly to the left, Minnesota has a strong conservative strain as well. The stimulus for the reform of welfare was not a desire to expand the state's program but rather criticism that it was too generous, attracting welfare families from other states and increasing the burden on the state. On many policy matters (but certainly not all!), Minnesota does tend to end up on the liberal side of the issue. To get there, however, a wide range of views, from very conservative to very liberal, struggle as they do everywhere, each to get as much of its vision incorporated into public policy as possible. The state is by no means politically homogeneous.

Minnesota's manner of dealing with conflict and stalemate in policy debates is also worth noting. Minnesotans possess a strong midwestern faith in reliable information informing enlightened policy. That faith, combined with an aversion to conflict, frequently (but, again, not always) leads policymakers to step back, gather volumes of facts, and consult widely with anyone who might have an interest in the issue. This process frequently leads to a softening of positions and a better understanding of where the consensus (or at least majority) view lies. Welfare reform is an example of how the building of a common body of knowledge combined with widespread consultation with communities slowly clarified and built support for appropriate actions.

The inclination to seek opinions from all and sundry derives in part from Minnesotans' strong populist traditions. Sizable remnants of the old-fashioned values of democracy, particularly a belief in the ultimate wisdom of the people, remain deeply embedded in Minnesota's culture. There is also a strong element of prairie pragmatism, a sense that when a problem or obstacle appears, the appropriate response is to find a solution and move on. Add to all of this the discomfort Minnesotans feel with conflict and the result is a tendency, in the face of differences of opinion, to consult widely, discussing issues until compromise is reached or one of the parties is exhausted and gives up.

Welfare reform in Minnesota also illustrates the important role of the private sector in the life of the state and in meeting the social-welfare needs of low-income families. Nonprofit organizations played a significant role in working through the issues of welfare reform. They continue to be important in administering the program, providing job training, counseling, chemical-dependency treatment, and other services to welfare recipients, sometimes under contract with counties, other times with their own resources. Many of the partnerships that were established, involving both nonprofits and employers, remain important in shaping the program at the local level. Private foundations also make their contribution, prominent among them McKnight's large and direct involvement, but also the continuing support of many Minnesota foundations for the ongoing work of the nonprofits.

Innovation in Minnesota: Health Care

The evolution of state strategies to expand health care in Minnesota had many similarities to the development of reforms in welfare. A state-subsidized health-insurance program for poor children, the first in the nation, was created by the legislature in 1987. The Children's Health Plan initially covered children up to the age of six and low-income pregnant women. Eligibility for the program was soon extended to children up to the age of eighteen and coverage expanded to include mental health and special education. In its first three and a half years, the program reached some thirty-eight thousand children.

The success of the Children's Health Plan encouraged liberal legislators to propose a series of bills addressing the needs of the broader population of uninsured Minnesotans. Bills were introduced in 1988 and 1989, failing each time. Again, as with welfare, disagreement led to the creation of a bipartisan group to look at the issues. The Health Care Access Commission was created in 1989 and charged with recommending to the governor and legislature "a plan to provide access to health care for all state residents."

The commission submitted its report in January of 1991, proposing legislation that would provide health insurance for the estimated 370,000 Minnesotans whose employers did not do so or who were too poor to afford to purchase it themselves. That year a bill with sweeping changes in the state's health-insurance program was passed by the legislature. The price tag on health coverage is high, however, and the bill was vetoed by Governor Carlson.

This did not stop the proponents of health coverage for all Minnesotans. A bipartisan committee of legislators was created to deal with the problems the governor had with the proposal. The result of their work, the HealthRight Bill, was passed by the legislature and, this time, signed by the governor. This bill committed the state to an expansion of access to health care for the uninsured population through a state-subsidized insurance program. It also put in place strategies for cost containment and medical-malpractice reform and created purchasing pools for health-care services. This bill, later renamed The MinnesotaCare Act to avoid a trademark fight over the original name, made the state a leader in health-care reform.

MinnesotaCare provides health-insurance coverage to low-income families for a sliding fee based on family size and income. It now covers more than one hundred thousand enrollees. A family of three with an income of as much as $38,000 per year is eligible, with some low-income children covered for premiums of $4 per month. The state contracts with nine different provider networks of clinics, doctors, and hospitals, negotiating the prices paid by the state each year. The program is not intended to replace employer-subsidized or privately purchased health insurance and has provisions to prevent that substitution.

This and other state-financed or federally financed health-care programs (such as Medicaid) cover approximately five hundred thousand Minnesotans who otherwise would not be able to afford health coverage. The results of the state's investments in health care are dramatic. Only 5.2 percent of the state's population is currently uninsured, a smaller percentage than a decade ago. By comparison, the national rate of uninsured people has been rising in recent years and is now about 16 percent.

As with welfare reform, Minnesota did not move directly or smoothly to within striking distance of health coverage for all. It involved partisan debate, gubernatorial vetoes, and commissions to sort out the different perspectives and to figure out how to achieve health-care goals within budget constraints. As with welfare, however, Minnesota policymakers developed solutions that the majority could support and have made great strides toward ensuring that all citizens of the state, particularly the poor, have access to reasonably priced health care.

More than welfare reform, however, health-care policy in Minnesota is under significant pressure. The system is extremely complex. Too many people, particularly children, remain without coverage, and costs have risen substantially in recent years. The health-plan organizations, which in Minnesota are by law nonprofit, are losing money on their contracts for some public programs and, understandably, are pushing for relief. The system is financed by an array of taxes, many of which are unpopular with doctors and administrators of health plans. In spite of a well-insured population, urban hospitals, like their counterparts elsewhere, face high costs for uncompensated care. While welfare in Minnesota needs fine-tuning, the whole health-care system, in spite of its accomplishments, is in need of a much more fundamental rethinking, a rethinking that the administration of Governor Jesse Ventura has promised to undertake.

Minnesota's Commitment to Social Welfare: Why?

Minnesota has over many decades demonstrated a commitment to social welfare and to the creation of reasonably enlightened policies that promote that welfare. There have been struggles over specifics, for certain, but those struggles usually have resulted in policies more innovative than in most other states.

The question is: why? One important explanation—probably the most significant—is the culture of the early settlers of the state and the values they held and built into the society they created. Studies demonstrate that how much a state commits to social services is heavily influenced by the political culture of that state. Daniel Elazar's concept of three political subcultures that have mixed together to form the American culture is described in detail elsewhere in this volume.[1] Minnesota clearly fits the criteria for what he calls the moralistic political subculture. Characteristics of this subculture include a more activist government, a more vigorous nonprofit sector, and a high level of comfort with partnerships between government and the private sector to get the job done. Minnesotans in large measure see the good society as one in which people have an undivided interest in the common good, in which citizens cooperate to create and maintain a government that will reflect commonly held moral values.

This is a state that believes in hard work and pragmatism. The frontier sensibilities are not so far away in a state that began with farming, lumbering, iron mining, and the processing and shipping associated with these raw materials. Two major waves of immigration into the region brought strong religious values that powerfully shaped the more secular values of the state. The earliest of these were people of European heritage, Yankees who had originally settled in New England but moved west, bringing with them the concept of the holy commonwealth, a public sector imbued with strong moral values. A later immigration brought Scandinavian and other northern European groups who reinforced the emerging moralistic political culture.

Minnesota's settlers brought a strong belief in the value of education, its importance in transmitting their religious beliefs and in producing citizens who, in their daily lives, would reflect those beliefs. Minnesota has one of the nation's highest high-school graduation rates—it has one of the most well-educated populations. And, for its population, it enjoys one of the largest groups of private, currently or originally church-related colleges and universities in the country.

As in many states, Minnesota's early approach to the provision of social services was local and private, growing from the dictates of faiths that called for charity to those in need. Support for the indigent, for orphaned or abandoned children, and for the mentally ill was in the early days of settlement the purview of local religious groups. Essential social services were a function of religious institutions, not government. Early attitudes toward the needy were characteristic of a pioneer culture, working hard to build a society in the wilderness. Governor John S. Pillsbury, for example, speaking in 1877, called poverty "a disease, cured by hard work . . . and as little charity as possible." Around the same time, a community leader was quoted in the largest-circulation Minneapolis newspaper to the effect that ". . . indiscriminate charity fosters and increases pauperism, vagrancy, and crime." Hardly soft liberalism.

Charity began as a local, private responsibility. Two forces, however, drew government into a greater role in social services. One was the growth in population. By the late 1800s, the poor population of the two large cities of Minnesota—St. Paul, the capital, and Minneapolis—had begun to strain small private service organizations. A number of such groups in St. Paul undertook a study, shades of strategies to come. They concluded that relief needed to be coordinated and that the community should move toward "more orderly plans for approaching the modern spirit of social services." The Associated Charities of St. Paul emerged from these discussions, a collaboration of individual relief organizations that coordinated their strategies and priorities and eventually the actual flow of money. This cooperative effort set the stage for larger-scale, governmental action.

Another force was the occasional natural disaster that struck the farmers of the state, creating demands for regional relief efforts of a scope that no private organization could manage. One such disaster, a grasshopper plague in 1877, led to a call for government intervention to assist thousands of affected farm families. So many farms came close to being wiped out that local churches and relief groups were overwhelmed. The government had to step in or watch the near ruin of the state's agricultural economy.

Even as the state recognized the need for government intervention, however, it insisted that responsibility for delivering relief be kept at the local level, in counties rather than the state. To this day, most social services continue to be delivered by counties, funded heavily by the state and federal governments as well as the counties themselves.

The values of early settlers of the state included a moralistic rationale for addressing the needs of the poor, strong work and community ethics, a preference for action at the local level, and an important role for churches and private charities. These values—and their persistence to this day—are the underpinnings of Minnesota's approach to social services.

Why have the values of early settlers remained so evident in this state when, in many others, they have evolved or been eroded? One reason is the conservatism, in the essential meaning of that term, associated with strong rural and religious communities. Values are to be held, transmitted to younger generations (recall the state's substantial commitment to education), and maintained, whether those values are left or right of center. The stability of the makeup of the population of Minnesota has also helped to ensure the endurance of early values. The white population, people of German, Scandinavian, Irish (particularly in St. Paul), and eastern European (in the north, on the Iron Range) extraction made up 99 percent of the total Minnesota population as late as 1950. Even today, 92 percent of the state's population is of European extraction. The vast majority of Minnesotans are still descendants of the original immigrant groups that settled the state.

Minnesota's leaders over the past 125 years have emerged from that Minnesota culture. Democrat or Republican, they have been people committed to government as an instrument of the highest values of the society, a positive force in meeting the needs of the citizenry. This is true as well of business leaders, many of whom over the decades have been homegrown Minnesotans who reflected the values of the community in their approach to business and its responsibilities to the community. From such business leaders emerged the Five Percent Club (corporations that pledge to give 5 percent of their pre-tax profits back to the community), the establishment of numerous world-class cultural institutions, museums, theaters, and orchestras, and the creation of private foundations that, on a per capita basis, give more per year than philanthropies in all but two other states.

A final reason can be suggested for Minnesota's persistent leadership in the social services: it has had the luxury of being able to afford it. Over many decades, Minnesota has enjoyed a relatively stable economy. This is a state that made an early transition from the production of raw materials—crops, lumber, and iron ore—to their processing, particularly of food products, to manufacturing, and then to technology and financial and medical services. The state's economy has been adept at moving on to the next wealth-producing activity. Remnants of each era have remained, leaving the state with a productive and diverse economy that is better cushioned against downdrafts in the business cycle than those of many other states. The state has suffered during recessions, yes. But it has also been able to fulfill much of the vision of its forebears, caring for its elderly, its poor, and its children as well as any state and better than most.

A Final Note

Minnesota has an unusual record of commitment to social welfare, to creativity and generosity in its programs. In recent years, however, many have begun to worry whether the "Minnesota Miracle" can endure. They worry about the erosion of those pioneer values that have persisted for so long as the state becomes more and more diverse. Minnesota has a growing Hispanic population as increasing numbers of migrant workers settle in the towns and cities. Minnesota has what is estimated to be the second largest population among the states (after California) of Hmong, tribal people from the highlands of Laos who migrated to Minnesota following the end of the Vietnam War. In recent years, increasing numbers of Somali, Ethiopians, and Bosnians have settled here.

Some observers feel that these changes make it inevitable that Minnesota will lose the singular characteristics of its common heritage. They bemoan a gradual loss of the old values and are convinced that Minnesota will soon take on a different character, more like states along the eastern seaboard and large cities like Chicago or Houston. More likely, what is happening is a revitalization of many of the state's traditional values—Minnesota's new settlers share a strong religious sense, a commitment to family, a thirst for education, and a willingness to work hard to achieve for themselves and their children. Quite likely the similarity of values new immigrants find is one reason this rather unlikely state is welcoming such numbers of people from elsewhere in the world.

Others worry about the changing face of business and the implications for community leadership and corporate philanthropy. Companies that were created here and led over the years by native Minnesotans have been bought by or merged with other companies headquartered elsewhere. Fewer chief executive officers of large companies grew up here, and some have attitudes toward community service decidedly different from those of their predecessors. Inevitably, the giving programs of such companies have also changed, in some cases dramatically.

There are also voices raising the alarm that Minnesota will be left in the dust in the next seismic shift in the economy, further toward high technology, biotechnology, genomics, a Web-based economy, and the Pacific Rim. Entrepreneurs seem to prefer the coasts, not the midlands. Other states are committing more to the development of emerging industries. In the view of some, Minnesota positively discourages such development with its high taxes and tough environmental and other standards.

There are counters to each of these observations. The argument goes back and forth at the tables of the Minneapolis Club, in academic discussions, in the media, and among state policymakers. One can probably expect that commissions will be formed, exhaustive information gathered, citizens' opinions heard, arguments engaged, and, perhaps, if Minnesota's luck holds, creative responses will emerge, in that cautiously radical way, and the Minnesota Miracle will continue.

Note

1. See Virginia Gray and Wyman Spano, "The Irresistible Force Meets the Immovable Object: Minnesota's Moralistic Political Culture Confronts Jesse Ventura" (previous chapter).

JON PRATT & EDSON W. SPENCER

Dynamics of Corporate Philanthropy in Minnesota

CORPORATE PHILANTHROPY has become a defining feature of Minnesota's civic life; a variety of explanations have been offered as to why business owners make public commitments to give away corporate profits for community projects. A new campaign by the Minneapolis Chamber of Commerce suggests that Minnesota's business contributions are perhaps a product of the environment, with the slogan "It must be something in the water" used to recruit new corporate generosity.

However, it was not until after World War II that Minnesota could be considered a leader in corporate philanthropy. Earlier in its history Minnesota's business culture was defined more by its agricultural economy, labor conflict, and a few business owners who made substantial contributions as individuals.

Long before it became a publicly held retailing giant, the Target Corporation (formerly the Dayton Hudson Corporation) had been a leader in corporate philanthropy in the Twin Cities. George Draper Dayton was supporting religious causes, including Macalester College, before the turn of the century. The family set aside the first funds to endow what would become the future Target Foundation in 1909. As a private company, Dayton's had set aside 5 percent of pretax profits for charitable gifts. The practice was continued when the family took the company public in the late 1950s.

While the Target Corporation and other companies were respected as business successes, Minnesota's group of postwar chief executives preferred to be recognized for their accomplishments on behalf of the community. The heady feeling that the growing corporations could simultaneously tackle urban problems and museum expansions was tempered by a fear that the new business ethic, and the accompanying corporate philanthropy, would disappear when the postwar business leadership retired. A number of other companies,

JON PRATT *is executive director of the Minnesota Council of Nonprofits.* EDSON W. SPENCER *is retired chief executive officer of Honeywell Inc.*

generally private or family controlled, adopted the five-percent rule. In 1976 the Minneapolis Chamber of Commerce created the Five Percent Club, now called the Keystone Program, to formalize the commitment of corporations allocating a fixed percentage of their earnings to philanthropy.

In 1976 the Five Percent Club was unique, and received both praise and criticism depending on one's view of the proper uses of corporate funds. The Five Percent Club drew John D. Rockefeller III to speak to the Minneapolis Chamber of Commerce in 1977:

> I heard so much about the city of Minneapolis, about its Chamber of Commerce, about the public spirit of its business community, about your remarkable Five Percent Club that I feel a bit like Dorothy in the Land of Oz. I had to come to the Emerald City myself to see if it really exists.[1]

While not quite the Emerald City, the Minneapolis-based Five Percent Club added participating companies and expanded its geographical scope to include businesses throughout the state. In 1994 the *Chronicle of Philanthropy* rated Minneapolis as having the highest level of charitable giving overall among fifty U.S. cities it studied, and the highest per capita level of corporate contributions. The *Chronicle* compared cities based on per capita contributions to national organizations, the United Way, and community foundations, and per capita contributions by corporate foundations, independent foundations, and community foundations.

By 1998 Minnesota had 4,410 financially active charities, with 209,664 employees and annual expenditures of $11.4 billion. Nonprofit employees now make up 8.45 percent of Minnesota's employed workforce, up from 6.8 percent in 1987. The last ten years have seen Minnesota's nonprofit sector grow faster than the state's economy as a whole, with total wages paid in the sector rising an average 6 percent per year (in constant dollars), and the number of firms and the number of employees both growing by 5 percent per year. This growth underscores the fact that nonprofits are a larger factor in Minnesota's economy than for the nation as a whole. Minnesota's 8.45 percent nonprofit share of the state's paid workforce is substantially higher than the national average of 6.8 percent.

IRS business filings verify that Minnesota's nonprofit sector is proportionally larger than the national average, as shown in an Urban Institute analysis.[2] While Minnesota ranks as the twentieth state by population, the state ranks eighteenth in total expenses by nonprofit organizations, seventeenth in total assets of nonprofit organizations, sixteenth in the amount of charitable contributions to these organizations, and thirteenth in the number of active non-profit organizations.

In addition to high levels of charitable giving and nonprofit activity, Minnesota ranks at or near the top for common quality-of-life measures in comparison with other states:

· first in longevity of women, and second for men;
· first in workforce participation by adult women, second for adult men;
· first for voter turnout;
· first for high-school graduation rate;
· top five ranking for SAT and ACT scores for the last twenty years;
· top of the states in rankings as a healthy place to live.[3]

Does the system of philanthropy in Minnesota deserve credit for creating this high quality of life, or is charitable activity simply the by-product of an otherwise successful economy and society? A critical shift, coincident with the growing public spirit among leading corporations, was an increase in state- and local-government expenditures—often in partnership with philanthropy. The state's history makes clear that Minnesota's charitable impulse is less the result of longstanding social attitudes and cultural habits than it is of a strategic intervention by leaders able to refocus attention from private conflicts to projects benefiting a broad public. A redefinition of the "Minnesota way of doing things" led to the creation of a strong base of charitable institutions and support organizations, backed by a widespread generosity and a conviction that "it has probably always been this way."

Historical Roots of Corporate Philanthropy

As a mostly rural, agriculture-based economy from statehood in 1858 until about 1945, Minnesota had mostly conservative business and political leaders and a small set of philanthropic and nonprofit institutions.

An influential corps of New England Yankees was recruited to form an industrial and financial class in the Minnesota Territory in the 1850s, many of whom brought their working capital with them. This group included George Draper Dayton (dry goods), Cadwallader Washburn (grain milling), Amherst Wilder (overland and river transport), Alexander Wilkin (riverboat and property insurance), Charles A. Pillsbury (grain milling), and Thomas Barlow Walker (logging). James J. Hill, builder and owner of the Great Northern Railroad, emigrated from Canada.

The picture of philanthropy in Minnesota before 1945 shows a broad mix of purposes and several generous families, perhaps most notably those noted above. The successful entrepreneurs of the nineteenth century believed philanthropy was a responsibility of their private wealth, not of their businesses.

By the turn of the century the state's mostly agricultural and logging economy had developed the Twin Cities into a railroad and flour-milling center for the Upper Midwest, with increasing revenue from iron-ore mining and light manufacturing. Political development and civic leadership were comparable to other states of that era; graft and corruption were commonplace.

From 1931—the year Floyd B. Olson was sworn in as the first Farmer-Labor Party governor—to 1944, when the Farmer-Labor Party merged with the Democratic Party, Minnesota's political environment was in turmoil. Farmers were battling banks and grain companies over prices and financing; labor was organizing for higher wages; and business leaders were united in opposition to both causes. In Minneapolis, business leaders were focused on opposition to labor unions and "agitators," and coordinated their efforts through the somewhat misleadingly named Citizens Alliance.

Olson's biggest legislative battle came in 1934 with the Republican-controlled Senate, which was blocking relief legislation, and with the state's largest banks, Northwest Bancorporation of Minneapolis and First Bank Stock Corporation of St. Paul. After bringing thousands of angry farmers into the capital, Olson finally got the senators to pass his program of a moratorium on farm-mortgage foreclosures, appropriation of relief funds, an old-age pension, and an emergency-banking act. It was in this atmosphere that the Farmer-Labor Party called for the abolition of private enterprise and the establishment of virtually total Socialism in its 1934 platform.

A chasm divided the political party ruling Minnesota and the leadership setting the business agenda. Both sides had successfully developed disciplined institutional networks and mobilized substantial resources, but were on an unsustainable course. Many business leaders were disgusted by the tactics of the Citizens Alliance, and many Farmer-Laborites were taken aback by the extreme language of the 1934 platform. Unions broadened their gains after the truckers' strike, and employers gradually accommodated their demands. Floyd B. Olson's death from cancer in 1936 left the Farmer-Labor Party without its key political strategist, and after diminished success at the polls it merged with the Democratic Party in 1944.

Institutionalizing Corporate Philanthropy: 1946 to the Present

The postwar era was ripe for a new generation of leaders. New faces on the political scene included Hubert Humphrey, elected as Democratic-Farmer-

Labor mayor of Minneapolis in 1944 and U.S. senator in 1948, and Orville Freeman, elected as the first DFL governor in 1954.

Minnesota's economy had been primarily agricultural since statehood; but in 1952, manufacturing displaced farming as the major source of income. At the same time a new political liberalism took hold, a second generation of business leaders took office at Dayton Hudson, Cowles Newspapers, Piper Jaffray, and other corporations. In 1946 each of these companies began donating 5 percent of their pretax profits to charitable causes, including the arts, human services, and sometimes their family churches.

In the early 1950s the Dayton's department stores in downtown Minneapolis and St. Paul were some of the most successful department stores in the nation. Each Saturday the Dayton brothers would first walk the floor to observe the retail business and then gather to discuss ideas for improvements. They discussed strategies to grow the business, but came to two key conclusions:

· with the highest market share of any department store in the United States, they could only grow through new locations, acquisitions, or product lines; and
· what happened outside the store was as important as what happened inside the store.

The first conclusion lead to geographic expansion and eventually to new types of stores for the company, including the Target discount stores. The second point was the underlying theory for corporate philanthropy: that attractive streets, a good economy, and an actively engaged community are the best climate for business success, not simply good merchandise on the inside. Ken Dayton described this approach later as "What's good for the community is good for the company"—a rephrasing of an older generation's view of corporate responsibility, as it had been expressed by Charles E. Wilson when, as president of General Motors, he asserted in congressional testimony that "What's good for the country is good for General Motors, and vice versa."[4]

The Dayton brothers concentrated their generosity on various institutions: Bruce on the Minneapolis Institute of Arts, Kenneth on the Minnesota Symphony and the Walker Art Center, Wallace on a number of environmental organizations (including the Nature Conservancy and several related to the Yellowstone National Park ecosystem), Douglas on the YMCA.

The Dayton brothers also advanced their commitment to corporate contributions through service on the boards of other leading Minnesota corporations. Bruce Dayton, as a Honeywell director, chided the board into increasing the amount allocated for charitable contributions; Ken Dayton did the same thing on the General Mills board. After several years of seeing management's recommendations for corporate charitable contributions increased by the board—following the Dayton brothers' suggestion—the CEO of General Mills called the CEO of Honeywell to say he was concerned that his public shareholders might complain, and asked what should be done. The answer was "Nothing." Annual contributions to the respective General Mills and Honeywell Foundations continued to increase.

During the 1960s the number of nonprofit organizations increased, both as a result of broadened knowledge of how to form and finance organizations and because of an increase in government contracting and grantmaking to organizations. As state institutions for the mentally ill and retarded were scaled back in the 1950s and 1960s, nonprofits became the preferred vehicle to provide community-based services with government funds.

The state preference for nonprofit health providers was written into state law, requiring that all health-provider organizations be nonprofit corporations. Despite a national wave of hospital conversions from nonprofit to for-profit auspices, Minnesota has only nonprofit or local-government-owned hospitals. By 1996, health care accounted for 56.8 percent of Minnesota nonprofit employment. Established in 1918, the Mayo Foundation—perhaps the most significant, and surely the best-known, Minnesota health-care institution— grew from the fairly modest vision of its founders, Drs. Charles and William Mayo, to Minnesota's largest health-care provider. In 1998, Mayo had 32,000 employees; provided health care for 478,000 clinic patients; had $4.5 billion in assets; and received $101 million in contributions, private research grants, and endowments.

The social needs focused on by philanthropic activities were not always so quiescent. In 1967, Minneapolis did not escape the urban riots of an angry black community. Buildings were burned; communities and the police clashed; people were injured. Minnesota had a long history of progressivism, liberalism, and populism, typified by the Floyd Olson government of the Depression years. The race riots of the mid-1960s catalyzed the philanthropic and corporate communities to focus on solving social problems with a new energy. A direct response to the riotous destruction on Plymouth Avenue in north Minneapolis was the establishment of the Urban Coalition. Steve Keating, CEO of Honeywell, was its first chairman; under his leadership the corporate community was mobilized to turn its money and its talented employees toward the most difficult and intractable urban problems.

New immigrants and growing minority populations also increased the diversity of organizations. The emergence of such groups as the Sabathani Community

Center (1967), Project for Pride in Living (1972), KMOJ Radio (1976), African American Family Services (1977), MIGIZI Communications (1977), Accessible Space (1978), and the Hmong American Partnership (1990) were milestones along this path. By the end of the 1990s new organizations sprang up to serve the needs of Somali, Sudanese, Russian, and Latin American immigrants.

In the mid-1970s, Dayton Hudson Corporation perceived a need to broaden the role of the business community in exercising leadership toward solving community problems. The company brought Wayne Thompson, former city manager of Oakland, California, to Minneapolis as their new vice president of community affairs. Three important new organizations grew out of a series of brainstorming meetings of a dozen CEOs under Thompson's leadership:

· The Minnesota Business Partnership, a statewide lobbying organization whose members are all CEOs;
· The Minnesota Meeting, which over its twelve-year life has grown into a nationally respected forum, bringing distinguished speakers to the Twin Cities to inform the business community on a variety of national issues;
· The Center for Corporate Responsibility, which is a training ground in philanthropy and community responsibility for second-level managers in large corporations and leaders of small companies.

Board members and fund-raisers for organizations serving low-income populations formed a coalition in 1983 to redirect corporate and foundation grants to their communities. Organizers felt that they were at a disadvantage in fund-raising, and did not receive the quantity or size of grants that were going to larger institutions—for example, four-year colleges and the University of Minnesota. The Philanthropy Project was a three-year effort with 130 organizational members, including the Urban Coalition, the Project for Pride in Living, the American Indian Center, and the Community Clinic Consortium.

The Philanthropy Project sponsored tours and presentations for trustees and foundation staff, and published three research studies documenting the extent to which foundation and corporate grants went to organizations that served low-income people, women, communities of color, and rural populations. The project's final report concluded that between 1981 and 1985, the share of Minnesota grant dollars going to disadvantaged constituencies had increased from 28 percent to 38 percent of total grants. After the Philanthropy Project ended in 1986, the project's staff and board formed the Minnesota Council of Nonprofits to address a broader range of issues, including the relationship between nonprofits and government.

Yet the Five Percent Club is the most visible evidence of Minnesota's corporate support base for philanthropy. A larger network of support organizations has reinforced these efforts, some initiated by business leaders and others formed by philanthropic and nonprofit leaders. The support organizations grew over an eighty-year period into a broad infrastructure with three main functions:

· increasing charitable contributions;
· increasing volunteer labor;
· enhancing the management capacity, earned income, and coordination of organizations.

Minnesota Philanthropic Support Organizations

The promotion of charitable activity through support organizations has increased over time, beginning with religiously sponsored charities and later purely secular efforts. Seven prewar support organizations were formed to aggregate financial contributions and devote them to broad community needs: Lutheran Social Service (1865), Catholic Charities (1869), Jewish Family and Children's Service (1910), the Minneapolis Foundation (1915), United Way of the Minneapolis Area (1919), United Way of the Saint Paul Area (1920), and the Saint Paul Foundation (1940). While each institution had a particular geographic or community focus, they shared the common goal of raising awareness of social needs and motivating contributors. This first set of philanthropic support organizations directly received contributions for community needs, and was complemented by later initiatives that did not distribute funds but existed to encourage greater charitable contributions, volunteer labor, and nonprofit management capacity.

Twenty more support organizations, with growing specialization, were formed over the next fifty years. Individually each of these support organizations has a specific task in supporting one or more aspects of nonprofit activity. For example, the Management Assistance Program for Nonprofits, started by Honeywell in 1979, provides technical and financial advice and support for struggling young nonprofits. Collectively, these institutions share in inculcating the population, but especially business leaders, in the belief that philanthropy and voluntary activity is not only a social good, but also an essential element of social legitimacy. They also promote positive public opinion toward charitable activity and the fund-raising efforts behind them. While comparable organizations in these categories exist in other states, the scope and magnitude of Minnesota activity are clearly on the high end.

INCREASING CHARITABLE CONTRIBUTIONS

The Minnesota Keystone Program (formerly the Five Percent Club) codified the new business leadership thinking of the 1950s and 1960s into a recognition program designed to spread the practice of business tithing:

> The Minnesota Keystone Program symbolizes the strong bridge between community needs and business resources. Successful businesses are essential to the survival of Minnesota's communities. Healthy, safe communities help businesses thrive. Through the Keystone Program, organizations are encouraged to make and maintain corporate investments in the community and are publicly recognized for those significant and generous actions.[5]

The Minneapolis Chamber of Commerce launched the Five Percent Club in 1976 with twenty-three participating companies, including Cowles Media Company, Dayton Hudson Corporation, Medtronic, Norwest Bank, and Piper Jaffray Companies. The program inspired business leaders in several U.S. cities and one other country, Costa Rica, to establish tithing clubs, which have been found to have a positive impact on giving.

The Keystone Program provides support to companies interested in beginning a contributions program. Program materials instruct companies how to develop corporate-giving programs able to realize real growth in the dollar value contributed, increased formality of budget and structure, better effectiveness through narrower subject focus and larger, longer commitments, and more employee involvement in decision-making.

Have the formalized expectations of the Keystone Program given Minnesota corporate philanthropy staying power? Two examinations of Twin Cities corporate grantmaking by Joseph Galaskiewicz (1979–1981 and 1987–1989) sought to identify the factors that explain changes in corporate giving. Galaskiewicz's first study had suggested that:

> The Twin Cities were witnessing the end of an era. Intensely personal networks of social influence orchestrated by an economically and powerful and socially prominent elite were going to be replaced by community institutions that would motivate, reward, and legitimate corporate community service.[6]

Part of the rationale for institutionalizing corporate-contribution levels was the impending retirement of the business leadership and a fear that new CEOs from outside the community would scrap donations to increase profits. Galaskiewicz found that while the CEOs turned over between the studies, the contributions did not drop. However, in Galaskiewicz's analysis of interviews, indicators such as CEO country-club memberships, friendship patterns, or birth locations, as well as corporate charitable commitments, convinced him that the credit belonged less to the Keystone Program and rather more to informal social structures. Informal social structures were more durable than the more organized efforts, and much giving in 1987–1989 was still driven by the CEOs' personal ties to local philanthropic leaders. The "new old-boy network" proved to be just as effective as the old old-boy network in soliciting funds and communicating expectations.

Galaskiewicz credited executive involvement in local business organizations, educational organizations, social-service agencies, and task forces as being an important factor, and recognized one strategy in particular:

> Clearly, networks were critical in sustaining the Twin Cities grants economy, but without the civic and voluntary associations to help build and nurture these ties, the networks would have atrophied and had a difficult time surviving.
>
> In interviews in both periods, I heard over and over again how important it was to recruit new CEOs onto the boards of nonprofit organizations and into business and social clubs. Stories were told about a new CEO in town who at first would slash the contributions budget but then suddenly increase contributions the next year, having served on a prominent cultural board. It was in these arenas that executives were solicited for contributions, socialized into the local culture, and where trust, mutual respect, and norms of reciprocity are created.[7]

Over half of the Twin Cities' CEOs have turned over since Galaskiewicz's second round of data collection, and rates of contribution have held steady. By 1998 the Keystone Program had added a new level—2 percent givers—and reported 158 participants at the 5 percent level and 94 organizations at the 2 percent level. In addition to maintaining participation, commitments (or the lack thereof) to enforcement of historic charitable obligations have played an important role in several corporate takeover battles and buyouts.

The first generation of corporate philanthropic leaders was personally engaged in the work of their company foundations and in active participation in philanthropic activities in the community. Community-affairs directors in their corporations reported directly to them—as did Wayne Thompson at Dayton Hudson, Ron Speed at Honeywell, Jim Shannon at General Mills, and others. Unfortunately, as a new generation of corporate leaders has taken over, as business has become national and global, and as CEOs travel more and manage more complicated businesses, the trend is for the community-affairs executive to be a part of a larger communications and public-relations department.

Pressures for stock performance and earnings targets have heightened awareness of short-term returns, influencing management thinking about what companies themselves might gain from their philanthropy. The development of cause-related giving, where corporate goals for publicity or product awareness are achieved by targeting donations to organizations closely identified with the need addressed by the company's products, has ironically decreased the amount of funds available for general community projects.

In response to attempted hostile takeovers of Dayton Hudson Corporation and the Saint Paul Companies, the Minnesota legislature held hearings and passed legislation favorable to maintaining local ownership. In both cases the companies' charitable contributions—and the relatively uncharitable track records of their pursuers—were major topics of discussion and dread. In the buyouts of Pillsbury, Cowles Media, and Piper Jaffray, the new owners felt obliged to pledge publicly that they would continue existing philanthropic commitments. Local norms, whether because of informal social networks or formal institutions, held sway.

With increases in the stock market, with higher asset values increasing private foundation payout requirements, and with increased profits tied to Keystone Program commitments, Minnesota is experiencing a boom in its grants economy.

FOUNDATIONS	YEAR FORMED	1998 GRANTS (IN MILLIONS)
McKnight Foundation	1953	$77.4
Bush Foundation	1953	$27.7
Andersen Foundation	1957	$18.5
Blandin	1945	$13.6
Otto Bremer	1940	$13.6
Community Foundations		
Saint Paul Foundation	1940	$27.9
Minneapolis Foundation	1915	$21.2
Corporations		
Target Corporation		$53.4
Norwest Bank Corporation		$26.0
US Bancorp		$19.5
General Mills		$16.8
St. Paul Companies		$16.6
3M		$16.1
Honeywell		$13.2
Cargill		$11.3

Source: Research conducted by the Minnesota Council of Nonprofits, 1999.

Institutionalizing philanthropy involves getting other people to be philanthropic. While virtually every nonprofit organization undertakes its own search for donations, one of the most common strategies is to organize community-wide drives in which peers perform the solicitation. The community foundations (the Minneapolis and Saint Paul Foundations), the United Way organizations, United Arts Fund, Cooperating Fund Drive, HealthFund of Minnesota, and the Minnesota Initiative Funds perform this function. The two largest community foundations have sponsored several of the most innovative philanthropic initiatives, including the AIDS Funding Consortium (1988–1994), the St. Paul Foundation's Diversity Endowment Fund, and the Bigelow Foundation's Children, Families and Community Initiative.

Law firms have not been noted for the generosity of their partners as a group, even though individual firm members may make sizeable contributions. Perhaps the largest charitable contribution in the country by a law firm was recently announced by Michael Cerisi and his partners. The Cerisi firm won a high fee for representing the state of Minnesota in a suit against tobacco companies, which ended in a $6 billion award to the state. The partners of the law firm are contributing $30 million to establish a fund at the Minneapolis Community Foundation. The designated areas for beneficiaries are in the fields of public health, social justice, and education; a leadership institute for schoolteachers; and awards for academic achievement in the arts.

Another interesting example of generosity is that of Emma Howe, who was—unusually—not a corporate leader or scion of a wealthy family. In 1915 she became one of the first three employees of Deluxe Check Printing Company, which was to grow to a leading firm in its industry. Miss Howe started emptying wastebaskets and keeping the office clean. She retired as a proofreader for the president. She lived alone in a small house in a modest neighborhood in northeast Minneapolis, and had no immediate family. Like other early employees of the company, she was paid partially in stock and felt it was disloyal to sell shares. Upon her death, the accumulated value of this stock had reached nearly $30 million.

After Emma Howe's death, the Minneapolis Community Foundation received a bequest of $28 million to establish the Emma Howe fund in the early 1990s. The fund today has assets of more than $50 million. The beneficiaries, designated in Miss Howe's will, are disadvantaged children.

Emma Howe's bequest was of course unusual for its source and its size. The Minneapolis and St. Paul Community Foundations, like other successful community foundations across the country, have received hundreds of donations to establish funds—from quite small to several millions of dollars—from

hundreds of individuals. The community foundation model is now beginning
to spread to smaller cities and towns throughout Minnesota.

Minnesota's foundations grew to make the state third-highest in the
United States for per capita foundation assets (after Michigan and New York),
with 180 foundations listed in the 1997 *Foundation Directory*, published by the
Foundation Center. Minnesota's two largest private foundations, Bush and
McKnight, were established in the 1950s with gifts of several million dollars in
3M stock, which had increased in value to over one billion dollars by 1997. Two
Minnesota founders of food product companies put more than $200 million
of their personal assets into charitable foundations: the Hormel Foundation
(1946) and the Schwan Foundation (1997).

The One Percent Club is the most recent organization to work toward
increasing charitable contributions, modeled after the earlier Five Percent
Club and inspired by Claude Rosenberg's advocacy of donating a portion of net
worth in his *Wealthy and Wise*.[8] The One Percent Club was organized in 1997
by Joe Selvaggio, former director of the Project for Pride in Living (an inner-city
social service organization) and Ken Dayton (one of the original founders of the
Five Percent Club). After three months, seventy-five people, mostly wealthy
people with substantial assets, signed the following pledge:

> I agree to contribute 1 percent or more of my net worth annually to the tax-
> deductible cause(s) of my choice. I understand this entitles me to membership
> in an association of 1 percent givers who believe strongly in the wisdom of
> philanthropy.

By 2000 there were 189 members, 171 of whom agreed to let their names
be known (risking increased solicitations). The One Percent Club actively
recruits additional signers onto its pledge, maintains a speakers bureau, and
seeks to lead by example. At least part of the appeal being made by the One
Percent Club advocates for philanthropy with a critique of government:

> We have a unique opportunity. For the first time in this country's history, we
> have both the wealth and the means, in the form of dedicated nonprofit
> organizations, to heal our nation's social and cultural ills. One percent can
> make a difference. Nonprofits have literally moved in next door to the
> problems in our communities. Like small businesses, they are more flexible,
> innovative, and cost effective than big government programs. When you
> invest in them, you are putting your dollars directly to work in the most
> efficient ways available today.[9]

INCREASING VOLUNTEER LABOR

People who volunteer and attend church services are more likely to make charitable contributions, though these behaviors are more concomitant than causal. Minnesotans have a high rate of volunteering, and the state is the second highest per capita as a source for Peace Corps volunteers.

Over fifty organizations and projects are structured along the lines of the Volunteer Resource Center in Minneapolis, which matches individuals to volunteer assignments. The Minnesota Office of Citizenship and Volunteer Services, a state agency in the Department of Administration, provides training and information for other volunteer programs. Similarly, the Management Assistance Program for Nonprofits recruits corporate volunteers to assist nonprofit organizations to improve their management. Another key initiative has been the establishment of the Virginia McKnight Binger Human Services Awards, begun by the McKnight Foundation to recognize the importance of individual volunteers, especially people who have proven their commitment through years of service. In addition to being part of a gracious event and publicity, the ten award recipients receive $7,500 each.

ENHANCING MANAGEMENT CAPACITY AND ABILITY TO GENERATE INCOME

While promotion of a philanthropic and volunteer ethic has been important in Minnesota, a comprehensive strategy involves both a push and a pull. One former Minnesota governor observed that it was not just that Minnesotans were so generous, but that the organizations making requests had become more effective at making requests.

Efforts to improve the capacity—and the accountability—of the demand side have received less attention, but have equally been a focus of activity. Active donors, seeking to ensure that their donations were going to organizations spending their money effectively, formed the Charities Review Council of Minnesota in 1946. So, too, the founding of the Minnesota Nonprofit Assistance Fund in 1980 by the Minneapolis Foundation and other local funders was intended, inter alia, to provide cash-flow loans and financial advice to struggling nonprofits. A former Control Data executive formed the National Center for Social Entrepreneurs in 1985 to help nonprofits become more successful at generating income from fees and sales while meeting community needs. The University of St. Thomas serves as home to the Center for Nonprofit Management, the Institute for Renewing Community Leadership, and the

Partners Internship Program, each furthering a different aspect of nonprofit leadership development.

Conspicuous among the failures of Minnesota philanthropy was the demise of low-income, constituency-controlled organizations in the 1980s and 1990s. Negative audit reports, deficits, and dissolution followed years of foundation grants and government contracts to The Way, the St. Paul American Indian Center, the Minnesota Clients Council, the Whittier Alliance, the Phoenix Group, People of Phillips, and others. The abundance of management and financial support available in the state did not help these organizations keep basic books and maintain cash flow.

Corporate contributions generally steer clear of groups critical of or antagonistic toward specific business interests. The Minnesota Tenants Union, which advocates for tenants' rights in disputes with landlords, has not received a corporate grant in twenty years. Even when corporations are not making a direct decision about the grantworthiness of a particular project, other community members sometimes act to squelch controversy on their behalf to avoid conflict or embarrassment.

An unusual example of the power of selection occurred in the late 1970s when a North Minneapolis low-income organization was concerned about the inability of neighborhood residents to get mortgages or loans from the city's largest banks. In this case the neighborhood organization was sponsored by a large social-service agency, which received the majority of its funds from the United Way. With the assistance of a young community organizer, the neighborhood group sent letters to the banks requesting lending data required under the Community Reinvestment Act.

Officials at one bank, a large United Way donor, contacted the United Way to ask why their institution was being targeted. The United Way asked the same question of the social-service agency, which in turn directed the neighborhood organization to end its inquiry. When the neighborhood residents persisted, the organizer assigned to their neighborhood by the social-service agency was fired and the group disbanded. Direct interventions such as this are rare, since most participants in the contributions interaction are knowledgeable about the practical bounds of corporate philanthropy.

More recent examples of cooperation among large nonprofits abound. In 1996, the Minnesota Council of Nonprofits, the Minnesota Council on Foundations, and the Minnesota Council of Churches joined to cosponsor a fund intended to assist nonprofits restructuring in response to welfare reform. The Minnesota Futures Fund received $1.3 million in contributions from Minnesota foundations and corporations, and $750,000 from the state of Minnesota.

In 1998, Urban Ventures was started by a retired businessman, Peter Heegaard, to expose up-and-coming middle managers to problems encountered by nonprofits working in such areas as urban renewal, low-cost housing, homeless shelters, and similar services. The organization's objective is to develop a pool of executives who understand the problems of nonprofits and can bring their corporate expertise to help as they rise through the ranks of their companies. Another successful effort to help economic development is the Loan Tech program of the Minneapolis Foundation. A rotating fund of loan money is made available to help inner-city entrepreneurs, small businesses, and struggling nonprofits as they work their way out of financial problems.

Several Minnesota nonprofits have used reliable philanthropic support to build substantial enterprises of earned income. The classic example is Minnesota Public Radio (MPR), which began merchandising *Prairie Home Companion* memorabilia and turned it into a multimillion-dollar catalog-and-music business, run by a for-profit subsidiary. Hazelden, an early pioneer in residential chemical dependency counseling, launched a publishing business with books, tapes, and calendars that now accounts for half its income. The economic success and entrepreneurship of many organizations was welcomed by the press and the public, but the use of for-profit subsidiaries has raised some hackles—especially concerning compensation for MPR executives paid both by the charity and its for-profit subsidiary.

Lessons from Minnesota Philanthropy

The growth of Minnesota's nonprofit sector and the increasing role of corporate philanthropy have come at a time of increasing population and a generally healthy economy. Since the state ranks fifteenth in median disposable income and sixteenth in per capita personal income, the economy does not explain the growth of Minnesota's commitment to philanthropy. The philosophy that "what is good for the community is good for business" is institutionally accepted and leads to public expectations of how present and future business and political leaders will perform. Several conclusions are possible:

First, the best customer for philanthropy is an educated person—and a young person, as indicated by poll results.[10] Not only does Minnesota have a high rate of charitable giving, but more information is publicly available regarding charities in Minnesota than any other state—including libraries stocked with the *Minnesota Nonprofit Directory*, toll-free telephone access to the Charities Review Council, and the Attorney General's Office Charities Division web site.

Next, business leadership influences the larger community. The location of fourteen Fortune 500 companies in the state is important, as is the visible, persistent leadership and formal structures of commitment—especially the Keystone Program.

Third, receptivity to social messages has been self-reinforcing, resulting from the repeated message of the value of charitable giving and volunteering from multiple channels, including the workplace, support organizations, and community leaders.

Furthermore, fairness in distribution of grants is an ongoing challenge. While major educational and cultural institutions have thrived—such as the Carlson School of Management and the Ordway Center for the Performing Arts—they operate in an unstated competition with health clinics, human-services agencies, environmental groups, neighborhood associations, and small nonprofits. Successful capital campaigns for the Minneapolis American Indian Center, Turning Point, and the Seed Academy showed that organizations serving communities of color can successfully pursue large contributions. A $20 million campaign by the Penumbra Theatre Company and Walker-West Music Academy, announced in 1998, raised the ante significantly.

Finally, an important unexplored area is the link between the public's decision to make charitable contributions and willingness to pay taxes. Minnesota is considered a high-tax state, ranking fifth among the states in personal tax load. While Minnesota's corporations, including the Keystone Program organizations, have long sought to lower the state's personal income tax and commercial/industrial tax rates, they have never pursued this campaign vigorously. Yet the state's high tax rates are matched by high rates of charitable giving, both individual and business, while states with lower tax rates generally report lower levels of charitable giving. How might this correlation be explained?

Minnesota is not the Cooperative Commonwealth that the Farmer–Laborites envisioned, or the open shop of the Citizens Alliance. Minnesota still has its share of persistent poverty, urban sprawl, and violence. However, the state has made sufficient peace in its politics and employment relations to achieve high workforce participation and a healthy, diverse economy, with one of the nation's lowest rates of unemployment for many years.

A defining feature of Minnesota that shows no signs of dissipating is the public spirit—a now institutionalized expectation of ongoing personal involvement and contributions from businesses and individuals. A highly visible and well networked third sector has emerged that influences how much Minnesota allocates, through philanthropy as well as public funds, to tackle social problems and improve the quality of life for all Minnesota citizens.

The Future of Corporate Philanthropy in Minnesota

With increased participation in programs like the Keystone, a jump in private foundation grants, continued support for tax exemptions and for giving, and improved management and board capacity in most nonprofit organizations, the future of Minnesota philanthropy appears to be bright. The balanced growth of nonprofit revenue—including strong charitable, government, and earned income—means that most community organizations are on a path of sustainable development.

Perhaps Minnesota's greatest challenge is to come to grips with the full potential of philanthropic and nonprofit activity, since it is a larger factor in its economy and public life than is the case in any other state. As a significant economic and political influence, can philanthropy and nonprofits reposition themselves in the public's eye from their current image as beneficial but disconnected, resource-short gap-fillers, to a new role as successful and essential to a healthy society?

The next progression needs to include increased linkages between institutional philanthropy and public officials. This requires greater coordination between support organizations emphasizing charitable giving and their counterparts focused on government relations. Just as in the early phase of the state's history, when business leadership moved from economic warfare to the common ground of philanthropy to support charitable institutions, there is a growing appreciation of the possibilities of collective action involving the Minnesota business community, government, and nonprofits together. Welfare-to-work programs, urban schools, and environmental mediation are bringing together all three sectors as players in a democratic, pluralistic society with a mixed economy. The results are often messy, but there is a growing experience base and comfort level with these multisector collaborations, and an expansion of what gets included in private expressions of the public spirit.

Corporate headquarters move out of Minnesota; turnover of corporate leadership speeds up; new, fast-growing companies with young CEOs replace the old corporations and their leaders; businesses tend to focus more on global than local issues. Corporations and wealthy individuals have raised one important question about the future of philanthropic contributions: What will happen to those contributions as the old leadership in the Twin Cities that funded so many of the institutions discussed in this essay passes from the scene? Of the approximately $3 billion in annual charitable contributions, 80 percent comes from individuals, and 90 percent of the balance comes from private and corporate foundations. Fortunately for the future, Minnesota has a long tradition of individual and corporate support for nonprofit organizations. The method of giving and the organizations to which the money flows have become institutionalized, making philanthropy easy and expected. The business community knows that it needs a healthy economic, social, medical, and educational community around it to keep business healthy. History and peer pressure will make it highly likely that the leaders of the future will continue in a pattern of generosity and involvement to assure a healthy level of philanthropy.

Notes

1. Quoted in "High Praise from High Places," *Minneapolis Star*, 1 July 1977, 4A.
2. Carol J. De Vita, "Viewing Nonprofits across the States," number one in the series *Charting Civil Society* (Washington, D.C.: The Urban Institute, Center on Nonprofits and Philanthropy, August 1997), 3. The report's table "Distribution of Public Charities in States by Activity, 1992" was based on 1993 U.S. Internal Revenue Service Exempt Organizations/Business Master File and Return Transaction File.
3. Minnesota Department of Trade and Economic Development, *Compare Minnesota: An Economic and Statistical Fact Book*, St. Paul, Minn., 1996, 17, 23, 36.
4. Charles E. Wilson, confirmation hearings, Washington, D.C., 15 January 1953; Ken Dayton, interview by the authors, Minneapolis, 13 October 1999.
5. Minnesota Keystone Program participants' brochure 1996 (Minneapolis: Greater Minneapolis Chamber of Commerce, 1996), 2.
6. Joseph Galaskiewicz, "An Urban Grants Economy Revisited: Corporate Charitable Contributions in the Twin Cities 1979–81, 1987–89," *Administrative Science Quarterly* (42) (September 1997): 467.
7. Ibid., 468.
8. Claude N. Rosenberg, *Wealthy and Wise: How You and America Can Get the Most Out of Your Giving* (Boston: Little, Brown, 1994).
9. One Percent Club brochure, Minneapolis, 1998.
10. Minnesota Center for Survey Research, *Minnesota State Survey*, Minneapolis, January 1998, 36; Robert Franklin, "8 in 10 in the State Donate to a Wide Variety of Charities," *Star Tribune*, 17 December 1995, 1A, 19A.

JOE DOWLING

Theater and the Arts: A Personal Reflection

EVEN AFTER FIVE YEARS, Minnesota continues to surprise and fascinate me. Coming from Ireland to run the Guthrie Theater in Minneapolis, I expected that the frozen north would be a daunting environment for theater and the arts. I feared that exposure to ice fishing, a much-loved annual ritual, might have blunted the state's finer sensibilities. I anticipated that the sheer misery of a climate that reached unbelievably low temperatures would have dampened the artistic impulse. While the fame of the Guthrie Theater had ensured Minneapolis name recognition among the theatrical cognoscenti, most of my friends and acquaintances expressed alarm that I was leaving the new cosmopolitanism of Dublin for the bleak tundra of the Upper Midwest. Those who knew anything about it recoiled in horror at stories of −60°F temperatures, and the urban myths of tongues frozen to lampposts were repeated with glee. The more geographically challenged asked if we intended to frequent car racing, confidently assuming that we were bound for Indianapolis. For many of them, both cities were merely names on a map vaguely remembered from the schoolroom.

Our arrival in February of 1995 confirmed many of the more Cassandra-like prophecies of family and friends. Traveling from London in a heated plane and then whisked to the hotel in an overheated car, my wife and I were lulled into a false sense of warmth and security. The clear blue sky and the bright winter sun added to the illusion of comfort and calm in our new surroundings. Anxious to get some air and to explore the city, we ignored the advice of more seasoned Minneapolitans and boldly ventured forth. Approximately twenty seconds later, we dived for cover into the nearest shop and stood for several seconds attempting to restore some semblance of circulation to our frozen limbs. Neither of us could speak, and we were wondering how, in the name of God, we were going to get back to the hotel. A cheerful voice behind us asked with some amusement, "So, where are you guys from?" The shop clerk had

JOE DOWLING *is Artistic Director of the Guthrie Theater.*

immediately recognized two weather virgins whose brutal introduction to their new life had left them speechless but infinitely wiser.

My wife returned to Dublin to complete professional and family obligations, intending to join me the following year. As the winter rolled on, I became increasingly disenchanted with its severity. I called her several times and urged her not to sell our comfortable Dublin home. I was less and less sure that I would survive the numerous ice storms and blizzards. However, although they were brutal to be caught in, they created a kind of austere beauty I had not witnessed before. The stillness of a winter morning after an ice storm with the sun highlighting the silver branches of the ice-sealed trees was breathtaking.

Winter, however, turned to spring and, half an hour later, to summer. Finally, I got it. At long last, I understood the attractions of a city surrounded by lakes whose tree-lined walks had seemed eerie and isolated during the long winter months. I began to appreciate the walkways and parklands and knew why they were recognized as among the best in the country. The sense of freedom and pleasure in strolling around the Lake of the Isles early on a Sunday morning, nodding to passing cyclists and avoiding instant death from in-line skaters, gave me a new appreciation of the quality of life and recreation available in this bijou city. The memory of the long winter with its terrifying bleakness and relentless ferocity faded fast. It was replaced by a feeling of freshness and an atmosphere of openness and community. While in winter months people scurry through the hermetically sealed skyways that link downtown buildings and dress in clothes that make the Michelin Man seem svelte, at the first glimmer of spring they strip to just this side of decency and parade their sunshine-deprived skin around the lakes with abandon. The change in mood is infectious and the natural Midwest friendliness drives away the mythic savageness of winter.

When Tyrone Guthrie, one of the most influential directors of twentieth-century English-speaking theater, decided to create a repertory theater in Minneapolis in the early 1960s, he was not sure why he was so anxious to locate it in the Twin Cities. Writing in *A New Theatre* in 1964 he asks the question, "Why? The weather? The people? The river? We have discussed it often and we simply do not know."[1] Later in the same book, he attempts to come up with an answer that explains his impulses to create a new form of theater in America. "It is an attempt to relate a theatre to its supporting community."[2] Since its founding, the Guthrie Theater has depended on the community it serves and, in return, it has provided that community with a quality of theater as high as anywhere in the world.

A surprising statistic about the Twin Cities is that, outside of New York, per head of population, this part of the upper Midwest has more theaters than anywhere in the United States. Much of this theatrical activity has been spawned by the continuing success of the Guthrie. Don Stolz, the head of the Old Log Theater, America's longest-running repertory theater, came to Tyrone Guthrie and expressed his concern that the new theater proposed for Minneapolis would do damage to his own business. The great man reassured him and promised that, with the arrival of the new theater, there would be an increase in enthusiasm for theater throughout the region. And so it proved. With the emergence of new theaters audiences were ready to experience a wide variety of dramatic offerings. The audiences in the Twin Cities are among the most literate and discerning in the country. They come prepared to listen and have an appetite for the unusual as well as a love of the classical. They expect a standard of presentation that has become a norm and are vocally critical of any work that falls below anticipated levels.

While the Guthrie Theater is the largest and best-funded theater in the region, we are certainly not the only attraction for the theater lover. Companies such as Theatre de la Jeune Lune offer a cosmopolitan feel to the theatrical landscape of Minnesota. Two of its four founders are French and two are American. They met at the Ecole Jacques Lecoq in Paris where the emphasis was on a physical theater emphasizing a combination of athleticism and a broad presentational style. Their work also incorporates a new take on classical plays that can be spellbinding. The combination of American actors and a French influence creates a unique blend that can, at its best, be thrilling and innovative. Much of the work of the company is created through improvisation and workshop and combines an emphasis on *commedia dell'arte* with an American directness and verve. Tours to other parts of the United States have introduced this Minnesotan marvel to a wider audience and to critical acclaim.

A wonderful children's theater offers a superb introduction to the art of drama to young Minnesotans. Many of the graduates of the Children's Theatre Company school become the adult actors who serve the many theaters all around the cities. It is a tribute to the philanthropic spirit of Minnesota that a theater devoted to children can operate at a level comparable to any adult theater in the country. The exciting thing about the work done at the Children's Theatre is that it does not patronize its young audience. The acting and technical work is first-class and the current artistic director, Peter Brosius, has a remarkable ability to choose work that challenges common perceptions of children's theater. The successive generations that have been weaned on the Children's Theatre and the educational work of the Guthrie Theater form the basis of a superb audience.

Another great asset to the Twin Cities is the Penumbra Theatre Company in St. Paul. Founded by Lou Bellamy in the late 1970s, it serves a crucial national function in fostering African American literature and presenting the experience of black life and culture on the stage. August Wilson, the Pulitzer Prize–winning dramatist, was a founding member of the company, and his plays have long been a highlight of Penumbra's work. In 1997, the Guthrie Theater hosted the Penumbra production of Wilson's *Fences*, bringing these two important institutions together and presenting Wilson's work at the Guthrie for the first time. It is the intention of both theaters to work together in the future to ensure that, collectively, they can achieve artistic results that individually would not be possible. The deep insight provided by Bellamy and his company, combined with the classical and technical experience of the Guthrie company and staff, provide a unique experience. This collaboration allowed a diverse audience in the spring of 2000 to experience a beautifully realized production of *The Darker Face of the Earth*, Rita Dove's treatment of the Oedipus story set in the antebellum South.

When you add such interesting companies as the Jungle Theater, recently relocated to a beautiful new theater in uptown Minneapolis, and the Illusion Theater, devoted to new work and also in a new venue, to the list, it is clear that the theatrical life in the Twin Cities continues to be well served. Young companies abound in tiny spaces all around the cities with varying degrees of skill and achievement. Among the most talented are Eye of the Storm, a company led by Casey Stangl, whose productions of contemporary work are always fresh, and the Frank Theatre, led by Wendy Knox, whose work is eclectic and breaks new ground with each new show. The Mixed Blood Theatre, led by a local treasure, Jack Reuler, is an important company that has worked diligently at breaking down barriers between the races. Their work has national significance, and constantly challenges stereotypes and demands a deeper understanding between people of all backgrounds.

While the focus of my time in Minnesota has been on theater, it has been fascinating to experience the range of other performing-arts possibilities available in the Twin Cities. With the Minnesota Orchestra, the Saint Paul Chamber Orchestra, and numerous other smaller offerings, musical life in the region is rich and filled with variety. The Minnesota Opera presents superb national and international artists in two sold-out seasons each year at the Ordway Center for the Performing Arts in St. Paul. The Minnesota Dance Alliance has both superb performances and a wide educational program to introduce the art of dance to a new generation. One of the liveliest and most eccentric companies is the Ballet of the Dolls. Headed by a gifted dancer and choreographer, Myron Johnson, this company undertakes a program that includes the classical rigors of ballet and combines them with a highly camp sensibility. The company's recent combination of *Swan Lake* with *Whatever Happened to Baby Jane?* provided one of the more unusual highlights of the season at the Loring Playhouse, a venue for all kinds of alternative events. A recent move to a new permanent home for Ballet of the Dolls will ensure the company's growth.

A network of skillfully restored theaters and arts centers around the state in diverse places such as St. Cloud, Duluth, Lanesboro, and many other communities belies the notion that Minnesota is a dour and weather-obsessed state. The misperception that entertainment in this state is confined to snowboards and the peculiar habit of digging holes in the ice, mounting portable huts over them, and waiting for the arrival of unsuspecting fish is hard to dislodge. For those whose only exposure to local culture is the movie *Fargo*, it can come as a surprise to experience the real Minnesota with a sophisticated and highly educated population and an authentic streak of independence in both politics and cultural life.

Coming from a European society that expects the state to play a large part in the funding of the arts, I found it a bit of a shock to discover how difficult it is for arts groups to ensure their survival for the long term. I still find it hard to accept that the arts are only possible in many communities around the country because of private donations and aggressive fund-raising. The acceptance of the arts as a vital and integral part of the fabric of society demands public investment. I worry that, without increased public involvement, the innovative, demanding work, the new expressions and the alternative viewpoints that are essential for the health of any society, will be driven underground and not find any mainstream expression in the United States. The distinguished British critic and former head of the BBC World Service was succinct and accurate in his book *Art Matters: Reflecting on Culture* when he declared: "The arts matter because they embrace, express and define the soul of a civilization. A nation without arts would be a nation that had stopped talking to itself, stopped dreaming, and had lost interest in the past and lacked curiosity about the future."[3]

The debates in recent years about the funding of the National Endowment for the Arts at the federal level were debilitating and futile. The accusations of pornography leveled against individual artists and institutions were always a smoke screen to hide a more fundamental fear. Those who would stifle artistic expression fear the questions the artist explores. The curiosity of the artist often demands answers and can create ripples in the smooth surface of a complacent society. I remember a visit to West Berlin in the late 1970s when, as artistic director of the Abbey Theatre, Ireland's national theater, I had the opportunity to meet many colleagues in the German theater. At that time, we were all envious of the levels of subsidy offered to the *Schauspielhäuser* throughout West Germany. Speaking to the intendant of the Schiller theater in Berlin, I asked about the level of subsidy his company received from the government. I was amazed at the enormous sums of money he mentioned and asked why he thought the German government was so generous. His answer struck home with great force. "So that it will never happen again." He did not need to state what "it" was. The recognition that the artist can, with persistent questioning, contribute to the balance within a society is a mature reflection on the value of the arts to the preservation of democracy. A dictator can destroy a constitution and a legal system, he can terrorize people into a bland conformity, but he can never stifle the imagination or the subversive irony and satire that have always served as oblique opposition to tyranny. A society that fears or ignores its artists lacks self-confidence and a belief in its own values.

The state of Minnesota has a proud record in the matter of arts funding that is in keeping with its fierce independent spirit. The Scandinavian sense of fair play and social equality still motivate much of the public thinking in this state. Again and again, the legislature and the governor have voted significant appropriations to the Minnesota State Arts Board. Before leaving office in 1998, Governor Arne Carlson took the unusual step of greatly increasing funding to the Arts Board. In a moving speech delivered to the entire arts community, he spoke of the value of the arts to the future of the state and of the lasting impact on young people of exposure to artistic expression. He was particularly emotional about the effect opera had on his father, a Swedish emigrant to the United States in the early part of the century. As a newcomer to the state, I was both impressed and moved by the passion and sincerity of a political leader who saw that, by judicious expenditure and investment of state money, the cultural infrastructure of the community could be developed and improved for the benefit of all its citizens.

While the current governor, the inimitable Jesse Ventura, is publicly opposed to the funding of the arts by the taxpayer, he did not reduce the appropriation to the Arts Board in his early budgets. However, he has made it clear that he will veto capital expenditure on arts buildings and improvements. Recently, he vetoed a bill providing planning money to the Guthrie Theater for a new building proposed on the Mississippi River, declaring that funding a specific theater would require him to fund all theaters. In a move that shocked many political observers and pundits, the legislature overrode his veto and restored the original $3 million in planning money voted as part of a state bonding bill. What made this event so spectacular was that legislators were bombarded with letters, phone calls, e-mails, and other communications from constituents around the state who believed in a vision for the Guthrie Theater and were determined that there would be public funding. There is a very real sense of ownership of the cultural institutions by a large majority of the citizens of the state.

Sponsorship and private funding are also a major feature of the artistic life of Minnesota, as they are in the rest of the country. Families such as the Daytons, the Pillsburys, the McKnights, the Cowleses, the Wurteles, and many others who have committed to the welfare of the community have been generous and farsighted in their support for theaters, orchestras, museums, and a wide variety of artists and artistic institutions. Many of the companies who are headquartered here also respond generously to the preservation of the arts in our community. Indeed, the joke goes that Minnesota is where fund-raisers die and go to heaven!

What makes this state such a Mecca for arts funding? In many ways, it is a measure of the pride and sense of independence people here feel about their community. This is a potentially isolated part of the world. Winter is long and harsh and the natural resources and many of the recreations are not available during those long months. Minnesota has a bleak reputation as a cold and remote place. The reality is very different, as many immigrants (including me) have found. When I came here I heard it said that Minnesota was the hardest place to recruit people to and the hardest place to recruit people from. One of the reasons why corporations, foundations, and individuals are so generous to the arts is to ensure that the quality of life is preserved and developed. In this way corporations can attract talented people to work here and to stay. As the world becomes more of a global village and the technological revolution allows people to work anywhere, the need to compete for the top talent will become even more marked. The arts in Minnesota provide a sense of cosmopolitanism and sophistication lacking in many similar sized cities and states in the country. The quality of life here is one of the best-kept secrets in the world—and many here would like to keep it that way.

The founding of the Guthrie Theater in 1963 was a kind of miracle in itself. Tyrone Guthrie, Oliver Rea, and Peter Zeisler—all working in New York—recognized that the future of American theater was in jeopardy if the focus of all activity remained on Broadway. In Guthrie's eyes, American theater had become more concerned with the high cost of rent in New York than with the pursuit of the art. He and his colleagues were determined to find a city far away from New York where they could create a theater that would offer a season ". . . not merely . . . of classics, but of classics which in origin, style and content would contrast interestingly one with another, would pose the implicit question: what is a classic and what has made it so?"[4]

They decided to consult Brooks Atkinson, then a critic for the *New York Times*. The following Sunday, Atkinson wrote of the plan to create a not-for-profit theater away from the commercial necessities of Broadway and asked cities around the country to demonstrate their interest and commitment. Seven applications were received. The hardy trio toured the country and interviewed the interested parties. The cities that survived the scrutiny were Milwaukee, Detroit, and Minneapolis. For various reasons, the first two fell by the wayside and Minneapolis was the chosen site. A steering committee led by John Cowles Jr. met with Guthrie in New York and persuaded him that they were seriously committed to the future of his project.

The Walker Art Center provided the land, and a brilliant architect, Professor Ralph Rapson of the University of Minnesota, was chosen to design the new theater. I do not believe that the original founders of the theater could have imagined how profound the effect would be on the health of American theater. What began as a reaction to the excesses of commercialism on Broadway has developed into an important national movement that has greatly improved the quality of life throughout the country and ensured that successive generations of young Americans have been introduced to the work of great playwrights. Some thirty-seven years after the founding of the Guthrie, regional theaters around the country form the backbone of a movement that is a *de facto* National Theater of America. Unlike many European countries, the United States has never made a concerted effort to create a national theater. The vastness of the country, the regional differences, and the inadequate structures of state funding have all conspired to frustrate this ambition. However, the theaters that form the League of Resident Theaters, situated in many cities and towns throughout America, share many personnel and plays. Directors, designers, and actors move from city to city forming a kind of national company. Indeed, a trend in recent years has been to create co-productions between theaters and perform the same production in several different cities. Much of the energy for this movement came from early pioneering theaters such as the Guthrie in Minneapolis, Arena Stage in Washington, D.C., the Alley Theatre in Houston, and others.

The Guthrie has grown immeasurably from its spectacular beginnings. What was intended as a theater with a four-play summer festival performed by a company in rotating repertory now performs year-round in two separate theaters to over four hundred thousand patrons each year. Such a huge increase in activity and the sophisticated demands of contemporary audiences have made the original building inadequate to the needs of the company. Most theaters around the country of similar importance have at least two performance spaces under the same roof, and, with increasing interest in the power of drama as an educational tool, dedicated spaces are needed for classes, seminars, and other educational programs.

In recent years, the board has decided to relocate the Guthrie, and the city of Minneapolis has provided a site on the Mississippi River to house a new and expanded theater. Plans are underway to select an architect and to begin a new phase in the history of Minnesota's most important theater. The intention is to create a new complex with three different auditoriums. The signature of the Guthrie Theater has been the thrust stage, which allows the action of the play to be brought close to the audience in a way unknown on a proscenium arch stage. In the current location, no audience member is more than fifty feet away from the stage. The wrap-around auditorium with its distinctive multicolored seats and a formation that links the parterre with the balcony is a unique arrangement. It is a vibrant and exciting theatrical space. Designed for Shakespeare and the classical authors, it is the perfect place to see works of size and movement. I know of no other stage where Shakespeare's language and imagery seem so natural and immediate. The relationship between actor and audience, which is at the heart of the theatrical experience, is ideal. The sweep of the thrust stage, the entrances from both backstage and from the audience, the direct connection that can be made with the language of each play—all conspire to create an excitement unknown in other spaces. For this reason, it has been determined that a new Guthrie Theater will always maintain its signature thrust stage. We will keep the asymmetrical auditorium and the intimacy between actor and audience as the hallmarks of our theater.

At the same time, we need to develop a greater diversity in our theatrical endeavors—engage contemporary writers who tell the story of our time and participate in the shaping of the theater of the future. In order to achieve these ambitions, it is essential to have more than one space available to our artists. Many of the works written in the second part of the last century, for example, feel out of place on our stage. Works conceived on a smaller scale and written in a naturalistic style that focus on the internal psychological motivations of characters or that demand concentration on a single penetrating image seem lost on our stage.

As the trend toward smaller theaters becomes more important in the American theater, the opportunity to produce contemporary works and collaborate with other companies on new and exciting projects will be lost unless the Guthrie takes appropriate action. To preserve a role as the flagship of the American theater, we must have a second space where we can work with writers, present international and national touring productions, and engage in projects that promote long-term relationships with other theaters around the region and the country. That space should have a flexible proscenium stage so that a contrast can be achieved with our signature thrust stage space.

Like many people working in the American theater, I am concerned that there is a drift of young talent away from the live stage. Graduates from acting programs enter the world of film and television without ever setting foot on stage to learn the basis of their craft. If we are to ensure the continuance of classical theater performance, we must begin to nurture the next generation of writers, actors, directors, and craftspersons who will fill our stages. For this purpose, the new Guthrie Theater will have a studio space that allows alternative works to be produced, to develop the imagination of young artists and excite a new generation with the power of live performance.

In many ways, this move and the expansion of activities fulfill the original ambitions of the founders to create a place where a variety of experiences could attract a wide audience with the aim, in Guthrie's own words, "not to uplift or to instruct, but to entertain, to delight."[5] The enthusiasm shown for the idea of The Guthrie on the River, as it has become known, has been overwhelming among local media and political authorities and confirms Guthrie's own prophesy that one day the river would come into its own:

> But the river itself was what most charmed and amazed us. It had not yet frozen over and was flowing with a lively sparkle through winding gorges which are still beautiful, although here, as everywhere else, the convenience of the waterway has been exploited. . . . Of course it will not always be so. Eventually the Twin Cities will realise that their river can be, and ought to be, a wonderful and life-giving amenity without losing any of its utility.[6]

When the new theater is built, I believe that the life-giving amenity Tyrone Guthrie speaks of will be a permanent reflection of the incredible spirit of openness and respect for the art of theater that he found here in the early 1960s and that continue to delight and amaze me every day.

Notes

1. Tyrone Guthrie, *A New Theatre* (New York: McGraw-Hill, 1964), 60.
2. Ibid., 178.
3. John Tusa, *Art Matters: Reflecting on Culture* (London: Methuen Publishing Ltd., 1999), 22.
4. Guthrie, *A New Theatre*, 41.
5. Ibid., 177.
6. Ibid., 50.

ROBERT J. WHITE

Minnesota and the World Abroad

The Almost Foreign Minister

IN THE SPRING OF 1991, with Yugoslavia on the brink of its slide toward bloody dismemberment, President Franjo Tudjman of Croatia prepared to welcome into his cabinet a new foreign minister. His name was Rudy Perpich, and his credentials included spending the previous eight years as governor of Minnesota.

Observers unfamiliar with the state and its people may see in that bit of recent history an example of Minnesota's sometimes quirky contradictions. This is, after all, a state that provoked national, even international, interest in a later governor. How, people wondered, could the sober-sided citizens of Minnesota elect in 1998 the former professional wrestler Jesse Ventura, especially when one of the other candidates carried the name Humphrey? How—in a further contradiction—had a political neophyte managed to gather such an impressive postelection brain trust? And why, a decade earlier, would a Balkan president name to his cabinet someone from presumably parochial mid-continent America? Perpich ultimately declined the invitation, troubled by doubts that he could simultaneously serve in a foreign government and retain his U.S. citizenship.

As will be evident, Tudjman's choice of Perpich was logical. Yet the episode illustrated Minnesota's global contradiction: its people are simultaneously insular and worldly-wise.

Perpich came from northern Minnesota: Iron Range country, where local loyalties run deep and people cast suspicious glances at the city slickers in the Minneapolis–St. Paul metropolis. If linguistic purists wince when today's governor gives the state a diphthong ("Minnesoahta"), they writhed when yesterday's governor spoke with strangled syntax. But most Minnesotans make allowance for Ventura, who only sounds like the rest of us. And they made allowance for Perpich; English was his second language, Croatian his first.

ROBERT J. WHITE *is the former editor of the editorial pages of the Minneapolis* Star Tribune.

However parochial Iron Rangers may appear, they know something of the old world from which their families came—as do the increasingly diverse families elsewhere in the state. They know something, too, about the new world of this new century.

Tudjman wanted Perpich as an envoy to the West precisely because he was from it. Here was a politician who knew the American heartland, and yet—when the Soviet Union was still intact—had persuaded Mikhail Gorbachev to visit Minnesota. Wags in the state capitol asked how soon the ex-governor would be campaigning for Tudjman's job, and the idea could have proved more than a joke. One wonders what Croatia might have become had Perpich surmounted the citizenship hurdle, had he not died in 1995, had he outlived Tudjman.

An Inland Worldview

Governors provide only one window into Minnesota's global contradiction, though an important one. When Harold Stassen was elected in 1938, the thirty-one-year-old governor brought with him openly internationalist convictions. Most Minnesotans at the time were at best uninterested in such ideas, yet they sent Stassen into office on a landslide. Nor was their aversion to foreign entanglements momentary. Votes on international matters by a state's congressional delegation give a fair indication of constituent sentiment; between 1933 and 1950 Minnesota was solidly isolationist.[1]

Opinion surveys offer more direct interpretations of public worldviews. The Minnesota Poll, established by the *Minneapolis Tribune* (now the *Star Tribune*), is one such source.[2] On issues of foreign aid, foreign relations, trade, and national security, the Minnesota surveys from 1944 to 1999 include nearly a thousand questions in fifty-six categories.

Although this is a rich inventory of public attitudes on international matters, it contains only a few indications of opinion on the same subject over time. A 1944 question—"When do you think the war will end in Europe?"—cannot be repeated a half-century later. There is, however, a pattern discernible through four decades in surveys that asked about foreign aid. Although not identical, the questions posed were sufficiently similar to suggest two conclusions. First, when the Cold War began to look permanent, isolationism declined. Second, the change in attitude—at least toward foreign aid—remained fairly constant in subsequent years.

In January of 1951, the Minnesota Poll asked whether respondents approved of a proposal for $90 million in U.S. aid to "the backward areas of Asia, Africa, and Latin America"; a strong majority (64 percent) said no. Four years later, however, responses to similar questions indicated acceptance of American financial responsibilities overseas. In that 1955 poll the percentage opposing aid—most of it proposed for Asia, but now an amount approaching $3.5 billion for the coming year—dropped to 37 percent. Forty-four percent approved, compared with 17 percent in 1951.

Polls in 1957, 1961, 1964, and 1965 offered evidence of firm, if not overwhelming, approval of overseas assistance. Each poll showed support by about half the Minnesota public for current or higher spending on foreign aid; less than half wanted aid reduced. Majorities in all but the 1957 poll thought the program had benefited the United States.

Taking a different approach to the same subject, the poll in 1983 questioned Minnesotans about obligations abroad rather than cost. When asked whether "Americans have a special responsibility" to provide food and health aid, prevent wars, and protect human rights, a majority in each instance said yes. Among those who gave that answer, a majority also favored continuing aid even if doing so caused a decline in American living standards. A similar set of questions in 1989 elicited similar answers.

There are no easy explanations for what influences respondents' answers in a particular poll. Perhaps Minnesota's 1951 opposition to Third World assistance was a sign of world-weariness; the Korean War was raging, and UN forces had just been driven back. But the contrasting acceptance of "special responsibility" registered in the 1980s polls came from Minnesotans who had no reason to envision a suddenly peaceful international environment; the Cold War had not ended, and the imprint of the Vietnam trauma remained vivid.

Still, the polls lend weight to this observation: In the last half of the twentieth century Minnesota's place in the world, and its citizens' perception of that place, became something substantially different from what it had been before. And even on the limited gauge of foreign aid these opinion surveys confirm the global contradiction: A slim majority of Minnesotans are sensitive to the needs of people beyond U.S. borders, and believe that helping to meet those needs is a Tocquevillian self-interest rightly understood. But a near majority repeatedly demurs. If the dissenters are not quite saying "Stop the world, I want to get off," they at least want it slowed.

Prairie Internationalism

While it is true that Minnesotans emerged from an isolationist cocoon after World War II, they had not always been insular. An early twentieth-century enterprise illustrates the global influence exerted by people in the American heartland.

The digging of the Panama Canal, writes the historian David McCullough, carried the blessing of an "unseen guiding spirit." The unlikely celestial being in McCullough's description is the Minnesota railroad baron James J. Hill: unlikely both because Hill's beatitudes tended toward testiness—President Theodore Roosevelt, he once said, had never done anything but "pose and draw a salary"[3]—and because Hill himself did not guide the project.

The visible guide was Hill's protégé, John Stevens, whom Roosevelt appointed in 1905 as chief engineer to take over the stalled canal enterprise. Roosevelt did so after Hill, despite his low opinion of the president, had recommended Stevens to him as the best construction engineer in the country and the right man for the Panama job.

Hill and Stevens had much in common. Like Hill, Stevens was blunt and independent. Like Hill, he became a legend in the Northwest, and it is appropriate that the foundation established by the Hill family is now called the Northwest Area Foundation. Stevens found the route to the Pacific that let Hill's Great Northern Railroad cross the Continental Divide at a lower elevation than any other railroad and by the most direct route. Stevens decided where to tunnel, where to bridge. He used the same skills to direct the construction of the Panama Canal.

Great Northern's Empire Builder was not only the name of the railroad's best-known train but its founder's self-description. Asia, Hill believed, would be essential to his company's commerce. An interesting footnote to Minnesota history is that only in part did Hill fulfill his dream of empire to the Pacific and beyond by building a railroad; his greater influence may well have been as the "guiding spirit" behind building a maritime shortcut between oceans.

Railroads, iron mining, lumber, shipping, farming, grain milling, commodity trading, finance, manufacturing—as these and other industries matured from the nineteenth to the twentieth centuries in Minnesota and elsewhere, they came to affect, and be affected by, events beyond the United States. Much the same can be said of Minnesota's people and institutions. One is tempted to assume that the familiarity with the world forced on mid-continent Americans by World War II, together with the ease of travel abroad after that time, led to a new awareness of things foreign.

Certainly the awareness exists. But it is not really new. In the peak immigration years of the late nineteenth and early twentieth centuries, the foreign-born as a percentage of total U.S. population rose to 15 percent, then began a decline that lasted until the 1970s. As a comparatively young and newly settled state one hundred years ago, Minnesota had more than double the national average of foreign-born residents. The state's 1890 election instructions were issued in nine languages.[4] So Minnesotans at that time had extensive continuing contact with the world beyond their state and nation.

Even though family connections with one's country of origin diminish in subsequent generations, the traces that remain are strong. Alexander Dubcek was the architect of Czechoslovakia's "Prague Spring," which Soviet tanks ended in 1968. Twenty-two years later, rehabilitated by the collapse of communism, Dubcek visited Minnesota. At an appearance in September of 1990, before a Twin Cities business audience, Dubcek was introduced by Robert Vanasek, then the speaker of the Minnesota House of Representatives. Vanasek, whose legislative district is New Prague, made the introduction in Slovak.

What *is* new is a surge in the diversity of Minnesotans' international connections. Some of this is attributable to population change. Compared with other states, Minnesota's population has a low percentage of minorities, less than 9 percent. But in recent decades the growth rate of its non-European population has been rapid, accelerating in the 1990s. According to the U.S. Census Bureau, Minnesota's total population increased 8 percent between 1990 and 1998. During that time its black, Hispanic, Asian, and American Indian population increased 43 percent.[5] Projections for 2025 show the minority population becoming 17 percent of the total—nearly twice the present level.[6]

One result is that Minnesotans of European descent are beginning to learn more about non-European cultures. They are also learning that people from two of those cultures are concentrated in this state. In 1999 the State Demographic Center estimated that Hmong in Minnesota numbered about sixty thousand; Somalis, about six thousand. While those numbers represent a small part of the minority total, many in the Hmong and Somali communities report that their Minnesota populations are the largest in the United States.[7] And although minorities, Hispanics in particular, have at times located in rural Minnesota, most are concentrated in the Minneapolis–St. Paul metropolitan area where about half the state's total population lives.[8] The concentration is evident in public education: Students in the central-city schools speak more than eighty languages.

Non-European ethnic diversity is new to Minnesota. It has made the Twin Cities a livelier place, most evident along a main thoroughfare named, ironically, for an early nineteenth-century French geographer. On Nicollet Avenue just south of downtown Minneapolis, few storefronts carry once-familiar European names. Now one sees, among many, Supermercado Las Americas and other markets with such titles as Hai Nguyen and Loc Loi; the Samaha family's restaurant and the Jerusalem, Safari, El Mariachi, Tijuana, Phuong, Trieu Chi, and Quang; the dentist Tung Thien Doan; the jewelers Kim Tin and Phuoc Lor Tho. On other Minneapolis and St. Paul streets are still more clusters of new-immigrant entrepreneurs: Suuq-Karmel, for example, a Somali mini-mall.

The new immigrants' connections with their countries of origin will no doubt lessen as the years pass and their children and grandchildren mature; much the same happened among Minnesota descendants of European immigrants. Lessen but not vanish. Celebrations of the country from which one's forebears migrated, Mexican as much as Swedish or Irish, continue even in faraway Minnesota. Knowledge of one's ancestors' country and, when possible, a visit to it are durable customs. And as those ties persist, extending to parts of the world scarcely heard of in Minnesota a generation ago, they cannot help but create a growing sense of global connectedness.

The link may look tenuous: James J. Hill in the nineteenth century looking for a commercial empire in Asia, a Hmong Minnesotan in the twenty-first looking for news of relatives in Laos. Disparate though such people appear, they have in common the ability to keep one eye on home and the other on distant lands.

"Wobegon" Minnesota?

Immigrants do not come to Minnesota because Minneapolis in January feels like Mogadishu. They come because others they know or know of have preceded them and stayed. They come because of employment opportunities. They come because energetic resettlement agencies have helped. They come because they have heard they will be welcome. The incentives seem like something out of Minnesota Public Radio's *A Prairie Home Companion*. It is as though a tolerance scale showed Minnesota to be an amplification of Garrison Keillor's Lake Wobegon, a state where not only the Wobegon children but everyone—young and old, rural and urban—is above average.

Not exactly. Concerned that immigrants are sometimes slighted or worse, President Emmett Carson and his colleagues at the Minneapolis Foundation developed an advertising campaign based on "Minnesota Nice." Minnesota Nice is the ethos said to characterize those who live here. Minnesota Nice implies such a surfeit of courtesy that when one is called a thief and scoundrel, one responds with a self-effacing shrug and a modest "You betcha."

In the fall of 1999 the foundation's "Nice or Not?" advertising appeared on billboards and posters, as well as in newspapers, magazines, and broadcasts. The ads made a barbed point. One, displaying pictures of snow and mosquitoes, read, "Living in Minnesota presents new immigrants with many challenges." It concluded: "Is one of them our attitude?" Carson wrote in a newspaper op-ed article of the mutual benefits resulting from the arrival of refugees and immigrants: Sudanese, Ethiopian, Bosnian, Russian, and others.[9] He noted Minnesota's unusual standing as the state with the largest population of Korean adoptees and the second largest of Tibetan adoptees. Asked later about public reaction (people had been invited to call for a free booklet), Carson said it had been overwhelming: larger than any of the foundation's previous community-service campaigns, with 95 percent of the thousands of responses favorable.

And the Minneapolis Foundation's is only one among many community efforts, government and nongovernment, to make Minnesota Nice apply to all. For example, the nonprofit organization Minnesota Advocates for Human Rights, long active in refugee and immigrant programs, has a three-year statewide project called BIAS (Building Immigrant Awareness And Support). Among the project's services are curriculum material for schools, teacher training, and education for attorneys and other professionals.

Minnesota's reputation, policies, and people make clear that foreign newcomers will be well treated. But some of the newcomers feel badly treated. So, further illustrating the state's global contradiction, the Minnesota community gathers its resources to alert the Minnesota community to the idea that awareness of interdependence is not enough; that overcoming insularity means reaching out to new neighbors.

Plowing Foreign Fields

Some Minnesotans in the second half of the twentieth century believed that reaching out to foreign peoples was not only an obligation but an opportunity. Perhaps the clearest evidence of that Minnesota mind-set is the origin of the Peace Corps.

The idea had its roots in the American tradition of overseas volunteerism, much of it undertaken by missionaries. Among proponents of a similar but secular enterprise was Robert Hewitt, a *Minneapolis Star* correspondent whose experience in North Africa and Asia had convinced him of the efficacy of such a program. The leading congressional advocate was Minnesota Senator Hubert H. Humphrey. In 1960 Humphrey introduced legislation for a "Youth Peace Corps." The proposal fit so well with John F. Kennedy's bear-any-burden philosophy that in his presidential campaign of that year Kennedy mentioned it in two speeches and, after his election, created the Peace Corps by executive order.[10]

Curiously, in Minnesota enthusiasm for the Peace Corps seems not to have inspired a sudden increase in nongovernmental foreign-affairs organizations. The predecessor of today's leading statewide provider of public discussion of foreign affairs, the Minnesota International Center, was the University of Minnesota's World Affairs Center, founded in 1948. Several private organizations, in place earlier, appealed principally to upper crustaceans: for example, a Minnesota branch of the Foreign Policy Association, whose dinner meetings in the 1930s were formal affairs, and a Committee on Foreign Relations (then an adjunct of the Council on Foreign Relations), formed by Twin Cities business and academic leaders concerned about isolationism as World War II loomed.

Records maintained by the Minnesota Council of Nonprofits show that, from the end of World War II until the 1980s, there was growth but no acceleration in the number of nonprofits dedicated to international matters. In the 1940s, the United Nations Association of Minnesota was formed; appropriately, since former Governor Harold Stassen had been a delegate to the San Francisco conference that created the UN. Slow growth continued until an explosion of international nonprofits in the 1980s and 1990s created more than two dozen new ones in Minnesota. The steady but slow growth in international nonprofits from the 1940s to the 1970s shows a substantial but not overwhelming interest in the world abroad. The blossoming of internationally oriented nonprofits in the 1980s confirms what polls tell us: a slight majority of Minnesotans were acknowledging a special American responsibility to aid others, prevent wars, and protect human rights.[11]

The increasing emphasis on aid and social activism during this period was reflected in the new organizations. Some resembled those in other parts of the country; others were unusual; one was unique. The Center for Victims of Torture, unique because it was the first of its kind in the United States, says a good deal about ingredients for creating a Minnesota-style antidote to an international illness. The formula called for private initiative, accompanied in this instance by political initiative. It required private generosity, sometimes supplemented by government aid. Idealism was essential too, along with an equal measure of practicality.

How Two Nonprofits Took Root

A Stanford University law student, also a volunteer for Amnesty International, discussed the idea of a victims-treatment center with his father. The father in question was Minnesota's governor, whose staff was occasionally able to catch up with his ideas on the occasions when they knew his whereabouts. Governor Perpich, he of the subsequent Croatian adventure, gathered advice and experts from the newly formed Minnesota Advocates for Human Rights, the University of Minnesota Law School, and the Mayo Clinic, and led them to Copenhagen to visit the world's first treatment center. He then appointed a forty-member task force to decide whether Minnesota should establish a similar American center. The answer was yes. In 1985 the Center for Victims of Torture came into being as a nonprofit, nongovernmental organization responsible for its own finances.[12] The budget—$200,000 at the outset (half from the foundation established by James J. Hill's descendants)—had risen to $3.3 million in 1999. Today, the center treats people from around the world.

Fifteen other centers elsewhere in the country now treat torture victims. According to estimates by the Minnesota center, there are four hundred thousand such victims in the United States, including fourteen thousand in Minnesota. Because even a nationwide network cannot treat all torture victims, the Minnesota center decided to place its emphasis on training, research, and public policy; the goal is to pass along to other care providers the lessons the center has learned.

State and federal governments have since begun to help. In 1998, Congress, in a rare demonstration of bipartisanship, approved the Torture Victims Relief Act. Former Senator Dave Durenberger, a moderate Republican who specialized in health policy, was among the legislation's early sponsors in 1994. Among its other advocates have been Minnesota Senators Paul Wellstone, a Democrat, and Rod Grams, a Republican whose conservatism is as staunch as the liberalism of his Democratic colleague. State support for torture victims was similarly bipartisan and included Perpich's successor as governor, Republican Arne Carlson.

None of this should leave an impression of great rivers of government cash flowing into the Center for Victims of Torture. One-third of its resources comes from individual donations, another third from foundations, and the last third from contracts. With a grant from the State Department, the center in late 1999 began a project in Guinea to assist people traumatized by violence in Liberia and Sierra Leone. Other Minnesotans—former Vice President Walter Mondale and Edson Spencer, former chairman of Honeywell Inc.—are working with the center to develop an international consensus about new human-rights tactics in which victim treatment would be a key element.

The necessary ingredients came together partly by accident, mostly by design. A law student happened to have a father who relished unorthodox ideas and, as governor, was able to translate ideas into actions. Human-rights lawyers and physicians joined forces with other talented people, in and out of government, to become a creative task force, then a board of directors. The board found in Douglas Johnson an executive director who combined idealism with practicality. Donors signaled with checkbooks their appreciation of both qualities. So did legislators, state and federal, from both major parties.

If the Center for Victims of Torture is an instructive example of nonprofit activity mainly *in* Minnesota for people *from* other countries, there is also something to be learned from an example of the reverse. The American Refugee Committee works *from* Minnesota to serve people *in* other countries. ARC is unusual because of its location far from Washington, D.C., where most other national organizations concerned with refugees are clustered.

Here, too, serendipity played a part. In the late 1970s Neal Ball, who had served in the Nixon administration, realized while working in Chicago that the challenge of resettling Southeast Asian refugees would persist for years. With support from Chicago business and community leaders he founded ARC.[13] But an obstacle confronted the new organization almost immediately: Stanley Breen, whom ARC wanted as executive director, lived in Minnesota and made clear that he had no interest in moving to Chicago. So ARC established its headquarters in Minneapolis, and in retrospect, the move was logical. Minnesota has a higher number of refugees per capita than any other state. And while ARC at first concentrated on refugee resettlement in America, it soon shifted its emphasis to focus on the poorly understood problems of refugees abroad who were living, precariously, near the places from which they had fled. Even less understood were the problems of those antiseptically described as "internally displaced"—refugees within their own countries. ARC recognized that the popular image of refugees seeking a better place to live is misleading; most want to go home.

ARC's first mission was to Thailand, bringing health care and health-care training to refugees from Cambodia. Since then, the organization has provided health and other assistance and training on three continents. It has five field offices in Africa, two in Asia, and six in the Balkan region of Europe. In the 1980s overseas staff came from Minnesota; in the 1990s, increasingly from overseas. Anthony Kozlowski, ARC's president since 1992, brought with him from Geneva, Switzerland, a dozen years' experience as head of a council of international voluntary groups. He considers the Twin Cities the "ideal place" for ARC because of transportation, communications, the availability of talented people, and public support (ARC's 1999 budget exceeded $22 million, compared to $3 million seven years earlier).

These observations about nonprofits may suggest that Minnesota is nirvana for international social improvers. Alas, such is not the case. An incident several years ago illustrates the persistence of the state's global contradiction, the coexistence of worldly wisdom and insularity. The incident involved farmers and bankers. Farmers tend to look closely at international trends, knowing that their livelihoods depend increasingly on the export of American agricultural products. They are no less interested in domestic economic trends affecting, among other things, equipment prices and lending rates. The urban owner of a bank in an agricultural corner of Minnesota sought to stimulate those interests, and enliven the bank's board meetings by introducing an occasional specialist from afar: an agricultural economist, perhaps, or a human-resources expert, or a plant pathologist. At the meeting in question a former physician, now a specialist in genetic structure, spoke of the changes made possible by research. The response of a prominent board member—"It's a communist plot"—may have been atypical.[14] But it was similar in spirit to a question addressed to Henry Kissinger by a radio correspondent during a 1975 visit to Minnesota by the then-secretary of state. The correspondent's remarks included the accusation that Kissinger was sympathetic to, maybe even (his voice tightening further) a member of, the Trilateral Commission and the Council on Foreign Relations.

Through a Glass Lightly: Church and Campus

Immigrants brought to nineteenth-century Minnesota strong beliefs in the importance of religion and education. The colleges they founded united the two convictions, and if Minnesotans often approach foreign affairs today with missionary zeal, they derive that attitude from long tradition.

Catholic and Lutheran church members together account (in nearly equal numbers) for about half the state's population. Yet the oldest college—Hamline, now a university—was established by Methodists in 1854 in the Mississippi River city of Red Wing, and later moved to St. Paul. (The University of Minnesota's charter preceded Hamline's, but the state university did not function as a higher-education institution until later.) By the start of the twentieth century Hamline had produced 263 graduates; many became educators, lawyers, and other professionals. Some became missionaries.[15]

The presence of foreign students on American campuses is so common that few people give it a second thought. With overseas travel now measured in hours rather than weeks, student exchange seems not only natural but recent. Exchange may be natural; it is not recent. Traveling in Japan in the 1980s, Stephen Lewis, president of Carleton College in Northfield, sensed uncertainty among his listeners when he described Carleton's international outlook until he mentioned that Carleton's first Japanese alumnus graduated in 1891. Like other colleges, Carleton offers faculty and students opportunities for study abroad. Unlike others, Carleton's intensive connections with China began in 1904 when the empress dowager asked the college to establish a medical mission in her country.[16]

Private colleges and universities reflect the state's predominant religions. Of the sixteen members of the Minnesota Private College Council seven are Catholic, six, Lutheran. In all the colleges, international themes play a prominent role. At Macalester College, founded in St. Paul by Presbyterians, 12 percent of the 1,700 students come from seventy foreign countries; as Macalester President Michael McPherson observes, it is no surprise that the United Nations Secretary General, Kofi Annan, is a Macalester graduate. Neither is it surprising that Gustavus Adolphus College, emphasizing its Swedish Lutheran tradition, has the Nobel Foundation's approval to hold an annual Nobel science conference. Still, there is something uncommon about a middle-America event that regularly brings to a campus sixty miles from the Twin Cities leading experts, including Nobel laureates, on subjects ranging from the nature of life to chaos theory to neuroscience. And if it is unsurprising that Minnesotans are interested in the other notable Nobel mission—the Peace Prize, awarded annually by the Norwegian Nobel Committee—the manifestation of that interest is nevertheless worth noting. Every year four Minnesota colleges founded in the Norwegian Lutheran tradition (together with Luther College of Iowa) hold a Peace Prize Forum on one of their campuses, bringing Nobel Peace Prize laureates and other experts to examine the current state of peacemaking.

This does not mean that educators are preoccupied with celebrity scholars. A 1,500-student Minneapolis Lutheran college, Augsburg, maintains a Center for Global Education that has staff in Namibia, Mexico, and three Central American countries, with study centers in four of the five. And there is something reassuring about the willingness of a northern Minnesota Lutheran college, Concordia in Moorhead, to run summertime foreign-language immersion camps for elementary- and secondary-school students from all over the United States: teaching German when the program originated in 1960, now offering a dozen languages, including Russian and Chinese.

Because Catholicism is by definition global, the depth of the international programs at Minnesota's Catholic colleges and universities is to be expected. Still, there are surprises here too. Central Minnesota is really less remote than it might seem from east of the Hudson River, but it is not the first place that comes to mind when one asks where the world's largest collection of microfilmed medieval manuscripts is housed. At St. John's University, the Hill Monastic Manuscript Library has built a collection of thirty million pages microfilmed in seventeen different countries since the library opened in 1965.[17] The job was not simple for the St. John's experts who went abroad. Even a Benedictine brother may find it difficult to persuade an abbot in Malta, Ethiopia, or Central Europe to let him riffle through the monastery's ancient volumes and photograph every page.

In the 1980s the state's governor suggested that the University of Minnesota establish an Austrian campus, using a castle available at the time. Even friendly critics, including this writer, thought the idea foolish; the proposal was interred. In the 1990s, the University of St. Thomas decided to establish an Italian campus, using a mansion available at the time. No one thought the idea foolish; the university bought the building. Circumstances surrounding the 1980s proposal were different from those of the 1990s, notably because the earlier proposal involved a public university. Still, responses to these two incidents suggest that the Minnesota contradiction of insularity and worldly wisdom is displayed not only by different groups but sometimes by the same individuals.

Among three comparable categories of higher-education institutions in Minnesota, enrollment is divided fairly evenly: in the fall of 1999, approximately 57,300 students were enrolled at private colleges and universities, 54,700 at state universities (which are in a system separate from the University of Minnesota), and 58,200 at the University of Minnesota's campuses in the Twin Cities and elsewhere.[18] As with the private colleges, the international emphasis in public universities is usually what one would expect—and sometimes what one would not. One campus of the Minnesota State College and University System is in northern Honshu, Japan.

The work of a major university is rarely inhibited by territorial constraints. Norman Borlaug won the Nobel Peace Prize because he applied what he learned at the University of Minnesota to increase crop yields in Latin America and Asia. The university's strength in agricultural sciences, applied worldwide, continues. So does its influence in other fields. In a 1999 letter to Walter Mondale, who earlier had been U.S. ambassador to Japan, a senior official in Japan's Ministry of Finance reminisced about his 1980s experience as a member of the university's economics faculty. That experience was the "foundation of my academic career," Takatoshi Ito wrote, and he went on to speak of his intellectual debts to Walter Heller and other Minnesota economist colleagues of the time.

Like similar institutions across the United States, the University of Minnesota has a number of international studies centers, some of them unique. The Center for Austrian Studies, for example, was established in 1977 when the Austrian government chose Minnesota over Yale and Stanford.[19] For the past decade the Center for Nations in Transition, at the university's Hubert H. Humphrey Institute of Public Affairs, has worked in Central and Eastern Europe to design post–Cold War institutions for education and sustainable development. The university's China Center is thriving because the university has the highest number of students and scholars from China in the United States. The first Chinese students came to Minnesota's land-grant university in 1914 to study agricultural development. The growing strength of educational ties between China and Minnesota is evident not only in student exchanges, but in institutional collaboration. In February of 2000 the university's Carlson School of Management announced the establishment of a partnership with Zhongshan University in Guangzhou, which will offer an Executive Master's of Business Administration program in China. The Carlson School will start a similar program in Austria, patterned—as is the China program—on one established earlier in Poland, and expects similar ventures in South Asia and Latin America.[20]

Minnesota's China connections are especially significant. They arose from no single event, but from sustained mutual interest and trust among business leaders, politicians, and scholars. The interest may be seen in the fact that more than a thousand of the state's elementary- and secondary-school students study Mandarin. Only California, New York, Massachusetts, and New Jersey show higher numbers, but all of them are more populous than Minnesota.[21] The trust is evident not only in academic exchanges and public-university programs like the Executive MBA program in China, but also in stirrings of interest among Chinese leaders in developing private colleges. Responding to an invitation from China, directors of the Minnesota Private College Council—college presidents, community leaders, and business board members—were to visit Beijing late in 2000 to explore such ideas with their counterparts in what the Minnesotans hope will be continuing seminars.[22]

Midwest Justice

The state's tradition of social justice at home and abroad, largely inspired by religious and academic leaders, endures. Many recall today that campus and community debates over the Vietnam War and Central America were as heated in Minnesota as anywhere, perhaps more so. Some recall a study critical of nuclear arms, "The Challenge of Peace," completed in 1983 by the National Council of Catholic Bishops after three years of deliberations. The council's president at the time was John Roach, archbishop of the Archdiocese of St. Paul and Minneapolis.

Fewer know of an ecumenical protest in 1933, when prejudice against Jews was on the rise in Minnesota and, as Richard Chapman notes elsewhere in this book, would make the Twin Cities known as America's capital of anti-Semitism. At Temple Israel in Minneapolis, Protestants and Catholics gathered with Jews to protest the treatment of Jews in Germany. A statement prepared for the occasion by the archbishop was remarkable for its unambiguous criticism of a foreign government: this at a time when many Minnesotans worshiped isolationism and considered neutrality the Eleventh Commandment. On that March day in 1933 Archbishop John Gregory Murray, referring to the new Nazi government, wrote "in protest against political action which adopts as its principal purpose the annihilation of the Jewish people and all other liberty-loving groups in the great country of Germany who are opposed to the chauvinistic and narrow-minded program of the nationalistic party." The archbishop went on to "beseech a civilized world to make articulate the conscience of humanity in behalf of those who have committed no other crime than to be members of a race which has given to the world the priceless boon of the most enlightened culture in antiquity. . . ."[23]

The explicitness of the Minnesota archbishop's condemnation was remarkable in light of the tensions in the Catholic Church in respect to Hitler's Germany. Although German bishops in early 1933 were opposed to Hitler, the German government's negotiations with the Vatican for a concordat (signed in July) were probably as well known in St. Paul as in Berlin.[24] In any case, the position of Minnesota political and religious leaders was clear. At the Temple Israel rally Protestant and Jewish leaders joined in the archbishop's protest, as did Governor Floyd B. Olson.

One might think that the enlightenment displayed by prominent Minnesotans in 1933 was a natural result of citizens' attitudes in earlier decades. Not so. Despite the mind-opening of education, so long valued by Minnesotans, and despite the tolerance expected of a well-churched population, a xenophobic strain had long prevailed. One of the ironies of the state's history is the public venom directed at Charles Lindbergh, father of the famous aviator. The author Barbara Stuhler writes that Lindbergh, who ended the last of his five terms in Congress just before the United States entered World War I, "gave Minnesota a gospel of radical isolationism." Yet Lindbergh, running unsuccessfully for governor during the war, was treated as a public enemy: newspaper editorials called him "the candidate of disloyalty" and a "Gopher Bolshevist." Infected with war fever, the legislature created the Minnesota

Commission of Public Safety, which targeted among others Lindbergh's allies in the Nonpartisan League, precursor of the Farmer-Labor Party. Targeted indeed: the commission's leader, a Minneapolis lawyer and former judge, suggested firing squads for dissidents.[25]

The commission spread its poison across the state, inspiring chauvinist cheers. The town of Edgerton, in a southwestern Minnesota farming area, provides an example. In the late nineteenth century Dutch immigrants began settling in Edgerton alongside the community's mainly Yankee founders. Establishing their own churches and clinging to their own language, the newcomers aroused suspicion during World War I. In 1917, the Edgerton *Enterprise* editorialized: "Our soldier boys will come home some day, perhaps unable to work; they can use some disloyal citizen's farm, residence, or bank account to a very good advantage."[26] Lest this seem an isolated and distant phenomenon, consider a 1992 remark by Edgerton resident Robert Schoone-Jongen: ". . . some of the animosities fueled by Minnesota's sad experiment in rule by edict and trial by innuendo linger just below the surface, even three-quarters of a century later."[27]

Thus the paradox: Despite Minnesotans' ethnic animosities during World War I, and the isolationism and anti-Semitism that prevailed in the following three decades, in the early 1930s respected moral leaders called resoundingly for justice for German Jews. There could hardly be a better example of Minnesota's global contradiction, its simultaneous insularity and worldly wisdom.

Minnesota Media

One day in 1996 Walker Lundy, editor of the *St. Paul Pioneer Press*, listened to Dave Beal propose a visit to China. Although Beal was a veteran business reporter and editor, Lundy at the outset saw no good reason to send a journalist with no foreign experience on such an assignment. But Lundy listened—and Beal was dispatched to China. A year earlier a *Pioneer Press* team had gone to Cambodia to report on the origins of St. Paul's large Hmong community. As Lundy aptly puts it, "The foreign story is the local story."

For Minnesota Public Radio, sometimes the foreign story is the foreign story—important to listeners as a matter of national interest, and therefore also of local interest. During the 1999 Kosovo war MPR devoted a full hour in the late morning, five days a week, to coverage of that crisis. A separate special report, "The Killers of Pec," was a seven-month project in Kosovo by an MPR producer and correspondent.

The *Star Tribune* in Minneapolis continues its post–World War II practice of sending reporters and editorial writers abroad. Although it no longer maintains foreign bureaus, in the 1980s and 1990s a Minneapolis-based *Star Tribune* correspondent traveled the world as his beat. A series of articles in 1999 illustrates the newspaper's willingness to explore international issues in depth. The subject was not a crisis of the moment, unless forty years qualify as a moment. The series' subject was the Cold War; how it ended and why, how it framed a generation's thinking.[28]

As these vignettes suggest, Minnesota media take seriously their responsibility to bring to their audience insights on the world abroad. They are criticized for doing too little of it, or too much. They rely on wire services or broadcast networks for most foreign news, but they add their own international reporting. John Cowles, an Iowan who with his brother bought the *Minneapolis Star* in 1935, was an internationalist in a sea of isolationists. Unsurprisingly, in 1940 the *Star Journal* (as it had become) urged Republicans to bypass the isolationist Senator Robert Taft in favor of the internationalist Wendell Willkie as their presidential nominee. Cowles himself wrote Willkie's acceptance speech.[29] He was as dedicated to widening Minnesotans' horizons as he was to making his newspaper business profitable.

Postwar horizon-broadening got a boost, too, from individual reporters for the Minneapolis newspapers. Although Carl Rowan was widely recognized as a Washington-based syndicated columnist for the thirty-five years until his death in 1999, his journalism career began at the *Minneapolis Tribune* shortly after World War II, when black reporters were rarities in this country's newsrooms. In twelve years at the *Tribune* Rowan won assignments ranging from the civil-rights movement in the American South to the 1956 Suez War in the Middle East. He also reported from Europe and Asia. Sam Romer, who had been an ambulance driver for the Republican side in the Spanish Civil War, became in later years a renowned labor reporter; his fluency in Spanish brought him an assignment to Cuba when Fidel Castro came to power. Before Graham Hovey joined the *New York Times* editorial board he wrote for *Tribune* readers about such events as the building of the Berlin Wall. In the *Minneapolis Star,* Robert Hewitt covered the Algerian revolt against France; in the *Tribune,* Ronald Ross covered the Vietnam War.

A Global Business Village

Along with the news media, the state's political leaders in both parties from the 1940s on were instrumental in leading Minnesota out of its isolationist past. Ties linking immigrants and their descendants to their countries of origin helped lift people's vision beyond America's shores. So did higher education, organized religion, the missionary impulse manifested in international nonprofits, and the country's second highest per capita number of Peace Corps volunteers. As always, war and rumor of war internationalized the public mindset. In 1914, Minnesotans learned to identify Sarajevo; in 1992 another generation learned to identify Sarajevo. Yet whatever weight one assigns to these links between Minnesota and the rest of the world, one stands out—commerce.

In the world of international business, Minnesota's comparative disadvantages became, paradoxically, an asset. The Twin Cities were not a Chicago-style rail hub. Minnesota is far from the coasts, though Duluth remains a useful port (except in winter). Rich resources of lumber and iron ore were depleted over time. Although agriculture was important, it did not set Minnesota apart from surrounding states. Minnesota flour milling was once a major industry; now urban planners began to devise new uses for vacant mill buildings. Minnesota adapted, becoming a place to manufacture a wide range of products, devising systems to move people and cargo, and providing all manner of services.

Tourism has become an important business in Minnesota. Here the outdoors is something close to a religion, and though the Department of Natural Resources does not quite resemble the Greek god Pan, it is the subject of worshipful overtures by legislators who want voters to amend the state constitution. The amendment in question would create an eternal monetary shrine to the outdoors by requiring a fixed percentage of state revenues to be spent on nature, thereby avoiding the pain of authorization and appropriation legislation inflicted on lesser deities like education and welfare. Given the reverence for the outdoors in the Land of 10,000 Lakes (the number is actually greater), the attractions for visitors, foreign as well as from within the United States, would seem to be self-evident. Not quite. In 1997, the last year reported by the state, the chief attraction for tourists was not hunting, fishing, or camping, as one might expect, but shopping. More visitors came from Canada than from all other countries combined. And the most popular tourist destination was the Twin Cities area.

International business mainly means multinational companies. A glance at a few of Minnesota's indicates their diversity: Minnesota Mining and Manufacturing Company (better known as 3M), Northwest Airlines Corp., Carlson Companies (hotels and travel), General Mills, Inc., and the St. Paul Companies, Inc. (insurance). Honeywell, long a familiar Minnesota corporate name, was acquired in 1999 by AlliedSignal, Inc., which in turn announced in

2000 that it would be acquired by General Electric Company. Pillsbury, another well-known company, remained in Minneapolis after it was sold in 1989 to a British corporation; but after a further sale, in 2000, Pillsbury will be merged into General Mills.

One reason for the success of major Minnesota corporations has been their ability to adapt quickly. For example, in the late 1970s General Mills saw the need for better worldwide distribution of its cereal products. Nestlé, headquartered in Switzerland and the world's largest food company, was better equipped for distributing than manufacturing the kind of products made by the Minnesota corporation. Bruce Atwater, then General Mills' CEO, was acquainted with his Nestlé counterpart, Helmut Maucher. Atwater recalls calling Maucher to suggest a joint venture. Within the week an agreement for a 50–50 venture was completed. The operation has been successful ever since.

Or consider 3M, a century-old company that began international operations in 1951. Its foreign sales in 1999 accounted for 52 percent of total sales. 3M's opening in China is a lesson in patient pursuit of a goal of greater value than might appear evident to the casual observer. After the United States ended its trade embargo on China in 1972, the company began exploring possibilities for doing business there. Under the guidance of 3M executive John Marshall, who later became director of international business development, the exploration continued for ten years. In 1983 Chinese authorities and 3M agreed on terms for the company to begin operations in China.[30] The agreement would have been of only moderate interest—other foreign corporations had done business in China longer—were it not for China's acceptance of 3M's greater goal. The company would establish a manufacturing plant in Shanghai. More important still, the operation would be wholly owned by 3M, the first of its kind in modern China, and no small achievement given Chinese sensitivities to foreign exploitation in an earlier era.

One Minnesota multinational perennially fascinating to people in the state and beyond is Cargill, Inc. By Minnesota standards it is an old company, founded in 1865. By any standard it is a large one: 81,600 employees in 65 countries, with 1998 revenues of $51 billion.[31] The fascination arises because Cargill is probably the largest privately held company in the world and, like other grain traders, for most of its corporate life disclosed little to the public about its business. That corporate culture began to change in 1972 with Senate hearings on grain sales to the Soviet Union, changed further in 1992 with the introduction of employee stock ownership, and changed still further in 1999 with a public relations and advertising campaign.[32] Openness is unlikely to mollify critics like Senator Paul Wellstone, who see in Cargill's acquisition of

Continental Grain another attempt to squeeze farmers driven to desperation by low prices (which in fact are caused by world market conditions rather than by conniving corporations). Whatever Minnesotans' opinions of Cargill may be, as they learn more about the company they also learn more about their connections to the wider world.

Another multinational makes an interesting comparison. Medtronic, Inc., a relative newcomer, was founded in 1949. Its shares are publicly traded. Although its growth has been widely reported, many may not know that in 1999 Medtronic's market value exceeded that of 3M (3M's revenues still exceed Medtronic's: in 1999, $15.7 billion for 3M, $4.1 billion for Medtronic). With twenty thousand employees in 120 countries, Medtronic is undeniably global. Like Cargill it claims a superlative—the world's leading medical technology company. Unlike Cargill, Medtronic has few critics. To review the awards the company has received is to wonder whether there are any it has yet to collect. Interviewed by a Minnesota business magazine reporter, a Medtronic executive summed up the change in the company's culture. His words could apply to the wider community: "We're no longer just parochial Minneapolis. It's not the white, Anglo-Saxon, Protestant, Scandinavian Medtronic anymore."[33]

With agile corporations, an educated workforce, a durable commitment to higher education, an admirable quality of life, and a well-developed civic conscience, Minnesota would seem perfectly poised for the knowledge-based global economy of the twenty-first century. But perversely, those very qualities threaten to turn Minnesota Nice into Minnesota Smug. That is not conjecture. Since the mid-1990s, study groups and task forces have issued warnings and proposed remedies.

The Citizens League is a Twin Cities organization that examines public-policy issues by bringing together interested members from diverse occupations to hear experts, examine data, reach conclusions, and issue reports. In 1996 the league found that the Twin Cities region "is perceived as 'insular' rather than 'international,'" that the "workforce is losing its competitive edge," and that "the region is behind the curve in embracing information and communication technologies"—keys to success in the global economy.[34] Another league report, on the University of Minnesota, noted its low national ranking in biomedical engineering despite the university's ties to the medical device industry (Medtronic and other companies). The report noted further that despite the rise (and subsequent meltdown) of Minnesota computer companies Control Data and Cray Research, computer science at the university ranked forty-seventh nationally in a 1993 National Research Council survey.[35]

In 1998 an unlikely duo established a roundtable to survey seventy-eight

Minnesota business executives and present their findings to community leaders. The survey dealt with the standing of the Twin Cities metropolitan area in the global economy. Its initiators were Randy Johnson, Republican chairman of the board of the state's most populous county, and Vance Opperman, a liberal Democratic businessman. Among the survey's findings was a consensus that while the metropolitan area competes well with comparable regions elsewhere in the country, it is slipping; that a growing shortage of skilled workers inhibits growth; and that Minnesota's major metropolitan area lacks the global strategy found in competing regions.

All these studies offer recommendations, and there are glimmers of collaborative response to them. The Johnson-Opperman initiative has grown into a nonprofit corporation called the Great North Alliance, looking at such questions as how to stimulate greater entrepreneurial energy. For example, why does more Minnesota venture capital flow out of the state rather than remain? Newspaper editorials are warning of public and corporate complacency. David Kidwell, dean of the University of Minnesota's Carlson School of Management, has argued at length that the need for action is urgent; that Minnesotans should not be lulled by the current "economic euphoria," but must realize that the state has opportunities nationally and globally that need to be seized.[36]

One question hovering over the discussions of Minnesota's future role in the world abroad is whether the new guard of Minnesota leaders will have the vision once shown by the old. At the end of an interview on the subject of this essay, the ever-energetic Walter Mondale—former senator, former vice president, former ambassador—was asked why, with all the world open to him, he returned to Minnesota. His reply was immediate: "This state gave me everything." Another "former," Arlen Erdahl, returned from Washington after serving as congressman and Peace Corps executive to head a Minnesota nonprofit giving overseas health-care training. Even as a state legislator in the 1960s he sought to alert his constituents to international issues. Erdahl recalls leaving home one evening with his children's globe as a lecture tool, when his son asked, "Daddy, what are you going to do with my world?"

Try to make it a little better, Minnesotans might answer, and try to give the state its rightful place in the twenty-first-century global economy. The problems are formidable, but people tend to see Minnesota as the city on the hill. Unfortunately, Minnesota is mostly flat.

Notes

1. Barbara Stuhler, *Ten Men of Minnesota and American Foreign Policy, 1898–1968* (St. Paul: Minnesota Historical Society, 1973), 10. In the study cited by Stuhler, votes in the House gave Minnesota a ranking of being the sixth most isolationist; in the Senate, between seventh and twelfth.

2. The Minnesota Poll, begun on 19 March 1944, is the second oldest continuous regional poll in the United States. The Iowa Poll began four months earlier.

3. David McCullough, *The Path Between the Seas* (New York: Simon and Schuster, 1977), 459–468.

4. Minnesota Advocates for Human Rights, "Minnesota's Immigrant Populations: Past and Present," Minneapolis, 1999.

5. Bob von Sternberg and David Westphal, "A Changing Ethnic Makeup," *Star Tribune*, 15 September 1999, 1A.

6. Martha McMurry, *Faces of the Future: Minnesota Population Projections 1995–2025* (St. Paul: State Demographic Center, Minnesota Department of Planning, 1998), 1, 4.

7. Minnesota Advocates for Human Rights, "Minnesota's Immigrant Populations: Past and Present," Minneapolis, 1999. Also, author's conversation with Tim Gordon, policy analyst in the Refugee Section of the Minnesota Department of Human Services. According to Gordon, the consensus among executive directors of community-based organizations in the Hmong and Somali communities is that the Minnesota populations of those communities are larger than in any other state. The consensus, however, is based on estimates rather than head counts.

8. The history of minorities in southwestern Minnesota and the responses of communities in that part of the state are well described in Joseph Amato, *To Call It Home* (Marshall, Minn.: Crossings Press, 1996).

9. "Immigrant Acculturation is a Two-way Street," *St. Paul Pioneer Press*, 10 October 1999, 23A.

10. Author's conversations with Robert Hewitt, 1960–1963; and Stuhler, *Ten Men of Minnesota*, 204.

11. There is no intent here to assert a cause-and-effect relationship between the sense of international responsibility registered in two opinion surveys and the numerical increase in international nonprofits. The findings are complementary, not conclusive.

12. Interview with Douglas Johnson, president of the Center for Victims of Torture, 11 December 1999; web site <http://www.cvt.org>.

13. Interview with Anthony Kozlowski, president of the American Refugee Committee, 1 December 1999, and ARC *Annual Report 1998*, Minneapolis, 1999.

14. This incident was described to the author by a participant in the meeting.

15. Merrill E. Jarchow, *Private Liberal Arts Colleges in Minnesota: Their History and Contributions* (St. Paul: Minnesota Historical Society, 1973), 1, 7–12.

16. Interview with Stephen R. Lewis Jr., 18 November 1999.

17. Russell Scott Smith, "Preserving the Word," *Minnesota Monthly* (December 1999): 47.

18. Minnesota Higher Education Services Office, "Preliminary Headcount in MN," 6 December 1999. Public community and technical colleges form the largest single enrollment category, with 92,000 students. Enrollment at private career and professional schools was 19,400. The head count does not differentiate between full- and part-time students.

19. Center for Austrian Studies web site <http://www.cas.umn.edu>.

20. News release, Carlson School of Management, 17 February 2000.

21. Author's conversation with Margaret Wong, teacher at Breck School, Golden Valley, Minn., January 2000.

22. Author's conversation with David B. Laird Jr., president of the Minnesota Private College Council, 29 March 2000.

23. "Jews Upheld by Archbishop," *Minneapolis Tribune*, 27 March 1933, 2.

24. A recent analysis of events leading to the concordat can be found in John Cornwell, *Hitler's Pope* (New York: Viking, 1999), 130–156. See also István Déak, "The Pope, The Nazis & the Jews," *The New York Review of Books* (23 March 2000): 44, for an interpretation less critical than Cornwell's.

25. Stuhler, *Ten Men of Minnesota*, 42–53.

26. Cited in Robert Schoone-Jongen, "Patriotic Pressures WWI," Southwest History Center, Southwest State University, Marshall, Minn., 1992, 4.

27. Ibid., 10.

28. Observations on Minnesota media are based on conversations with Dave Beal, Ron Clark, and Walker Lundy of the *St. Paul Pioneer Press*, a conversation with Bill Buzenberg of Minnesota Public Radio, and the author's experience at the *Star Tribune*.

29. James A. Alcott, *A History of Cowles Media Company* (Minneapolis: Cowles Media Company, 1998). The Cowles family's ownership of the *Star Tribune* ended with the newspaper's sale to McClatchy Newspapers, Inc. in 1998.

30. "3M's Pioneer in Shanghai," *3M Today* (January 1995): 8; "3M Establishes Wholly Owned Company in China," *International Ambassador* (November/December 1983): 2. *3M Today* and *International Ambassador* are 3M publications.

31. Liz Brissett, "Still the One," *Corporate Report* (May 1999): 32.

32. Wayne G. Broehl Jr., *Cargill: Going Global* (Hanover, N.H.: University Press of New England, 1998), 364.

33. Liz Brissett, "Size Matters," *Corporate Report* (March 1999): 69.

34. Citizens League, "Compete Globally, Thrive Locally," September 1996.

35. Citizens League, "A Competitive Place in the Quality Race," January 1998.

36. David Kidwell, "Has the Twin Cities Economy Lost its Blue-Chip Status?" speech at the First Tuesday Luncheon Series, Radisson Hotel Metrodome, Minneapolis, 7 March 2000.

INDEX

Colleges, 5, 18, 101, 109, 125, 126, 271n18; denominational, 138, 139, 140; and student aid, 195, 201; foreign students and, 259–60

Committee on Foreign Relations, 256

Commodities, 85–86, 96

Common good, 173–74, 187, 196, 203

Communist movement, 9, 34, 35

Communist Party, 12, 34

Communities, 98; ethnic, 56–58, 139; imagined, 63–64; isolation of, 136, 137; activism of, 145–46, 203; moralism and, 191–92

Community Clinic Consortium, 226

Community Fund, 142

Community Reinvestment Act, 234

Community service, 111, 112

Computer industry, 14, 16, 19–20, 268

Concordia College, Moorhead, 138, 260

Concordia College, St. Paul, 138

Congregational churches, 140

Conservatism, conservatives, 17, 95, 217

Continental Grain, 268

Control Data, 19, 268

Cooperating Fund Drive, 231

Cooperatives, 10, 17, 95

Cornishmen, 7

Corporations, 172; philanthropy of, 98, 220–21, 222–23, 224–25, 228–31, 237–38

Corruption, 184, 185, 187

Costa Rica, 228

Counterculture, 17

Counties, 94. *See also by name*

Covenant churches, 140

Cowles, John, 173, 265

Cowles, John, Jr., 246

Cowles family, 245

Cowles Media Company, 228, 230

Cowles Newspapers Corporation, 224

Cray Research, 268

Creation story, Ojibwe, 117–18, 132n2, 135

Croats, 152, 249

Crookston, 109

Cultural diversity, 21–22, 95–96, 136

Cultural identity, 95–96, 99, 125, 132

Cuyuna Range, 87

Czechs, 140

Dakota (Sioux), 3, 117, 118, 129, 139; warfare with, 4–5; and fur trade, 28–29; land of, 32, 91; communities, 41, 120, 121; education of, 125, 132; traditional economy of, 126–27

Dakota War, Dakota Conflict, 4, 22, 29–30, 121

Dance, 242–43

Danes, 137

Dawes Severality Act. *See* General Allotment Act of 1887

Dayton, Bruce, 224

Dayton, Douglas, 224

Dayton, George Draper, 220, 222

Dayton, Kenneth, 224, 232

Dayton, Wallace, 224

Dayton family, 245

Dayton Hudson Corporation, philanthropy of, 172, 220, 224–25, 226, 228, 229, 230. *See also* Target Corporation

Deer, 76–77, 81

Deluxe Check Printing Company, 231

Democratic-Farmer-Labor (DFL) Party, 14, 164, 168, 223; control of, 12, 161; power of, 15, 184, 190

Democratic National Convention, 39–40

Democratic Party, 39, 141, 159; and DFL, 12, 168, 183–84; power of, 160, 163; political offices and, 161, 162, 167

Demography, 52, 99, 152

Department of Human Services, 210–11

Department of Natural Resources (DNR), 78, 79, 81, 266

Depression, *see* Great Depression

DFL. *See* Democratic-Farmer-Labor Party

Disciples of Christ, 148

Discrimination, 8, 144; against Germans, 9, 37; against African Americans, 35, 36. *See also* Racism, Anti-Semitism

Donnelly, Ignatius, 143

Dove, Rita, 242

Dubcek, Alexander, 253

Ducks, 77

Duluth, 13, 18, 109, 120, 183; iron industry in, 7, 87; as port city, 16, 88

Dunne, Dennis, 176

Durenberger, David, 165, 257

Dylan, Bob, 16, 27

Eastern Europeans, 217. *See also various ethnic groups*

Eastern Orthodox, 147

Eastern Rite Catholicism, 139

Economy, 85; of Twin Cities, 48, 223; rural sector, 52–53, 58, 95; small-town, 54–

National Endowment for the Arts, 243
Nationalization, 97–98, 99
National Labor Relations Act, 7, 10, 11
National Labor Relations Board, 20
National Park Service, 79, 82
Native Americans, 13, 21, 83, 96, 132, 152,
253; and fur trade, 3–4, 29, 127; tribal
governments of, 18, 122; gaming and,
23, 128–30; reservations for, 41, 121;
and land, 116–17; migrations of, 118–
20; education of, 122–26; economies
of, 126–28; and treaty rights, 130–31.
See also various tribes; communities
Nature Conservancy, 224
Nazism, 263
Nebraska, 89, 121
Neerland, Charles, 176
Neighborhood-improvement organizations, 111
Nelson, Knute, 9
Nelson Act, 42
Nestlé, 267
New Age, religion, 17
New Right, 151
Newspapers, 5–6, 95; Minneapolis, 7–8; and
politics, 173, 199–200. *See also various
papers*
Nicollet Avenue, 253–54
Ninth Federal Reserve District, 7
Nixon, Richard M., 162
Nobel Foundation, 260; prize, 38, 261
Nonpartisan League, 9, 11, 160, 161, 264
Nonprofit organizations, 221, 225; and
welfare reform, 212–13; CEOs and,
228–29; leadership in, 233–34;
cooperation in, 234–35; and
international issues, 256–59. *See also
various organizations*
Nonprofit sector, 221; cooperation among,
234–35
Norris, Kathleen, 149
North American Manufacturing Belt, 85
North Dakota, 19, 86, 92
North Star State, imagery as, 47, 48
Northern Pacific Railroad, 35
Northern States Power Company (NSP), 19
Northfield College, 33
Northwest Airlines Corp., 266
Northwest Area Foundation, 98, 252
Northwest Bancorporation, 223
Northwestern Bible Schools, 17
Norwegians, 8, 9, 94, 137; as immigrants, 33–35

Norwest Bank, 228
Norwest Corporation, 103
Nuclear energy plants, 19

Ojibwe, 3, 5, 91, 121, 123, 125, 132, 152, 155;
economic and political issues of, 11,
41–42, 106, 129; creation story of, 117–
18, 132n2, 135; migration of, 118–20;
traditional economy of, 126–27;
Christianity and, 139–40. *See also
Native Americans*
Old Log Theater, 241
Olesen, Anna Dickie, 160
Olson, Floyd B., 10–11, 160, 223, 263
One Percent Club, 232
Opinion polls, 250–51
Opperman, Vance, 269
Ordway Center for the Performing Arts,
236, 242
Orthodox Judaism, 139
Ottawa, 3, 119
Our Lady of Guadalupe parish, 13, 153
Outmigration, 100, 104

Pacific Islanders, 21
Packinghouses, 13, 53
Palestinians, 144
Panama Canal, 96, 252
Parks, 191
Partridge, 77
Peace Corps, 233, 255
Pearlstein, Mitchell, 177
Penny, Tim, 177
Pentecostals, 148, 149
Penumbra Theatre Company, 236, 242
Perot, Ross, 184
Perpich, Rudolph, 20, 167, 168–69, 207,
249, 250, 257
Pheasants, 77
Philanthropy, 112–13, 146, 172, 227, 233;
corporate, 98, 220–21, 222–23, 224–25,
228–31, 237–38; urban areas and, 225–
26; sources of, 231–32; levels of, 235–36
Philanthropy Project, 226
"Phonegate," 186
Pilgrim Baptist church, 139
Pillsbury, Charles A., 222
Pillsbury, John S., 216
Pillsbury, Richard, 70
Pillsbury family, 245
Pillsbury, 47, 103, 172, 230, 267

University of St. Thomas, 139, 233, 261
Upper Midwest, defined, 86
Upper Sioux community, 41, 120, 121
Urban Coalition, 225, 226
Urban sector, 71, 225–26. *See also* Twin
  Cities Metropolitan Area; *various cities
  by name*
Urban Ventures, 235
Urbanization, 6, 13, 14, 22–23, 95, 97, 100

Valelly, Richard M., 160
Vanasek, Robert, 253
Vanderpoel, Peter, 176
Veblen, Thorstein, 9
Ventura, Jesse, 47, 60, 164; election of, 24,
  99, 186, 193–94, 249; perceptions of,
  131, 194–95; governance of, 171, 179–80,
  197–98, 200–201, 244; Independence
  Party and, 184, 198–99; and moralistic
  culture, 195–96; book, 196–97; and
  media, 199–200, 202n16, n17
Vermilion Range, 87
Vietnam War, 111, 262
Vietnamese, 152
Volstead, Andrew, 9
Volunteer Resource Center, 233
Volunteerism, 233
Voting, 186; same-day, 185, 194
Voyageurs National Park, 16, 79–80

Wages, 8. *See also* Income
Wagner, Steven, 193–94
Wahl, Rosalie, 18
Walker, Thomas Barlow, 222
Walker Art Center, 224, 246
Walker-West Music Academy, 235
Wallace, Henry A., 12
Wal-Mart, 107
War Chest, 142
War on Poverty, 206
Warfare, Dakota-Euro-American, 4–5, 29–
  30, 121
Washburn, Cadwallader, 222
Washburn-Crosby, 10
Washington, Booker T., 35
Washington, Mrs. Booker T., 36
Watercraft, 74–75

Waterskiing, 75
Wealth, personal, 98
Weaver, Charles, 166
Weber, Vin, 177
Welfare, reform of, 204, 205–13
Wellstone, Paul, 24, 49, 60, 164, 257, 267–68
West Duluth, 7
West Publishing Company, 36
Western Federation of Miners, 7
Weyerhauser family, 9
Wheat, 5, 94; flour industry, 10, 266. *See
  also* Grain industry
Whipple, Benjamin Henry, 140
White Earth Reservation, 41, 121, 126, 129
Wild rice, 127
Wilder, Amherst, 222
Wilderness, 3, 16; value of, 71, 72; use of,
  75–76; noise in, 80–81
Wilkin, Alexander, 222
Willkie, Wendell, 265
Wilson, August, 242
Wilson, Charles E., 224
Wind farms, 19
Winona, 137
Winter Carnival, 83–84
Wisconsin, 23, 86, 88, 89, 118, 211
Women, in politics, 13–14, 18; and
  recreation, 70–71; employment of,
  105–6
Woodcock, 77
World Affairs Center, 256
World War I, 6, 9, 36, 37, 142, 264, 266
World War II, 11, 12, 38, 96
World Wrestling Federation, 196, 202n16
Wounded Knee, 4–5, 18
Wrestling, 73
Wurtele family, 245
Wynia, Ann, 177

Yankees, 140–41, 222
Yellowstone National Park, 224
YMCA, 36, 74, 80, 224
Youngdahl, Luther W., 12, 146, 162
Yugoslavia, 111, 249, 250
YWCA, 74

Zeisler, Peter, 245

MINNESOTA, REAL & IMAGINED was designed and set in Martin Majoor's typefaces Scala and Scala Sans by Greg Britton. The cover was designed by Will Powers using David P. Bradley's painting, *Minnesota Lake*. The book was printed and bound by Hignell Printing, Winnipeg.